Writing Creative Nonfiction

THE LITERATURE
OF REALITY

GAY TALESE
Barbara Lounsberry
University of Northern Iowa

HarperCollinsCollegePublishers

Senior Acquisitions Editor: Patricia A. Rossi
Developmental Editor: Lynne Cattafi
Project Coordination: Interactive Composition Corporation
Text and Cover Design: Interactive Composition Corporation
Cover Photographs: Richard H. Smith, FPG International
                   Lori Sklar, FPG International
                   Mark Harmel, FPG International
                   R. Pleasant, FPG International
Electronic Production Manager: Eric Jorgensen
Manufacturing Manager: Hilda Koparanian
Electronic Page Makeup: Interactive Composition Corporation
Printer and Binder: RR Donnelley & Sons Company
Cover Printer: Phoenix Color Corp.

For permission to use copyrighted material and photographs, grateful acknowledgment is made to the copyright holders on pp. 333–335 which are hereby made part of this copyright page.

Writing Creative Nonfiction: The Literature of Reality

Talese, Gay.
    Writing creative nonfiction: the literature of reality / by Gay
  Talese and Barbara Lounsberry.
        p.   cm.
    Includes index.
    ISBN 0-06-046587-5
    1. Reportage literature—Authorship—Problems, exercises, etc.
  2. Journalism—Authorship—Problems, exercises, etc. 3. English
  language—Rhetoric. 4. Exposition (Rhetoric) 5. Creative Writing.
  6. College readers. I. Lounsberry, Barbara. II. Title.
  PN3377.5.R45T35 1995
  808'.0427—dc20   95-7544
                                                          CIP

96 97 98 9 8 7 6 5 4 3 2

TO
NONFICTION
ARTISTS

PAST, PRESENT, AND FUTURE

CONTENTS

PART III

PREFACE

As more and more young journalists, magazine writers, biographers, and other writers are conducting their research and writing with the aid of tape recorders, word processors, and other timesaving devices resulting from new technology, we are presenting in this volume the old-fashioned techniques of literary crafters whose methods emulate the laborious dedication of stonecutters, but whose words carry weight with discerning readers and with those who appreciate all things of lasting merit.

Some of the writers featured in this anthology might be accused of investing unnecessary lengths of time in their research, their writing and revising; indeed, one of our contributors, the venerable Joseph Mitchell of *The New Yorker*—whose work leads our anthology—has been known to take *years* to produce a single article. Nevertheless, his contribution here, which was originally published a half-century ago, retains its appeal like an exquisite piece of sculptured marble.

All twenty-nine selections in this anthology are examples of "nonfiction"—an unfortunately negative sounding name perhaps, but one with untold possibilities when practiced by writers of literary distinction. In my opinion—although I confess to a bias cultivated during my years as a college teacher and strong advocate of literary nonfiction—this form can be as artful and dramatic and significant as the best efforts of our most revered dramatists, poets, and authors of fiction. What distinguishes nonfiction is that it is—or should be—based on facts, on material chosen from (and remaining a verifiable part of) the real world, and *not* invented or created in the author's mind. And yet creativeness in writing and organization is a legitimate part of literary nonfiction—as is made obvious within these pages by such creative individuals as Annie Dillard, Norman Mailer, Joan Didion, William Least Heat-Moon, Melissa Fay Greene, Tobias Wolff, Art Spiegelman, and many others. I will later have more to say about all the writers and their techniques in this book, which is separated into three sections, each of which highlights a singular aspect of literary nonfiction—but which, collectively, link the many themes embraced by *The Literature of Reality*.

If there is one writer who is eminently qualified to personify this reality, and to compose the introduction to this volume, it is Gay Talese, who remains today perhaps more concerned than even I with the increasing reliance of nonfiction writers on such gadgets as the tape recorder. Mr. Talese fears that the tape recorder undermines the "art of listening" and has introduced "sound bites" into the pages of many current magazines and books. The "Question and Answer" interview, he points out, is now a common feature in such traditional periodicals as the *New York Times Sunday Magazine*. Many book-length biographies distributed by leading publishing houses are drawn from manuscripts made up of juxtaposed transcripts of tape-recorded interviews of dozens of people all commenting on a single subject. Consequently, according to Mr. Talese, the "voice" of the nonfiction writer is increasingly surrendering to sounds recorded on the spinning plastic wheels of tape machines. All the more reason, he adds, for our emphasizing in this anthology what is possible if nonfiction is taken seriously. Mr. Talese also tells us in his Introduction what it was that inspired him as a young writer, how he developed his style, and how his personal background—as the son of newcomers to America—provided him with a special way of seeing and feeling that later gave to his writing a tone and style that is both unique and uniquely literary.

Following is his "Origins of a Nonfiction Writer."

— Barbara Lounsberry

ORIGINS OF A NONFICTION WRITER

GAY TALESE

Part I

I come from an island and a family that reinforced my identity as a marginal American, an outsider, an alien in my native nation. But while this may have impeded my assimilation into the mainstream, it did guide me through the wayward yet interesting path of life that is familiar to many searching people who become writers.

My origins are Italian. I am the son of a dour but debonair custom tailor from Calabria and an amiably enterprising Italian-American mother who successfully operated our family dress business. I was educated by Irish-Catholic nuns and priests in a poor parish school on the Protestant-controlled island of Ocean City, off the southern coastline of New Jersey, where I was born in 1932.

This breezy, sand-swept community had first been established as a religious retreat in 1879 by Methodist ministers wishing to secure the presence of God on the beach, to shade the summer from the corrupting exposure of the flesh, and to eliminate the temptations of alcohol and other evil spirits they saw swirling around them as freely as the mosquitoes from the nearby marshlands. While these sober ministers did not achieve all of their virtuous ambitions, they did instill on the island a sense of Victorian restraint and hypocrisy that exists to this day.

The sale of liquor remains forbidden. Most businesses are closed on the sabbath. The steeples of churches rise prominently in an unpolluted sky. In the center of town are white gingerbread houses with large porches, turrets and finials that retain the look of late ninteenth-century America. In my youth a voluptuous young woman who strolled on the beach wearing a slim bikini would often prompt mild frowns from the town's proper matrons, if not from the middle-aged men concealing their interest behind dark sunglasses.

In this setting where sensuality and sin are always in delicate balance, I cultivated a rampant curiosity that coexisted with my nun-numbed

1

sexuality. Often I went clam digging after supper with my boyhood friends, but at times I strayed alone toward the beachfront bulkheads behind which the island's most amorous teenaged couples necked every night; later, however, I conformed to the bedtime rules of my parochial school: I slept on my back, with my arms across my chest, and my hands resting on opposite shoulders—a presumably pious posture that made masturbation impossible. At dawn I served Mass as the acolyte to a whisky-scented priest, and after school I worked as an errand boy in my family's dress shop that catered to decorous women of ample figures and means. These were the ministers' wives, the bankers' wives, the bridge players, the tale bearers. They were the white-gloved ladies who in summer avoided the beach and the boardwalk to spend considerable amounts of time and money along the main avenue in places like my parents' shop, where, amid the low humming of the fans and the attentive care of my mother in the dressing rooms, they would try on clothes while discussing their private lives and the happenings and misadventures of their friends and neighbors.

The shop was a kind of talk-show that flowed around the engaging manner and well-timed questions of my mother; and as a boy not much taller than the counters behind which I used to pause and eavesdrop, I learned much that would be useful to me years later when I began interviewing people for articles and books.

I learned to listen with patience and care, and never to interrupt even when people were having great difficulty in explaining themselves, for during such halting and imprecise moments (as the listening skills of my patient mother taught me) people often are very revealing— what they hesitate to talk about can tell much about them. Their pauses, their evasions, their sudden shifts in subject matter are likely indicators of what embarrasses them, or irritates them, or what they regard as too private or imprudent to be disclosed to another person at that particular time. However, I have also overheard many people discussing candidly with my mother what they had earlier avoided— a reaction that I think had less to do with her inquiring nature or sensitively-posed questions than with their gradual acceptance of her as a trustworthy individual in whom they could confide. My mother's best customers were women less in need of new dresses than the need to communicate.

Most of them were born of privileged Philadelphia families of Anglo-Saxon or Germanic stock, and they were generally tall and large-sized in a way typified by Eleanor Roosevelt. Their suntanned, leathery, handsome faces were browned primarily as a result of their devotion to gardening, which they described to my mother as their favorite summertime hobby. They acknowledged not having gone to the beach in years, wearing during those years what I assume were bathing suits too modestly designed to prompt a lifeguard's second look.

My mother had been reared in a Brooklyn neighborhood populated primarily by Italian and Jewish immigrant families, and while she had acquired a certain worldliness and fashion-consciousness during the four premarital years she had worked as a buyer for the borough's largest department store, she had known very little about Protestant America until she married my father. He had left Italy to live briefly in Paris and Philadelphia before residing on the white-bread island of Ocean City, where he started a tailoring and dry cleaning business, and later, in partnership with my mother, the dress boutique. Although my father's reserved and exacting manner, and the daily care he attached to his appearance, gave him a semblance of compatibility with the town's most scrupulous leading men, it was my convivial mother who established our family's social ties to the island's establishment, doing so through the women she cultivated first as customers and eventually as friends and confidantes. She welcomed these women into her shop as if into her home, guiding them to the red leather chairs outside the dressing rooms while offering to send me out to the corner drugstore for sodas and iced tea. She did not permit telephone callers to interrupt her discussions, relying on my father or one of the employees to take messages; and while there were one or two women who abused her forbearance as a listener, droning on for hours and ultimately inducing her to hide in the stock room when she next saw them coming, most of what I heard and witnessed in the shop was much more interesting and educational than what I learned from the black-robed censors who taught me in parochial school.

Indeed, in the decades since I have left home, during which time I have retained a clear memory of my eavesdropping youth and the women's voices that gave it expression, it seems to me that many of the social and political questions that have been debated in America in the second half of the twentieth century—the role of religion in the bedroom, racial equality, women's rights, the advisability of films and publications featuring sex and violence—all were discussed in my mother's boutique as I grew up during the war and postwar years of the 1940s.

While I remember my father listening late at night to the war news on his shortwave radio in our apartment above the store (his two younger brothers were then in Mussolini's army opposing the Allied invasion of Italy), a more intimate sense of the conflict came to me from a weeping woman who visited our shop one afternoon with word of her son's death on an Italian battlefield, an announcement that drew my mother's deepest sympathy and compassion—while my troubled father remained behind the closed door of his tailoring room in the rear of the building. I recall other women complaining during these years of their daughters leaving school to "run off" with servicemen, or to do volunteer work in hospitals from which they frequently did not return home at night, and of middle-aged husbands who were seen bar-hopping in Atlantic City after attributing their absences from home to their supervisory jobs in Philadelphia defense plants.

The exigencies of the war, and the excuses it provided, were of course evident and available everywhere; but I think that large events influence small communities in ways that are uniquely illuminating with regard to the people involved, for the people *are* more involved in places where almost everybody knows everybody else (or think they do), where there are fewer walls behind which to hide, where sounds carry further, and where a less-hurried pace allows a longer look, a deeper perception, and, as personified by my mother, the leisure and luxury of listening.

From her I not only learned this first lesson that would be essential to my later work as a nonfiction writer pursuing the literature of reality, but I also gained from my store-centered upbringing an understanding of another generation, one that represented a variety in style, attitude, and background beyond what I could have encountered in my normal experiences in school or at home. In addition to my mother's customers and their husbands who occasionally accompanied them, the place was frequented by the female employees who helped my mother with the selling and bookkeeping during the busy summer months; the elderly semi-retired tailors who worked with my father in the back room altering suits and dresses (and, not infrequently, trying to remove whisky stains from the clothes of the town's many furtive drinkers); the high school senior boys who drove the plant's delivery trucks; and the itinerant black men who operated the pressing machines. All the pressers were flat-footed and had been rejected for military service during World War II. One of these was a militant Moslem who first made me aware of black anger in this period when even the United States Army was racially segregated. "Draft or no draft," I heard him say often, "they never gonna get *me* to fight in this white man's war!"

Another presser who then worked in the shop, a massive man with a shaved head and knife-scarred forearms, had a small, feisty wife who regularly entered the steaming back room to berate him loudly because of his all-night gambling habits and other indiscretions. I was reminded of her aggressiveness many years later, in 1962, while I was researching an article for *Esquire* on the ex-heavyweight champion Joe Louis, a man with whom I had cavorted through several New York night clubs on the evening before our flight back to his home in Los Angeles. At the baggage claim area in Los Angeles, we were met by the fighter's wife (his third), and she promptly provoked a domestic quarrel that provided me with the opening scene of the magazine article.

After my colleague Tom Wolfe had read it, he publicly credited it with introducing him to a new form of nonfiction, one that brought the reader into close proximity to real people and places through the use of accurately reported dialogue, scene-setting, intimate personal details, including the use of interior monologue—[my mother would inquire of her friends: *What were you* thinking *when you did such-and-such?* and I asked the same question of those I later wrote about]—in addition to other techniques that had long been associated with fiction writers and playwrights. While Mr. Wolfe heralded my Joe Louis piece as emblematic of what he called "The New Journalism," I think his complimenting me was undeserved, for I had not written then, or since then, anything I consider to be stylistically "new," since my approach to research and storytelling had evolved out of my family's store, drawing its focus and inspiration primarily from the sights and sounds of the elderly people I saw interacting there every day like characters in a Victorian play—the white-gloved ladies sitting in the red leather chairs, indulging in mid-afternoon chats while gazing beyond the storefront awning out into the hot, sun-burnished business district in a time that seemed to be passing them by.

I think of them now as America's last generation of virgin brides. I see them as representing non-active statistics in the Kinsey Report—women who did *not* partake in pre-marital sex, or extra-marital sex, or even masturbation. I imagine that most of them have now departed from the planet, taking with them their old-fashioned values laced tight by bindings of restraint. At other times I feel something of their reincarnated vitality (together with the vigilance of my parochial school's nuns) in the spirit of 1990s neo-Victorianism—their hands in the writing of the Antioch College dating code, their voices in harmony with antiporn feminism, their presence hovering over our government like a governess.

But my memory of the white-gloved ladies remains benign, for they and the other people who patronized or worked in my parents' store (plus the curiosity transferred by my mother) sparked my early interest in small town society, in the common concerns of ordinary people. Each of my books, in fact, draws inspiration in some way from the elements of my island and its inhabitants who are typical of the millions who interact familiarly each day in stores and coffee shops and along the promenades of small towns, suburban villages, and urban neighborhoods everywhere. And yet, unless such individuals become involved in crimes and horrible accidents, their existence is generally ignored by the media as well as by historians and biographers, who tend to concentrate on people who reveal themselves in some blatant or obvious way, or who stand out from the crowd as leaders, or achievers, or are otherwise famous or infamous.

One result is that "normal" everyday life in America is portrayed primarily in "fiction"—in the works of novelists, playwrights, and short story writers such as John Cheever, Raymond Carver, Russell Banks, Tennessee Williams, Joyce Carol Oates and others possessing the creative talent to elevate ordinary life to art, and to make memorable the commonplace experiences and concerns of men and women worthy of Arthur Miller's plea in behalf of his suffering salesman: "Attention must be paid."

And yet I have always believed, and have hoped to prove with my efforts, that attention might also be paid to "ordinary" people in *non*fiction, and that *without changing the names or falsifying the facts,* writers might produce what in this anthology is called the "Literature of Reality." Different writers, of course, reflect differing definitions of reality. In my case, it reflects the perspective and sensibilities of a small town American outsider whose exploratory view of the world is accompanied by the essence of the people and place I have left behind, the overlooked non-newsworthy population that is everywhere, but rarely taken into account by journalists and other chroniclers of reality.

My first book, *New York—a Serendipiter's Journey,* published in 1961, presents the small town character of New York neighborhoods, and reveals the interesting lives of certain obscure individuals dwelling within the shadows of the towering city. My next book, *The Bridge,* published in 1963, focuses on the private lives and loves of steelworkers as they link a bridge to an island, altering the character of the land and its inhabitants. My first best seller in 1969, entitled *The Kingdom and the Power,* describes the family backgrounds and interpersonal relationships of my former colleagues on the *New York Times,* where I worked from 1955 through 1965. This was my only full time job, and I spent all my years there in the main newsroom on Forty-third Street off Broadway. This newsroom was my "store."

My next best seller, *Honor Thy Father,* was written in reaction to my defensive father's embarrassment over the prevalence of Italian names in organized crime. I grew up hearing him claim that the American press exaggerated the power of the Mafia and the role of Italian gangsters within it. While my research would prove him wrong, the book that I completed in 1971 (having gained access to the Mafia through an Italian-American member whose friendship and trust I cultivated) was less about gun battles than about the island-like insularity that characterizes the private lives of gangsters and their families.

In response to the sexual repression and hypocrisy that was evident in my formative years, I wrote, almost in dedication to the patrons of my mother's boutique, *Thy Neighbor's Wife.* Published in 1980, it traces the definition and redefinition of morality from my adolescence in the 1930s through the sexually-liberating pre-AIDS era that continued into the 1980s—a half-century of social change that I described in the context of the ordinary lives led by typical men and women around the country.

The final chapter in that book refers to the research I did among nude sunbathers at a private beach located twenty miles downstream from my native island—a beach I visited without clothing and on which I would soon discover myself being observed by voyeurs standing with binoculars aboard the several anchored vessels they had

sailed over from the Ocean City Yacht Club. In my earlier book about
the *Times, The Kingdom and the Power,* I had referred to my onetime
profession as voyeuristic. But here on this nudist beach, without press
credentials or a stitch of clothing, my role was suddenly reversed.
Now *I* was being observed, rather than doing the observing. And there
is no doubt that my next and most personal book, *Unto the Sons,* published in 1991, progressed from that final scene in *Thy Neighbor's
Wife.* It is the result of my willingness to expose in a book of nonfiction
myself and my past influences, without changing the names of the
people or the place that shaped my character. It is also a modest example of what is possible for nonfiction writers in these times of increased candor, of more liberal laws with regard to libel and the invasion of privacy, and of expanding opportunities to explore a wide
variety of subjects even, as in my case, from the narrow confines of
an island.

Part II

I left the island in the autumn of 1949 to attend the University of
Alabama. I was then seventeen, acne-scarred, and socially inse-
cure in ways I had not been when younger. The comfort I had
found among my elders during my errand-boy days in my parents'
shop, and the polite and highly personalized "store manners" that I
had inherited from my mother and that had ingratiated me with the elite
women who patronized her boutique in summertime, had provided me
with no headstart advantages during the previous damp and deserted
months of the off-season when I had attended high school. To most
of the teenagers with whom I spent four scholastic years in a chilly
brick building two blocks from the ocean, I was a classmate in
name only.

I was variously looked upon as "aloof," "complicated," "vague,"
"smug," "quirky," "in another world"—or so I was described by a
few former students years later at a class reunion I attended. They also
recalled that during our school days I had somehow seemed to be
"older" than the rest of them, an impression I attribute partly to my
being the only student who came to class daily wearing a jacket and
tie. But even if I appeared to be older, I did not feel senior to anyone,
and certainly never a leader in any of those areas by which we judged
one another—athletically, socially, or academically.

In sports, I was too slightly built and insufficiently fast to make the football team; in basketball I was a bench-warming substitute guard; and in baseball I was a fair contact hitter and a shortstop with "good hands" but an erratic throwing arm, and I was inserted into the starting lineup by the coach hesitantly and irregularly. My main athletic contributions usually came *after* the games, when I returned home and used the store's typewriter to write about the contests for the town's weekly newspaper, and sometimes for the daily paper published in nearby Atlantic City. This was not an assignment I had initially sought. It had long been the obligation of one of the assistant coaches to phone-in to the press the scores and accounts of those games that the editors deemed too unimportant to be covered by any of their own personnel. But one afternoon during my junior year, the assistant coach of our baseball team protested that he was too busy to perform this chore; and for some reason the head coach asked me to do it, possibly because at the time he saw me standing nearby in the locker room doing nothing, and because he also knew that I subscribed to sports magazines (which he frequently borrowed and never returned). On the mistaken assumption that relieving the athletic department of its press duties would gain me the gratitude of the coach and get me more playing time, I took the job and even embellished it by using my typing skills to compose my own accounts of the games rather than merely relaying the information to the newspapers by telephone. Sometimes this resulted in my receiving bylines on articles in which I was obliged to acknowledge my inadequacies as an athlete— . . . *the game got out of hand in the eighth inning when, with the bases loaded, Talese' wild throw from shortstop bounced beyond the first-baseman's reach and rolled under the stands, ...*

Although there were many young women in high school to whom I was attracted, I was too self-conscious, especially after my bout with acne, to ask any of them out on dates. And while I devoted hours every evening to my school books, what most engaged my interest in those books were ideas and observations that my teachers invariably considered inconsequential, and never included in the questions they formed for our quizzes and examinations. Except for my excellent marks in typing class, taught by a buxom, flaxen-braided opera buff who was a friend of my mother's—and who sent my spirits soaring one day when she compared my nimble-fingered hands to those of a young classical pianist that she admired—my grades were below average in almost every subject; and in the late spring of 1949, I graduated from high school in the lower third of my class.

Adding to my dismay later that summer was being rejected by each of the dozen colleges to which I had applied in and around my home state of New Jersey. After I had contacted our principal's secretary, seeking the names and addresses of additional colleges to which I might apply, the principal himself paid a rare and unexpected visit to my parents' shop. At the time I was up in my father's balcony office that overlooked the main room of the shop, seated at his desk reviewing the list of late-afternoon delivery stops I was about to make in connection with my summertime job as a driver of one of the dry cleaning trucks. I was not aware of the principal's presence until I heard his familiar stentorian voice greeting my mother, who was standing at a dress rack putting price tags on some of the new fall merchandise I had earlier unpacked.

While I watched anxiously, crouching behind one of the potted palms placed along the ledge of the balcony, I saw my father coming out from the tailoring room to shake hands with the principal before joining my mother in front of a counter while the principal cleared his throat loudly, as he always did in our assembly hall prior to making announcements. A lean and bespectacled man with curly gray hair, he was dressed as usual in a white round-collared shirt adorned with a polka dot bowtie, and hung from a gold watchchain strung across the vest of his three-piece beige suit was his diamond-studded Phi Beta Kappa key that I could see sparkling from a distance of 30 feet. My custom-tailored father, being his own best customer, was also nattily attired, but there was a lofty bearing about the principal that somehow diminished my father, or so it seemed to me, and it made me uncomfortable even though it had no apparent effect upon my father. He stood there calmly next to my mother with his arms crossed, leaning ever-so-lightly back against the counter waiting for the principal to speak.

"I'm really sorry to burden you both with this," he began, not sounding sorry at all, "for I know your son is a fine young man. But I'm afraid he is not college material. He persists in sending out applications, which I've always advised him against, and now I'm appealing to you to try to discourage him." He paused, as if expecting some objection. When my parents remained silent, he continued in a softer tone, even sympathetically: "Oh, I know you both want the best for your son. But you both work very hard for your money. And I would hate to see you waste it on his tuition. I really think it would be better for you, and for your son as well, if you would keep him here in your business, and perhaps prepare him to take it over one day, rather than to entertain any thoughts of his going on to college, and . . ."

As my parents continued to listen quietly, I stared down at the three of them, humiliated but not surprised by what I was hearing, and yet I was disappointed that my parents had said nothing on my behalf. It was not that I resented the idea of taking over their business. As their only son, and the older of their two children, I sometimes thought of it as inevitable and perhaps my best prospect. But I was also eager to escape the familiarity of this island that in wintertime especially was so forlorn; and I had looked upon college as a way out, a destination toward which I had always saved my store earnings and to which my parents had also promised to provide whatever I lacked financially. Still, I was not sure how a college education would serve my career, since I was uncertain I would ever have a career—except, as the principal was cogently suggesting, within the boundaries of the shop.

In recent weeks, perhaps in reaction to my mounting rejection mail, my father had often repeated an offer he had first made months earlier about sending me to Paris to study tailoring on the classical level it was practiced by his Italian cousins on the Rue de la Paix. I might ultimately develop into a high-fashion designer of suits and dresses for women, my father explained, zestfully adding: "Ah, *there's* where the money is!" The renowned dress designer, Emanuel Ungaro, had once worked as a tailoring apprentice in the firm of my father's cousin, and I myself had not dismissed the idea of seeking such an apprenticeship during this uncertain summer after high school.

Another possible option for me existed in journalism. In addition to the sports reporting I did for the town weekly, I had volunteered during my junior year to do a non-athletic feature called "High School Highlights," a column devoted to student programs and activities in drama, art, music, community work, and such social events as the class dances and proms I had always avoided. The editor liked my idea and accepted it on the condition that I expect no higher payment than our already established sports rate, which was ten cents for every inch of my writing as measured within the newspaper's published pages. From the "Highlights" column and sportswriting combined, I soon was receiving weekly checks in the range of two to four dollars—a sum far below what was paid even to the lowest apprentice tailor in Paris, my father reminded me; but I was being rewarded in extra ways that were privately satisfying.

Although I continued to forgo asking young women to dances, I sometimes did go alone in my new role as a social columnist. For individuals who were as shy and curious as myself, journalism was an ideal preoccupation, a vehicle that transcended the limitations of reticence. It also provided excuses for inquiring into other people's lives, asking them leading questions and expecting reasonable answers; and it could as well be diverted into serving any number of hidden personal agendas.

For instance, when my pet mongrel ran away one day while I was at school during my senior year—[despite my mother's insistent denials, I've always believed that she gave my dog away, or had him "put away," because of my repeated failures at keeping him out of the store]—I persuaded the editor to let me write a feature article about the local animal shelter, an idea inspired entirely out of my wishful thinking that I would find my dog there, or at least confirm there my worst suspicions about my mother, whose graciousness toward customers did not extend to animals. After three prolonged visits to the shelter, however, where I discovered no evidence of my dog's life or death, I did learn for the first time about the "power of the press"—or rather about the many privileges and courtesies that could be accrued by self-interested people like myself while masquerading as an objective journalist. The town's leading animal rights advocates, including the philanthropists who helped to support the shelter financially, welcomed me cordially every time I arrived there to examine each howling and vibrating steel cage bearing newly arrived animals; and I was also given access (unattended) to the office filing cabinets that contained not only public documents and statistics about lost-and-found pets but also several unpaid parking tickets tagged to the dog-catcher's private car, along with a few fading, mistakenly-filed love letters received long ago by one of the shelter's deceased volunteer secretaries. In the files I found mortuary records pertaining to a pet cemetery that I never knew existed in the outskirts of Atlantic City; and when I mentioned this to the shelter's director, he insisted on driving me there—filling me with renewed hope and fear that I might at last discover the final destiny of my missing mongrel.

But after being introduced to the head groundskeeper of the sprawl-ing, tree-shaded burial grounds jutted with stone statuary, crosses, and other monuments honoring the memory of some eight hundred pets—dogs, horses, cats, monkeys, guinea pigs, canaries, parrots, goats, mice—I was assured that no mongrel matching my description had recently been brought there. Yet my interest in the pet cemetery continued unabated, and with the groundskeeper's permission I subsequently returned several times alone, driving my dry cleaning truck after work to the site that was ten miles inland beyond the is-land's bridge. Remaining until twilight to stroll past the gravestones that often displayed the pet's pictures along with their names and their owner's words of affection, I was no longer searching for signs of my own dog but was responding instead to the vast sadness and sense of loss that now allied me to this place.

Here were mourners lamenting the death of their animals in human terms, decorating the gravesites with flowers, and, as the groundskeeper told me, often interring their pets in white lambskin caskets within concrete vaults, and placing silk handkerchiefs over their animal's faces while services were said, services accompanied at times by funeral processions, pallbearers, and requiem music. Many affluent and famous people whose pets had died while the owners were visiting or working in Atlantic City had chosen this place for the burial, and among those who did this were the financier J. P. Morgan, the songwriter Irving Berlin, and the film actress Paulette Goddard. Some of the buried animals had achieved distinction on their own: here were the remains of "Amaz the Wild," a celebrated show dog re-puted to be the last of the great Russian wolfhounds raised by the Ro-manoff family; "Cootie," the revered mascot of Infantry Company 314 of World War I history; and "Rex," a dog which performed for years on stage in Atlantic City and throughout the nation.

The cemetery had been founded in the early 1900s by an animal-loving couple who resided in the Atlantic City area and whose prac-tice of providing their dead pets with funeral rites and gravestones in their backyard had gained the approval of their pet-owning neighbors, and then the desire of these neighbors to share the space and the cost of its upkeep. After the original couple's death, the cemetery was bought and enlarged upon by a woman who was in her mid-seventies when the groundskeeper introduced me to her; and from her—after a minimum of coaxing—I obtained all the cooperation I needed to write what I hoped would be a lengthy and poignant article about the cemetery. This story had the elements that appealed to me. I was connected to it personally. It had enduring human appeal. And it was centered in an obscure place that until now had eluded the attention or interest of other writers and journalists. Since I had already satisfied my obligation to my editor regarding the island's animal shelter—I had written a brief unsigned piece announcing the director's latest fund-raising campaign—I was free to submit this more interesting story in a place where I might attract more readers, namely the *Atlantic City Press*. From a *Press* copyreader that I knew from my sports assignments, I obtained the name of the Suburban Editor to whom I should submit the article; and two weeks after I had mailed it to him, I received a note of acceptance together with a check in a sum sufficiently awesome to impress my father temporarily—twenty-five dollars.

The 2,000-word piece was run with my byline at the top of the suburban section under a double-decked four-column headline accompanied by a large picture of the burial grounds taken by a staff photographer. While I was then years away from the understated literary style I would aspire to during my *Esquire* magazine-writing period, the cemetery piece showed early signs of my continuing interest in providing readers with precise details (. . . *Mr. Hillelson gave his dog, Arno, a funeral with six pallbearers and a three-car procession through the streets* . . .) although it also came with a bit of bathos that the cemetery owner had recounted to me and that I could not resist (. . . *as the old blind man's dog was lowered into the ground, he rose and cried, "Oh God! first you take away my eyes, and then my dog."*)

The response to the article was immediate. I received many complimentary telephone calls and letters from readers as far away as Trenton and Philadelphia, along with comments both from the Suburban Editor and my island editor indicating that I might have a future in some aspect of reporting or writing. Neither of these men had attended college, which were facts I had elicited from them when it began to seem that this would also be my fate. But it had not been "fate" in their cases, they had emphasized; they had eschewed college by choice, as had many journalists of their generation, believing that it induced an effeteness in a tough profession then smitten by the flamboyant spirit of the "Front Page," of reporters who talked like big-city detectives, and who typed, if at all, with two fingers.

I do not know if I was finding consolation in this imagery as I sat eavesdropping in the balcony while my principal was characterizing me as ill-prepared for university life. All I recall, as I mentioned earlier, was a certain recurring shame about my lowly academic status, and disappointment that my parents had not challenged the principal's assessment of me, leading me to wonder if perhaps they might even be secretly relieved; insofar as the store was concerned, the question of succession was now resolved.

After the principal had departed, and while my parents now began communicating quietly at the counter, I sank softly into my father's chair and listlessly glanced at my delivery route spread out on the desk. I remained there for several minutes, not knowing what to do next, not even knowing if my parents were aware that I was up there—until I suddenly heard my father's voice calling from the bottom of the staircase.

"Your principal is not very smart," he announced, removing an envelope from his breast pocket, and summoning me down to read it. And with a slight smile he added: "You're going to college."

The envelope contained a letter of admission from the University of Alabama. Unknown to me until it was later explained, my father had discussed my difficulties a month earlier with a fellow Rotarian for whom he made suits—an Alabama-born physician who had practiced medicine on the island since the mid-1920s. He was also our family doctor and, lucky for me, an influential graduate of the University of Alabama. In addition to this, his sister-in-law was my typing teacher, whose limited but laudatory view of my talents represented the most impressive vote of confidence I could ever hope to get from the local faculty; and she, together with the doctor, apparently had written so positively and persuasively about me to the Alabama dean, contending that I had a growth potential beyond what was indicated by my school grades, that I was admitted into the University's freshman class.

Also in my favor perhaps was the desire of many Southern colleges in those days to bring to their then lily-white and heavily home-bred campuses some out-of-state diversity that might include students with backgrounds that were Slovak, Greek, Italian, Jewish, Moslem, or anything but black. Long before the terms "affirmative action" and minority "quotas" came into use, such sentiments existed unofficially in places like Alabama with regard to the offspring of people that the Klan might define as marginally white; and I think I was a beneficiary of this slow-moving trend toward tolerance. When I read my father's letter, however, I realized that I did not know where Alabama *was*; and after locating it on a map, I felt some anxiety about attending a college so far away from home. But during the Labor Day weekend, as many of my fellow graduates from high school were preparing to leave the island for campuses within the state, or within neighboring New York and Pennsylvania, I was happy that I'd be far away from them. Where I was going no one would know me. No one would know who I was, who I had been. My high school records were as good as burned. I would have a fresh start, a second chance. As my parents and young sister escorted me on a balmy fall afternoon in early September of 1949 past the stone columns of the Philadelphia train station, where I would soon board one of the silver-paneled rail cars across which was painted a dark streamline-lettered sign reading *The Southerner,* I imagined that I was feeling what my father had been feeling twenty-five years before when he left Europe at seventeen for America. I was an immigrant starting a new life in a new land.

The train moved slowly and jerkily through the night down past the Shenandoah Valley of Virginia into the Carolinas and Tennessee and the northwestern tip of Georgia. The car was filled with attractive, friendly and neatly dressed young men and women who chatted amiably and laughed often, and who traveled with their tweed jackets and camel's hair coats folded carelessly up in the overhead racks next to suitcases plastered with stickers announcing: "Duke," "Sweet Briar," "Georgia Tech," "LSU," "Tulane"—and none, I was happy to note, "Alabama." I was still pursuing a singular route.

I did not linger in the club car, where a crap game was being conducted on the floor by several shouting men in their mid-twenties who were students on the GI Bill. I learned this from overhearing two black porters complaining to one another about the ruckus; since neither made any attempt to stop it, it continued through the eighteen hours I remained on board. I spent most of that time staring out the window at a blurred nocturnal landscape, trying to memorize some of the strange and faintly lit station names of the small towns we raced through; and, since I could not sleep, I read a few chapters from *The Young Lions* by one of my favorite authors, Irwin Shaw—[I think my being seen on two occasions carrying novels by Irwin Shaw and John O'Hara into senior English had not endeared me to the Virginia Woolf-loving woman who taught the class]—and on the train I also perused the Alabama registration catalogue that had arrived on the eve of my departure. I planned to major in journalism. Although I still was not convinced that this would become my career, I believed that taking journalism would challenge me the least in an academic sense. I wanted every chance to remain in school and protect my student-deferment status from the clutches of my draft board.

After the train had arrived at a town in central western Alabama called Tuscaloosa, where I was the single departing passenger, I handed the two cracked leather suitcases I had borrowed from my father down to a top-hatted black jitney driver who soon transported me into what could have been a movie set for *Gone With The Wind*. Stately antebellum buildings loomed wherever I looked from the jitney's windows, structures that were part of the older section of the University of Alabama. Some had been restored after the campus had been attacked and torched by Union soldiers during the Civil War. Now all them were being put to use for classroom study or as social or residential centers for students, faculty, and alumni.

My dormitory was a half-mile beyond, built on lowlands near a swamp that had become an expanding locale of postwar building resulting from the student increase magnified by the GI Bill. My quarters were small, dank, and, as I would discover soon enough, penetrated regularly by wind blown musky odors emanating from a papermill located outside the school grounds off the main highway. The dormitory was also invaded by the nightly return of ex-GI students from the beer halls that flourished beyond the "dry" county that encompassed the campus—serenading revelers eager to begin playing cards and shooting dice with the vigor I had seen exhibited by those other veterans on the club car.

But far from being disturbed by the nightly commotion—though I contributed very little to it even as I began making friends during the succeeding weeks—I became drawn to these older men more than to my contemporaries. In my comfortable role as an observer and listener, I liked watching the veterans playing blackjack and gin rummy, and hearing their war stories, their barracks language, their dirty jokes. Up half the night, and rarely cracking a book, they rose daily to attend classes, or cut classes, with no apparent fear of ever failing a course—an attitude that left some of them open for surprises. Not all the survivors of the war survived their first college year.

I of course did not follow their example, lacking the confidence at this point to be casual about anything; but being around these men loosened me up a bit, spared me from having to compare myself exclusively and perhaps unfavorably with my age group, and it seemed to have a favorable effect on my health and school work. My acne had all but vanished within six months of my arrival, a cure I could attribute to the festive atmosphere of the dorm and maybe even the salubrious, if foul-smelling, fragrance that floated in from the papermill. I made passing grades in all of my freshman courses, and near the end of the term I had my first coffee date, then movie date, then first French kiss with a blonde sophomore from Birmingham. She was studying journalism, but would have a career in advertising.

As a journalism student I was usually ranked in the middle of the class, even during my junior and senior years when I was active on the college weekly and worked as the campus correspondent for the Scripps–Howard daily, the *Birmingham Post–Herald.* The faculty tended to favor the reportorial style of the conservative though very reliable *Kansas City Star,* where some of them had previously worked as editors and staff writers. They had definite views of what constituted "news" and how news stories should be presented. The "five W's"— who, what, when, where, why—were questions they thought should be answered succinctly and impersonally in the opening paragraphs of an article. Since I sometimes resisted the formula, and might try instead to communicate the news through the personal experience of the single person most affected by it—being doubtless influenced more by the fiction writers I preferred reading to the practitioners of "objective" nonfiction—I was never a faculty favorite.

It should not be inferred, however, that there was any unpleasantness between us, or that I was a rebellious student. They were reflecting an era that predated the rise of television as the dominant force in spot-news reporting. I was reflecting my own peculiar background in my ambivalence about who and what was important. In reading through old newspapers and other antiquated periodicals in the school library and elsewhere, as I sometimes did in my leisure time, it seemed that most of the news printed on the front pages was historically and socially less revealing of the time than what was published in the classified and the display advertising spread through the middle and back pages. The advertising offered detailed sketches and photographs showing the then current fashion in clothing, the body styles of cars, where rental apartments were obtainable and at what cost, what jobs were available to the white-collar and the laboring classes; while the front pages were largely concerned with the words and deeds of many seemingly important people who were no longer important.

Throughout my college days that ended in 1953, and in the years following at the *Times*, I sought assignments that were unlikely candidates for page one. Even when I specialized in writing sports, whether it was at Alabama or at the *Times,* the final results interested me less than who played the game; and if given the choice of writing about people who personified the Right Stuff or the Wrong Stuff, I'd invariably choose the latter. When I became the sports editor of my college newspaper in my junior year, I took full advantage of my position to describe the despair of the infielder whose errant throw lost the game; of the basketball benchwarmer who saw action only during scrimmages; and of many other ill-starred characters on the fringes of the playing field. One of the sports features I wrote for the college paper concerned a big, seven-foot student from the backwoods hill country who did not know how, and did not want to learn how, to play any games. I also wrote about an elderly black man, the grandson of slaves, who was the athletic department's chief locker room attendant; and how in this time and place where there was no interracial contact in sports, the all-white 'Bama football team began each game by stroking the black man's head for good luck. If I wrote more compassionately about losers than winners during my sportswriting days, it was because the losers' stories to me were more interesting, a view I retained long after leaving the Alabama campus. As a *Times* sportswriter I became enamored of a heavyweight fighter, Floyd Patterson, who was constantly being knocked down, but who kept getting up. I wrote more than thirty different pieces about him in the daily paper and the *Times Sunday Magazine,* and finally did a long piece about him in *Esquire* entitled "The Loser" that Barbara Lounsberry has included in Part II of this anthology.

This was done when I was engaged in what Tom Wolfe called the "New Journalism," but, as I hope is obvious, it is founded in old-fashioned legwork, hanging out with the story's subject day after day (just as I'd hung out in my parents' shop as a juvenile observer and listener)—the "Art of Hanging Out," I've sometimes called it—and it is an indispensable part of what motivates my work, together with that other element that I have maybe mentioned too much already, that gift from my mother: curiosity. My mother also knew that there is a difference between curiosity and nosiness, and this distinction has always guided me with regard to the people I interviewed and how I presented them in print. I never wrote about anyone for whom I did not have at least a considerable measure of respect, and this respect is evident in the effort I take with my writing and the length I will go in trying to understand and express their viewpoints and the social and historical forces that contributed to their character—or lack of character.

Writing for me has always been difficult, and I would not invest the necessary time and effort on people merely to ridicule them; and I say this having written about gangsters, pornographers, and others who have earned society's disapproval and contempt. But there was in these people also a redeeming quality that I found interesting, a prevailing misconception that I wanted to correct, or a dark streak upon which I hoped to cast some light because I believed it would also illuminate a larger area in which a part of us all live. Norman Mailer and Truman Capote have achieved this in writing about murderers, and other writers—Thomas Keneally and John Hersey—show it to us out of the gas chambers of Nazi Germany and the fatal fumes over Hiroshima.

Nosiness represents mainly the interests of the mean-spirited, the one-night-stand temperament of tabloid journalists and even mainstream writers and biographers seizing every opportunity to belittle big names, to publicize a public figure's slip of the tongue, to scandalize every sexual dalliance even when it bears no relevance to that person's political or public service.

I have avoided writing about political figures, for so much about them is of temporary interest; they are dated people, victims of the recycling process of politics, doomed if they openly say what they truly think. My curiosity lures me, as I've said, toward private figures, unknown individuals to whom I usually represent their first experience in being interviewed. I could write about them today, or tomorrow, or next year and it will make no difference in the sense of their topicality. These people are dateless. They can live as long as the language used to describe them lives, *if* the language is blessed with lasting qualities.

My very first writing in the *Times,* in the winter of 1953 following my June graduation from Alabama, dealt with an obscure man who worked in the center of "the Crossroads of the World," Times Square.

I was then a copyboy, a job I'd gotten after walking into the paper's personnel department one afternoon and impressing the director with my fast and accurate typing and my herringbone tailored suit (she later told me). Some months after I'd gotten the job, I was on my lunch hour, wandering awkwardly around the theater district when I began to concentrate on the five-foot high electric light sign that rotated in glittering motion the world's latest headlines around the tall, three-sided building overlooking Forty-second Street. I was not really reading the headlines; I was wondering instead: *how does that sign work? how do the words get formed by those lights? who's behind all this?*

I entered the building and found a staircase. Walking up to the top, I discovered a large, high-ceilinged room, like an artist's loft, and there on a ladder was a man putting chunks of wooden blocks into what looked like a small church organ. Each of these blocks formed letters. With one hand he held a clipboard on which the latest headline bulletins were attached—the headlines changed constantly—and in the other hand he held blocks that he inserted into the organ that created lettering along the exterior wall's three-sided sign containing 15,000 twenty-watt bulbs.

I watched him for a while, and when he stopped I called to him, saying I was a copyboy from the *Times*, which was located a half-block away but which also owned this smaller building with the sign. The man greeted me, and, taking a coffee break, he came down the ladder and talked to me. He said his name was James Torpey, adding that he had been standing on that ladder setting headlines for the *Times* since 1928. His first headline was on the night of the Presidential election, and it read: *HOOVER DEFEATS SMITH!* For twenty-five years this man Torpey had been on that ladder, and even with my limited experience in New York journalism I knew that *that* was some kind of story. After writing some notes about Mr. Torpey on the folded paper I always kept in my pocket, I returned to the main office and typed a short memo about him and put it in the mail box of the City Editor. I wasn't being paid to write, only to run errands and perform other menial tasks; but within a few days, I received word from the editor that he would welcome a few paragraphs from me on the high life of the lightbulb man—and this was published (without my byline) on the second day of November in 1953.

That article—and also my bylined piece in the *Times'* Sunday Travel section three months later about the popularity of the three-wheeled rolling chairs that people rode on the Atlantic City boardwalk—brought me to the attention of the editors. Other pieces followed, including a Sunday magazine article that the *Times* published in 1955 while I was on leave with the Army. The piece was about a woman old enough to be one of my mother's most venerable customers—a silent screen actress named Nita Naldi, who had once been Valentino's leading lady in Hollywood. But in 1954, decades after Nita Naldi's exit from the film business, it was announced that a new musical called *The Vamp,* inspired by the actress' life, and starring Carol Channing, would soon be coming to Broadway.

I had read this item in a tabloid's theater column one morning while riding the subway to work, months before leaving for the army. The column mentioned that Nita Naldi was then living as a recluse in a small Broadway hotel, but the hotel was not named. New York then had close to 300 small hotels in the Broadway area. I spent hours looking in the yellow pages in the *Times* newsroom when I was not otherwise occupied; then I jotted down the hotel numbers and later began placing calls from one of the rear phones that copyboys could use without being in visual range of the City Editor's desk clerks, who liked to assert their authority over copyboys.

I phoned about eighty hotels over a four day period, asking each time to be connected to Miss Naldi's suite, speaking always in a confident tone that I hoped might convey the impression that I *knew* she was staying there. But none of the hotel people had ever heard of her. Then I called the Wentworth Hotel, and, to my amazement, I heard the gruff voice of a man say, "Yeah, she's here—who wants her?" I hung up. I hurried over to the Wentworth Hotel in person.

The telephone, to me, is second only to the tape recorder in undermining the art of interviewing. In my older years, especially while doing publicity tours for one of my books, I myself have been interviewed by young reporters carrying tape recorders; and as I sit answering their questions I see them half listening, relaxing in the knowledge that the little plastic wheels are rolling. But what they are getting from me (and I assume from other people they talk to) is not the insight that comes from deep probing and perceptive analysis and much legwork; it is rather the first-draft drift of my mind, a once-over-lightly dialogue that too frequently reduces the exchanges to the level of talk radio on paper. Instead of decrying this trend, most editors tacitly approve of it, because a taped interview that is faithfully transcribed can protect the periodical from those interviewees who might later claim that they had been damagingly misquoted—accusations that, in these times of impulsive litigation and soaring legal fees, cause much anxiety, and sometimes timidity, among even the most independent and courageous of editors. Another reason editors are accepting of the tape recorder is that it enables them to obtain publishable articles from the influx of facile freelancers at pay rates below what would be expected and deserved by writers of more deliberation and commitment. With one or two interviews and a few hours of tape, a relatively inexperienced journalist today can produce a 3,000-word article that relies heavily on direct quotation and (depending largely on the promotional value of the subject at the newsstand) will gain a writer's fee of anywhere from approximately $500 to slightly more than $2,000—which is fair payment, considering the time and skill involved, but it is less than what was being paid for articles of similar length and topicality when I began writing for some of these same national magazines, such as the *Times' Sunday Magazine* and *Esquire,* back in the 1950s and 1960s.

The telephone is another inadequate instrument for interviewing, because, among other things, it denies you from learning a great deal from observing a person's face and manner, to say nothing of the surrounding ambience. I also believe people will reveal more of themselves to you if you are physically present; and the more sincere you are in your interest, the better will be your chances of obtaining that person's cooperation.

The house phone of the Hotel Wentworth, which I knew I had to use in announcing myself to Nita Naldi, did not present the same obstacle that a regular phone might have: I would, after all, be calling within her own building, *I was already there,* an undeniable presence!

"Hello, Miss Naldi," I began, having asked the operator to be directly connected without my having first announced myself to one of the hotel's desk clerks, a courtesy that—suspecting their mercenary nature—might have boomeranged to my disadvantage. "I'm a young man from the *Times,* and I'm downstairs in your hotel lobby, and I'd like to meet you for a few minutes, and talk about doing an article for the *Sunday Magazine.*"

"You're *downstairs?*" she asked, in a dramatic voice of mild alarm. "How did you know where I lived?"

"I just called all the Broadway hotels I could."

"You must have spent a lot of money, young man," she said, in a calmer voice. "Anyway, I don't have much time."

"May I just come up to introduce myself, Miss Naldi?"

After a pause, she said: "Well, give me five minutes, then come up. Room 513. Oh, the place is a perfect mess!"

I went up to the fifth floor, and will never forget the place. She occupied a small suite with four parrots, and the suite was decorated like a turn-of-the-century movie set. And she was dressed in a style that would have no doubt appealed to Rudolph Valentino himself, and perhaps *only* to him. She had dark arched eyebrows and long earrings and a black gown, and jet black hair which I'm sure she dyed daily. Her gestures were very exaggerated, as in the silent screen era they had to be; and she was very amusing. I took notes, went back to my apartment after finishing work that day, and I wrote the story, which probably took three or four days, or even longer to complete. I turned it into the Sunday editor who handled show business subjects, and asked if he would be kind enough to read it.

A week later, he called to say he would like to use the article. His response marked one of the happiest days of my young life. The magazine would definitely publish it, he repeated, adding he did not know exactly when. It lay in type for a few months. But finally it did appear, on October 16, 1955, while I was serving in the tank corps in Fort Knox, Kentucky. My parents sent me a telegram. I called them back from a telephone booth, collect, and my mother read the published article to me over the phone. It began:

> In order that Carol Channing be flawlessly vampish, beguiling and pleasingly unwholesome as the star of the musical on the silent movie era which comes to Broadway Nov. 10 and is called, not unexpectedly, "The Vamp," she has had as a kind of adviser, aide de camp, critic and coach, that exotic former siren named Nita Naldi. When it comes to vamping roles, no one is a more qualified instructor than Miss Naldi. In her heyday, in the Twenties, Nita Naldi was the symbol of everything passionate and evil on the silent screen. . . .

And it ended:

> . . . still very dark and buxom, Miss Naldi is recognized surprisingly often as she travels about. "Women don't seem to hate

me anymore," she says with satisfaction. She is often stopped in the street and asked, "What was it really like kissing Valentino?" Young people will remark, "Oh, Miss Naldi, my father has told me so-o-o much about you!" to which the actress manages to respond graciously. Not too long ago a man approached her on the corner of Forty-sixth Street and Broadway and exclaimed in wonder, "You're Nita Naldi, the Vampire!" It was as if he had turned the clock back, restoring Miss Naldi to the world she had inhabited thirty years ago. Eager to live in the present, the actress replied in a tone that mixed resentment and resignation, "Yes, do you mind?"

My mother ordered several dozen copies of the magazine and mailed them out to all the customers who had known me as a boy in the store, and she included in her package my address at the base. In the fan mail I later received from them was also a letter from the City Editor of the *Times* informing me that, after I was discharged and had returned to the paper, I would no longer be employed as a copyboy. I was being promoted to the writing staff, and assigned to the Sports Department.

In a postscript, he added: "You're on your way."

Writing Creative Nonfiction

THE LITERATURE
OF REALITY

AN ANTHOLOGY

ANTHOLOGY INTRODUCTION

T raditionally readers have often divided the nonfiction universe into categories highlighting the specific real world focus:

lives (*diaries, memoirs, autobiographies, biographies*)

events (*histories, journalism*)

places (*travel writing, nature writing, science writing*) and

ideas (*essays,* including religious and philosophical works).

We maintain that each of these nonfiction genres must be further divided into
"nonliterary" and "literary." In so doing, we acknowledge that much nonfiction writing has no literary aspiration—nor even the slightest wish for immortality. It is as
perishable as the daily newspaper.

Journalism, therefore, can be ordinary, or it can be as "new" and stylish and
snapping with energy and vitality as nonfiction artists like Tom Wolfe can make it
(see pages 145–160). Travel writing, likewise, can be serviceable, ordinary, and
dated, like a *Fodor's Guide,* or it can be as artful and eternal as Annie Dillard's "An
Expedition to the Pole" (see pages 312–331). We have all read histories, science
writing, and nature writing which are textbook dull in language and equally unremarkable in form. On the other hand, such writing can be as vivid, singular, and
lasting as John Hersey's classic history of the dropping of the atomic bomb on Hiroshima, Lewis Thomas's transcendent *Lives of the Cell,* and William Least Heat-
Moon's bountiful *PrairyErth* (also showcased in this volume).

May more of these works flourish!

What, then, is the difference between artless and artful prose? Between ordinary
and literary nonfiction? We believe there are three distinguishing qualities and we
highlight them in this volume.

The anthology's first section, "Reality Researched," focuses formally upon the
exhaustive research which is one of the most notable features of the Literature of
Reality. Recognizing that remarkable subjects are all about them in the world, nonfiction writers return to their subjects again and again to enrich their perspectives.
Alternately, they simply stay with their subjects (in the library and on the scene) for
extended periods of time. Their thorough research shows. Such research yields rich
strands of information for the nonfiction writer to weave in the composing process.

"Reality Researched," of course, is only the beginning. It is, however, this extensive research which allows the writer to be an artist. "Reality Presented—with

Style," our extensive second section, then showcases nine techniques most often used by writers of literary nonfiction when presenting their material. These are techniques any writer can try. They include scenic construction; simultaneous, sequential, and substitutionary narration; interior monologue; and the artful use of imagery, allusion, humor, and even the pyrotechniques of print itself. "Reality Presented—with Style" reveals the second distinguishing feature of literary nonfiction: the fact that certain nonfiction writers fully intend to be artful (in language and form), for they are writing for the future as well as for the present.

Indeed, as "Reality Enlarged," our final celebratory section makes clear, the nonfiction writer's goal ultimately is to enlarge our understanding of the world. This desire to expand the public's understanding—to bring forward the unnoticed from the shadows of neglect, or to offer revisionary portraits of well-known persons and events—has propelled nonfiction writers throughout history. Artful nonfiction is much older than the novel which is a mere babe among the ancient sequoias of literature. Early artful histories (Herodotus and Thucydides), biographies (Plutarch's *Lives*), autobiographies (Saint Augustine's *Confessions*), travel writing (Marco Polo), essays (Montaigne) and journalism (Addison and Steele) emerged well before Moll Flanders and Tom Jones began cavorting across fictional pages in the England of the 1700s.

Writers of literary nonfiction have always understood they have the best of all worlds. They can be as artful in language and form as the most ambitious poet, dramatist, or novelist, yet they have the bonus of built-in reader credulity, for the moments they re-present have existed in time. These moments can become the certifiable Literature of Reality. What amusing contortions fiction writers like Miguel de Cervantes and Nathaniel Hawthorne have put themselves through (in the prefaces to *Don Quixote* and *The Scarlet Letter*) in order to convince readers their "fictions" are founded in fact!

We come down finally to the odd declaration that in our time literary nonfiction is a form of writing with a distinguished history, untold possibilities, and a terrible name. Literary *nonfiction* is certainly *not fiction*—although some works read like novels. Artful nonfiction is more than fiction, offering the satisfying truths of fact and the "universal truths" of art. Today many of our best writers are finding great maneuvering room in the spacious (yet scarcely trammeled) "real estate" of literary nonfiction.

GUIDELINES

1. Research deeply. The deeper you dig, the more freedom you will find.
2. Cultivate close relationships with your subjects over extended periods of time, in order to: a) establish trust; b) absorb information; c) observe change; and d) know the individuals so well you can describe their thoughts, feelings, and attitudes with confidence.
3. Never invent or change facts or events. This is not necessary.
4. Avoid the composite portrait. The universal resides in the individual.

5. Accept the challenge of writing with style on the highest literary level. The Literature of Reality should have the texture, the rhythm, the pacing, the coloring, and the drama of a work of art, yet it should hold to the standard of verifiable truth. The Literature of Reality is an art form, and those who practice it can be artists as great as any poet, dramatist, or novelist.
6. Bring to real people an enlarged sense of their lives.
7. Bring to real events an enlarged sense of their meaning.
8. Have faith in the value and importance of human beings and human events, no matter how small or ignored. There is more to us—and to the world—than we acknowledge.

Acknowledgments

We have recognized in these pages only a few of the great artists of nonfiction. We would also like to express our thanks to others who have contributed to this volume. Special gratitude goes to Philip Leininger, who first conceived of this book. The following scholars also have reviewed these pages and offered helpful suggestions: Chris Anderson, Oregon State University; John Hellmann, Ohio State University; Robert McClory, Northwestern University; Norman Sims, University of Massachusetts at Amherst; Richard Veit, University of North Carolina; and Ronald Weber, University of Notre Dame. Barbara Lounsberry wishes to thank the following Iowa colleagues for reading and commenting on various portions of the volume: Nancy Price, Ann Struthers, Grace Ann Hovet, Charlene Eblen, and Jane Palen Severin. We also want to thank HarperCollins editor Patricia Rossi for her patience and encouragement.

P A R T   I

R E A L I T Y
R E S E A R C H E D

This section is less about writing than about research. Each of the following selections—Joseph Mitchell's "The Rats on the Waterfront," John McPhee's "Oranges," Tracy Kidder's "House," and Gay Talese's "The Bridge"—exhibits a writer's energetic pursuit of a subject, and the writer's awareness that we are always within range of subjects rare and wonderful. Often when we start writing, we think the only good subjects are exotic ones, found in distant locales. In reality, subjects are all around us waiting to be explored, as the following selections reveal.

Reading Joseph Mitchell, one concludes he literally hounded the rats of New York in order to write about them. One glimpses him lurking in the shadows of waterfront pilings, waiting patiently for the appearance of his unsuspecting subjects to reveal the hidden aspects of their lowlife. John McPhee has sought the orange in all its manifestations. He follows its trail through history and in art, as well as to groves throughout the world. From tree to processing plant to market and breakfast table, he invites us to peel the orange and savor its incomparable facets. Tracy Kidder, in contrast, whisks us from the lore of animals and vegetation to the human world of house building. Rarely budging from one New England site, we witness the craft and conflicts of home construction as architect, contractors, and the young couple who has hired them seek to hammer their separate visions into one agreeable whole. Connection, too, is sought by Gay Talese's bridge builders whose work and lives he shadowed for three years. In "The Bridge" Talese offers almost a bridge-building manual and, at the same time, a complex cultural portrait of the daring "boomers" who link everything but their lives.

Readers should not underestimate the patience and legwork necessary for writing of this kind. When done well, it looks so easy. "Reality Researched" means immersing yourself in your subject. It means absorbing everything of importance written on the topic, starting, perhaps, with an encyclopedia article to get a general overview; then moving deeper, digesting each of the nuances of the subject through books and articles, reports, letters, and diaries. Extensive interviewing of experts and practitioners in the field becomes a way, both of verifying what you have read, and becoming aware of the latest developments on the "cutting edge." Personal observation is equally essential. Like Henry David Thoreau with his nature note-books, you will want to return to your subject again and again to note changes and enrich your perspective. Eventually you may decide you will learn most by staying with your subject for long stretches of time.

🖋   🖋   🖋

THE RATS ON THE WATERFRONT

J O S E P H   M I T C H E L L

Editor's Note: "A newspaper can have no bigger nuisance than a reporter who is always trying to write literature," asserts Joseph Mitchell, himself one of those nuisances, and one of the writers most admired by fellow authors of literary nonfiction. This North Carolina-born writer had never lived in a town of more than 2,700 when he arrived in New York City in 1929 and took a job with the Herald Tribune. *Mitchell wanted to become a political reporter, but he soon found his calling writing about the offbeat inhabitants of the city—including rats. Mitchell wrote about fan dancers, tattoo artists, and wrestling managers for the* Tribune, The World, *and later for the* New York World-Telegram *before finding a permanent home in 1938 at* The New Yorker. *Now in his eighties, he remains one of the magazine's most admired and painstaking writers, his works including* My Ears Are Bent *(1938),* McSorley's Wonderful Saloon *(1943),* Old Mr. Flood *(1948),* Joe Gould's Secret *(1965),* The Bottom of the Harbor *(1960), and* Up in the Old Hotel and Other Stories *(1992).*

Mitchell will labor months, even years, over a single article, reading and interviewing authorities, prowling about the scene, then crafting a style as quiet as a mouse—if not a rat. "The Rats on the Waterfront," first published in 1944 in The New Yorker, *conveys practically all the known information of the time regarding those true inspirers of the delirium tremens.*

A close examination of the way Mitchell structures this selection will reveal the wide range of research sources he tapped. Mitchell draws on interviews with Department of Health inspectors to report where rats live, as well as for accounts of their viciousness. Tapping others' personal observations and his own, he activates all our senses as he re-creates images of rats:

> steal[ing] along as quietly as spooks in the shadows close to the building line, or in the gutters, peering this way and that, sniffing, quivering, conscious every moment of all that is going on around them.

He combines observation with historical context—and involves the reader in the process—when he writes that:

> Anyone who has been confronted by a rat in the bleakness of a Manhattan dawn and has seen it whirl and slink away, its claws rasping against the pavement, thereafter understands fully why this beast has been for centuries a symbol of the Judas and the stool pigeon, of soullessness in general.

Having captured our concern and cultivated our sense of horror in this way, Mitchell feels safe (in paragraph four) to introduce his scientific research into the several rat species—including their scientific names. He follows with description of rats' alarming rate of reproduction and—drawing on interviews with exterminators—the variety of ways people seek to trap and kill them. In the final third of this selection, Mitchell mines histories and presents the testimony of public health physicians in order to portray the dramatic history of the Black Death (the plague), carried by flea-infested rats, and the danger it still poses to human life.

Direct quotations from sources bolster a writer's credibility. They also lend variety to a story, since they introduce other voices. But how do writers know when to quote their sources directly, and when to present the information in their own words? Mitchell's choices regarding direct quotations are instructive. In this 20-paragraph article, he uses six quotations of varying lengths: two short (two sentences each), two medium length (four and five sentences each), and two remarkably long. He selects for direct quotation only the pithiest, liveliest, most quotable lines: sentences he could not improve on himself. Indeed, he often lets his sources tell the best stories.

"The Rats on the Waterfront" illustrates how extensive research can aid a writer. Such research uncovers rich material. It yields strands of information that the nonfiction writer can artfully weave in the composing process.

I n New York City, as in all great seaports, rats abound. One is occasionally in their presence without being aware of it. In the whole city relatively few blocks are entirely free of them. They have diminished greatly in the last twenty-five years, but there still are millions here; some authorities believe that in the five boroughs there is a rat for every human being. During wars, the rat populations of seaports and of ships always shoot up. A steady increase in shipboard rats began to be noticed in New York Harbor in the summer of 1940, less than a year after the war started in Europe. Rats and rat fleas in many foreign ports are at times infected with the plague, an extraordinarily ugly disease that occurs in several forms, of which the bubonic, the Black Death of the Middle Ages, is the most common. Consequently, all ships that enter the harbor after touching at a foreign port are examined for rats or for signs of rat infestation by officials of the United States Public Health Service, who go out in cutters from a quarantine station on the Staten Island bank of the Narrows. If a ship appears to be excessively infested, it is anchored in one of the bays, its crew is taken off, and its holds and cabins are fumigated with a gas so poisonous that a whiff or two will quickly kill a man, let alone a rat. In 1939 the average number of rats killed in a fumigation was 12.4. In 1940 the average rose abruptly to 21, and two years later it reached 32.1. In 1943, furthermore, rats infected with the plague bacteria, *Pasteurella pestis*, were discovered in the harbor for the first time since 1900. They were taken out of an old French tramp, the *Wyoming*, in from Casablanca, where the Black Death has been intermittent for centuries.

The biggest rat colonies in the city are found in run-down structures on or near the waterfront, especially in tenements, live-poultry markets, wholesale produce markets, slaughterhouses, warehouses, stables, and garages. They also turn up in more surprising places. Department of Health inspectors have found their claw and tail tracks in the basements of some of the best restaurants in the city. A few weeks ago, in the basement and sub-basement of a good old hotel in the East Forties, a crew of exterminators trapped two hundred and thirty-six in three nights. Many live in crannies in the subways; in the early-morning hours, during the long lulls between trains, they climb to the platforms and forage among the candy-bar wrappers and peanut hulls. There are old rat paths beneath the benches in at least two ferry sheds. In the spring and summer, multitudes of one species, the brown rat, live in twisting, many-chambered burrows in vacant lots and parks. There are great colonies of this kind of rat in Central Park. After the first cold snap they begin to migrate, hunting for warm basements. Packs have been seen on autumn nights scuttering across the boulevards and transverses in the Park and across Fifth Avenue and across Central Park West. All through October and November, exterminating firms get frantic calls from the superintendents of many of the older apartment houses on the avenues and streets adjacent to the Park; the majority of the newer houses were ratproofed when built. The rats come out by twos and threes in some side streets in the theatrical district practically every morning around four-thirty. The scow-shaped trucks that collect kitchen scraps from restaurants, night clubs, and saloons all over Manhattan for pig farms and soap factories in New Jersey roll into these streets at that time. Shortly after the trucks have made their pick-ups, if no people are stirring, the rats appear and search for dropped scraps; they seem to pop out of the air.

The rats of New York are quicker-witted than those on farms, and they can out-think any man who has not made a study of their habits. Even so, they spend most of their lives in a state of extreme anxiety, the black rats dreading the brown and both species dreading human beings. Away from their nests, they are usually on the edge of hysteria. They will bite babies (now and then, they bite one to death), and they will bite sleeping adults, but ordinarily they flee from people. If hemmed in, and sometimes if too suddenly come upon, they will attack. They fight savagely and blindly, in the manner of mad dogs; they bare their teeth and leap about every which way, snarling and snapping and clawing the air. A full-grown black rat, when desperate, can jump three feet horizontally and make a vertical leap of two feet two inches, and a brown rat is nearly as spry. They are greatly feared by firemen. One of the hazards of fighting a fire in a junk shop or in an old warehouse is the crazed rats. It is dangerous to poke at them. They are able to run right up a cane or a broomstick and inflict deep, gashlike bites on their assailant's hands. A month or so ago, in broad daylight, on the street in front of a riding academy on the West Side, a stable-boy tried to kill a rat with a mop; it darted up the mop handle and tore the thumbnail off the boy's left hand. This happening was unusual chiefly in that the rat was foraging in the open in the daytime. As a rule, New York rats are nocturnal. They rove in the streets in many neighborhoods, but only after the sun has set. They steal along as quietly as spooks in the shadows close to the building line, or in the gutters, peering this way and that, sniffing, quivering, conscious every moment of all that is going on around them. They are least cautious in the two or three hours before dawn, and they are encountered most often by milkmen, night watchmen, scrubwomen, police-men, and other people who are regularly abroad in those hours. The average person rarely sees one. When he does, it is a disquieting experience. Anyone who has been confronted by a rat in the bleakness of a Manhattan dawn and has seen it whirl and slink away, its claws rasping against the pavement, thereafter understands fully why this beast has been for centuries a symbol of the Judas and the stool pigeon, of soul-lessness in general. Veteran exterminators say that even they are unable to be calm around rats. "I've been in this business thirty-one years and I must've seen fifty thousand rats, but I've never got accustomed to the look of them," one elderly exterminator said recently. "Every time I see one my heart sinks and I get the belly flutters." In alcoholic wards the rat is the animal that most frequently appears in the visual hallucinations of patients with delirium tremens. In these wards, in fact, the D.T.'s are often referred to as "seeing the rat."

There are three kinds of rats in the city—the brown (*Rattus norvegicus*), which is also known as the house, gray, sewer, or Norway rat; the black (*Rattus rattus*), which is also known as the ship or English rat; and the Alexandrian (*Rattus rattus alexandrinus*), which is also known as the roof or Egyptian rat and is a variety of the black rat. In recent years they have been killed here in the approximate proportion of ninety brown to nine black and one Alexandrian. The brown is hostile to the other kinds; it usually attacks them on sight. It kills them by biting their throats or by clawing them to pieces, and, if hungry, it eats them.

The behavior and some of the characteristics of the three kinds are dissimilar, but all are exceedingly destructive, all are hard to exterminate, all are monstrously procreative, all are badly flea-bitten, and all are able to carry a number of agonizing diseases. Among these diseases, in addition to the plague, are a form of typhus fever called Brill's disease, which is quite common in several ratty ports in the South; spirochetal jaundice, rat-bite fever, trichinosis, and tularemia. The plague is the worst. Human beings develop it in from two to five days after they have been bitten by a flea that has fed on the blood of a plague-infected rat. The onset is sudden, and the classic symptoms are complete exhaustion, mental confusion, and black, intensely painful swellings (called buboes) of the lymph glands in the groin and under the arms. The mortality is high. The rats of New York are all ridden with a flea, the *Xenopsylla cheopis*, which is by far the most frequent transmitting agent of the plague. Several surveys of the prevalence in the city of the *cheopis* have been made by Benjamin E. Holsendorf, a consultant on the staff of the Department of Health. Mr. Holsendorf, an elderly Virginian, is a retired Passed Assistant Pharmacist in the Public Health Service and an international authority on the rat-proofing of ships and buildings. He recently supervised the trapping of many thousands of rats in the area between Thirty-third Street and the bottom of Manhattan, and found that these rats had an average of eight *cheopis* fleas on them. "Some of these rats had three fleas, some had fifteen, and some had forty," Mr. Holsendorf says, "and one old rat had hundreds on him; his left hind leg was missing—probably lost it in a trap, probably gnawed it off himself—and he'd take a tumble every time he tried to scratch. However, the average was eight. None of these fleas were plague-infected, of course. I don't care to generalize about this, but I will say that if just one plague-infected rat got ashore from a ship at a New York dock and roamed for only a few hours among our local, uninfected rats, the resulting situation might be, to say the least, quite sinister."

Rats are almost as fecund as germs. In New York, under fair conditions, they bear from three to five times a year, in litters of from five to twenty-two. There is a record of seven litters in seven months from a single captured pair. The period of gestation is between twenty-one and twenty-five days. They grow rapidly and are able to breed when four months old. They live to be three or four years old, although now and then one may live somewhat longer; a rat at four is older than a man at ninety. "Rats that survive to the age of four are the wisest and the most cynical beasts on earth," one exterminator says. "A trap means nothing to them, no matter how skillfully set. They just kick it around until it snaps; then they eat the bait. And they can detect poisoned bait a yard off. I believe some of them can read." In fighting the rat, exterminating companies use a wide variety of traps, gases, and poisons. There are about three hundred of these companies in the city, ranging in size from hole-in-the-wall, boss-and-a-helper outfits to corporations with whole floors in midtown office buildings, large laboratories, and staffs of carefully trained employees, many of whom have scientific degrees. One of the largest is the Guarantee Exterminating Company ("America's Pied Piper"), at 500 Fifth Avenue. Among its clients are hospitals, steamship lines, railroad terminals, department stores, office buildings, hotels, and apartment houses. Its head is E. R. Jennings, a second-generation exterminator; his father started the business in Chicago, in 1888. Mr. Jennings says that the most effective rat traps are the old-fashioned snap or break-back ones and a thing called the glueboard.

"We swear by the glueboard," he says. "It's simply a composition shingle smeared on one side with a thick, strong, black glue. We developed this glue twenty-five years ago and it's probably the stickiest stuff known to man. It has been widely copied in the trade and is used all over. The shingle is pliable. It can be laid flat on the floor or bent around a pipe. We place them on rat runs—the paths rats customarily travel on—and that's where skill comes in; you have to be an expert to locate the rat runs. We lay bait around the boards. If any part of the animal touches a board, he's done for. When he tries to pull away, he gets himself firmly caught in the glue. The more he struggles, the more firmly he's caught. Next morning the rat, glueboard and all, is picked up with tongs and burned. We used to bait with ground beef, canned salmon, and cheese, but we did some experimenting with many other foods and discovered that peanut butter is an extremely effective rat bait. Rats have to be trapped, poisoned, or gassed. Cats, if they're hungry enough, will kill rats, but you can't really depend on them—in many cases, they're able to keep the number of rats down, but they're seldom able to exterminate them.

"Insects, particularly cockroaches and bedbugs, are the Number One exterminating problem in New York. Rats come next. Then mice. Perhaps I shouldn't tell this, but most good exterminators despise rat jobs because they know that exterminating by itself is ineffective. You can kill all the rats in a building on a Monday and come back on a Wednesday and find it crawling with them. The only way rats can be kept out is to ratproof the building from sub-basement to skylight. It's an architectural problem; you have to build them out. Killing them off periodically is a waste of time. We refuse to take a rat job unless the owner or tenant promises to stop up every hole and crack through which rats can get in, and seal up or eliminate any spaces inside the building in which they can nest. That may sound like cutting our own throats, but don't worry: insects are here to stay and we'll always have more work than we can do. Twenty-five years ago there were easily two rats for every human being in the city. They gradually decreased to half that, for many reasons. Better sanitary conditions in general is one reason. Fewer horses and fewer stables is another. The improved packaging of foods helped a lot. An increase in the power of the Department of Health is an important reason. Nowadays, if a health inspector finds rat tracks in a grocery or a restaurant, all he has to do is issue a warning; if things aren't cleaned up in a hurry, he can slap on a violation and make it stick. The most important reason, however, is the modern construction of buildings and the widespread use of concrete. It's almost impossible for a rat to get inside some of the newer apartment houses and office buildings in the city. If he gets in, there's no place for him to hide and breed."

None of the rats in New York are indigenous to this country. The black rat has been here longest. Its homeland is India. It spread to Europe in the Middle Ages along trade routes, and historians are quite sure that it was brought to America by the first ships that came here. It is found in every seaport in the United States, and inland chiefly in the Gulf States. It has bluish-black fur, a pointed nose, and big ears. It is cleaner and not as fierce as the brown rat but more suspicious and harder to trap. It is an acrobatic beast. It can rapidly climb a drapery, a perpendicular drain or steam-heat pipe, an elevator cable, or a telephone or electric wire. It can gnaw a hole in a ceiling while clinging to an electric wire. It can run fleetly on a taut wire, or on a rope whether slack or taut. It uses its tail, which is slightly longer than its body, to maintain balance. It nests in attics, ceilings, and hollow walls, and in the superstructures of piers, away from its enemy, the ground-loving brown rat. Not all piers are infested, a few of the newer ones, which are made of concrete, have none at all. It keeps close to the waterfront, and until recently was rarely come across in the interior of the city. Whenever possible, it goes aboard ships to live. While docked here, all ships are required to keep three-foot metal disks, called rat guards, set on their hawsers and mooring cables. These guards sometimes get out of whack—a strong wind may tilt them, for example—and then a black or an Alexandrian can easily clamber over them. Occasionally a rat will walk right up or down a gangplank. It is almost impossible to keep a ship entirely free of them. Some famous ships are notoriously ratty. One beautiful liner—it was in the round-the-world cruise service before the war—once came in with two hundred and fifty aboard. Public Health Service officials look upon a medium-sized ship with twenty as excessively infested. The record for New York Harbor is held by a freighter that came in from an Oriental port with six hundred, all blacks and Alexandrians. The black and the Alexandrian are very much alike, and the untrained eye cannot tell them apart. The Alexandrian is frequently found on ships from Mediterranean ports. It is a native of Egypt, and no one seems to know, even approximately, when it first appeared in this country. It has never been able to get more than a toehold in New York, but it is abundant in some Southern and Gulf ports.

The brown rat, the *R. norvegicus*, originated somewhere in Central Asia, began to migrate westward early in the eighteenth century, and reached England around 1730. Most authorities believe that it got to this country during the Revolutionary War. From ports all along the coast it went inland, hot on the heels of the early settlers, and now it thrives in every community and on practically every farm in the United States. Its spread was slowest in the high and dry regions of the West; it didn't reach Wyoming until 1919 and Montana until 1923. Its nose is blunt, and its ears are small and alert, and its eyes are sharp and shiny and joyless and resentful and accusing. Its fur is most often a grimy brown, but it may vary from a pepper-and-salt gray to nearly black. Partial albinos occasionally show up; the tame white rat, which is used as a laboratory animal and sometimes kept as a pet, is a sport derived from the brown.

In addition to being the most numerous, the brown rat is the dirtiest, the fiercest, and the biggest. "The untrained observer," a Public Health Service doctor remarked not long ago, "invariably spreads his hands wide apart when reporting the size of a rat he has seen, indicating that it was somewhat smaller than a stud horse but a whole lot bigger than a bulldog. They are big enough, God protect us, without exaggerating." The average length of adult brown rats is ten inches, not counting the tail, which averages seven inches. The average weight is three-quarters of a pound. Once in a while a much heavier one is trapped. One that weighed a pound and a half and measured twenty and a half inches overall (that is, counting the tail) was recently clubbed to death in a Manhattan brewery; brewery and distillery rats feed on mash and many become obese and clumsy. Some exterminators have maintained for years that the biggest rats in the country, perhaps in the world, are found in New York City, but biologists believe that this is just a notion, that they don't get any bigger in one city than they do in another. The black and the Alexandrian are about two-thirds the size of the brown.

The brown rat is distributed all over the five boroughs. It customarily nests at or below street level—under floors, in rubbishy basements, and in burrows. There are many brownstones and red-bricks, as well as many commercial structures, in the city that have basements or sub-basements with dirt floors; these places are rat heavens. The brown rat can burrow into the hardest soil, even tightly packed clay, and it can tunnel through the kind of cheap mortar that is made of sand and lime. To get from one basement to another, it tunnels under party walls; slum-clearance workers frequently uncover a network of rat tunnels that link all the tenements in a block. Like the magpie, it steals and hoards small gadgets and coins. In nest chambers in a system of tunnels under a Chelsea tenement, workers recently found an empty lipstick tube, a religious medal, a skate key, a celluloid teething ring, a belt buckle, a shoehorn, a penny, a dime, and three quarters. Paper money is sometimes found. When the Civic Repertory Theatre was torn down, a nest constructed solely of dollar bills, seventeen in all, was discovered in a burrow. Exterminators believe that a high percentage of the fires that are classified as "of undetermined origin" are started by the brown rat. It starts them chiefly by gnawing the insulation off electric wires, causing short circuits. It often uses highly inflammable material in building nests. The majority of the nests in the neighborhood of a big garage, for example, will invariably be built of oily cotton rags.

The brown rat is as supple as rubber and it can squeeze and contort itself through openings half its size. It has strong jaws and long, curved incisors with sharp cutting edges. It can gnaw a notch big enough to accommodate its body in an oak plank, a slate shingle, or a sun-dried brick. Attracted by the sound of running water, it will gnaw into lead pipe. It cannot climb as skillfully as the black and the Alexandrian, it cannot jump as far, and it is not as fleet, but it is, for its size, a remarkable swimmer. A Harbor Police launch once came upon three brown rats, undoubtedly from New Jersey, in the middle of the Hudson; in an hour and twenty-five minutes, swimming against the wind in tossing water, they reached the pilings of one of the Barclay Street ferry slips, where the policemen shot them. The brown rat is an omnivorous scavenger, and it doesn't seem to care at all whether its food is fresh or spoiled. It will eat soap, oil paints, shoe leather, the bone of a bone-handled knife, the glue in a book binding, and the rubber in the insulation of telephone and electric wires. It can go for days without food, and it can obtain sufficient water by licking condensed moisture off metallic surfaces. All rats are vandals, but the brown is the most ruthless. It destroys far more than it actually consumes. Instead of completely eating a few potatoes, it takes a bite or two out of dozens. It will methodically ruin all the apples and pears in a grocery in a night. To get a small quantity of nesting material, it will cut great quantities of garments, rugs, upholstery, and books to tatters. In warehouses, it sometimes goes berserk. In a few hours a pack will rip holes in hundreds of sacks of flour, grain, coffee, and other foodstuffs, spilling and fouling the contents and making an overwhelming mess. Now and then, in live-poultry markets, a lust for blood seems to take hold of the brown rat. One night, in the poultry part of old Gansevoort Market, alongside the Hudson, a burrow of them bit the throats of over three hundred broilers and ate less than a dozen. Before this part of the market was abandoned, in 1942, the rats practically had charge of it. Some of them nested in the drawers of desks. When the drawers were pulled open, they leaped out, snarling.

So far, in the United States, the bubonic plague has been only a menace. From 1898 to 1923, 10,822,331 deaths caused by the plague were recorded in India alone; in the United States, in this period, there were fewer than three hundred deaths. The plague first occurred in this country in 1900, in the Chinatown of San Francisco. It is generally believed that the bacteria were brought in by infected rats that climbed to the docks from an old ship in the Far Eastern trade that caught afire while being unloaded. This epidemic killed a hundred and thirteen people and lasted until the end of 1903. The plague broke out again in 1907, a year after the earthquake. In the same year there was an epidemic in Seattle. There have been two epidemics in New Orleans—one in 1914 and one in 1919 and 1920—and there was one in Los Angeles in 1924 and 1925. Since then there have been only sporadic cases. However, there is a vast and ominous reservoir of plague infection in the rural rodents of the West. During the first epidemic in San Francisco, many rats fled the city and infected field rodents, chiefly ground squirrels, in the suburbs. In 1934, thirty years later, Public Health Service biologists turned up the fact that the plague had slowly spread among burrowing animals—ground squirrels, prairie dogs, chipmunks, and others—as far east as New Mexico and Wyoming. Late last year it appeared fifty miles inside the western border of North Dakota. Public Health Service officials say that there is no reason to assume that the infection will not infiltrate into rodents of the Great Plains, cross the Mississippi, and show up in the East. Most of the diseased rodents inhabit thinly settled sections and come in contact with human beings infrequently. Even so, every year several people, usually hunters, are bitten by infected rodent fleas and come down with the plague. There is an ever-present possibility that a few infected rodents may stray from rural areas and communicate the disease to town and city rats. If the disease ever gets loose among city rats, epidemics among human beings are apt to follow.

There has never been an outbreak of the plague in New York. There have, however, been two narrow escapes. In 1900, plague-infected rats were found in ships in the harbor of New York, as well as in the harbors of San Francisco and Port Townsend, Washington. They got ashore only in San Francisco, causing the first Black Death epidemic in North America. Plague rats were found in New York Harbor for the second time early in January of 1943. Among themselves, health officials refer to this discovery as "the *Wyoming* matter." The history of the *Wyoming* matter was told to me in 1944 by Dr. Robert Olesen, medical director of the New York Quarantine Station of the Public Health Service. Mr. Holsendorf sent me to see Dr. Olesen; they were colleagues years ago in the Public Health Service and are old friends. I saw Dr. Olesen in his office in an old, red-brick building overlooking the Narrows, in Rosebank, on Staten Island.

"The *Wyoming* matter has been one of the best-kept secrets in the history of the Public Health Service, and I'm proud of that," Dr. Olesen said, "but I agree with what Ben Holsendorf has been saying lately—there's no reason at all to keep it secret any longer. I'll tell you about it.

"First of all, I'd better explain how we inspect ships. Every ship in foreign trade that comes into the harbor is boarded by a party made up of a customs officer, an immigration officer, a plant-quarantine man from the Department of Agriculture, a Public Health doctor, and a sanitary inspector, whose main job is to determine the degree of rat infestation aboard. While the doctor is examining the crew and passengers for quarantinable diseases, the sanitary inspector goes through the ship looking for rat tracks, gnawings, droppings, and nests. Rats have a smell that is as distinctive as the smell of cats, although not as rank, and an experienced inspector can detect their presence that way. The inspector pays particular attention to ships that have touched at plague ports. There are quite a few of these ports right now; Suez had an outbreak the other day and was put on the list. After he's made his search, he reports to the doctor, who orders a fumigation if things look bad. If infestation is slight and if the ship comes from a clean port, the doctor probably won't insist on a fumigation. I won't give you any wartime figures, but in one peacetime month, for example, we inspected five hundred and sixty ships, found that a hundred and thirty-two were infested to some degree, and fumigated twenty-four, recovering eight hundred and ten rats.

"We've been short-handed since the war began, and most of our fumigating is done by a group of twenty-two Coast Guardsmen. They were assigned to us early in the war and we trained them to make rat inspections and fumigations. We use hydrocyanic gas, which is one of the most lethal of poisons. An infested ship is anchored and a fumigation party of four or five Coast Guardsmen goes aboard. First, they send the entire crew ashore, carefully checking them off one by one. Then one of the Coast Guardsmen goes through the ship, shouting, banging on bulkheads with a wrench, and making as much racket as possible. He shouts, 'Danger! Fumigation! Poison gas!' Then the Coast Guardsmen put on gas masks and toss some tear-gas bombs into the holds. That's to fetch out any stowaways who might be aboard. During the first months we used hydrocyanic, we killed a number of stowaways. A few weeks ago, in the hold of a South American freighter, the tear gas brought out eight weeping stowaways who had been hiding in an empty water tank. Two fellows in the crew had smuggled them aboard in Buenos Aires and had been feeding them. These fellows had kept their mouths shut and gone ashore, leaving the stowaways to be killed, for all they cared. When the Coast Guardsmen are satisfied a ship is empty of human beings, they seal the holds and cabins and open cans of hydrocyanic, liberating the gas. They even fumigate the lifeboats; rats often hide in them. After a certain number of hours—ten for a medium-sized ship—the holds are opened and aired out, and the Coast Guardsmen go below and search for dead rats. The rats are dropped in wax-paper bags and brought to a laboratory in the basement here. They are combed for fleas. The fleas are pounded in a mortar, put into a solution, and injected into guinea pigs. Then the rats are autopsied, and bits of livers and spleens are snipped out and pounded up. These are also put into a solution and injected into guinea pigs. If the fleas or the rats are infected, the pigs sicken and die. We began this work in 1921, and for twenty-two years we injected scores of generations of pigs with the fleas and livers and spleens of rats from practically every port in the world without turning up a single Black Death germ. We didn't want to find any, to be sure, but there *were* days when we couldn't help but look upon our work as routine and futile.

"Now then, late in the evening of January 10, 1943, the French freighter *Wyoming* arrived from Casablanca, North Africa, with a miscellaneous cargo, mainly wine and tobacco. A big convoy came in that evening, sixty or seventy ships, and we didn't get to the *Wyoming* until next day. Casablanca was on the plague list at that time; there had been an outbreak in December, shortly before the *Wyoming* sailed. The crew was carefully examined. No sign of illness. Then the captain brought out a deratization certificate stating that the ship had recently been fumigated—in Casablanca, if I remember correctly—and was free of rats; looking back, I feel sure the official who signed this certificate had been bribed. She was allowed to dock at Pier 34, Brooklyn, where she discharged some bags of mail. Next day she proceeded to Pier 84, Hudson River, and began discharging her cargo. Some rats were seen in her by longshoremen, and on January 13th we went over her and found evidence of infestation. She was allowed to continue unloading. On January 18th we fumigated her right at her dock and found twenty rats. We combed and autopsied the rats, and inoculated a guinea pig. Four days later the pig sickened and died. An autopsy indicated plague infection and cultures from its heart blood showed an oval organism which had all the characteristics of *Pasteurella pestis*. We made a broth of tissue from this pig and inoculated a second pig. It sickened and died. It was the Black Death, no doubt about it. We had found it in the harbor for the first time in forty-three years.

"In the meantime, the *Wyoming* had moved from the Hudson to Pier 25, Staten Island, for repairs. On January 29th we went aboard her, removed all excess dunnage and gear to the decks, and ripped open all the enclosed spaces in the holds; we were afraid the hydrocyanic hadn't penetrated to these spaces. Then we refumigated. Twelve more dead rats were found. On the same day we got in touch with Dr. Stebbins, the Commissioner of Health for the city, and told him about the situation. We were terribly apprehensive. The *Wyoming* had touched at piers in rat-infested sections in three boroughs and there was, of course, a distinct possibility that infected rats had got ashore and were at that moment wandering around the waterfront, coming in contact with local rats and exchanging fleas. Mr. Holsendorf, in his capacity as the Health Department's rat consultant, quickly got together some crews of trappers and put them to work setting break-back traps on the Brooklyn pier, the Manhattan pier, and the Staten Island pier, and in buildings in the vicinity of each pier. The trapping was done unobtrusively; we were afraid a newspaper might learn of the matter and start a plague scare. Early in February the first batch of rats was sent for autopsies to the laboratory of the Willard Parker Hospital, a hospital for contagious diseases, on the East River at Fifteenth Street. We sent them there, rather than bring them way down here to our laboratory, in order to get a report on them as quickly as possible. We waited for the report with considerable anxiety. It was negative on every rat, and we began to breathe easier. Mr. Holsendorf and his crews trapped from the end of January to the middle of May and the reports continued to come in negative. At the end of May we concluded that no *Wyoming* rats had got ashore, and that the city was safe."

From ORANGES

J O H N   M C P H E E

*Editor's Note: John McPhee occasionally teaches a course at Princeton called
"The Literature of Fact," a course described in the university's catalog as "the
application of creative writing techniques to journalism and other forms of
nonfiction." McPhee is even more famous for his articles and books as a staff
writer for* The New Yorker. *He is one of Joseph Mitchell's successors.*

*Just as novelist William Faulkner created his own fictional "Yoknapatawpha
County" in Mississippi, McPhee has shown that nonfiction writers can find ample
material in their own backyards—but none of it invented. McPhee has mined his
home state better than any other nonfiction writer. He has celebrated New Jersey's*
Pine Barrens. *He has followed its noteworthy citizens, such as former Princeton
basketball star and current U.S. Senator Bill Bradley (in* A Sense of Where You
Are *and "Open Man"). His "Search for Marvin Gardens" took him through the
real Monopoly board of Atlantic City, and he has written of more modest New
Jersey enterprises, such as the attempt to revive the blimp for commercial aviation
through an unlikely contraption christened* The Deltoid Pumpkin Seed. *McPhee's
sojourn in orange country, excerpted here, probably began in his Princeton office
where he keeps a refrigerator stocked with sweet Valencias.*

*In doing research, McPhee says he reads just enough to get going, and then a
great deal after his on-site research. He urges students never to stop at the first
source, but to go through as many sources as possible "until you meet yourself
coming out the other side." McPhee's research rule is this: "When you keep
encountering the same facts and stories again and again, then you know you* may
be right."

*McPhee will prepare some questions in advance for interviews, but not many.
He prefers to be with people and see what develops. In fact, McPhee's special gift
is for arranging ingenious travels or situations to showcase his subjects. In order
to write of wild food genius Euell Gibbons, for example, he arranged a one-week
foraging expedition in Pennsylvania, with Gibbons adding a new wild ingredient
at each meal. To explore the* Levels of the Game *of tennis, he took turns reviewing
a videotaped match with players Arthur Ashe and Clark Graebner, ascertaining
point-by-point their recollections and their reactions to each other. Like Gay
Talese, McPhee avoids the tape recorder in his research. "How," he queries
pointedly, "do you know when to turn it off?" Instead, McPhee prefers narrow
notepads and pencils. When white water rafting on the Colorado River for*
Encounters with the Archdruid, *he would place his notebook in a plastic bag to
keep it dry.*

*Besides conceptual ingenuity, another research talent McPhee possesses is
remarkable clarity of mind. Theodore Taylor, the former bomb designer turned
nuclear safeguard advocate, observed this gift during their travels for McPhee's
1974 volume* The Curve of Binding Energy. *"John would open his notebook at 5
A.M. and begin asking questions, and often wouldn't close it till 9 at night," Taylor*

recalls. "He would amaze physicists by listening to highly technical explanations, stopping them if he didn't understand something, and then restating it for verification in a form infinitely clearer than first told. 'Exactly,' they would say. 'I wish I had said it like that.'" Because of this lucidity, McPhee explores technical subjects confidently, from nuclear physics to geology.

McPhee seeks to come at his subject from every perspective; his vision, ultimately, is panoptic. McPhee's work is proof that the extraordinary is to be found in the most ordinary object or human enterprise, and that if writers will only look about them and trust in subjects toward which they instinctively gravitate, they will find an audience. In his own case, McPhee has said his best subjects have been interests he had as a boy. As a Princeton undergraduate, McPhee answered questions on animals, vegetables, and minerals on the radio program "Twenty Questions." Following graduation in 1953, he wrote for Time *magazine while collecting rejection letters from* The New Yorker *before finally having a piece accepted and joining the staff in 1964. Since then, McPhee has published more than twenty volumes, many on nature and ecology. He has been nominated twice for the National Book Award, and has attracted a loyal, almost cult, readership.*

The custom of drinking orange juice with breakfast is not very widespread, taking the world as a whole, and it is thought by many peoples to be a distinctly American habit. But many Danes drink it regularly with breakfast, and so do Hondurans, Filipinos, Jamaicans, and the wealthier citizens of Trinidad and Tobago. The day is started with orange juice in the Colombian Andes, and, to some extent, in Kuwait. Bolivians don't touch it at breakfast time, but they drink it steadily for the rest of the day. The "play lunch," or morning tea, that Australian children carry with them to school is usually an orange, peeled spirally halfway down, with the peel replaced around the fruit. The child unwinds the peel and holds the orange as if it were an ice-cream cone. People in Nepal almost never peel oranges, preferring to eat them in cut quarters, the way American athletes do. The sour oranges of Afghanistan customarily appear as seasoning agents on Afghan dinner tables. Squeezed over Afghan food, they cut the grease. The Shamouti Orange, of Israel, is seedless and sweet, has a thick skin, and grows in Hadera, Gaza, Tiberias, Jericho, the Jordan Valley, and Jaffa; it is exported from Jaffa, and for that reason is known universally beyond Israel as the Jaffa Orange. The Jaffa Orange is the variety that British people consider superior to all others, possibly because Richard the Lionhearted spent the winter of 1191–92 in the citrus groves of Jaffa. Citrus trees are spread across the North African coast from Alexandria to Tangier, the city whose name was given to tangerines. Oranges tend to become less tart the closer they are grown to the equator, and in Brazil there is one kind of orange that has virtually no acid in it at all. In the principal towns of Trinidad and Tobago, oranges are sold on street corners. The vender cuts them in half and sprinkles salt on them. In Jamaica, people halve oranges, get down on their hands and knees, and clean floors with one half in each hand. Jamaican mechanics use oranges to clear away grease and oil. The blood orange of Spain, its flesh streaked with red, is prized throughout Europe. Blood oranges grow well in Florida, but they frighten American women. Spain has about thirty-five million orange trees, grows six billion oranges a year, and exports more oranges than any other country, including the United States. In the Campania region of Italy, land is scarce; on a typical small patch, set on a steep slope, orange trees are interspersed with olive and walnut trees, grapes are trained to cover trellises overhead, and as many as five different vegetables are grown on the ground below. The over-all effect is that a greengrocer's shop is springing out of the hillside. Italy produces more than four billion oranges a year, but most of its citrus industry is scattered in gardens of one or two acres. A Frenchman sits at the dinner table, and, as the finishing flourish of the meal, slowly and gently disrobes an orange. In France, peeling the fruit is not yet considered an inconvenience. French preferences run to the blood oranges and the Thomson Navels of Spain, and to the thick-skinned, bland *Maltaises*, which the French import not from Malta but from Tunisia. France itself only grows about four hundred thousand oranges each year, almost wholly in the Department of the *Alpes Maritimes*. Sometimes, Europeans eat oranges with knives and forks. On occasion, they serve a dessert orange that has previously been peeled with such extraordinary care that strips of the peel arc outward like the petals of a flower from the separated and reassembled segments in the center. The Swiss sometimes serve oranges under a smothering of sugar and whipped cream; on a hot day in a Swiss garden, orange juice with ice is a luxurious drink. Norwegian children like to remove the top of an orange, make a little hole, push a lump of sugar into it, and then suck out the juice. English children make orange-peel teeth and wedge them over their gums on Halloween. Irish children take oranges to the movies, where they eat them while they watch the show, tossing the peels at each other and at the people on the screen. In Reykjavik, Iceland, in greenhouses that are heated by volcanic springs, orange trees yearly bear fruit. In the New York Botanical Garden, six mature orange trees are growing in the soil of the Bronx. Their trunks are six inches in diameter, and they bear well every year. The oranges are for viewing and are not supposed to be picked. When people walk past them, however, they sometimes find them irresistible.

The first known reference to oranges occurs in the second book of the *Five Classics*, which appeared in China around 500 B.C. and is generally regarded as having been edited by Confucius. The main course of the migration of the fruit—from its origins near the South China Sea, down into the Malay Archipelago, then on four thousand miles of ocean current to the east coast of Africa, across the desert by caravan and into the Mediterranean basin, then over the Atlantic to the American continents—closely and sometimes exactly kept pace with the major journeys of civilization. There were no oranges in the Western Hemisphere before Columbus himself introduced them. It was Pizarro who took them to Peru. The seeds the Spaniards carried came from trees that had entered Spain as a result of the rise of Islam. The development of orange botany owes something to Vasco da Gama and even more to Alexander the Great; oranges had symbolic importance in the paintings of Renaissance masters; in other times, at least two overwhelming invasions of the Italian peninsula were inspired by the visions of paradise that oranges engendered in northern minds. Oranges were once the fruit of the gods, to whom they were the golden apples of the Hesperides, which were stolen by Hercules. Then, in successive declensions, oranges became the fruit of emperors and kings, of the upper prelacy, of the aristocracy, and, by the eighteenth century, of the rich bourgeoisie. Another hundred years went by before they came within reach of the middle classes, and not until early in this century did they at last become a fruit of the community.

Just after the Second World War, three scientists working in central Florida surprised themselves with a simple idea that resulted in the development of commercial orange-juice concentrate. A couple of dozen enormous factories sprang out of the hammocks, and Florida, which can be counted on in most seasons to produce about a quarter of all the oranges grown in the world, was soon putting most of them through the process that results in small, trim cans, about two inches in diameter and four inches high, containing orange juice that has been boiled to high viscosity in a vacuum, separated into several component parts, reassembled, flavored, and then frozen solid. People in the United States used to consume more fresh oranges than all other fresh fruits combined, but in less than twenty years the per-capita consumption has gone down seventy-five per cent, as appearances of actual oranges in most of the United States have become steadily less frequent. Fresh, whole, round, orange oranges are hardly extinct, of course, but they have seen better days since they left the garden of the Hesperides.

Fresh oranges have become, in a way, old-fashioned. The frozen product made from them is pure and sweet, with a laboratory-controlled balance between its acids and its sugars; its color and its flavor components are as uniform as science can make them, and a consumer opening the six-ounce can is confident that the drink he is about to reconstitute will taste almost exactly like the juice that he took out of the last can he bought. Fresh orange juice, on the other hand, is probably less consistent in flavor than any other natural or fermented drink, with the possible exception of wine.

The taste and aroma of oranges differ by type, season, county, state, and country, and even as a result of the position of the individual orange in the framework of the tree on which it grew. Ground fruit—the orange that one can reach and pick from the ground—is not as sweet as fruit that grows high on the tree. Outside fruit is sweeter than inside fruit. Oranges grown on the south side of a tree are sweeter than oranges grown on the east or west sides, and oranges grown on the north side are the least sweet of the lot. The quantity of juice in an orange, and even the amount of Vitamin C it contains, will follow the same pattern of variation. Beyond this, there are differentiations of quality inside a single orange. Individual segments vary from one another in their content of acid and sugar. But that is cutting it pretty fine. Orange men, the ones who actually work in the groves, don't discriminate to that extent. When they eat an orange, they snap out the long, thin blades of their fruit knives and peel it down, halfway, from the blossom end, which is always sweeter and juicier than the stem end. They eat the blossom half and throw the rest of the orange away.

An orange grown in Florida usually has a thin and tightly fitting skin, and it is also heavy with juice. Californians say that if you want to eat a Florida orange you have to get into a bathtub first. California oranges are light in weight and have thick skins that break easily and come off in hunks. The flesh inside is marvelously sweet, and the segments almost separate themselves. In Florida, it is said that you can run over a California orange with a ten-ton truck and not even wet the pavement. The differences from which these hyperboles arise will prevail in the two states even if the type of orange is the same. In arid climates, like California's, oranges develop a thick albedo, which is the white part of the skin. Florida is one of the two or three most rained-upon states in the United States. California uses the Colorado River and similarly impressive sources to irrigate its oranges, but of course irrigation can only do so much. The annual difference in rainfall between the Florida and California orange-growing areas is one million one hundred and forty thousand gallons per acre. For years, California was the leading orange state, but Florida surpassed California in 1942, and grows three times as many oranges now. California oranges, for their part, can safely be called three times as beautiful.

The color of an orange has no absolute correlation with the maturity of the flesh and juice inside. An orange can be as sweet and ripe as it will ever be and still glisten like an emerald in the tree. Cold—coolness, rather—is what makes an orange orange. In some parts of the world, the weather never gets cold enough to change the color; in Thailand, for example, an orange is a green fruit, and traveling Thais often blink with wonder at the sight of oranges the color of flame.

From HOUSE

T R A C Y   K I D D E R

Editor's Note: Since 1981, Tracy Kidder has written a trilogy about "non-famous people at work." For his first volume, the Pulitzer Prizewinning The Soul of a New Machine, *Kidder spent eight months in the windowless basement of Data General Corporation's suburban Boston headquarters watching computer designers create a super-mini computer. "It is a rather painful feeling not to know what the people around you are talking about. But that's also an impetus to figure it out," stresses Kidder. "I tried to keep out of the way when I could. I think if I had created any important problems the engineers would have thrown me out."*

For the third volume of his trilogy, Among Schoolchildren *(1989), Kidder went back to school. He spent the entire 1986–1987 school year at the back of Chris Zajac's fifth grade classroom in Holyoke, Massachusetts. "I had nothing to do but watch for details," he notes. Kidder's 340-page account of the interplay between one dedicated teacher and 20 ten-year-olds came from the 100 notebooks he filled during the school year, one 1,000-page rough draft, and two rewrites.*

In between computer and school, Kidder found himself drawn to that instinctive habit of all species: home construction. In his 1985 volume, House, *excerpted below, he describes the building of one Greek Revival home on the outskirts of Amherst, Massachusetts, and the delicate tension created by the desires of the owners, the architect's effort to translate them into something functional yet beautiful, and the builders' concerns for the budget, deadlines, and craft. Into this dramatic story, Kidder manages to weave short essays on groundbreaking, architecture, the lumber business, and the pleasures of physical labor.*

"I enjoy research, once I get lost in it," Kidder acknowledges. "Writing is an awfully nice profession because I'm able to meet a lot of different and interesting people and get into a lot of fascinating subjects. . . . My tendency is to write about individuals and let the general take care of itself."

Kidder's latest book, Old Friends, *is a study of aging and of life within one Massachusetts nursing home.*

Jim Locke sets gently on the undisturbed earth a mahogany box, opens it, and takes out his transit, which looks like a spyglass. It is a tool for imposing levelness on an irregular world.

Locke's transit is made of steel with small brass adjusting wheels and is as old as the century, more than twice as old as Locke, who is thirty-six. He uses it near the beginnings of jobs and first of all for guiding bulldozers. Locke erects the transit on a tripod. He turns the brass wheels until the bubble, encased in glass beneath the eyepiece, floats to the center of its chamber. Then, bending over, putting one eye to the lens of the transit and squinting the other, he transforms his view of this patch of open ground into a narrow, well-lighted tunnel divided by cross hairs. Oliver

Wendell Holmes once said, in another context, "The art of civilization is the act of drawing lines." And of course it has also been the act of drawing level ones.

This piece of ground was once part of a New England hayfield. It lies on the southern outskirts of Amherst, Massachusetts, a college and university town, the kind of place that has a fine public school system and a foreign policy. The site has been studied all winter. It commands pretty views. There's a deep-looking woods on one edge. On another, there's a pasture, which turns into the precipitous, forested, publicly owned hills known as the Holyoke Range. And to the north and east there's a panorama. Look north and you see a hillside orchard topped with two giant maples locally known as Castor and Pollux. Look a little east and your view extends out over a broad valley, all the way to the Pelham Hills, which have turned blue at this morning hour.

The air has some winter in it. On this morning in mid-April 1983 a New England spring snow is predicted. The sky looks prepared. It has a whitening look. Several weeks must pass before dandelions, but the urge to build has turned New England's April into May. While Locke prepares for the transformation of this ground, four others pace around, killing time. They have their collars turned up and their hands thrust deep into coat pockets. They wait with reddening noses. None of the onlookers needs to be here, but none would have willingly stayed away. Among them is a very tall man, named Bill Rawn. He is the architect. He has driven all the way from Boston to witness the birth of the first house he has ever designed, and he grins while he waits. There are Judith and Jonathan Souweine, the woman and the man of the house to be. (Their surname is French and is pronounced "Suh-wayne," or if one is in a hurry, "Swayne.") They have spent months planning for this moment, and they have imagined it for many more. Judith and Jonathan smile at each other. Judith takes a few snapshots while Jim Locke works with the transit.

Turning her camera on Locke, Judith sees a refined-looking young man. When she met him about two months ago, she thought, "Obviously, his upbringing was very upper middle class. Even if I hadn't known who his father was, I could have told. Everything about him was—well, you know. He's made a conscious decision not to be a white-collar professional." Locke is wearing jeans and work boots and an old brown jacket, a workingman's uniform. His clothes are clean and he is clean-shaven. He has straight brown hair, neatly trimmed and combed, and a long, narrow jaw. There is a delicacy in his features. You can imagine his mother in him. He has a thoughtful air. He studies his transit a moment, laying two fingers against his lips. Then as he bends again to the eyepiece, he wipes his hair off his forehead and for a moment he looks boyish and defiant.

The building site slopes gently. Locke calculates by how much it does so. He turns the scope of the transit until he sees the cross hairs rest upon a numeral inscribed on a long, numbered staff. Judith's father has volunteered to carry the staff. Locke directs him to and fro. For a benchmark, Locke has chosen an electrical box planted in the ground nearby. He sends his staff-bearer to that spot first. The numbers Locke reads through his scope tell him how far below his transit's scope the benchmark rests. He sends the staff-bearer to a stake that represents the south-eastern corner of the house to come, and through the scope he determines how far below the benchmark that corner lies. Locke checks these numbers against ones inscribed on a blueprint opened on the ground beside him. Soon he knows the relative elevations of the land at each corner of the house. He will be able to tell through his spyglass when the cellar hole has been dug to the proper depth. The ceremony can begin, as soon as the bulldozer arrives.

When Locke has begun to wonder whether it is coming at all, it appears—a small, yellow machine on a large trailer. Locke gives the driver his instructions, while the others hang back. The bulldozer puffs smoke, and clanks down off the trailer.

The first pass the machine makes over the ground, ripping the hair off the earth, looks like an act of great violence. The bulldozer does resemble a beast, but the creature is both unruly and extremely methodical. Gradually, the sense of disruption goes out of the scene. The machine makes its first cuts. It goes back over the same suddenly dark ground. Piles of earth mount up. The hole deepens and, as sand appears, turns orange. Watching the bulldozer work is restful and mesmerizing. Its noise discourages speech, leaving each of the party alone and thoughtful for moments.

Ground breaking: On every continent and many islands, people used to undertake elaborate rituals when they undertook to build. Augury assisted choices and planning of sites. In northern Ireland, for example, lamps were placed on stones that marked two corners of an incipient house, and the site was deemed safe to build on if the lamps stayed lit for a few nights. Elsewhere, to ensure the strength and safety of a building, human and surrogate victims—animals and various objects—were entombed under foundation stones. In the Balkans, as recently as the late 1800s, builders digging a foundation hole would entice a passer-by near so that the innocent victim's shadow would fall into the excavation. The builders would cover the shadow with a stone, or mark out the shadow's length and breadth and bury the measurement of it. The ritual ensured the foundation's durability. The victim, it was thought, would die within the year.

No bodies are being buried in this deepening cellar hole. No one has watched for omens. There is only desire. This group does have a few worries. They have not settled all the details of the plan. They have not arrived at a final price for the house. They have not yet signed a contract. Jim Locke wanted all of that done before this day. Locke felt he had to go ahead, knowing that if he delayed he might not get the excavator for weeks. But Locke can imagine events that would leave him holding the bill for this work. Both he and the Souweines have begun to build on faith, without much knowledge of each other.

The party lingers awhile. The bulldozer's cab begins to sink beneath the level of the field.

2

For eight years, Judith and Jonathan shared a duplex with another young couple, but both families grew too large for the place, and reluctantly they all agreed that the time for moving on had come. Judith's parents had settled in a new house on about twenty sloping acres. Jonathan and Judith looked around. They decided that they'd like to buy a piece of her parents' property. Jonathan and Judith liked the idea of locating three generations of their family on adjoining land. It was a traditional arrangement that had grown uncommon. They imagined many advantages. They also thought it was a slightly risky undertaking, but they like to see themselves as people who are not afraid of taking chances. Actually, the only obvious problem was that Judith sometimes bickers with her father, Jules Wiener. She remembers Jules closing out disputes, when she was still a child, by saying to her, "My house, my rules." Now when he visits her house and takes out a cigar, she says, "My house, my rules. No cigars." She smiles when she says her lines, but the joke sometimes leads to sharper words. "I'm pretty direct with my father, and he's pretty direct with me," she explains. "As they say, I come by it honest." As for Jonathan, he is hardly a typical son-in-law. He adores Judith's mother, Florence, and he and Jules have been friends ever since Jonathan was seventeen and came courting Judith. Like Jonathan, Jules is a lawyer, and it's a family joke that if Jonathan and Judith ever sued each other for divorce, Jules would opt to represent his son-in-law.

So Judith and Jonathan made their offer to her parents, who concealed momentarily their great delight, lest they seem too eager and stir up second thoughts. Jules made some vows to himself. "I can see a steady stream of grandchildren coming our way. The door's open. But it's not going the other way. If twenty cars are here for a party, I'm not walking over to say, 'What's going on?'" Jules and Florence deeded to Jonathan and Judith about four acres of land. The Souweines would have a house built on it by the time their twins entered kindergarten in the fall of 1983.

Jonathan is polite and very direct. In conversation he tends to curtness, but let him get on a subject that truly engages him, such as a coming election, and he becomes positively garrulous, tapping his listener's arm for emphasis, talking so swiftly that his words slur. He looks his best at such moments, or running a meeting, or speaking in front of a political gathering, or striding down a street. He clearly likes command. He is an inch below six feet. He has broad shoulders. He comes at you a little sleepy-eyed, wearing a small crooked grin, and carrying his arms out from his body in a way that makes you think of impending showdowns in Westerns.

Jonathan started college on a basketball scholarship, and even now, in a business suit, his hair in middle-aged retreat, he looks like a busy play-making guard—what sportswriters call the spark plug type. He was a good athlete and a better student. He gave up his scholarship, went to Columbia, participated in protests against the Vietnam War and campaigned for a liberal, antiwar congressman, and went on to Harvard Law School. He imagined himself becoming a lawyer who would work for the public good. He spent a year clerking for a federal judge and another in the department of consumer protection of the Massachusetts attorney general's office; in between he took command of the Massachusetts Public Interest Research Group (MassPIRG) and in that capacity led a number of lobbying campaigns, for solar energy and a bottle bill and against white-collar crime. Then Jonathan ran for district attorney of Hampshire and Franklin counties. It was now or probably never, he told Judith. Against all predictions—he was a newcomer, outspoken, and even a little left-wing—Jonathan won the Democratic primary. He lost the general election, and soon afterward he became a country lawyer. For the sake of his family, he gave up running for office, but he has kept his hand in as an epistolary politician. He writes letters to editors assessing political candidates. He writes about burning issues of the day and also about local fund-raising events. He has written so many letters and so many have been published locally that a Jonathan Souweine letter to the editor has become a virtual institution in Amherst and the towns nearby. Some people think he is still running for office, but clearly he is writing letters instead.

A former lieutenant in Jonathan's campaign remembers a quiet day in their office, when a stranger, a middle-aged man, walked in off the street and asked what sort of name was Souweine.

"French." said Jonathan.

The man looked greatly relieved. "Thank God. I thought you were Jewish."

"I am," said Jonathan pleasantly.

"He looked right at the guy," his former lieutenant remembers. "Jonathan told him he hoped that religion wouldn't be an issue in the election. He talked to the guy for about ten minutes, and I remember as I watched, thinking, 'This is Jonathan in one of his best moments.'"

A squash partner of Jonathan's had believed that winning mattered more than most things to Jonathan, and then one day Jonathan made him wonder if he had ever had the slightest idea who Jonathan was. They had played to a dead heat. They were in their fifth and deciding game. The score was tied. It was Jonathan's serve. But Jonathan held the ball. He turned to his opponent and declared that this had been such a fine and even match it seemed a shame to spoil it by going on. Wearing his cockeyed grin, Jonathan offered his hand.

Jonathan says, "If I'm confronted, I'll instantly fight." He has observed in others—in a law partner, in Bill the architect—a quieter way of contending. "What I call Protestant good manners." He has seen that approach succeed where his own had failed. "I haven't been able to integrate it into my life," he says. "But I can *see* it now." Sometimes—after he's spoken his mind at a school committee meeting, for instance—Jonathan leaves a roiled-up wake. Some people dislike him—that proves he's alive. And maybe he ought to occupy a wider sphere than the one he has chosen. But Jonathan has fun.

He does not deny himself the pleasure of a gaudy necktie now and then. He has a way with children. He emerges from a movie about Robin Hood—his favorite hero—teaching his boys how to swashbuckle down the street. He says, "I love trials. I love the intensity, the action." Losing the race for D.A., he insists, was a fine, enlightening experience, nearly as rewarding as winning, he guesses. After he had lost, he wrote a letter to the local paper, and in it he quoted Teddy Roosevelt, that Achilles of American politicians, as follows:

> Far better it is to dare mighty things, to win glorious triumphs, even though
> checkered by failure, than to take rank with those poor spirits who neither
> enjoy much nor suffer much, because they live in the gray twilight that
> knows not victory nor defeat.

Jonathan seems to believe in coming home with his shield or else on it. Judith likes to mix it up now and then, too. She is small, with black curly hair. She hopes to become a representative to the Amherst Town Meeting, a yearly congress on town affairs that usually lasts for days. It's some people's idea of torture, and her idea of fun. Of the fights between her teachers' union and the local school board, battles in which she will participate all during the building of her new house, she says, "There's one guy on our team who's not confrontational. But me? My idea is you yell, you scream, you pack the room and have emotional floor fights. What could be better? So we lose. At least we'll go down kicking and screaming." She explains, "If you grow up with a lot of yelling and screaming, yelling and screaming doesn't scare ya. In fact, you kind of like it."

Jonathan and Judith had imagined in some detail a house that would suit them functionally. Jonathan had already begun making lists. But they were stuck on the question, among others, of what style of house theirs should be. How should it look to their new neighbors, to their friends, and to people passing by on Bay Road, the old road to Boston, down at the bottom of the hill?

Judith and Jonathan had not rearranged their political philosophy to suit fashion or their growing affluence, and they did not want to display their bank account in the facade of their new house. "I won't be a brilliant lawyer," Jonathan once remarked. "I work hard and I'm a good lawyer, and that's good enough for almost any situation, and it's good enough for me." A plain-styled, sturdy house would have suited him best. And Judith's first impulse was utilitarian. "It's the structural details that can change the quality of your life." They had made up their minds, though, to buy a house of 3000 square feet, in a region where custom-made houses cost about $50 per foot. "By any standard," Jonathan would say, "it's a lot of house and a lot of money." Neither he nor Judith wanted to spend what looked to them like an enormous sum and end up with what Judith called "just a big box."

Judith grew up in a large and stylish house. It had a foyer and a graceful stair and a full butler's pantry. When the time came to sell it, her mother could scarcely bring herself to sign the papers. Judith did not imagine a reproduction of that house. It would have cost too much, and anyway, she did not want to imprison herself in the past. But she had been happy in that lovely house, and she did think back to it sometimes when she thought ahead to her new one. So did Jonathan. "I grew up in a Long Island subdivision, in a split-level house. All the houses were the same. I didn't mind. I didn't think about it. Then I met Judith, and Judith lived in this beautiful Colonial house. It was just gorgeous. It made me aware that there was something other than split-levels. It made me aware."

Between Amherst and the Connecticut River lies a little bit of Iowa—some of New England's most favored farmland. The summer and fall of 1982 Judith bicycled, alone and with Jonathan, down narrow roads between fields of asparagus and corn, and she saw the constructed landscape with new eyes, not just looking at houses but searching for ones that might serve as models for her own. She liked the old farmhouses best, their porches and white, clapboarded walls. "This New England farmhousey thing," she called that style. She found one house she liked especially, but did not get much further than that.

Although she and Jonathan considered many options, they began to feel that they didn't have all the right skills to invent their new house by themselves. And time was running out. Finally, late in January 1983, they decided to call in an architect. "We basically hired an architect because we felt the problems of building a house were too complex for us, and we're great believers in professionalism," said Judith afterward. "It looked like a difficult piece of land. We wanted to get someone with a lot of aesthetic ideas, too. Aesthetics are not as important to us as the function. They're important, but they're not where we start."

* * *

... on a Monday in late April, Jim walks into Jonathan's office carrying a zippered leather case, wedged tightly under his arm. Any purse snatcher would know that something inside is worth caring about. The case contains Jim's final price for the house and, on many sheets of yellow legal paper, the history of that price. It started at $162,000. The Souweines subtracted the garage and half a dozen other expensive items. The price fell to about $139,000. It started back up again, as the Souweines and Bill made new substitutions and additions. Jim's case contains the estimated cost of materials from Apple Corps's usual supplier; firm estimates on foundation work, plumbing, heating, wiring, painting, insulating, from Apple Corps's usual subcontractors; and Apple Corps's estimate of its members' own labor. Jim has put all those figures together and to the total he has added 10 percent, to cover overhead and profit and fear of miscalculation. Jim has come up with a hill-town Yankee's price. It is an exact-looking figure, rounded to the nearest ten dollars.

From his last meeting with Jonathan, Jim knows that the Souweines hope for concessions on the price, and he's not sure that even as it stands, his final price is high enough to cover the cost of this house and a modest profit for Apple Corps. The builders have turned down all other jobs for this one, though. In planning this house, Jim has invested at least two weeks' time, for which he hasn't yet been paid. Losing this job would rank among the large setbacks in Apple Corps's history. Jim feels nervous. He says so, rather nervously, to Judith and Jonathan.

Judith sits knitting in a chair in front of Jonathan's desk. She smiles at Jim and trades some small talk.

Just to build the house they want—and never mind the purchase of the land— Judith and Jonathan must borrow, at 13 percent interest, $100,000, the maximum that the local savings and loans will lend for house construction. To raise the remaining tens of thousands, whatever they come to exactly, the Souweines hope for a good and timely sale of their old house, and, of course, houses aren't always easy to sell. Jonathan hasn't lost much sleep over the money, but the sheer amount makes Judith nervous. She confesses later to a slightly embattled feeling—"It's us against the world, you know." The world is a troupe of unknown lumber dealers and workers, with a building contractor at their head. You turn everything over to a gang of people who don't really know you or have any reason to care about you. You turn over dreams, pride, and money. It's a frightening gamble. Judith and Jonathan don't intend to undertake it without some reassurances and some measure of control.

They once read a book called *It Takes "Jack" to Build a House*. It's a story of woe, with chapters that bear such titles as "The House Is Framed—So Are You." The woman who wrote it chose her builder carefully. He came highly recommended. He talked a good game. He cheated her. Jonathan and Judith feel certain of

Jim's competence and honesty, as certain as anyone could be of those qualities in a virtual stranger. They're ready to be guided by him, but not bossed around. Jim should be their partner in this undertaking. Jonathan hopes Jim's final price will be around $142,000. He fears it will be more, and if it is, he'll ask Jim to lower it, if only to get proof that Jim will compromise with them—as indeed Jim already has, on the matter of the windows.

Judith is a trained psychologist, among other things. She can foresee an argument. The prospect doesn't frighten her. She smiles and knits. A button on the lapel of her blazer reads, "GOOD CONTRACT GOOD EDUCATION," a token of the role she plays in negotiations elsewhere. If she feels at all nervous, it's well concealed in the thrust and parry of her needles.

It may not be deliberate, but Jonathan, who's dressed in a cable-knit sweater and corduroys, is still busy about his office. He says hello to Jim, hands Jim a set of specs, and goes back to examining papers on his desk, occasionally crumpling a sheet and chucking it into the wastebasket.

Jim reads the specs, still standing by the desk. He looks very nervous. He sucks at his lips. He is, unmistakably, not at home.

They begin. "Okay, Judith, tell him," says Jonathan.

"I will really go crazy if I have to live with my father for a month. My sense was it was absolutely clear we'd be in by September first," says Judith to Jim. She smiles.

There's intimacy in this plea. Jim turns to her and leans in her direction. "What can I say? I can't build it any faster. I would like to do it sooner."

Evidently, Judith has resigned herself to October 31.

"Okay," says Jonathan, smiling at Jim. "How much are you going to build this house for?"

"I still don't have the prices on the window casings," says Jim. "My supplier let me down. He went to a banquet tonight. But in theory, with narrow casings, it's one hundred forty-six thousand six hundred and sixty. The reason I'm so nervous, I've been over and over this so many times I don't really understand the numbers anymore. My partner Richard looked at the plans today, and he said, 'It's okay, we can build it for that.' So I guess it's all right."

"What are the high points?" asks Judith. "What have we changed?" She knits. Jim extracts his yellow pad from his case and reads numbers, all the deletions they've made, all the additions.

"Does that make sense?" asks Jim.

No one speaks.

"Something bothers you?" Jim says to Jonathan.

Jonathan has been studying his own sheaf of yellow paper. He looks up abruptly, like a man awakening. "No," he says pleasantly.

Again, there is silence. Again, Jim breaks into it. "I have no idea how to value Bill's time," he says, referring to the architect. "I know I'd have had to do more drawings without him. I know I've been to more meetings than I ever have before, and I don't know if that's because of him. And on the other concerns you had, Jonathan, we just didn't add very much as a fudge factor in our original bid.

Frankly, there are a couple of things we left out and we haven't put them back in. So I've allowed two hundred dollars for Bill's work and that two hundred dollars is the only one of the things we talked about that I'm willing to remove."

Judith knits. Jonathan leans a contemplative elbow on his desk. Finally, Judith speaks up. "You and I," she says to Jonathan, "I think we should talk about it."

Judith might just have fired a starter's gun. Jonathan jumps up. Judith arises. They vanish into another room.

Jim's price exceeds the one that Jonathan hoped for by several thousand dollars. Jonathan knows that an estimate on something as large and complex as a house can't be as precise as Jim's figure suggests. To Jonathan, Jim's price begs for some negotiation. To Jim, the price represents hours and hours of honest addition and subtraction. For his part, Jonathan believes that Jim has been honest, and though disappointed, he's prepared to find the several thousand more than he hoped he'd have to pay, if Jim in turn will round the number down to the nearest thousand. "I think he's gonna go nuts," Judith says. Jonathan stands firm. He just wants Jim to come down a little on the price, and she agrees Jim should.

They're gone only a few minutes. They reseat themselves as briskly as they left. Jim laughs out loud, at nothing in particular. "Okay," says Jonathan. "Some of the things I brought up Saturday I still believe. But what can I say? I came here hoping the price would be somewhere between one-forty and one-forty-five." He studies his papers. He looks up, the trace of a smile on his face. "I don't want to bargain or anything. You take off six hundred and sixty dollars and we have a deal."

Jim is sitting very stiffly. He opens his hands. "Why do you want to dicker?" he says.

"You call that dickering?" says Jonathan. "I call that a round number." It'll cost him $4000 for appliances, he explains, and removing the $660, then adding in the appliances, will bring the grand total to $150,000. "So when my friends ask, I can say it's a hundred-and-fifty-thousand-dollar house."

"Why don't you leave the six hundred and sixty in, and *tell* them it cost a hundred and fifty thousand?" says Jim.

Silence takes over again. Someone's stomach growls. Jonathan has picked up his calculator. Jim has pulled his out. It is hard to imagine what is left to compute. Judith smiles. "Look at this. The war of the calculators."

"That's my proposal," says Jonathan, that brief electronic skirmish over. "We make the deal, I won't bug you or complain."

"It makes me uncomfortable," says Jim. "I'm bargaining with three other guys' money." He adds quickly, "I know that's not your problem."

"I just talked to *my* partner," says Judith, still smiling.

Jim shifts in his chair. "It's stupid, you know. Here I am worried about six hundred dollars on a one-hundred-forty-six-thousand-dollar job." He adds, "But so are you."

"Actually, I'm worried about a lot more," says Jonathan.

Jim laughs. "I feel foolish."

"Don't feel foolish," says Jonathan. "Talk to your partners."

"I've got to," says Jim, who is no longer laughing, all of a sudden. "If it were just me, I'd say, 'No way.' "

The tone of the discussion changes now. "One thing I worry about, Jim. You're building my house, you have to make decisions. I have partners. If I want to move the office, I'll call a general meeting, but not if I'm just going to buy paper clips." Jim stares at a point on the wall. "I don't want you to feel bad or pressured," Jonathan adds.

"You gotta make a deal, Jim!" says Judith, not unkindly. "You gotta make a deal."

"I'm not used to bargaining," Jim says to her.

"Hey, I bargain," says Jonathan. "Judith bargains, and this—I'm kind of annoyed because I thought I was being magnanimous."

"My job's not bargaining. You accepted the bid!" says Jim.

"Do you think they just built the Empire State Building? They didn't bargain over the price?" says Jonathan.

"It feels to me like if you don't make a little deal out of it, you won't feel good about it," says Jim.

"I want to loosen you up, Jim," says Jonathan.

"Loosen me up how?" says Jim, raising his voice. "By the purse strings?"

"I want the six hundred dollars," says Jonathan, softly. "But you don't go up on a mountain and return with the truth. You can't tell me your estimate is the only possible number. I think there's got to be a little more give and take, a little more bending, a little more suppleness."

Jim looks at no one, and no one speaks. Then Jonathan sighs. "I really did think I was being magnanimous. I have a short office meeting. I'm available if there's anything else to talk about. I don't think there's anything else to talk about."

Jonathan leaves. Jim gets up, but leans against a chair a moment, to speak to Judith.

"How does he want to loosen me up?" he asks her. "I think I have a pretty good sense of humor."

"I didn't say you had no sense of humor," she says. "Rigid, yes."

Jim purses his lips.

"I don't believe you, Jim," she says gently. "Everybody has to make deals."

"Our usual procedure doesn't include bargaining," Jim answers. "We don't do that many contract jobs."

"I think you make bargains every day," she says. "Say you want some kitchen cabinets. There's no magic number. There's nothing sacred about those numbers you get on an estimate."

"Then why do estimates?" asks Jim.

"Those may be close estimates, but then the person comes in and says, 'I'll give you a little less.'"

"I just don't understand what the deal is, for that amount of money." Jim seems truly puzzled, but calm.

"It strikes me as a bit holy to think that you don't bargain, Jim," says Judith. "High Moral Tone. HMT," she says. "And I think that's the thing that really gets to Jonathan and me, High Moral Tone."

Jim departs on the instant. He walks out like a person who has found himself in the wrong neighborhood, wishing but not daring to run.

"There's nothing like a political campaign. But this comes close to it, in terms of intensity," says Judith. She sits in the reception room, waiting for Jonathan to finish his office meeting. "Do you know who his father is?" she says, speaking of Jim. "Number one in workmen's comp. He wrote the book." She gestures across the room toward a bookcase of legal texts. And there it is, in fact. *Massachusetts Practice: Volume 29*, by Laurence S. Locke. Judith adds, with a sad-looking face and a shrug, "Now he's involved with more lawyers, and he doesn't like it."

She calls Jim "very rigid, very rigid." She says, "Jonathan and I are controlling, but we're not rigid. We want things our way. We push people around. But we're not rigid."

Judith sighs. "I thought I was making things better, until I realized I was making them worse. He's mad."

"I wasn't mad," Jim tells Sandy Warren, sitting at their kitchen table. "I was embarrassed. I felt like I was being handled. It was a real familiar feeling. It felt like something that happened to me when I was little. I was put off balance by somebody I expected was going to be allied with me and turned out not to be."

In the bar downstairs from his office, Jonathan tells Judith that he has given up bargaining. He intends to make no more concessions.

A few days before, the other contractor who had bid on this job called Jonathan, offering his services at a reduced price if for some reason the deal with Apple Corps went awry. Jonathan insisted that he had a moral commitment to Apple Corps, but the other builder's call made him realize he felt that he was going to pay for it—the other builder had good credentials, too. By his own standards, Jonathan has negotiated very gently with Jim and has asked for only a small, token concession. He assumed Jim would accept, and he imagined a handshake and in the next day or two another ceremonial gathering of the Souweines and the carpenters at the site. It was just a small daydream, which Jim has destroyed. Jonathan is openly angry, at last.

He says to Judith, "If you go in to buy a truck, you don't care about the person you buy it from. But if somebody builds a house for you, he becomes a very important person in your life for six months. I'll tell you the truth. He makes me uptight. I feel as if I say the wrong thing, he'll get offended. Tell you the truth, I'm not worried about the money. I'm worried about the deal. If he can't pull it together on one night, how's he going to pull it together on the house?"

Judith worries about the money. "I'm flabbergasted that we're going to spend a hundred and fifty thousand dollars and not have a garage." Of the $660, she remarks, "It's somewhat symbolic, obviously. But it's not totally symbolic. It's six hundred and sixty dollars we've gotta earn, you know."

Now in the bar, Jonathan takes her arm. "Let's go home."

Jim and Sandy sit up till past midnight. "I don't mind the money so much as the way I'm being treated," he says. "I'm being handled and I don't like somebody saying the reason I'm feeling that way is because I have High Moral Tone. It's like going to buy a used car. Well, maybe not. He wants me to be less rigid. It's like he's trying to reform me. The bit about my loosening up. What do they mean? What do they care about what I do? Is that how you welcome someone into your family?"

"Weren't they saying, 'Come on, you're not as pure as that'?" Sandy asks. "'You're cheating us by at least this much money.' What they said to you over and over is that everybody bargains. They've got to shake that out of you."

"If I keep feeling the way I do," Jim tells her, "the job won't come out as well as it would have this morning. It'll come out less than six hundred and sixty dollars good, and that's what bothers me. I hate that, because that's not the way I want to work."

Sandy looks sad. She says, "I just don't want to face another summer of your getting up and going to a job just because you have to."

Just before they turn in, Sandy remembers their mortgage. Have they paid it? "It's not the end of the month yet," says Jim, touching her shoulder. "Don't worry about it. You don't have to pay mortgages until the end of the month."

Six hundred sixty dollars represents a very small fraction of what the Souweines will pay for their new house. Divided among Apple Corps, it comes to a little more than a day's pay for each carpenter, against a whole summer of wages, and perhaps, if the estimate holds, a profit of some fifteen thousand dollars. Money is merely the form of the argument. They have asked each other for gestures. They have really just wanted to be friends. They have let each other down.

Jim calls Jonathan and accepts Jonathan's terms. A few days later, they sign the contract. Jim goes over each detail with care. He offers his hand to Jonathan, and Jonathan, glad the hard bargaining is over, takes it with an enthusiasm that surprises Jim. Jonathan gets the better grip, consequently. Afterward, Jonathan feels pleased at Jim's approach to the contract. "My last builder would always say 'Yes,' and he didn't always live up to it. But a man who says he's worried about putting his name on a piece of paper is a man who cares about his word. Jim is a person of integrity. I feel very comfortable having him build my house."

Jim leaves contemplating the handshake. Even in that transaction, he thinks, Jonathan insisted on getting the better of him.

From **THE BRIDGE**

GAY TALESE

Editor's Note: Gay Talese's book The Bridge *began in 1959 with the public announcement that a bridge would be built connecting Staten Island to Brooklyn, New York. As with all his works, he was drawn to the subject by curiosity. "If you watch a great construction project, the building of a bridge or a skyscraper, you see this magnificent work being done at high altitudes—and sometimes at great peril," he explains. "I knew books had been written about bridges, but never about the people who built them, the obscure people we see from a distance only in silhouette."*

From the shore's edge Talese watched barges floating within view carrying loads of steel, and as he watched he wanted to know what it was like to be a bridge builder, to be up there courting danger while building something that is going to outlive you, as all great bridges outlive the people who create them. Talese returned to the bridge site again and again to watch the slow progress. Eventually he decided to spend all his free time in the next three years, not only watching the miraculous work being done with steel and cable, but becoming acquainted with the men who so adroitly performed this remarkable feat.

From early 1960 to late 1962, Talese practiced the fine art of "hanging out." "I was so regularly in attendance at the bridge in my off hours and vacations from the New York Times *that I was practically considered one of the staff of U.S. Steel," he recalls. Talese read all the books he could find on bridge building and on famous bridges and bridge builders. He interviewed O. H. Ammonn, the designer of this new Verrazano-Narrows Bridge, and he walked across the narrow beams, wobbling in the wind, to feel firsthand the danger. Indeed, Talese spent so much time with the bridge builders that they invited him to their homes on weekends, even the Indians who raced on Friday evenings 100 mph to reach their homes on a reservation near Montreal—an exploit that seemed more risky to Talese than the feats they performed 500 feet above the water.*

The Bridge *explores the recurring injuries and death inherent in the romantic, daring lifestyle of these American macho heroes. By titling this volume* The Bridge, *Talese joined his own vision to that of Hart Crane's poem "The Bridge" and Walt Whitman's famous "Crossing Brooklyn Ferry." This title, like the titles of Talese's other major works* (The Kingdom and the Power, Honor Thy Father, Thy Neighbor's Wife, *and* Unto the Sons), *transforms the story of one profession into an ironic American morality tale: a tale of the success—and failure—of the American Dream.*

They drive into town in big cars, and live in furnished rooms, and drink whiskey with beer chasers, and chase women they will soon forget. They linger only a little while, only until they have built the bridge; then they are off again to another town, another bridge, linking everything but their lives.

They possess none of the foundation of their bridges. They are part circus, part gypsy—graceful in the air, restless on the ground; it is as if the wide-open road below lacks for them the clear direction of an eight-inch beam stretching across the sky six hundred feet above the sea.

When there are no bridges to be built, they will build skyscrapers, or highways, or power dams, or anything that promises a challenge—and overtime. They will go anywhere, will drive a thousand miles all day and night to be part of a new building boom. They find boom towns irresistible. That is why they are called "the boomers."

In appearance, boomers usually are big men, or if not always big, always strong, and their skin is ruddy from all the sun and wind. Some who heat rivets have charred complexions; some who drive rivets are hard of hearing; some who catch rivets in small metal cones have blisters and body burns marking each miss; some who do welding see flashes at night while they sleep. Those who connect steel have deep scars along their shins from climbing columns. Many boomers have mangled hands and fingers sliced off by slipped steel. Most have taken falls and broken a limb or two. All have seen death.

They are cocky men, men of great pride, and at night they brag and build bridges in bars, and sometimes when they are turning to leave, the bartender will yell after them, "Hey, you guys, how's about clearing some steel out of here?"

Stray women are drawn to them, like them because they have money and no wives within miles—they liked them well enough to have floated a bordello boat beneath one bridge near St. Louis, and to have used upturned hardhats for flowerpots in the red-light district of Paducah.

On weekends some boomers drive hundreds of miles to visit their families, are tender and tolerant, and will deny to the heavens any suggestion that they raise hell on the job—except they'll admit it in whispers, half proud, half ashamed, fearful the wives will hear and then any semblance of marital stability will be shattered.

Like most men, the boomer wants it both ways.

Occasionally his family will follow him, living in small hotels or trailer courts, but it is no life for a wife and child.

The boomer's child might live in forty states and attend a dozen high schools before he graduates, *if* he graduates, and though the father swears he wants no boomer for a son, he usually gets one. He gets one, possibly, because he really wanted one, and maybe that is why boomers brag so much at home on weekends, creating a wondrous world with whiskey words, a world no son can resist because this world seems to have everything: adventure, big cars, big money and gambling on rainy days when the bridge is slippery, and booming around the country with Indians who are sure-footed as spiders, with Newfoundlanders as shifty as the sea they come from, with roaming Rebel riveters escaping the poverty of their small Southern towns, all of them building something big and permanent, something that can be revisited years later and pointed to and said of: "See that bridge over there, son—well one day, when I was younger, I drove twelve hundred rivets into that goddamned thing."

Building a bridge is like combat; the language is of the barracks, and the men are organized along the lines of the noncommissioned officers' caste. At the very bottom, comparable to the Army recruit, are the apprentices—called "punks." They climb catwalks with buckets of bolts, learn through observation and turns on the tools, occasionally are sent down for coffee and water, seldom hear thanks. Within two or three years, most punks have become full-fledged bridgemen, qualified to heat, catch, or drive rivets; to raise, weld, or connect steel—but it is the last job, connecting the steel, that most captures their fancy. The steel connectors stand highest on the bridge, their sweat taking minutes to hit the ground, and when the derricks hoist up new steel, the connectors reach out and grab it with their hands, swing it into position, bang it with bolts and mallets, link it temporarily to the steel already in place, and leave the rest to the riveting gangs.

Connecting steel is the closest thing to aerial art, except the men must build a new sky stage for each show, and that is what makes it so dangerous—that and the fact that young connectors sometimes like to grandstand a bit, like to show the old men how it is done, and so they sometimes swing on the cables too much, or stand on unconnected steel, or run across narrow beams on windy days instead of straddling as they should—and sometimes they get so daring they die.

Once the steel is in place, riveting gangs move in to make it permanent. The fast, four-man riveting gangs are wondrous to watch. They toss rivets around as gracefully as infielders, driving in more than a thousand a day, each man knowing the others' moves, some having traveled together for years as a team. One man is called the "heater," and he sweats on the bridge all day over a kind of barbecue pit of flaming coal, cooking rivets until they are red—but not so red that they will buckle or blister. The heater must be a good cook, a chef, must think he is cooking sausages not rivets, because the other three men in the riveting gang are very particular people.

Once the rivet is red, but not too red, the heater tong-tosses it fifty, or sixty, or seventy feet, a perfect strike to the "catcher," who snares it out of the air with his metal mitt. Then the catcher relays the rivet to the third man, who stands nearby and is called the "bucker-up"—and who, with a long cylindrical tool named after the anatomical pride of a stud horse, bucks the rivet into the prescribed hole and holds it there while the fourth man, the riveter, moves in from the other side and begins to rattle his gun against the rivet's front end until the soft tip of the rivet has been flattened and made round and full against the hole. When the rivet cools, it is as permanent as the bridge itself.

Death on the Bridge

It was a gray and windy morning. At 6:45 A.M. Gerard McKee and Edward Iannielli left their homes in two different parts of Brooklyn and headed for the bridge.

Iannielli, driving his car from his home in Flatbush, got there first. He was already on the catwalk, propped up on a cable with one leg dangling 385 feet above the water, when Gerard McKee walked over to him and waved greetings.

The two young men had much in common. Both were the sons of bridgemen, both were Roman Catholics, both were natives of New York City, and both were out to prove something—that they were as good as any boomer on the bridge.

They quietly resented the prevailing theory that boomers make the best bridgemen. After all, they reasoned, boomers were created more out of necessity than desire; the Indian from the reservation, the Southerner from the farm, the Newfoundlander from the sea, the Midwesterner from the sticks—those who composed most of the boomer population—actually were escaping the poverty and boredom of their birthplaces when they went chasing from boom town to boom town. Iannielli and McKee, on the other hand, did not have to chase all over America for the big job; they could wait for the job to come to them, and did, because the New York area had been enjoying an almost constant building boom for the last ten years.

And yet both were impressed with the sure swagger of the boomer, impressed with the fact that boomers were hired on jobs from New York to California, from Michigan to Louisiana, purely on their national reputations, not on the strength of strong local unions.

This realization seemed to impress Iannielli a bit more than McKee. Perhaps it was partly due to Iannielli's being so small in this big man's business.

He desperately wanted to prove himself, but he would make his mark not by cutting big men to size, or by boasting or boozing, but rather by displaying cold nerve on high steel—taking chances that only a suicidal circus performer would take—and by also displaying excessive pride on the ground.

Iannielli loved to say, "I'm an *iron*worker." (Bridges are now made of steel, but iron was the first metal of big bridges, and the first bridgemen were called "iron-workers." There is great tradition in the title, and so Iannielli—and all bridgemen with pride in the past—refer to themselves as *iron*workers, never *steel*workers.)

When Edward Iannielli first became an apprentice ironworker, he used to rub orange dust, the residue of lead paint, into his boots before taking the subway home; he was naïve enough in those days to think that passengers on the subway would

associate orange dust with the solution that is coated over steel during construction to make it rustproof.

"When I was a little kid growing up," he had once recalled, "my old man, Edward Iannielli, Sr., would bring other ironworkers home after work, and all they'd talk about was ironwork, ironwork. That's all we ever heard as kids, my brother and me. Sometimes my old man would take us out to the job, and all the other ironworkers were nice to us because we were Eddie's sons, and the foreman might come over and ask, 'You Eddie's sons?' and we'd say, 'Yeah,' and he'd say, 'Here, take a quarter.' And that is how I first started to love this business.

"Later, when I was about thirteen or fourteen, I remember going out to a job with the old man and seeing this big ladder. And I yelled to my father, 'Can I climb up?' and he said, 'Okay, but don't fall.' So I began to climb up this thing, higher and higher, a little scared at first, and then finally I'm on the top, standing on this steel beam way up there, and I'm all alone and looking all around up there, looking out and seeing very far, and it was exciting, and as I stood up there, all of a sudden, I am thinking to myself, '*This* is what I want to do!'"

After his father had introduced him to the business agent of Local 361, the iron-workers' union in Brooklyn, Edward Iannielli, Jr., started work as an apprentice.

"I'll never forget the first day I walked into that union hall," he had recalled. "I had on a brand-new pair of shoes, and I saw all those big men lined up, and some of them looked like bums, some looked like gangsters, some just sat around tables playing cards and cursing.

"I was scared, and so I found a little corner and just sat there, and in my pocket I had these rosaries that I held. Then a guy walked out and yelled, 'Is young Iannielli here?' and I said, 'Here,' and he said, 'Got a job for you.' He told me to go down and report to a guy named Harry at this new twelve-story criminal court building in downtown Brooklyn, and so I rushed down there and said to Harry, 'I'm sent out from the hall,' and he said, 'Oh, so you're the new apprentice boy,' and I said, 'Yeah,' and he said, 'You got your parents' permission?' and I said, 'Yeah,' and he said, 'In writing?' and I said, 'No,' and so he said, 'Go home and get it.'

"So I get back on the subway and go all the way back, and I remember running down the street, very excited because I had a job, to get my mother to sign this piece of paper. Then I ran all the way back, after getting out of the subway, up to Harry and gave him the piece of paper, and then he said, 'Okay, now I gotta see your birth certificate.' So I had to run all the way back, get another subway, and then come back, and now my feet in my new shoes are hurting.

"Anyway, when I gave Harry the birth certificate, he said, 'Okay, go up that ladder and see the pusher,' and when I got to the top, a big guy asked, 'Who you?' I tell 'im I'm the new apprentice boy, and he says, 'Okay, get them two buckets over there and fill 'em up with water and give 'em to the riveting gang.'

"These buckets were two big metal milk cans, and I had to carry them down the ladder, one at a time, and bring them up, and this is what I did for a long time—kept the riveting gangs supplied with drinking water, with coffee and with rivets—no ifs and buts either.

"And one time, when I was on a skyscraper in Manhattan, I remember I had to climb down a ladder six floors to get twenty coffees, a dozen sodas, some cake and everything, and on my way back, holding everything in a cardboard box, I remember slipping on a beam and losing my balance. I fell two flights. But luckily I fell in a pile of canvas, and the only thing that happened was I got splashed in all that steaming hot coffee. Some ironworker saw me laying there and he yelled, 'What happened?' and I said, 'I fell off and dropped the coffee,' and he said, '*You dropped the coffee!* Well, you better get the hell down there fast, boy, and get some more coffee.'

"So I go running down again, and out of my own money—must have cost me four dollars or more—I bought all the coffee and soda and cake, and then I climbed back up the ladder, and when I saw the pusher, before he could complain about anything, I told him I'm sorry I'm late."

After Edward Iannielli had become a full-fledged ironworker, he fell a few more times, mostly because he would run, not walk across girders, and once—while working on the First National City Bank in Manhattan—he fell backward about three stories and it looked as if he was going down all the way. But he was quick, light and lucky—he was "The Rabbit," and he landed on a beam and held on.

"I don't know what it is about me," he once tried to explain, "but I think it all has something to do with being young, and not wanting to be like those older men up there, the ones that keep telling me, 'Don't be reckless, you'll get killed, be careful.' Sometimes, on windy days, those old-timers get across a girder by crawling on their hands and knees, but I always liked to run across and show those other men how to do it. That's when they all used to say, 'Kid, you'll never see thirty.'

"Windy days, of course, are the hardest. Like you're walking across an eight-inch beam, balancing yourself in the wind, and then, all of a sudden, the wind stops—and you *temporarily lose your balance*. You quickly straighten out—but it's some feeling when *that* happens."

Edward Iannielli first came to the Verrazano-Narrows job in 1961, and while working on the Gowanus Expressway that cut through Bay Ridge, Brooklyn, to the bridge, he got his left hand caught in a crane one day.

One finger was completely crushed, but the other, cleanly severed, remained in his glove. Dr. Coppola was able to sew it back on. The finger would always be stiff and never as strong as before, of course; yet the surgeon was able to offer Edward Iannielli two choices as to how the finger might be rejoined to his hand. It could either be set straight, which would make it less conspicuous and more attractive, or it could be shaped into a grip-form, a hook. While this was a bit ugly, it would mean that the finger could more easily be used by Iannielli when working with steel. There was no choice, as far as Iannielli was concerned; the finger was bent permanently into a grip.

When, in the fall of 1963, Gerard McKee met Edward Iannielli and saw the misshapen left hand, he did not ask any questions or pay any attention. Gerard McKee was a member of an old family of construction workers, and to him malformation was not uncommon, it was almost a way of life. His father, James McKee, a big, broadshouldered man with dark hair and soft blue eyes—a man whom Gerard strongly resembled—had been hit by a collapsing crane a few years before, had had his leg permanently twisted, had a steel plate inserted in his head, and was disabled for life.

James McKee had been introduced to ironwork by an uncle, the late Jimmy Sullivan. The McKee name was well known down at Local 40, the union hall in Manhattan, and it had been quite logical for James McKee, prior to his accident, to take his three big sons down to the hall and register them in the ironworkers' apprentice program.

Of the three boys, Gerard McKee was the youngest, tallest and heaviest—but not by much. His brother John, a year older than Gerard, was 195 pounds and six feet two inches. And his brother Jimmy, two years older than Gerard, was 198 pounds and six feet three inches.

When the boys were introduced to union officials of Local 40, there were smiles of approval all around, and there was no doubt that the young McKees, all of them erect and broad-shouldered and seemingly eager, would someday develop into superb ironworkers. They looked like fine college football prospects—the type that a scout would eagerly offer scholarships to without asking too many embarrassing questions about grades. Actually the McKee boys had never even played high school football. Somehow in their neighborhood along the waterfront of South Brooklyn, an old Irish neighborhood called Red Hook, the sport of football had never been very popular among young boys.

The big sport in Red Hook was swimming, and the way a young boy could win respect, could best prove his valor, was to jump off one of the big piers or warehouses along the waterfront, splash into Buttermilk Channel, and then swim more than a mile against the tide over to the Statue of Liberty.

Usually, upon arrival, the boys would be arrested by the guards. If they weren't caught, they would then swim all the way back across Buttermilk Channel to the Red Hook side.

None of the neighborhood boys was a better swimmer than Gerard McKee, and none had gotten back and forth through Buttermilk Channel with more ease and speed than he. All the young boys of the street respected him, all the young girls who sat on the stoops of the small frame houses admired him—but none more than a pretty little Italian redhead named Margaret Nucito, who lived across the street from the McKees.

She had first seen Gerard in the second grade of the parochial school. He had been the class clown—the one the nuns scolded the most, liked the most.

At fourteen years of age, when the neighborhood boys and girls began to think less about swimming and more about one another, Margaret and Gerard started to date regularly. And when they were eighteen they began to think about marriage.

In the Red Hook section of Brooklyn, the Catholic girls thought early about marriage. First they thought about boys, then the Prom, then marriage. Though Red Hook was a poor neighborhood of shanties and small two-story frame houses, it was one where engagement rings were nearly always large and usually expensive. It was marriage before sex in this neighborhood, as the Church preaches, and plenty of children; and, like most Irish Catholic neighborhoods, the mothers usually had more to say than the fathers. The mother was the major moral strength in the Irish church, where the Blessed Virgin was an omnipresent figure; it was the mother who, after marriage, stayed home and reared the children, and controlled the family purse strings, and chided the husband for drinking, and pushed the sons when they were lazy, and protected the purity of her daughters.

And so it was not unusual for Margaret, after they tentatively planned marriage and after Gerard had begun work on the bridge, to be in charge of the savings account formed by weekly deductions from his ironworker's earnings. He would only fritter the money away if he were in control of it, she had told him, and he did not disagree. By the summer of 1963 their account had reached $800. He wanted to put this money toward the purchase of the beautiful pear-shaped diamond engagement ring they had seen one day while walking past Kastle's jewelry window on Fulton Street. It was a one-and-one-half carat ring priced $1,000. Margaret had insisted that the ring was too expensive, but Gerard had said, since she had liked it so much, that she would have it. They planned to announce their engagement in December.

On Wednesday morning, October 9, Gerard McKee hated to get out of bed. It was a gloomy day and he was tired, and downstairs his brothers were yelling up to him, "Hey, if you don't get down here in two minutes, we're leaving without you."

He stumbled down the steps. Everyone had finished breakfast and his mother had already packed three ham-and-cheese sandwiches for his lunch. His father, limping around the room, was quietly cross at his tardiness.

He had not been out late the night before. He had gone over to Margaret's briefly, then had had a few beers at Gabe's, a neighborhood saloon with a big bridge painted across the backbar. He had been in bed by about midnight, but this morning he ached, and he suspected he might be getting a cold.

They all left the house at 6:45 A.M. and caught a bus near the corner; then at Forty-ninth Street they got a cab and rode it to One Hundred and First Street in Bay Ridge, and then they walked, with hundreds of other ironworkers, down the dirt road toward the Brooklyn anchorage of the Verrazano-Narrows Bridge.

"Wait, let me grab a container of coffee," Gerard said, stopping at a refreshment shack along the path.

"Hurry up."

"Okay," he said. He gulped down the coffee in three swallows as they walked, and then they all lined up to take the elevator up to the catwalk. That morning Jimmy and John McKee were working on the section of the catwalk opposite Gerard, and so they parted on top, and Gerard said, "See you tonight." Then he headed off to join Iannielli.

Edward Iannielli seemed his spry self. He was sitting up there on the cable, whistling and very chipper.

"Good morning," he said, and McKee waved and forced a smile. Then he climbed up on the cable, and soon they began to tighten the seven bolts on the top of the casting.

After they had finished, Iannielli slid down from the cable and McKee handed the ratchet wrench down to him. Iannielli then fitted the wrench to the first of the seven lower bolts.

It was now about 9:30 A.M. It was cloudy and windy, though not as windy as it had been in the first week of October. Iannielli pushed his hardhat down on his head. He gazed down the catwalk and could see hundreds of men, their khaki shirts and jackets billowing in the breeze, all working on the cable—bolting it, banging it with tools, pushing into it. Iannielli took the big wrench he held, fixed it to a bolt, and pressed hard. And then, suddenly, from the bottom of the cable he heard a voice yelling, *"Eddie, Eddie . . . help me, Eddie, help me . . . please, Eddie . . . "*

Iannielli saw, hanging by his fingers from the south edge of the catwalk, clutching tightly to the thin lower wires of the hand rail, the struggling figure of Gerard McKee.

"God," Iannielli screamed, "dear God," he repeated, lunging forward, lying across the catwalk and trying to grab onto McKee's arms and pull him up. But it was very difficult.

Iannielli was only 138 pounds, and McKee was more than 200. And Iannielli, with one finger missing on his left hand from the crane accident, and with the resewn second finger not very strong, could not seem to pull McKee's heavy body upward even one inch. Then McKee's jacket and shirt came loose, and he seemed to be just hanging there, dead weight, and Iannielli kept pleading, "Oh, God, God, please bring him up . . . bring him up . . . "

Other men, hearing the screams, came running and they all stretched down, grabbing wildly for some part of McKee's clothing, and Gerard kept saying, "Hurry, hurry please, I can't hold on any longer." And then, a few moments later, he said, "I'm going to go . . . I'm going to go . . ." and he let go of the wire and dropped from the bridge.

The men watched him fall, feet first for about one hundred feet. Then his body tilted forward, and Iannielli could see McKee's shirt blowing off and could see McKee's bare back, white against the dark sea, and then he saw him splash hard, more than 350 feet below, and Iannielli closed his eyes and began to weep, and then he began to slip over, too, but an Indian, Lloyd LeClaire, jumped on top of him, held him tight to the catwalk.

Not far from where Gerard McKee hit the water, two doctors sat fishing in a boat, and also nearby was a safety launch. And for the next thirty seconds, hysterical and howling men's voices, dozens of them, came echoing down from the bridge, "Hey, grab that kid, grab that kid . . . hurry, grab that kid . . . "

Even if Gerard McKee had landed within a yard of the safety boat, it would have been no use; anyone falling from that altitude is sure to die, for, even if his lungs hold out, the water is like concrete, and bodies break into many pieces when they fall that far.

The remains of Gerard McKee were taken out of the water and put into the safety launch and taken to Victory Memorial Hospital. Some of the men up on the bridge began to cry, and, slowly, all of them, more than six hundred of them, removed their hardhats and began to come down. Work was immediately suspended for the day. One young apprentice ironworker, who had never seen a death like this before, froze to the catwalk and refused to leave; he later had to be carried down by three others.

Jimmy and John McKee went home to break the news and be with their parents and Margaret, but Edward Iannielli, in a kind of daze, got into his automobile and began to drive away from the bridge, without any destination. When he saw a saloon he stopped. He sat at the bar between a few men, shaking, his lips quivering. He ordered one whiskey, then another, then three beers. In a few minutes he felt loose, and he left the bar and got into his car and began to drive up the Belt Parkway. He drove about fifty miles, then, turning around, he drove fifty miles back, seeing the bridge in the distance, now empty and quiet. He turned off the Belt Parkway and drove toward his home. His wife greeted him, very excitedly, at the door, saying that the bridge company had called, the safety officer had called, and what had happened?

Iannielli heard very little of what she was saying. That night in bed all he could hear, over and over, was "Eddie, Eddie, help me . . . help me." And again and again he saw the figure falling toward the sea, the shirt blowing up and the white back exposed. He got out of bed and walked through the house for the rest of the night.

The next day, Thursday, October 10, the investigation was begun to determine the cause of McKee's death. Work was again suspended on the bridge. But since nobody had seen how McKee had gotten off the cable, nobody knew whether he had jumped onto the catwalk and bounced off it or whether he had tripped—and they still do not know. All they knew then was that the morale of the men was shot, and Ray Corbett, business agent for Local 40, began a campaign to get the bridge company to string nets under the men on the bridge.

This had not been the first death around the bridge. On August 24, 1962, one man fell off a ladder inside a tower and died, and on July 13, 1963, another man slipped off the approach road and died. But the death of Gerard McKee was somehow different—different, perhaps, because the men had watched it, had been helpless to stop it; different, perhaps, because it had involved a very popular young man, the son of an ironworker who had himself been crippled for life.

What ever the reason, the day of Gerard McKee's death was the blackest day on the bridge so far. And it would have made little difference for any company official to point out that the Verranzano-Narrows' safety record—just three deaths during thousands of working hours involving hundreds of men—was highly commendable.

McKee's funeral, held at the Visitation Roman Catholic Church in Red Hook, was possibly the largest funeral ever held in the neighborhood. All the ironworkers seemed to be there, and so were the engineers and union officials. But of all the mourners, the individual who seemed to take it the worst was Gerard's father, James McKee.

"After what I've been through," he said, shaking his head, tears in his eyes, "I should know enough to keep my kids off the bridge."

P A R T II

REALITY
PRESENTED—
WITH
STYLE

Gathering information requires patience and persistence. Assembling the facts into a coherent whole—for yourself and for others—calls again for these virtues, and for an artful writing style besides. "Reality Researched," therefore, is just the beginning. Reality must be *presented* (or "re-presented"), and here the greatest artists of nonfiction fully intend to be artful. They make use of scenic construction, narrative strategies, interior monologue, imagery and symbolism, allusion, and many of the other literary techniques showcased in this section— and they were doing this even before the novel came on the scene.

In *A Journal of a Plague Year*, published in 1722, Daniel Defoe drew on his uncle's diary to re-create that uncle's life in England during the Black Plague of 1665. Defoe interwove scenes of the plague with sections of medical advice, religious exhortation, and tables of the ever-mounting mortality figures. The result was an arresting hybrid genre: narrated scenes grounded in fact and written in a style both uncommon and enduring.

Oliver Wendell Holmes assayed a gentler blend of essay and narrated scene when he conjured his Autocrat (a character much like himself) and created a love story around the Autocrat's breakfast table in his 1850s *Atlantic Monthly* magazine columns.

Readers of the time warmed to this blend of essay and story, as did those reading Mark Twain and W. E. B. DuBois, Virginia Woolf and Ernest Hemingway, George Orwell, James Agee and others who followed with impressive experiments in artful nonfiction.* These writers found, as have many authors since World War II, that when facts are presented in a literary style—a style drawing on the narrative techniques of fiction yet with content true and verifiable—the facts come alive with impressive reverberations.

The finest artists of nonfiction have a repertoire of literary techniques at their fingertips. They also cultivate writing styles best conveying their own personalities and visions. *Style*, as C. Hugh Holman and William Harmon remind us, is

> the arrangement of words in a manner best expressing the individuality
> of the author and the idea and intent in the author's mind. The best style,
> for any given purpose, is that which most nearly approximates a perfect
> adaptation of one's language to one's ideas.

Just as no two personalities are alike, no two writing styles are alike—nor should they be. Style is as individual as your walk, your laugh, your handwriting, or your DNA.

Joan Didion is one of the premier prose stylists of our time. In this section, we have chosen her article "Some Dreamers of the Golden Dream" to illustrate her brilliant writing style and also how *symbols* can be employed in a nonfiction writer's work. In describing her method of writing, Didion suggests a way apprentice writers can begin to hone in on their own distinctive writing styles. "To shift the structure of a sentence alters the meaning of that sentence, as definitely and inflexibly as the position of a camera alters the meaning of the object photographed," Didion explains:

> Many people know about camera angles now, but not so many know
> about sentences. The arrangement of the words matters, and the
> arrangement you want can be found in the picture in your mind. The
> picture dictates whether this will be a sentence with or without
> clauses, a sentence that ends hard or a dying-fall sentence, long or
> short, active or passive. The picture tells you how to arrange the words

---

*Besides Defoe's *A Journal of a Plague Year* and Holmes's *The Autocrat of the Breakfast-Table, The Poet at the Breakfast-Table,* and *The Professor at the Breakfast-Table,* we recommend as instructive models of artful nonfiction Mark Twain's *Roughing It, The Innocents Abroad,* and *Life on the Mississippi*; W. E. B. DuBois's melodic and moving *The Souls of Black Folk*; Virginia Woolf's *A Room of One's Own, Three Guineas,* and *Flush: A Biography*; Ernest Hemingway's *Death in the Afternoon, Green Hills of Africa,* and *A Moveable Feast*; George Orwell's *Down and Out in Paris and London, Homage to Catalonia,* and *The Road to Wigan Pier*; and James Agee's *Let Us Now Praise Famous Men:*

and the arrangement of the words tells you, or tells me, what's going
on in the picture.

Following Didion's advice, writers seeking to develop a distinctive writing style
should begin with the picture their material creates in their minds, and then seek to
reproduce that picture in appropriate sentences. The style may suddenly "click in,"
or it may slowly unfold, mental picture by mental picture. After a while, you may
begin to recognize certain rhythms, images, arrangements of ideas, and other stylistic touches as singularly your own. Someone may even write a parody of your style
which is the ultimate compliment. Like Ernest Hemingway's, Tom Wolfe's, and
Joan Didion's, your style is recognizably yours.

A writer's style can and does change, however, and you should be ready for
this to happen. It may vary as your material varies, and it may change as you age.
Shakespeare's early style (with many rhymes), for example, is not his late style
(with few rhymes).

The following section offers a cornucopia of striking literary *styles*, as well as
nine techniques often used by writers who aspire to link reality with the highest
standards of literature. It begins with examples of *scenic construction* (Thomas
Keneally's *Schindler's List*), followed by illustrations of four forms of narration:
simultaneous narration (John Hersey's *Hiroshima*), *sequential narration* (Truman
Capote's *In Cold Blood*), *substitutionary narration* (Norman Mailer's *The
Executioner's Song*), and *interior monologue* (Gay Talese's "The Loser"). Next
come models of artful use of *imagery* and *symbolism* (Joan Didion's "Some
Dreamers of the Golden Dream"), *allusion* (Thomas Thompson's *Blood and
Money*), and the *pyrotechniques of print* (Tom Wolfe's dazzling "Las Vegas
(What?). Las Vegas (Can't Hear You! Too Noisy) Las Vegas!!!!"). It closes with
three samples of literary *humor* (James Thurber's classic "University Days," S. J.
Perelman's "No Starch in the Dhoti, S'il Vous Plaît" as an illustration of artful let-
ters, and John McNulty's heartbreaking "Two Bums Here Would Spend Freely
Except for Poverty").

We showcase these literary techniques with the caveat that they do not exhaust
all the possibilities. The excitement of the Literature of Reality is that its greatest
artists continue to discover new literary techniques to re-create their worlds.

From SCHINDLER'S LIST

T H O M A S   K E N E A L L Y

Editor's Note—The Scene: The presence of a scene or scenes in nonfiction writing is one of the easiest ways to recognize the Literature of Reality. *At some point the journalist, historian, essayist, travel writer, nature writer, scientist, biographer, or autobiographer will stop merely "reporting" or "discussing" what happened, and instead cast the happening in a dramatic scene. The remarkable effect of this transformation is that the past is reprised; it lives again, yet with the subtle lights and shadings of the author's vision. However, as Part I of this anthology makes clear, it is only after exhaustive research that a writer can dare to re-create authentic, factually accurate, scenes.*

In the case of the best-selling 1982 volume Schindler's List, *Australian writer Thomas Keneally interviewed 50 survivors of the Nazi holocaust who owed their lives to the courageous acts of German manufacturer Oskar Schindler. Keneally's interviews took him to seven nations and to Yad Vashem, The Martyrs' and Heroes' Remembrance Authority in Israel, where Jews rescued by Schindler deposited their testimonies. Most of these survivors were workers in Emalia, Schindler's manufacturing plant in Poland, but Keneally also interviewed Schindler's wartime business associates and postwar friends. He examined Schindler's papers and letters and—perhaps most important for a writer seeking to re-create scenes—he visited each of the locations he was preparing to depict, accompanied by a major figure in the story. Finally, he submitted his completed manuscript to three survivors for verification.*

The result, as the following excerpts demonstrate, is a re-creation of one of the most horrifying moments in human record.* In "Prologue, Autumn, 1943," *Keneally offers a scene in miniature. With his opening four words—*"In Poland's deepest autumn"*—he illustrates how a writer can swiftly locate the reader in place and time. He follows immediately with description of his central character— in appearance and action. By the second paragraph Oskar Schindler is already engaged in conversation, and Keneally spends the remaining paragraphs of his short "Prologue" stepping away from the action to allow his narrator to enlarge philosophically on the meaning of* "this small winter scene."

The second excerpt offers a more extended scene. At times Keneally will quote his historical figures directly; at other times he avoids quotation marks, suggesting, perhaps, that he is providing an approximation of what was said—rather than the speaker's precise words. (After a while, readers are hardly aware of this judicious technique, for they feel like eye-witnesses to history.) However, at the same time Keneally is re-presenting reality, he is able to comment on Schindler's philosophical innocence, and on the horror of an evil few at that time could totally comprehend.

---

*Keneally's dramatic scenes caught the eye of filmmaker Stephen Spielberg whose film of *Schindler's List* won the Academy Award as the Best Film of 1993.

Prologue

AUTUMN, 1943

In Poland's deepest Autumn, a tall young man in an expensive overcoat, double-breasted dinner jacket beneath it and—in the lapel of the dinner jacket—a large ornamental gold-on-black-enamel *Hakenkreuz* (swastika) emerged from a fashionable apartment building [. . .] on the edge of the ancient center of Cracow, and saw his chauffeur waiting with fuming breath by the open door of an enormous and, even in this blackened world, lustrous Adler limousine.

"Watch the pavement, Herr Schindler," said the chauffeur. "It's as icy as a widow's heart."

In observing this small winter scene, we are on safe ground. The tall young man would to the end of his days wear double-breasted suits, would—being something of an engineer—always be gratified by large dazzling vehicles, would—though a German and at this point in history a German of some influence—always be the sort of man with whom a Polish chauffeur could safely crack a lame, comradely joke.

But it will not be possible to see the whole story under such easy character headings. For this is the story of the pragmatic triumph of good over evil, a triumph in eminently measurable, statistical, unsubtle terms. When you work from the other end of the beast—when you chronicle the predictable and measurable success evil generally achieves—it is easy to be wise, wry, piercing, to avoid bathos. It is easy to show the inevitability by which evil acquires all of what you could call the *real estate* of the story, even though good might finish up with a few imponderables like dignity and self-knowledge. Fatal human malice is the staple of narrators, original sin the mother-fluid of historians. But it is a risky enterprise to have to write of virtue.

"Virtue" in fact is such a dangerous word that we have to rush to explain; Herr Oskar Schindler, risking his glimmering shoes on the icy pavement in this old and elegant quarter of Cracow, was not a virtuous young man in the customary sense. In this city he kept house with his German mistress and maintained a long affair with his Polish secretary. His wife, Emilie, chose to live most of the time at home in Moravia, though she sometimes came to Poland to visit him. There's this to be said for him: that to all his women he was a well-mannered and generous lover. But under the normal interpretation of "virtue," that's no excuse.

Likewise, he was a drinker. Some of the time he drank for the pure glow of it, at other times with associates, bureaucrats, SS men for more palpable results. Like few others, he was capable of staying canny while drinking, of keeping his head. That again, though—under the narrow interpretation of morality—has never been an excuse for carousing. And although Herr Schindler's merit is well documented, it is a feature of his ambiguity that he worked within or, at least, on the strength of a corrupt and savage scheme, one that filled Europe with camps of varying but consistent inhumanity and created a submerged, unspoken-of nation of prisoners. The best thing, therefore, may be to begin with a tentative instance of Herr Schindler's strange virtue and of the places and associates to which it brought him.

* * *

On June 3, Abraham Bankier, [Herr Schindler's] office manager, didn't turn up [for work]. Schindler was still at home, drinking coffee [. . .], when he got a call from one of his secretaries. She'd seen Bankier marched out of the ghetto [. . .] straight to the Prokocim depot. There'd been other Emalia workers in the group too. There'd been Reich, Leser . . . as many as a dozen.

Oskar [Schindler] called for his car to be brought to him from the garage. He drove over the river and down toward Prokocim. There he showed his pass to the guards at the gate. The depot yard itself was full of strings of cattle cars, the station crowded with the ghetto's dispensable citizens standing in orderly lines, convinced still—and perhaps they were right—of the value of passive and orderly response. It was the first time Oskar had seen this juxtaposition of humans and cattle cars, and it was a greater shock than hearing of it; it made him pause on the edge of the platform. Then he saw a jeweler he knew. Seen Bankier? he asked. "He's already in one of the cars, Herr Schindler," said the jeweler. "Where are they taking you?" Oskar asked the man. "We're going to a labor camp, they say. Near Lublin. Probably no worse than . . ." The man waved a hand toward distant Cracow.

Schindler took a pack of cigarettes from his pocket, found some 10-zloty bills and handed the pack and the notes to the jeweler, who thanked him. They had made them leave home without anything this time. They said they'd be forwarding the baggage.

Late the previous year, Schindler had seen in the SS *Bulletin of Budget and Construction* an invitation for bids for the construction of some crematoria in a camp southeast of Lublin. Belzec. Schindler considered the jeweler. Sixty-three or - four. A little thin; had probably had pneumonia last winter. Worn pin-striped suit, too warm for the day. And in the clear, knowing eyes a capacity to bear finite suffering. Even in the summer of 1942 it was impossible to guess at the connections between such a man as this and those ovens of extraordinary cubic capacity. Did they intend to start epidemics among the prisoners? Was that to be the method?

Beginning from the engine, Schindler moved along the line of more than twenty cattle cars, calling Bankier's name to the faces peering down at him from the open grillwork high above the slats of the cars. It was fortunate for Abraham that Oskar did not ask himself why it was Bankier's name he called, that he did not pause and consider that Bankier's had only equal value to all the other names loaded aboard the *Ostbahn* rolling stock. An existentialist might have been defeated by the numbers at Prokocim, stunned by the equal appeal of all the names and voices. But Schindler was a philosophic innocent. He knew the people he knew. He knew the name of Bankier. "*Bankier! Bankier!*" he continued to call.

He was intercepted by a young SS *Oberscharführer*, an expert railroad shipper from Lublin. He asked for Schindler's pass. Oskar could see in the man's left hand an enormous list—pages of names.

My workers, said Schindler. Essential industrial workers. My office manager. It's idiocy. I have Armaments Inspectorate contracts, and here you are taking the workers I need to fulfill them.

You can't have them back, said the young man. They're on the list. . . . The SS NCO knew from experience that the list conferred an equal destination on all its members.

Oskar dropped his voice to that hard murmur, the growl of a reasonable man, well connected, who wasn't going to bring up all his heavy guns yet. Did the *Herr Oberscharführer* know how long it would take to train experts to replace those on the list? At my works, Deutsche Email Fabrik, I have a munitions section under the special protection of General Schindler, my namesake. Not only would the *Oberscharführer's* comrades on the Russian Front be affected by the disruption of production, but the office of the Armaments Inspectorate would demand explanations as well.

The young man shook his head—just a harassed transit official. "I've heard that kind of story before, sir," he said. But he was worried. Oskar could tell it and kept leaning over him and speaking softly with an edge of menace. "It's not my place to argue with the list," said Oskar. "Where is your superior officer?"

The young man nodded toward an SS officer, a man in his thirties wearing a frown above his spectacles. "May I have your name, *Herr Untersturmführer?*" Oskar asked him, already pulling a notebook from his suit pocket.

The officer also made a statement about the holiness of the list. For this man it was the secure, rational, and sole basis for all this milling of Jews and movement of rail cars. But Schindler got crisper now. He'd heard about the list, he said. What he had asked was what the *Untersturmführer's* name was. He intended to appeal directly to *Oberführer* Scherner and to General Schindler of the Armaments Inspectorate.

"Schindler?" asked the officer. For the first time he took a careful look at Oskar. The man was dressed like a tycoon, wore the right badge, had generals in the family. "I believe I can guarantee you, *Herr Untersturmführer,*" said Schindler in his benign grumble, "that you'll be in southern Russia within the week."

The NCO going ahead, Herr Schindler and the officer marched side by side between the ranks of prisoners and the loaded cattle cars. The locomotive was already steaming and the engineer leaning from his cabin, looking down the length of the train, waiting to be dispatched. The officer called to *Ostbahn* officials they passed on the platform to hold up. At last they reached one of the rear cars. There were a dozen workers in there with Bankier; they had all boarded together as if expecting a joint deliverance. The door was unlocked and they jumped down— Bankier and Frankel from the office; Reich, Leser, and the others from the factory. They were restrained, not wanting to permit anyone to detect their pleasure at being saved the journey. Those left inside began chattering merrily, as if they were fortunate to be traveling with so much extra room, while with emphasis in his pen strokes, the officer removed the Emalia workers one at a time from the list and required Oskar to initial the pages.

As Schindler thanked the officer and turned to follow his workers away, the man detained him by the elbow of his suit coat. "Sir," he said, "it makes no difference to us, you understand. We don't care whether it's this dozen or that."

The officer, who had been frowning when Oskar first saw him, now seemed calm, as if he had discovered the theorem behind the situation. You think your thirteen little tinsmiths are important? We'll replace them with another thirteen little tinsmiths and all your sentimentality for these will be defeated. "It's the inconvenience to the list, that's all," the officer explained.

Plump little Bankier admitted that the group of them had neglected to pick up *Blauscheins* from the old Polish Savings Bank. Schindler, suddenly testy, said to attend to it. But what his curtness covered was dismay at those crowds at Prokocim who, for want of a blue sticker, stood waiting for the new and decisive symbol of their status, the cattle car, to be hauled by heavy engine across their range of vision. Now, the cattle cars told them, we are all beasts together.

From HIROSHIMA

J O H N   H E R S E Y

Editor's Note—Simultaneous Narration: Once writers decide to cast their factual material in scenes, techniques of narration become immediately important. Each of the following four selections demonstrates a different narrative approach: simultaneous narration *(John Hersey's* Hiroshima*);* sequential narration *(Truman Capote's* In Cold Blood*);* substitutionary narration *(Norman Mailer's* The Executioner's Song*); and the* interior monologue *(Gay Talese's "The Loser").*

The opening chapter of John Hersey's famous account of the dropping of the first atomic bomb on Hiroshima illustrates the technique of simultaneous narration: *narrating consecutively what different individuals are doing* at the same moment in time.* *From his hundreds of interviews in the spring following the August 6, 1945 atomic detonation, Hersey selected six representative persons. He uses these six as vehicles for representing what actually happened to residents of Hiroshima at the moment of the blast, in the hours immediately following, in the subsequent six-month period when delayed radiation effects began to be known, and in the 40 years after.*[†]

In the following selection, Hersey describes, by turns, what each of the six was doing at 8:15 A.M., the precise moment of the blast. Through this narrative approach he is able, not only to suggest the range of experiences of Hiroshima survivors, but to re-create the horror of the detonation in the reader's mind— again and again and again. Another effective narrative technique Hersey employs is to halt each person's story at a critical moment—with Mrs. Nakamura searching for her children, or Miss Sasaki buried beneath books. In this way Hersey sustains continuous narrative suspense, despite the fact that readers already know the general outcome of his story (that is, that these people survived).

Hersey's Hiroshima *occasioned unprecedented international attention when it appeared in the August 31, 1946 issue of* The New Yorker. *For the first time in its history,* The New Yorker *gave over its entire editorial space to one article, and the issue sold out at newsstands within hours. Albert Einstein acquired 1,000 copies, the U.S. Army ordered texts for its education service, and Bernard Baruch for the Atomic Energy Commission. Newspapers in North and Central America were granted permission to reprint* Hiroshima, *and the American Broadcasting Company (ABC) canceled all its regular radio broadcasts on four successive evenings to read the work over the air to millions—as did the British Broadcasting*

---

*Note that Gay Talese employs *simultaneous narration* in his "Death on the Bridge" section of *The Bridge.* He describes first what Edward Iannielli was doing in the hours and minutes before the accident, and then Gerard McKee's actions (see pages 63–73).

[†]In 1985, in response to many requests, Hersey added a fifth chapter ("The Aftermath") to his 1946 *Hiroshima,* bringing readers up to date on the final fates of the six survivors.

Company (BBC) and stations in Canada and Australia. The Book-of-the-Month Club distributed hundreds of thousands of copies of Hiroshima *free to its subscribers because, as Harry Scherman stated, "We find it hard to conceive of anything being written that could be of more importance at this moment to the human race."*

Hersey's scenes, like the preceding scenes from Schindler's List, *contain little dialogue or direct quotation. This is because both Hersey and Keneally found themselves in the position of interviewing their subjects long enough after the actual event that relying on their memories of precise conversations could be dangerous. Reported memories are thus presented in the authors', rather than the characters', words—a most legitimate technique. Nevertheless, so exacting was Hersey's research that he can describe which way Miss Sasaki turns her head at the moment of the explosion, and in which hand Dr. Sasaki holds his test tube of blood.*

In 1950 Norman Cousins, editor of the Saturday Review of Literature, *journeyed to Japan to investigate the accuracy of Hersey's work. Dr. Fujii, one of the book's six characters, told Cousins: "Everything in* Hiroshima *was just as he said it was. It was remarkable to see how accurate and careful he was with the facts. . . . It was very interesting to see that he remembered every word of our three-hour conversation."*

Hersey himself insisted that: "Much nonsense has been written about 'journalistic' novels. The novel of contemporary history is an established form. It has dignity, purpose, and separateness."

I

A NOISELESS FLASH

At exactly fifteen minutes past eight in the morning, on August 6, 1945, Japanese time, at the moment when the atomic bomb flashed above Hiroshima, Miss Toshiko Sasaki, a clerk in the personnel department of the East Asia Tin Works, had just sat down at her place in the plant office and was turning her head to speak to the girl at the next desk. At that same moment, Dr. Masakazu Fujii was settling down crosslegged to read the *Osaka Asahi* on the porch of his private hospital, overhanging one of the seven deltaic rivers which divide Hiroshima; Mrs. Hatsuyo Nakamura, a tailor's widow, stood by the window of her kitchen, watching a neighbor tearing down his house because it lay in the path of an air-raid-defense fire lane; Father Wilhelm Kleinsorge, a German priest of the Society of Jesus, reclined in his underwear on a cot on the top floor of his order's three-story mission house, reading a Jesuit magazine, *Stimmen der Zeit*; Dr. Terufumi Sasaki, a young member of the surgical staff of the city's large, modern Red Cross Hospital, walked along one of the hospital corridors with a blood specimen for a Wassermann test in his hand; and the Reverend Mr. Kiyoshi Tanimoto, pastor of the Hiroshima Methodist Church, paused at the door of a rich man's house in Koi, the city's western suburb, and prepared to unload a handcart full of things he had evacuated from town in fear of the massive B–29 raid which everyone expected Hiroshima to suffer. A hundred thousand people were killed by the atomic bomb, and these six were among the survivors. They still wonder why they lived when so many others died. Each of them counts many small items of chance or volition—a step taken in time, a decision to go indoors, catching one streetcar instead of the next—that spared him. And now each knows that in the act of survival he lived a dozen lives and saw more death than he ever thought he would see. At the time, none of them knew anything.

The Reverend Mr. Tanimoto got up at five o'clock that morning. He was alone in the parsonage, because for some time his wife had been commuting with their year-old baby to spend nights with a friend in Ushida, a suburb to the north. Of all the important cities of Japan, only two, Kyoto and Hiroshima, had not been visited in strength by *B-san*, or Mr. B, as the Japanese, with a mixture of respect and unhappy familiarity, called the B–29; and Mr. Tanimoto, like all his neighbors and friends, was almost sick with anxiety. He had heard uncomfortably detailed accounts of mass raids on Kure, Iwakuni, Tokuyama, and other nearby towns; he was sure Hiroshima's turn would come soon. He had slept badly the night before, because there had been several air-raid warnings. Hiroshima had been getting such warnings almost every night for weeks, for at that time the B–29s were using Lake Biwa, northeast of Hiroshima, as a rendezvous point, and no matter what city the Americans planned to hit, the Superfortresses streamed in over the coast near Hiroshima. The frequency of the warnings and the continued abstinence of Mr. B with respect to Hiroshima had made its citizens jittery; a rumor was going around that the Americans were saving something special for the city.

Mr. Tanimoto is a small man, quick to talk, laugh, and cry. He wears his black hair parted in the middle and rather long; the prominence of the frontal bones just above his eyebrows and the smallness of his mustache, mouth, and chin give him a strange, old-young look, boyish and yet wise, weak and yet fiery. He moves nervously and fast, but with a restraint which suggests that he is a cautious, thoughtful man. He showed, indeed, just those qualities in the uneasy days before the bomb fell. Besides having his wife spend the nights in Ushida, Mr. Tanimoto had been carrying all the portable things from his church, in the close-packed residential district called Nagaragawa, to a house that belonged to a rayon manufacturer in Koi, two miles from the center of town. The rayon man, a Mr. Matsui, had opened his then unoccupied estate to a large number of his friends and acquaintances, so that they might evacuate whatever they wished to a safe distance from the probable target area. Mr. Tanimoto had had no difficulty in moving chairs, hymnals, Bibles, altar gear, and church records by pushcart himself, but the organ console and an upright piano required some aid. A friend of his named Matsuo had, the day before, helped him get the piano out to Koi; in return, he had promised this day to assist Mr. Matsuo in hauling out a daughter's belongings. That is why he had risen so early.

Mr. Tanimoto cooked his own breakfast. He felt awfully tired. The effort of moving the piano the day before, a sleepless night, weeks of worry and unbalanced diet, the cares of his parish—all combined to make him feel hardly adequate to the new day's work. There was another thing, too: Mr. Tanimoto had studied theology at Emory University, in Atlanta, Georgia; he had graduated in 1940; he spoke excellent English; he dressed in American clothes; he had corresponded with many American friends right up to the time the war began; and among a people obsessed with a fear of being spied upon—perhaps almost obsessed himself—he found himself growing increasingly uneasy. The police had questioned him several times, and just a few days before, he had heard that an influential acquaintance, a Mr. Tanaka, a retired officer of the Toyo Kisen Kaisha steamship line, an anti-Christian, a man famous in Hiroshima for his showy philanthropies and notorious for his personal tyrannies, had been telling people that Tanimoto should not be trusted. In compensation, to show himself publicly a good Japanese, Mr. Tanimoto had taken on the chairmanship of his local *tonarigumi*, or Neighborhood Association, and to his other duties and concerns this position had added the business of organizing air-raid defense for about twenty families.

Before six o'clock that morning, Mr. Tanimoto started for Mr. Matsuo's house. There he found that their burden was to be a *tansu*, a large Japanese cabinet, full of clothing and household goods. The two men set out. The morning was perfectly clear and so warm that the day promised to be uncomfortable. A few minutes after they started, the air-raid siren went off—a minute-long blast that warned of approaching planes but indicated to the people of Hiroshima only a slight degree of danger, since it sounded every morning at this time, when an American weather plane came over. The two men pulled and pushed the handcart through the city streets. Hiroshima was a fan-shaped city, lying mostly on the six islands formed by the seven estuarial rivers that branch out from the Ota River; its main commercial and residential districts, covering about four square miles in the center of the city, contained three-quarters of its population, which had been reduced by several evacuation programs from a wartime peak of 380,000 to about 245,000. Factories and other residential districts, or suburbs, lay compactly around the edges of the city. To the south were the docks, an airport, and the island-studded Inland Sea. A rim of mountains runs around the other three sides of the delta. Mr. Tanimoto and Mr. Matsuo took their way through the shopping center, already full of people, and across two of the rivers to the sloping streets of Koi, and up them to the outskirts and foothills. As they started up a valley away from the tight-ranked houses, the all-clear sounded. (The Japanese radar operators, detecting only three planes, supposed that they comprised a reconnaissance.) Pushing the handcart up to the rayon man's house was tiring, and the men, after they had maneuvered their load into the driveway and to the front steps, paused to rest awhile. They stood with a wing of the house between them and the city. Like most homes in this part of Japan, the house consisted of a wooden frame and wooden walls supporting a heavy tile roof. Its front hall, packed with rolls of bedding and clothing, looked like a cool cave full of fat cushions. Opposite the house, to the right of the front door, there was a large, finicky rock garden. There was no sound of planes. The morning was still; the place was cool and pleasant.

Then a tremendous flash of light cut across the sky. Mr. Tanimoto has a distinct recollection that it travelled from east to west, from the city toward the hills. It seemed a sheet of sun. Both he and Mr. Matsuo reacted in terror—and both had time to react (for they were 3,500 yards, or two miles, from the center of the explosion). Mr. Matsuo dashed up the front steps into the house and dived among the bedrolls and buried himself there. Mr. Tanimoto took four or five steps and threw himself between two big rocks in the garden. He bellied up very hard against one of them. As his face was against the stone, he did not see what happened. He felt a sudden pressure, and then splinters and pieces of board and fragments of tile fell on him. He heard no roar. (Almost no one in Hiroshima recalls hearing any noise of the bomb. But a fisherman in his sampan on the Inland Sea near Tsuzu, the man with whom Mr. Tanimoto's mother-in-law and sister-in-law were living, saw the flash and heard a tremendous explosion; he was nearly twenty miles from Hiroshima, but the thunder was greater than when the B–29s hit Iwakuni, only five miles away.)

When he dared, Mr. Tanimoto raised his head and saw that the rayon man's house had collapsed. He thought a bomb had fallen directly on it. Such clouds of dust had risen that there was a sort of twilight around. In panic, not thinking for the moment of Mr. Matsuo under the ruins, he dashed out into the street. He noticed as he ran that the concrete wall of the estate had fallen over—toward the house rather than away from it. In the street, the first thing he saw was a squad of soldiers who had been burrowing into the hillside opposite, making one of the thousands of dugouts in which the Japanese apparently intended to resist invasion, hill by hill, life for life; the soldiers were coming out of the hole, where they should have been safe, and blood was running from their heads, chests, and backs. They were silent and dazed.

Under what seemed to be a local dust cloud, the day grew darker and darker.

At nearly midnight, the night before the bomb was dropped, an announcer on the city's radio station said that about two hundred B–29s were approaching southern Honshu and advised the population of Hiroshima to evacuate to their designated "safe areas." Mrs. Hatsuyo Nakamura, the tailor's widow, who lived in the section called Nobori-cho and who had long had a habit of doing as she was told, got her three children—a ten-year-old boy, Toshio, an eight-year-old girl, Yaeko, and a five-year-old girl, Myeko—out of bed and dressed them and walked with them to the military area known as the East Parade Ground, on the northeast edge of the city. There she unrolled some mats and the children lay down on them. They slept until about two, when they were awakened by the roar of the planes going over Hiroshima.

As soon as the planes had passed, Mrs. Nakamura started back with her children. They reached home a little after two-thirty and she immediately turned on the radio, which, to her distress, was just then broadcasting a fresh warning. When she looked at the children and saw how tired they were, and when she thought of the number of trips they had made in past weeks, all to no purpose, to the East Parade Ground, she decided that in spite of the instructions on the radio, she simply could not face starting out all over again. She put the children in their bedrolls on the floor, lay down herself at three o'clock, and fell asleep at once, so soundly that when planes passed over later, she did not waken to their sound.

The siren jarred her awake at about seven. She arose, dressed quickly, and hurried to the house of Mr. Nakamoto, the head of her Neighborhood Association, and asked him what she should do. He said that she should remain at home unless an urgent warning—a series of intermittent blasts of the siren—was sounded. She returned home, lit the stove in the kitchen, set some rice to cook, and sat down to read that morning's Hiroshima *Chugoku*. To her relief, the all-clear sounded at eight o'clock. She heard the children stirring, so she went and gave each of them a handful of peanuts and told them to stay on their bedrolls, because they were tired from the night's walk. She had hoped that they would go back to sleep, but the man in the house directly to the south began to make a terrible hullabaloo of hammering, wedging, ripping, and splitting. The prefectural government, convinced, as everyone in Hiroshima was, that the city would be attacked soon, had begun to press with threats and warnings for the completion of wide fire lanes, which, it was hoped, might act in conjunction with the rivers to localize any fires started by an incendiary raid; and the neighbor was reluctantly sacrificing his home to the city's safety. Just the day before, the prefecture had ordered all able-bodied girls from the secondary schools to spend a few days helping to clear these lanes, and they started work soon after the all-clear sounded.

Mrs. Nakamura went back to the kitchen, looked at the rice, and began watching the man next door. At first, she was annoyed with him for making so much noise, but then she was moved almost to tears by pity. Her emotion was specifically directed toward her neighbor, tearing down his home, board by board, at a time when there was so much unavoidable destruction, but undoubtedly she also felt a generalized, community pity, to say nothing of self-pity. She had not had an easy time. Her husband, Isawa, had gone into the Army just after Myeko was born, and she had heard nothing from or of him for a long time, until, on March 5, 1942, she received a seven-word telegram: "Isawa died an honorable death at Singapore." She learned later that he had died on February 15th, the day Singapore fell, and that he had been a corporal. Isawa had been a not particularly prosperous tailor, and his only capital was a Sankoku sewing machine. After his death, when his allotments stopped coming, Mrs. Nakamura got out the machine and began to take in piecework herself, and since then had supported the children, but poorly, by sewing.

As Mrs. Nakamura stood watching her neighbor, everything flashed whiter than any white she had ever seen. She did not notice what happened to the man next door; the reflex of a mother set her in motion toward her children. She had taken a single step (the house was 1,350 yards, or three-quarters of a mile, from the center of the explosion) when something picked her up and she seemed to fly into the next room over the raised sleeping platform, pursued by parts of her house.

Timbers fell around her as she landed, and a shower of tiles pommelled her; everything became dark, for she was buried. The debris did not cover her deeply. She rose up and freed herself. She heard a child cry, "Mother, help me!," and saw her youngest—Myeko, the five-year-old—buried up to her breast and unable to move. As Mrs. Nakamura started frantically to claw her way toward the baby, she could see or hear nothing of her other children.

In the days right before the bombing, Dr. Masakazu Fujii, being prosperous, hedonistic, and at the time not too busy, had been allowing himself the luxury of sleeping until nine or nine-thirty, but fortunately he had to get up early the morning the bomb was dropped to see a house guest off on a train. He rose at six, and half an hour later walked with his friend to the station, not far away, across two of the rivers. He was back home by seven, just as the siren sounded its sustained warning. He ate breakfast and then, because the morning was already hot, undressed down to his underwear and went out on the porch to read the paper. This porch—in fact, the whole building—was curiously constructed. Dr. Fujii was the proprietor of a peculiarly Japanese institution: a private, single-doctor hospital. This building, perched beside and over the water of the Kyo River, and next to the bridge of the same name, contained thirty rooms for thirty patients and their kinfolk—for, according to Japanese custom, when a person falls sick and goes to a hospital, one or more members of his family go and live there with him, to cook for him, bathe, massage, and read to him, and to offer incessant familial sympathy, without which a Japanese patient would be miserable indeed. Dr. Fujii had no beds—only straw mats—for his patients. He did, however, have all sorts of modern equipment: an X-ray machine, diathermy apparatus, and a fine tiled laboratory. The structure rested two-thirds on the land, one-third on piles over the tidal waters of the Kyo. This overhang, the part of the building where Dr. Fujii lived, was queer-looking, but it was cool in summer and from the porch, which faced away from the center of the city, the prospect of the river, with pleasure boats drifting up and down it, was always refreshing. Dr. Fujii had occasionally had anxious moments when the Ota and its mouth branches rose to flood, but the piling was apparently firm enough and the house had always held.

Dr. Fujii had been relatively idle for about a month because in July, as the number of untouched cities in Japan dwindled and as Hiroshima seemed more and more inevitably a target, he began turning patients away, on the ground that in case of a fire raid he would not be able to evacuate them. Now he had only two patients left—a woman from Yano, injured in the shoulder, and a young man of twenty-five recovering from burns he had suffered when the steel factory near Hiroshima in which he worked had been hit. Dr. Fujii had six nurses to tend his patients. His wife and children were safe; his wife and one son were living outside Osaka, and another son and two daughters were in the country on Kyushu. A niece was living with him, and a maid and a manservant. He had little to do and did not mind, for he had saved some money. At fifty, he was healthy, convivial, and calm, and he was pleased to pass the evenings drinking whiskey with friends, always sensibly and for the sake of conversation. Before the war, he had affected brands imported from Scotland and America; now he was perfectly satisfied with the best Japanese brand, Suntory.

Dr. Fujii sat down cross-legged in his underwear on the spotless matting of the porch, put on his glasses, and started reading the Osaka *Asahi*. He liked to read the Osaka news because his wife was there. He saw the flash. To him—faced away from the center and looking at his paper—it seemed a brilliant yellow. Startled, he began to rise to his feet. In that moment (he was 1,550 yards from the center), the hospital leaned behind his rising and, with a terrible ripping noise, toppled into the river. The Doctor, still in the act of getting to his feet, was thrown forward and around and over; he was buffeted and gripped; he lost track of everything, because things were so speeded up; he felt the water.

Dr. Fujii hardly had time to think that he was dying before he realized that he was alive, squeezed tightly by two long timbers in a V across his chest, like a morsel suspended between two huge chopsticks—held upright, so that he could not move, with his head miraculously above water and his torso and legs in it. The remains of his hospital were all around him in a mad assortment of splintered lumber and materials for the relief of pain. His left shoulder hurt terribly. His glasses were gone.

Father Wilhelm Kleinsorge, of the Society of Jesus, was, on the morning of the explosion, in rather frail condition. The Japanese wartime diet had not sustained him, and he felt the strain of being a foreigner in an increasingly xenophobic Japan; even a German, since the defeat of the Fatherland, was unpopular. Father Kleinsorge had, at thirty-eight, the look of a boy growing too fast—thin in the face, with a prominent Adam's apple, a hollow chest, dangling hands, big feet. He walked clumsily, leaning forward a little. He was tired all the time. To make matters worse, he had suffered for two days, along with Father Cieslik, a fellow-priest, from a rather painful and urgent diarrhea, which they blamed on the beans and black ration bread they were obliged to eat. Two other priests then living in the mission compound, which was in the Nobori-cho section—Father Superior LaSalle and Father Schiffer—had happily escaped this affliction.

Father Kleinsorge woke up about six the morning the bomb was dropped, and half an hour later—he was a bit tardy because of his sickness—he began to read Mass in the mission chapel, a small Japanese-style wooden building which was without pews, since its worshipers knelt on the usual Japanese matted floor, facing an altar graced with splendid silks, brass, silver, and heavy embroideries. This morning, a Monday, the only worshipers were Mr. Takemoto, a theological student living in the mission house; Mr. Fukai, the secretary of the diocese; Mrs. Murata, the mission's devoutly Christian housekeeper; and his fellow-priests. After Mass, while Father Kleinsorge was reading the Prayers of Thanksgiving, the siren sounded. He stopped the service and the missionaries retired across the compound to the bigger building. There, in his room on the ground floor, to the right of the front door, Father Kleinsorge changed into a military uniform which he had acquired when he was teaching at the Rokko Middle School in Kobe and which he wore during air-raid alerts.

After an alarm, Father Kleinsorge always went out and scanned the sky, and in this instance, when he stepped outside, he was glad to see only the single weather plane that flew over Hiroshima each day about this time. Satisfied that nothing would happen, he went in and breakfasted with the other Fathers on substitute coffee and ration bread, which, under the circumstances, was especially repugnant to him. The Fathers sat and talked awhile, until, at eight, they heard the all-clear. They went then to various parts of the building. Father Schiffer retired to his room to do some writing. Father Cieslik sat in his room in a straight chair with a pillow over his stomach to ease his pain, and read. Father Superior LaSalle stood at the window of his room, thinking. Father Kleinsorge went up to a room on the third floor, took off all his clothes except his underwear, and stretched out on his right side on a cot and began reading his *Stimmen der Zeit*.

After the terrible flash—which, Father Kleinsorge later realized, reminded him of something he had read as a boy about a large meteor colliding with the earth—he had time (since he was 1,400 yards from the center) for one thought: A bomb has fallen directly on us. Then, for a few seconds or minutes, he went out of his mind.

Father Kleinsorge never knew how he got out of the house. The next things he was conscious of were that he was wandering around in the mission's vegetable garden in his underwear, bleeding slightly from small cuts along his left flank; that all the buildings round about had fallen down except the Jesuits' mission house, which had long before been braced and double-braced by a priest named Gropper, who was terrified of earthquakes; that the day had turned dark; and that Murata-*san*, the housekeeper, was nearby, crying over and over, "*Shu Jesusu, awaremi tamai*! Our Lord Jesus, have pity on us!"

On the train on the way into Hiroshima from the country, where he lived with his mother, Dr. Terufumi Sasaki, the Red Cross Hospital surgeon, thought over an unpleasant nightmare he had had the night before. His mother's home was in Mukaihara, thirty miles from the city, and it took him two hours by train and tram to reach the hospital. He had slept uneasily all night and had wakened an hour earlier than usual, and, feeling sluggish and slightly feverish, had debated whether to go to the hospital at all; his sense of duty finally forced him to go, and he had started out on an earlier train than he took most mornings. The dream had particularly frightened him because it was so closely associated, on the surface at least, with a disturbing actuality. He was only twenty-five years old and had just completed his training at the Eastern Medical University, in Tsingtao, China. He was something of an idealist and was much distressed by the inadequacy of medical facilities in the country town where his mother lived. Quite on his own, and without a permit, he had begun visiting a few sick people out there in the evenings, after his eight hours at the hospital and four hours' commuting. He had recently learned that the penalty for practicing without a permit was severe; a fellow-doctor whom he had asked about it had given him a serious scolding. Nevertheless, he had continued to practice. In his dream, he had been at the bedside of a country patient when the police and the doctor he had consulted burst into the room, seized him, dragged him outside, and beat him up cruelly. On the train, he just about decided to give up the work in Mukaihara, since he felt it would be impossible to get a permit, because the authorities would hold that it would conflict with his duties at the Red Cross Hospital.

At the terminus, he caught a streetcar at once. (He later calculated that if he had taken his customary train that morning, and if he had had to wait a few minutes for the streetcar, as often happened, he would have been close to the center at the time of the explosion and would surely have perished.) He arrived at the hospital at seven-forty and reported to the chief surgeon. A few minutes later, he went to a room on the first floor and drew blood from the arm of a man in order to perform a Wassermann test. The laboratory containing the incubators for the test was on the third floor. With the blood specimen in his left hand, walking in a kind of distraction he had felt all morning, probably because of the dream and his restless night, he started along the main corridor on his way toward the stairs. He was one step beyond an open window when the light of the bomb was reflected, like a gigantic photographic flash, in the corridor. He ducked down on one knee and said to himself, as only a Japanese would, "Sasaki, *gambare!* Be brave!" Just then (the building was 1,650 yards from the center), the blast ripped through the hospital. The glasses he was wearing flew off his face; the bottle of blood crashed against one wall; his Japanese slippers zipped out from under his feet—but otherwise, thanks to where he stood, he was untouched.

Dr. Sasaki shouted the name of the chief surgeon and rushed around to the man's office and found him terribly cut by glass. The hospital was in horrible confusion: heavy partitions and ceilings had fallen on patients, beds had overturned, windows had blown in and cut people, blood was spattered on the walls and floors, instruments were everywhere, many of the patients were running about screaming, many more lay dead. (A colleague working in the laboratory to which Dr. Sasaki had been walking was dead; Dr. Sasaki's patient, whom he had just left and who a few moments before had been dreadfully afraid of syphilis, was also dead.) Dr. Sasaki found himself the only doctor in the hospital who was unhurt.

Dr. Sasaki, who believed that the enemy had hit only the building he was in, got bandages and began to bind the wounds of those inside the hospital; while outside, all over Hiroshima, maimed and dying citizens turned their unsteady steps toward the Red Cross Hospital to begin an invasion that was to make Dr. Sasaki forget his private nightmare for a long, long time.

Miss Toshiko Sasaki, the East Asia Tin Works clerk, who is not related to Dr. Sasaki, got up at three o'clock in the morning on the day the bomb fell. There was extra housework to do. Her eleven-month-old brother, Akio, had come down the day before with a serious stomach upset; her mother had taken him to the Tamura Pediatric Hospital and was staying there with him. Miss Sasaki, who was about twenty, had to cook breakfast for her father, a brother, a sister, and herself, and—since the hospital, because of the war, was unable to provide food—to prepare a whole day's meals for her mother and the baby, in time for her father, who worked in a factory making rubber earplugs for artillery crews, to take the food by on his way to the plant. When she had finished and had cleaned and put away the cooking things, it was nearly seven. The family lived in Koi, and she had a forty-five-minute trip to the tin works, in the section of town called Kannonmachi. She was in charge of the personnel records in the factory. She left Koi at seven, and as soon as she reached the plant, she went with some of the other girls from the personnel department to the factory auditorium. A prominent local Navy man, a former employee, had committed suicide the day before by throwing himself under a train—a death considered honorable enough to warrant a memorial service, which was to be held at the tin works at ten o'clock that morning. In the large hall, Miss Sasaki and the others made suitable preparations for the meeting. This work took about twenty minutes.

Miss Sasaki went back to her office and sat down at her desk. She was quite far from the windows, which were off to her left, and behind her were a couple of tall bookcases containing all the books of the factory library, which the personnel department had organized. She settled herself at her desk, put some things in a drawer, and shifted papers. She thought that before she began to make entries in her lists of new employees, discharges, and departures for the Army, she would chat for a moment with the girl at her right. Just as she turned her head away from the windows, the room was filled with a blinding light. She was paralyzed by fear, fixed still in her chair for a long moment (the plant was 1,600 yards from the center).

Everything fell, and Miss Sasaki lost consciousness. The ceiling dropped suddenly and the wooden floor above collapsed in splinters and the people up there came down and the roof above them gave way; but principally and first of all, the bookcases right behind her swooped forward and the contents threw her down, with her left leg horribly twisted and breaking underneath her. There, in the tin factory, in the first moment of the atomic age, a human being was crushed by books.

From IN COLD BLOOD

TRUMAN CAPOTE

Editor's Note—Sequential Narration: Although Truman Capote never acknowledged the debt, readers may wonder if John Hersey's achievement in Hiroshima *lay in Capote's subconscious when he came to write* In Cold Blood, *his 1965 "nonfiction novel" about the murder of a respected Kansas family. Like* Hiroshima, *Capote's volume centers on six major characters. Like* Hiroshima, *it is structured in four long chapters, each composed of many short, often ironically juxtaposed, vignettes. Both works, furthermore, are about unexpected and unimaginable violence, blasts which dramatically change the lives of six people.* *

While Hersey employs simultaneous narration in Chapter 1 of Hiroshima, *recording consecutively what each of his six characters is doing at precisely 8:15* A.M., *Capote uses* sequential narration, *overlapping but* forward moving *sequences of action.*† *In the following excerpts, Capote alternates events in the last day in the lives of the four members of the Clutter family with those of their murderers, Perry Smith and Dick Hickock, whose black Chevrolet moves inexorably toward River Valley Farm. Through this contrapuntal narration, Capote instills a sense, not only of horror at the coming event, but of cosmic predestination. The mass murder seems almost an unavoidable intersection of the dark and the bright sides of the American Dream.*

These excerpts reveal ways writers can create artful transitions as they move from one sequence of action to another. After introducing "the master of River Valley Farm, Herbert William Clutter" *in his first narrative sequence, Capote smoothly segues to present Mr. Clutter's murderer with the intriguing three-word opening phrase:* "Like Mr. Clutter, *the young man breakfasting in a cafe called the Little Jewel never drank coffee" (see page 97). He uses* sounds *(a car's honking, a brother calling) to segue smoothly back from the murderers to introduce his heroine, sixteen-year-old Nancy Clutter (see pages 98–99). Such artful transitions bring unity to a narrative which is, in reality, jumping back and forth between two sets of characters and varying geographical locales.*

Capote's research methods for In Cold Blood *(as well as his handling of* sequential narration*) can be a model for aspiring artists of nonfiction. After reading of the 1959 Clutter murder in a short article in the* New York Times, *Capote journeyed to Holcomb, Kansas, where he lived for months interviewing*

---

*I am grateful to former University of Northern Iowa graduate student Lucille Lettow for drawing my attention to these parallels.

†This term is used by Donald Pizer in "Documentary Narrative as Art: William Manchester and Truman Capote," in *The Reporter as Artist: A Look at the New Journalism Controversy,* ed. Ronald Weber (New York: Hastings House, 1974): 207–219. John Hersey employs *sequential narration* in Chapters 2–5 of *Hiroshima.*

anyone even slightly connected with the murder. He was in the crowd when Perry Smith and Dick Hickock were finally returned to Garden City for indictment; he traveled to every stop they made on their long evasion of capture; and during their six years in prison, he wrote to each of them once a week. Indeed, when his life came to an end, Perry Smith willed Capote all his possessions. ·

In Cold Blood *took Capote almost six years to write. He trained himself to become a human tape recorder for this book by recording friends talking or reading, and then immediately writing down all he remembered and checking it against the tape. Capote claimed he practiced until he was 97 percent accurate in his transcriptions.*

In Cold Blood *has been included in this reader because it brilliantly illustrates* sequential narration *and because many consider it to be one of the foremost examples of artful nonfiction. Unfortunately, the factual accuracy of this work is now a matter of controversy. Several articles have cited instances in which Capote seems to have departed from the facts of the Clutter murder story in order to create a more sympathetic portrait of the murderer Perry Smith.* Capote resolutely denied these charges. "One doesn't spend almost six years on a book, the point of which is factual accuracy, and then give way to minor distortions," he told the* New York Times Book Review.

For some readers the issue of factual fidelity will not matter. One of the (many) remarkable features of narrative nonfiction is that if readers do not know that the "characters" actually existed and the events actually occurred, they can easily take such works for fiction. For many practitioners and admirers of the Literature of Reality, *however, factual fidelity is fundamental.*

Until one morning in mid-November of 1959, few Americans—in fact, few Kansans—had ever heard of Holcomb. Like the waters of the river, like the motorists on the highway, and like the yellow trains streaking down the Santa Fe tracks, drama, in the shape of exceptional happenings, had never stopped there. The inhabitants of the village, numbering two hundred and seventy, were satisfied that this should be so, quite content to exist inside ordinary life—to work, to hunt, to watch television, to attend school socials, choir practice, meetings of the 4H Club. But then, in the earliest hours of that morning in November, a Sunday morning, certain foreign sounds impinged on the normal nightly Holcomb noises—on the keening hysteria of coyotes, the dry scrape of scuttling tumbleweed, the racing, receding wail of locomotive whistles. At the time not a soul in sleeping Holcomb heard them—four shotgun blasts that, all told, ended six human lives. But afterward the townspeople, theretofore sufficiently unfearful of each other to seldom trouble to lock their doors, found fantasy re-creating them over and again—those somber

*See Phillip K. Tompkins' "In Cold Fact," *Esquire* 65 (June 1966): 125, 127, 166–168, 170–171, and John Hersey's "The Legend on the License," *The Yale Review* 70 (Autumn 1980): 1–15.

explosions that stimulated fires of mistrust in the glare of which many old neighbors viewed each other strangely, and as strangers.

The master of River Valley Farm, Herbert William Clutter, was forty-eight years old, and as a result of a recent medical examination for an insurance policy, knew himself to be in first-rate condition. Though he wore rimless glasses and was of but average height, standing just under five feet ten, Mr. Clutter cut a man's-man figure. His shoulders were broad, his hair had held its dark color, his square-jawed, confident face retained a healthy-hued youthfulness, and his teeth, unstained and strong enough to shatter walnuts, were still intact. He weighed a hundred and fifty-four— the same as he had the day he graduated from Kansas State University, where he had majored in agriculture. He was not as rich as the richest man in Holcomb—Mr. Taylor Jones, a neighboring rancher. He was, however, the community's most widely known citizen, prominent both there and in Garden City, the close-by county seat, where he had headed the building committee for the newly completed First Methodist Church, an eight-hundred-thousand-dollar edifice. He was currently chairman of the Kansas Conference of Farm Organizations, and his name was everywhere respectfully recognized among Midwestern agriculturists, as it was in certain Washington offices, where he had been a member of the Federal Farm Credit Board during the Eisenhower administration.

Always certain of what he wanted from the world, Mr. Clutter had in large measure obtained it. On his left hand, on what remained of a finger once mangled by a piece of farm machinery, he wore a plain gold band, which was the symbol, a quarter-century old, of his marriage to the person he had wished to marry—the sister of a college classmate, a timid, pious, delicate girl named Bonnie Fox, who was three years younger than he. She had given him four children—a trio of daughters, then a son. The eldest daughter, Eveanna, married and the mother of a boy ten months old, lived in northern Illinois but visited Holcomb frequently. Indeed, she and her family were expected within the fortnight, for her parents planned a sizable Thanksgiving reunion of the Clutter clan (which had its beginnings in Germany; the first immigrant Clutter—or Klotter, as the name was then spelled—arrived here in 1880); fifty-odd kinfolk had been asked, several of whom would be traveling from places as far away as Palatka, Florida. Nor did Beverly, the child next in age to Eveanna, any longer reside at River Valley Farm; she was in Kansas City, Kansas, studying to be a nurse. Beverly was engaged to a young biology student, of whom her father very much approved; invitations to the wedding, scheduled for Christmas Week, were already printed. Which left, still living at home, the boy, Kenyon, who at fifteen was taller than Mr. Clutter, and one sister, a year older—the town darling, Nancy.

In regard to his family, Mr. Clutter had just one serious cause for disquiet—his wife's health. She was "nervous," she suffered "little spells"—such were the sheltering expressions used by those close to her. Not that the truth concerning "poor Bonnie's afflictions" was in the least a secret; everyone knew she had been an on-and-off psychiatric patient the last half-dozen years. Yet even upon this shadowed terrain sunlight had very lately sparkled. The past Wednesday, returning from two weeks of treatment at the Wesley Medical Center in Wichita, her customary place of retirement, Mrs. Clutter had brought scarcely credible tidings to tell her husband; with joy she informed him that the source of her misery, so medical opinion had at last decreed, was not in her head but in her spine—it was *physical*, a matter of misplaced vertebrae. Of course, she must undergo an operation, and afterward—well, she would be her "old self" again. Was it possible—the tension, the withdrawals, the pillow-muted sobbing behind locked doors, all due to an out-of-order backbone? If so, then Mr. Clutter could, when addressing his Thanksgiving table, recite a blessing of unmarred gratitude. [. . .]

Passing through the orchard, Mr. Clutter proceeded along beside the river, which was shallow here and strewn with islands—midstream beaches of soft sand, to which, on Sundays gone by, hot-weather Sabbaths when Bonnie had still "felt up to things," picnic baskets had been carted, family afternoons whiled away waiting for a twitch at the end of a fishline. Mr. Clutter seldom encountered trespassers on his property; a mile and a half from the highway, and arrived at by obscure roads, it was not a place that strangers came upon by chance. Now, suddenly a whole party of them appeared, and Teddy, the dog, rushed forward roaring out a challenge. But it was odd about Teddy. Though he was a good sentry, alert, ever ready to raise Cain, his valor had one flaw: let him glimpse a gun, as he did now—for the intruders were armed—and his head dropped, his tail turned in. No one understood why, for no one knew his history, other than that he was a vagabond Kenyon had adopted years ago. The visitors proved to be five pheasant hunters from Oklahoma. The pheasant season in Kansas, a famed November event, lures hordes of sportsmen from adjoining states, and during the past week plaid-hatted regiments had paraded across the autumnal expanses, flushing and felling with rounds of birdshot great coppery flights of the grain-fattened birds. By custom, the hunters, if they are not invited guests, are supposed to pay the landowner a fee for letting them pursue their quarry on his premises, but when the Oklahomans offered to hire hunting rights, Mr. Clutter was amused. "I'm not as poor as I look. Go ahead, get all you can," he said. Then, touching the brim of his cap, he headed for home and the day's work, unaware that it would be his last.

Like Mr. Clutter, the young man breakfasting in a café called the Little Jewel never drank coffee. He preferred root beer. Three aspirin, cold root beer, and a chain of Pall Mall cigarettes—that was his notion of a proper "chow-down." Sipping and smoking, he studied a map spread on the counter before him—a Phillips 66 map of Mexico—but it was difficult to concentrate, for he was expecting a friend, and the friend was late. He looked out a window at the silent small-town street, a street he had never seen until yesterday. Still no sign of Dick. But he was sure to show up; after all, the purpose of their meeting was Dick's idea, his "score." And when it was settled—Mexico. The map was ragged, so thumbed that it had grown as supple as a piece of chamois. Around the corner, in his room at the hotel where he was staying, were hundreds more like it—worn maps of every state in the Union, every Canadian province, every South American country—for the young man was an incessant conceiver of voyages, not a few of which he had actually taken: to Alaska, to Hawaii and Japan, to Hong Kong. Now, thanks to a letter, an invitation to a "score," here he was with all his worldly belongings: one cardboard suitcase, a guitar, and two big boxes of books and maps and songs, poems and old letters, weighing a quarter of a ton. (Dick's face when he saw those *boxes*! "Christ, Perry. You carry that junk *everywhere*?" And Perry had said, "*What* junk? One of them books cost me thirty bucks.") Here he was in little Olathe, Kansas. Kind of funny, if you thought about it; imagine being back in Kansas, when only four months ago he had sworn, first to the State Parole Board, then to himself, that he would never set foot within its boundaries again. Well, it wasn't for long.

Ink-circled names populated the map. COZUMEL, an island off the coast of Yucatán, where, so he had read in a men's magazine, you could "shed your clothes, put on a relaxed grin, live like a Rajah, and have all the women you want for $50-a-month!" From the same article he had memorized other appealing statements: "Cozumel is a hold-out against social, economic, and political pressure. No official pushes any private person around on *this* island," and "Every year flights of parrots come over from the mainland to lay their eggs." ACAPULCO connoted deep-sea fishing, casinos, anxious rich women; and SIERRA MADRE meant gold, meant *Treasure of the Sierra Madre*, a movie he had seen eight times. (It was Bogart's best picture, but the old guy who played the prospector, the one who reminded Perry of his father, was terrific, too. Walter Huston. Yes, and what he had told Dick was true: He *did* know the ins and outs of hunting gold, having been taught them by his father, who was a professional prospector. So why shouldn't they, the two of them, buy a pair of pack horses and try their luck in the Sierra Madre? But Dick, the practical Dick, had said, "Whoa, honey, whoa. I seen that show. Ends up everybody nuts. On account of fever and bloodsuckers, mean conditions all around. Then, when they got the gold—remember, a big wind came along and blew it all away?") Perry folded the map. He paid for the root beer and stood up. Sitting, he had seemed a more than normal-sized man, a powerful man, with the shoulders, the arms, the thick, crouching torso of a weight lifter—weight lifting was, in fact, his hobby. But some sections of him were not in proportion to others. His tiny feet, encased in short black boots with steel buckles, would have neatly fitted into a delicate lady's dancing slippers; when he stood up, he was no taller than a twelve-year-old child, and suddenly looked, strutting on stunted legs that seemed grotesquely inadequate to the grown-up bulk they supported, not like a well-built truck driver but like a retired jockey, overblown and muscle-bound. [. . .]

A car horn honked. At last—Dick.

"Good grief, Kenyon! I *hear* you."

As usual, the devil was in Kenyon. His shouts kept coming up the stairs: "Nancy! Telephone!"

Barefoot, pajama-clad, Nancy scampered down the stairs. There were two telephones in the house—one in the room her father used as an office, another in the kitchen. She picked up the kitchen extension: "Hello? Oh, yes, good morning, Mrs. Katz."

And Mrs. Clarence Katz, the wife of a farmer who lived on the highway, said, "I *told* your daddy not to wake you up. I said Nancy must be *tired* after all that wonderful acting she did last night. You were lovely, dear. Those white ribbons in your hair! And that part when you thought Tom Sawyer was dead—you had real tears in your eyes. Good as anything on TV. But your daddy said it was time you got up; well, it *is* going on for nine. Now, what I wanted, dear—my little girl, my little Jolene, she's just dying to bake a cherry pie, and seeing how you're a champion cherry-pie maker, always winning prizes, I wondered could I bring her over there this morning and you show her?"

Normally, Nancy would willingly have taught Jolene to prepare an entire turkey dinner; she felt it her duty to be available when younger girls came to her wanting help with their cooking, their sewing, or their music lessons—or, as often happened, to confide. Where she found the time, and still managed to "practically run that big house" and be a straight-A student, the president of her class, a leader in the 4H program and the Young Methodists League, a skilled rider, an excellent musician (piano, clarinet), an annual winner at the county fair (pastry, preserves, needlework, flower arrangement)—how a girl not yet seventeen could haul such a wagonload, and do so without "brag," with, rather, merely a radiant jauntiness, was an enigma the community pondered, and solved by saying, "She's got *character*. Gets it from her old man." Certainly her strongest trait, the talent that gave support to all the others, derived from her father: a fine-honed sense of organization. Each moment was assigned; she knew precisely, at any hour, what she would be doing, how long it would require. And that was the trouble with today: she had overscheduled it. She had committed herself to helping another neighbor's child, Roxie Lee Smith, with a trumpet solo that Roxie Lee planned to play at a school concert; had promised to run three complicated errands for her mother; and had arranged to attend a 4H meeting in Garden City with her father. And then there was lunch to make and, after lunch, work to be done on the bridesmaids' dresses for Beverly's wedding, which she had designed and was sewing herself. [. . .]

By midafternoon the black Chevrolet had reached Emporia, Kansas—a large town, almost a city, and a safe place, so the occupants of the car had decided, to do a bit of shopping. They parked on a side street, then wandered about until a suitably crowded variety store presented itself.

The first purchase was a pair of rubber gloves; these were for Perry, who, unlike Dick, had neglected to bring old gloves of his own.

They moved on to a counter displaying women's hosiery. After a spell of indecisive quibbling, Perry said, "I'm for it."

Dick was not. "What about my eye? They're all too light-colored to hide that."

"Miss," said Perry, attracting a salesgirl's attention. "You got any black stockings?" When she told him no, he proposed that they try another store. "Black's foolproof."

But Dick had made up his mind: stockings of any shade were unnecessary, an encumbrance, a useless expense ("I've already invested enough money in this operation"), and, after all, anyone they encountered would not live to bear witness. "*No* witnesses," he reminded Perry, for what seemed to Perry the millionth time. It rankled in him, the way Dick mouthed those two words, as though they solved every problem; it was stupid not to admit that there might be a witness they hadn't seen. "The ineffable happens, things *do* take a turn," he said. But Dick, smiling boastfully, boyishly, did not agree: "Get the bubbles out of your blood. Nothing can go wrong." No. Because the plan was Dick's, and from first footfall to final silence, flawlessly devised.

Next they were interested in rope. Perry studied the stock, tested it. Having once served in the Merchant Marine, he understood rope and was clever with knots. He chose a white nylon cord, as strong as wire and not much thicker. They discussed how many yards of it they required. The question irritated Dick, for it was part of a greater quandary, and he could not, despite the alleged perfection of his over-all design, be certain of the answer. Eventually, he said, "Christ, how the hell should I know?"

"You damn well better."

Dick tried. "There's him. Her. The kid and the girl. And maybe the other two. But it's Saturday. They might have guests. Let's count on eight, or even twelve. The only *sure* thing is every one of them has got to go."

"Seems like a lot of it. To be so sure about."

"Ain't that what I promised you, honey—plenty of hair on them-those walls?"

Perry shrugged. "Then we'd better buy the whole roll."

It was a hundred yards long—quite enough for twelve.

From THE EXECUTIONER'S SONG

N O R M A N   M A I L E R

Editor's Note—Subsitutionary Narration: *When* The Executioner's Song *appeared in 1979, it surprised many readers. Where was Norman Mailer, the conspicuous central character of Mailer's previous artful nonfiction? In* The Executioner's Song, *Mailer is completely absent as a character or identifiable consciousness, for he is employing the technique of* substitutionary narration *in which the author narrates the story* in the accents and diction of the work's characters.

Substitutionary narration is a challenging technique to master for it requires a superb ear for human speech and the ability to "put on" others' personalities. It is worth noting, however, that Mailer had access to extensive tape recordings of the "Western Voices" that dominate his story. He also had the letters of Gary Gilmore, the media-hounded Utah double-murderer who wished only to die. In addition, he personally interviewed (and thus heard firsthand the voices of) all the major figures in his Pulitzer Prizewinning volume (save Gilmore himself who had been executed), and he could replay the tapes and reread Gilmore's hundreds of letters to Nicole Baker to capture individual cadences.

Mailer titles the first half of his "true life novel," Western Voices, *and readers will observe that the book's very typography, with its short paragraphs separated by large white spaces, imitates the West's open terrain—as well as the gaps in the sensibilities of many of the story's western figures. While a regional similarity can be found in the spare sentences used by all three of the "western voices" presented here—those of Gilmore's cousin Brenda, his love Nicole, and Gilmore himself—each voice is slightly different: Brenda's tough and slangy; Nicole's slightly "spacey"; and Gilmore's chilling in its terse mental movement from slight to retaliation.*

Substitutionary narration can lend an aura of authenticity to a story. It also can provide lively narrative voices. When Mailer writes of Gary's cousin Brenda, "She was six and he was seven and she thought he was swell," *we can imagine Brenda saying to Mailer during an interview: "I was six and he was seven and I thought he was swell." Here, the author's work may have been only to switch the pronouns from first to third person: from "I" to "she." At other times, however, a voice will seem to burst forth from the narrative, for example when Mailer writes that Brenda* "remembered liking Gary so well she would not bother to see who else was there— Hi, Grandma, can I have a cookie?—come on, Gary, let's go." *By omitting quotation marks in this sentence, Mailer avoids claiming these were Brenda's exact words.**

Though the author seems absent from such works, which appear to be narrated by their own characters, in reality the author's craft is most subtly demanded, and the writer's artfulness (witness the A., B., C., and D. in the final excerpt) is everywhere at hand.

---

*Thomas Keneally makes use of this same technique in *Schindler's List* (see pages 78-82).

The First Day

1

Brenda was six when she fell out of the apple tree. She climbed to the top and the limb with the good apples broke off. Gary caught her as the branch came scraping down. They were scared. The apple trees were their grandmother's best crop and it was forbidden to climb in the orchard. She helped him drag away the tree limb and they hoped no one would notice. That was Brenda's earliest recollection of Gary.

She was six and he was seven and she thought he was swell. He might be rough with the other kids but never with her. When the family used to come out to Grandpa Brown's farm on Decoration Day or Thanksgiving, Brenda would only play with the boys. Later, she remembered those parties as peaceful and warm. There were no raised voices, no cussing, just a good family get-together. She remembered liking Gary so well she would not bother to see who else was there— Hi, Grandma, can I have a cookie?—come on, Gary, let's go.

Right outside the door was a lot of open space. Beyond the backyard were orchards and fields and then the mountains. A dirt road went past the house and up the slope of the valley into the canyon.

Gary was kind of quiet. There was one reason they got along. Brenda was always gabbing and he was a good listener. They had a lot of fun. Even at that age he was real polite. If you got into trouble, he'd come back and help you out.

Then he moved away. Gary and his brother Frank Jr., who was a year older, and his mother, Bessie, went to join Frank Sr., in Seattle. Brenda didn't see any more of him for a long time. Her next memory of Gary was not until she was thirteen. Then her mother, Ida, told her that Aunt Bessie had called from Portland, and was in a very blue mood. Gary had been put in Reform School. So Brenda wrote him a letter, and Gary sent an answer all the way back from Oregon, and said he felt bad putting his family through what he did.

On the other hand, he sure didn't like it in Reform School. His dream when he came out, he wrote, was to be a mobster and push people around. He also said Gary Cooper was his favorite movie star.

Now Gary was the kind of boy who would not send a second letter until he received your reply. Years could go by but he wasn't going to write if you hadn't answered his last. Since Brenda, before long, was married—she was sixteen and thought she couldn't live without a certain guy—her correspondence lapsed. She might mail a letter from time to time, but Gary didn't really get back into Brenda's life until a couple of years ago when Aunt Bessie called again. She was still upset about Gary. He had been sent from Oregon State Penitentiary to Marion, Illinois, and that, Bessie informed Ida, was the place they built to replace Alcatraz. She was not accustomed to thinking of her son as a dangerous criminal who could be kept only in a Maximum Security prison. [. . .]

Brenda started writing to Gary once more. Before long, they were into quite a correspondence. Gary's intelligence was really coming through. He hadn't reached high school before they put him in the Reformatory, so he must have done a lot of reading in prison to get this much education together. He certainly knew how to use big words. Brenda couldn't pronounce a few of the longer ones, let alone be sure of their meaning.

Sometimes, Gary would delight her by adding little drawings in the margin; they were damn good. She spoke of trying to do some artwork herself, and mailed a sample of her stuff. He corrected her drawing in order to show the mistakes she was making. Good enough to tutor at long distance.

Once in a while Gary would remark that having been in prison so long he felt more like the victim than the man who did the deed. Of course, he did not deny having committed a crime or two. He was always letting Brenda know he was not Charley Good Guy.

The House in Spanish Fork

1

Just before the time her mother and father split up, Nicole found a little house in Spanish Fork, and it looked like a change for the better. She wanted to live alone and the house made it easier.

It was very small, about ten miles from Provo, on a quiet street at the start of the foothills. Her little place was the oldest building on the block, and next to all those ranch bungalows lined up on each sidewalk like pictures in supermarket magazines, the house looked as funky as a drawing in a fairy tale. It was kind of pale lavender stucco on the outside with Hershey-brown window trim, and inside, just a living room, bedroom, kitchen and bathroom. The roofbeam curved in the middle, and the front door was practically on the sidewalk—that's how long ago it had been built.

In the backyard was a groovy old apple tree with a couple of rusty wires to hold the branches together. She loved it. The tree looked like one of those stray mutts that doesn't get any attention and doesn't care—it's still beautiful.

Then, just as she was really settling in, getting to like herself for really taking care of her kids this once, and trying to put her head together so her thoughts wouldn't rattle when she was alone, why just then Kathryne and Charles chose to split, her poor mom and dad married before they were hardly in high school, married for more then twenty years, five kids, and they never did get, Nicole always thought, to like each other, although maybe they'd been in love from time to time. Anyway, they were split. That would have dislocated her if she hadn't had the house in Spanish Fork. The house was better than a man. Nicole amazed herself. She had not slept with anybody for weeks, didn't want to, just wanted to digest her life, her three marriages, her two kids, and more guys than you wanted to count.

Well, the groove continued. Nicole had a pretty good job as a waitress at the Grand View Cafe in Provo and then she got work sewing in a factory. It was only one step above being a waitress, but it made her feel good. They sent her to school for a week, and she learned how to use the power sewing machines, and was making better money than she had ever brought in before. Two-thirty an hour. Her take-home came to $80 a week.

Of course, the work was hard. Nicole didn't think of herself as being especially well coordinated, and certainly she was not fast—her head was too bombed-out for sure. She would get flustered. They would put her on one machine and just about the time she started getting the hang of it, and was near the hourly quota, they put her on another. Then the machine would fuck up when she least expected.

Still it wasn't bad. She had a nest of a hundred bucks from screwing welfare out of extra money they'd once given her in some mix-up of checks, and put another $75 together from working. So she was able to pay out in cash $175 for an old Mustang that she bought from her next-door neighbor's brother. He had wanted up to $300, but he liked her. She just got a little lucky.

On the night Nicole met Gary, she had taken Sunny and Jeremy for a drive—the kids loved the car. With her was her sister-in-law. While she and Sue Baker weren't tight exactly, they did spend a lot of time together, and Sue was in the dumps at this point, being pregnant and split up from Rikki.

On the drive, Nicole passed about a block from her cousin's house, and Sue suggested they drop in. Nicole agreed. She figured Sue liked Sterling and must have heard that he had also split up with his old lady, just this week, baby and all.

It was a cool dark night, one of those nights in May when the mountain air still had the feel of snow. Except not that cold because Sterling's door was open a little bit. The girls knocked and walked in. Nicole wasn't wearing anything but her Levi's and some kind of halter, and there was this strange-looking guy sitting on the couch. She thought he was just plain strange looking. Hadn't shaved in a couple of days, and was drinking a beer.

Nicole on the River

1

By now, Nicole wanted to hear about Gary's life. Only he didn't want to talk about himself. Preferred to listen to her. It took a while for Nicole to realize that having spent his adolescence in jail and just about every year since, he was more interested to learn what went on in her little mind. He just hadn't grown up with sweet things like herself.

In fact, if he did tell a story it was usually about when he was a kid. Then she would enjoy the way he talked. It was like his drawing. Very definite. He gave it in a few words. A happened, then B and C. Conclusion had to be D.

A. His seventh-grade class voted on whether they should send Valentines to each other. He thought they were too old. He was the only one to vote against it. When he lost, he bought Valentines to mail to everybody. Nobody sent him one. After a couple of days he got tired of going to the mailbox.

B. One night, he was passing a store that had guns in the window. Found a brick and broke the window. Cut his hand, but stole the gun he wanted. It was a Winchester semiautomatic that cost $125 back in 1953. Later he got a box of shells and went plinking. "I had these two friends," Gary told her, "Charley and Jim. They really loved that .22. And I got tired of hiding it from my old man—when I can't have something the way I want it, then I don't really want it. So I said, 'I'm throwing the gun in the creek, if you guys have the guts to dive for it, it's yours.' They thought I was bullshitting until they heard the splash. Then Jim jumped and hurt his knee on a big old sharp rock. Never got the gun. The creek was too deep. I laughed my ass off."

C. On his thirteenth birthday his mother let him pick between having a party or getting a $20 bill. He chose the party and invited just Charley and Jim. They took the money their folks gave them for Gary and spent it on themselves. Then they told him.

D. He had a fight with Jim. Got angry and beat him half to death. Jim's father, a rough-and-tumble fucker, pulled Gary off. Told him, "Don't come around here again." Soon after, Gary got in trouble for something else and was sent to Reform School.

When his stories got too boiled down, when it got like listening to some old cowboy cutting a piece of dried meat into small chunks and chewing on them, why then he would take a swallow of beer and speak of his Celestial Guitar. He could play music on it while he slept. "Just a big old guitar," he would tell Nicole, "but it has a ship's wheel with hand spokes, and in my dreams, music comes out as I turn the wheel. I can play any tune in the world."

THE LOSER

GAY TALESE

Editor's Note—Interior Monologue: Interior monologue is the reporting of a person's internal (often unspoken) thoughts and feelings. Critics often make too much of the barriers to interior monologue. Discovering what people are feeling and thinking at key moments in their lives takes time, but it is no trick, as this Esquire *profile of boxer Floyd Patterson reveals.*

Talese first began to write of Patterson in 1957. By the time he came to write "The Loser" in 1964, he had written 37 articles on the heavyweight fighter, each one representing at least one extended visit. Talese had lived with Patterson at his training camp. He had jogged beside him during roadwork. "I had become almost an interior figure in his life," Talese acknowledges. "I was his second skin."

The second section of this article contains the most extensive direct quotation Talese has ever used in his work. In this extended monologue, Patterson relives his second humiliating defeat by Sonny Liston and tells what it feels like to be knocked out. When Patterson spoke this extraordinary monologue, Talese was sitting beside him on the sofa at his training camp. Patterson was thinking and looking at the floor. "I felt at this moment like a witness to his private thoughts, a partner in his privacy with permission to write about this privacy," Talese recalls. "I was hearing, I felt, what echoes inside a man who feels absolutely alone."

The art of interviewing is as subtle as the fine art of "hanging out." Because Talese knew Patterson so well and had gained his trust, he was able at times to break into his monologue, sometimes to slow Patterson down, sometimes to push him deeper into himself. After describing the surprising euphoria he experienced in the first moments of the knockdown, Patterson began pacing and continued: "But then this good feeling leaves you. You realize where you are, and what you're doing there, and what has just happened to you. And what follows is a hurt, a confused hurt." *At this moment Talese repeated the fighter's last words as a question:* "A confused hurt?" *This spurred Patterson to say:* "Not a physical hurt—it's a hurt combined with anger; it's a what-will-people-think hurt." *Again Talese softly queried:* "A what-will-people-think hurt?" *Patterson went deeper:* "It's an ashamed-of-my-own-ability hurt." *By using this gentle probing technique Talese was actually going inside with his source. "I was helping him," he explains. "I was also getting a more refined quote. He was not only going deeper; he was rewriting himself. This is a technique any interviewer can use."*

This first extended monologue was spoken aloud. In the article's third section, Talese placed in italics the continuation of Patterson's remembrance of his loss— this time unspoken, but reported to him soon after. "I put this interior monologue in italics, not only because it was purely interior, but also to put a frame around it because I felt that in the short space of a magazine article I was moving almost too fast," Talese explains. "I had a man flying to rescue his daughter, and his fear of flying was part of that, and that evoked his memory of flying away from the

Liston fight, his flight against fear. I felt I had to keep the reader's attention on all this and used italics to do so."

The reader, of course, will guess that Talese was an eyewitness to most of the other scenes in this article. He was sitting in the back of the Cessna and in the back seat of Patterson's station wagon at the school. "The Loser" also offers Talese's other stylistic trademarks. Precisely chosen details of setting, such as an abandoned country clubhouse and an untuned piano, establish psychological mood from the outset, while dramatic tension is created from a bottle hurtling through a window, by a man denying his name.

Once again Talese presents a story of the American Dream: "the whole nation hoping you'll win, including the president." *Yet he presents, as always, a complex story of a poor boy's rise to greatness. Patterson's growth into a sensitive human being, one who recognizes that boxing* "isn't a nice thing," *makes him a winner as a person—but a loser in the ring.*

At the foot of a mountain in upstate New York, about sixty miles from Manhattan, there is an abandoned country clubhouse with a dusty dance floor, upturned barstools, and an untuned piano; and the only sounds heard around the place at night come from the big white house behind it—the clanging sounds of garbage cans being toppled by raccoons, skunks, and stray cats making their nocturnal raids down from the mountain.

The white house seems deserted, too; but occasionally, when the animals become too clamorous, a light will flash on, a window will open, and a Coke bottle will come flying through the darkness and smash against the cans. But mostly the animals are undisturbed until daybreak, when the rear door of the white house swings open and a broad-shouldered Negro appears in grey sweat clothes with a white towel around his neck.

He runs down the steps, quickly passes the garbage cans and proceeds at a trot down the dirt road beyond the country club toward the highway. Sometimes he stops along the road and throws a flurry of punches at imaginary foes, each jab punctuated by hard gasps of his breathing—*"hegh-hegh-hegh"*—and then, reaching the highway, he turns and soon disappears up the mountain.

At this time of morning farm trucks are on the road, and the other drivers wave at the runner. And later in the morning other motorists see him, and a few stop suddenly at the curb and ask:

"Say, aren't *you* Floyd Patterson?"

"No," says Floyd Patterson. "I'm his brother, Raymond."

The motorists move on, but recently a man on foot, a disheveled man who seemed to have spent the night outdoors, staggered behind the runner along the road and yelled, "Hey, Floyd Patterson!"

"No, I'm his brother, Raymond."

"Don't tell *me* you're not Floyd Patterson. I know what Floyd Patterson looks like."

"Okay," Patterson said, shrugging, "if you want me to be Floyd Patterson, I'll be Floyd Patterson."

"So let me have your autograph," said the man, handing him a rumpled piece of paper and a pencil.

He signed it—"Raymond Patterson."

One hour later Floyd Patterson was jogging his way back down the dirt path toward the white house, the towel over his head absorbing the sweat from his brow. He lives alone in a two-room apartment in the rear of the house, and has remained there in almost complete seclusion since getting knocked out a second time by Sonny Liston.

In the smaller room is a large bed he makes up himself, several record albums he rarely plays, a telephone that seldom rings. The larger room has a kitchen on one side and, on the other, adjacent to a sofa, is a fireplace from which are hung boxing trunks and T-shirts to dry, and a photograph of him when he was the champion, and also a television set. The set is usually on except when Patterson is sleeping, or when he is sparring across the road inside the clubhouse (the ring is rigged over what was once the dance floor), or when, in a rare moment of painful honesty, he reveals to a visitor what it is like to be the loser.

"Oh, I would give up anything to just be able to work with Liston, to box with him somewhere where nobody would see us, and to see if I could get past three minutes with him," Patterson was saying, wiping his face with the towel, pacing slowly around the room near the sofa. "I *know* I can do better. . . . Oh, I'm not talking about a rematch. Who would pay a nickel for another Patterson-Liston fight? I know I wouldn't. . . . But all I want to do is get past the first round."

Then he said, "You have no idea how it is in the first round. You're out there with all those people around you, and those cameras, and the whole world looking in, and all that movement, that excitement, and *The Star-Spangled Banner*, and the whole nation hoping you'll win, including the President. And do you know what all this does? It blinds you, just blinds you. And then the bell rings, and you go at Liston and he's coming at you, and you're not even aware that there's a referee in the ring with you.

". . . Then you can't remember much of the rest, because you don't want to. . . . All you recall is, all of a sudden you're getting up, and the referee is saying, 'You all right?' and you say 'Of *course* I'm all right,' and he says, 'What's your name?' and you say, 'Patterson.'

"And then, suddenly, with all this screaming around you, you're down again, and you know you have to get up, but you're extremely groggy, and the referee is pushing you back, and your trainer is in there with a towel, and people are all standing up, and your eyes focus directly at no one person—you're sort of floating.

"It is not a *bad* feeling when you're knocked out," he said. "It's a *good* feeling, actually. It's not painful, just a sharp grogginess. You don't see angels or stars; you're on a pleasant cloud. After Liston hit me in Nevada, I felt, for about four or five seconds, that everybody in the arena was actually in the ring with me, circled around me like a family, and you feel warmth toward all the people in the arena after you're knocked out. You feel lovable to all the people. And you want to reach out and kiss everybody—men and women—and after the Liston fight somebody told me I actually blew a kiss to the crowd from the ring. I don't remember that. But I guess it's true because that's the way you feel during the four or five seconds after a knockout. . . .

"But then," Patterson went on, still pacing, "this good feeling leaves you. You realize where you are, and what you're doing there, and what has just happened to you. And what follows is a hurt, a confused hurt—not a physical hurt—it's a hurt combined with anger; it's a what-will-people-think hurt; it's an ashamed-of-my-own-ability hurt . . . and all you want then is a hatch door in the middle of the ring—a hatch door that will open and let you fall through and land in your dressing room instead of having to get out of the ring and face those people. The worst thing about losing is having to walk out of the ring and face those people. . . ."

Then Patterson walked over to the stove and put on the kettle for tea. He remained silent for a few moments. Through the walls could be heard the footsteps and voices of the sparring partners and the trainer who live in the front of the house. Soon they would be in the clubhouse getting things ready should Patterson wish to spar. In two days he was scheduled to fly to Stockholm and fight an Italian named Amonti, Patterson's first appearance in the ring since the last Liston fight.

Next he hoped to get a fight in London against Henry Cooper. Then, if his confidence was restored, his reflexes reacting, Patterson hoped to start back up the ladder in this country, fighting all the leading contenders, fighting often, and not waiting so long between each fight as he had done when he was a champion in the ninety-percent tax bracket.

His wife, whom he finds little time to see, and most of his friends think he should quit. They point out that he does not need the money. Even he admits that, from investments alone on his $8,000,000 gross earnings, he should have an annual income of about $35,000 for the next twenty-five years. But Patterson, who is only twenty-nine years old and barely scratched, cannot believe that he is finished. He cannot help but think that it was something more than Liston that destroyed him—a strange, psychological force was also involved, and unless he can fully understand what it was, and learn to deal with it in the boxing ring, he may never be able to live peacefully anywhere but under this mountain. Nor will he ever be able to discard the false whiskers and moustache that, ever since Johansson beat him in 1959, he has carried with him in a small attaché case into each fight so he can slip out of the stadium unrecognized should he lose.

"I often wonder what other fighters feel, and what goes through their minds when they lose," Patterson said, placing the cups of tea on the table. "I've wanted so much to talk to another fighter about all this, to compare thoughts, to see if he feels some of the same things I've felt. But who can you talk to? Most fighters don't talk much anyway. And I can't even look another fighter in the eye at a weigh-in, for some reason.

"At the Liston weigh-in, the sportswriters noticed this, and said it showed I was afraid. But that's not it. I can never look *any* fighter in the eye because . . . well, because we're going to fight, which isn't a nice thing, and because . . . well, once I actually did look a fighter in the eye. It was a long, long time ago. I must have been in the amateurs then. And when I looked at this fighter, I saw he had such a nice face . . . and then he looked at *me* . . . and *smiled* at me . . . and *I* smiled back! It was strange, very strange. When a guy can look at another guy and smile like that, I don't think they have any business fighting.

"I don't remember what happened in that fight, and I don't remember what the guy's name was. I only remember that, ever since, I have never looked another fighter in the eye."

The telephone rang in the bedroom. Patterson got up to answer it. It was his wife. Sandra. So he excused himself, shutting the bedroom door behind him.

Sandra Patterson and their four children live in a $100,000 home in an upper-middle-class white neighborhood in Scarsdale, New York. Floyd Patterson feels uncomfortable in this home surrounded by a manicured lawn and stuffed with furniture, and, since losing his title to Liston, he has preferred living full time at his camp, which his children have come to know as "daddy's house." The children, the eldest of whom is a daughter named Jeannie now seven years old, do not know exactly what their father does for a living. But Jeannie, who watched the last Liston-Patterson fight on closed-circuit television, accepted the explanation that her father performs in a kind of game where the men take turns pushing one another down; he had his turn pushing them down, and now it is their turn.

The bedroom door opened again, and Floyd Patterson, shaking his head, was very angry and nervous.

"I'm not going to work out today," he said. "I'm going to fly down to Scarsdale. Those boys are picking on Jeannie again. She's the only Negro in this school, and the older kids give her a rough time, and some of the older boys tease her and lift up her dress all the time. Yesterday she went home crying, and so today I'm going down there and plan to wait outside the school for those boys to come out, and. . . ."

"How old are they?" he was asked.

"Teenagers," he said. "Old enough for a left hook."

Patterson telephoned his pilot friend, Ted Hanson, who stays at the camp and does public-relations work for him, and has helped teach Patterson to fly. Five minutes later Hanson, a lean white man with a crew cut and glasses, was knocking on the door; and ten minutes later both were in the car that Patterson was driving almost recklessly over the narrow, winding country roads toward the airport, about six miles from the camp.

"Sandra is afraid I'll cause trouble; she's worried about what I'll do to those boys; she doesn't want trouble!" Patterson snapped, swerving around a hill and giving his car more gas. "She's just not firm enough! She's afraid . . . she was afraid to tell me about that groceryman who's been making passes at her. It took her a long time before she told me about that dishwasher repairman who comes over and calls her 'baby.' They all know I'm away so much. And that dishwasher repairman's been to my home about four, five times this month already. That machine breaks down every week. I guess he fixes it so it breaks down every week. Last time, I laid a trap. I waited forty-five minutes for him to come, but then he didn't show up. I was going to grab him and say, 'How would you like it if I called *your* wife *baby*? You'd feel like punching me in the nose, wouldn't you? Well, that's what I'm going to do—if you ever call her *baby* again. You call her Mrs. Patterson; or Sandra, if you know her. But you don't know her, so call her Mrs. Patterson.' And then I told Sandra that these men, this type of white man, he just wants to have some fun with colored women. He'll never marry a colored woman, just wants to have some fun. . . ."

Now he was driving into the airport's parking lot. Directly ahead, roped to the grass airstrip, was the single-engine green Cessna that Patterson bought and learned to fly before the second Liston fight. Flying was a thing Patterson had always feared—a fear shared by, maybe inherited from, his manager, Cus D'Amato, who still will not fly.

D'Amato, who took over training Patterson when the fighter was seventeen or eighteen years old and exerted a tremendous influence over his psyche, is a strange but fascinating man of fifty-six who is addicted to Spartanism and self-denial and is possessed by suspicion and fear: he avoids subways because he fears someone might push him onto the tracks; never has married; never reveals his home address.

"I must keep my enemies confused," D'Amato once explained. "When they are confused, then I can do a job for my fighters. What I do not want in life, however, is a sense of security; the moment a person knows security, his senses are dulled—and he begins to die. I also do not want many pleasures in life; I believe the more pleasures you get out of living, the more fear you have of dying."

Until a few years ago, D'Amato did most of Patterson's talking, and ran things like an Italian *padrone*. But later Patterson, the maturing son, rebelled against the Father Image. After losing to Sonny Liston the first time—a fight D'Amato had urged Patterson to resist—Patterson took flying lessons. And before the second Liston fight, Patterson had conquered his fear of height, was master at the controls, was filled with renewed confidence—and knew, too, that even if he lost, he at least possessed a vehicle that could get him out of town, fast.

But it didn't. After the fight, the little Cessna, weighed down by too much luggage, became overheated ninety miles outside of Las Vegas. Patterson and his pilot companion, having no choice but to turn back, radioed the airfield and arranged for the rental of a larger plane. When they landed, the Vegas air terminal was filled with people leaving town after the fight. Patterson hid in the shadows behind a hangar. His beard was packed in the trunk. But nobody saw him.

Later the pilot flew Patterson's Cessna back to New York alone. And Patterson flew in the larger, rented plane. He was accompanied on this flight by Hanson, a friendly, forty-two-year-old, thrice-divorced Nevadan who once was a crop duster, a bartender, and a cabaret hoofer; later he became a pilot instructor in Las Vegas, and it was there that he met Patterson. The two became good friends. And when Patterson asked Hanson to help fly the rented plane back to New York, Hanson did not hesitate, even though he had a slight hangover that night—partly due to being depressed by Liston's victory, partly due to being slugged in a bar by a drunk after objecting to some unflattering things the drunk had said about the fight.

Once in the airplane, however, Ted Hanson became very alert. He had to, because, after the plane had cruised a while at 10,000 feet, Floyd Patterson's mind seemed to wander back to the ring, and the plane would drift off course, and Hanson would say, "Floyd, Floyd, how's about getting back on course?", and then Patterson's head would snap up and his eyes would flash toward the dials. And everything would be all right for a while. But then he was back in the arena, reliving the fight, hardly believing that it had really happened. . . .

"... And I kept thinking, as I flew out of Vegas that night, of all those months of training before the fight, all the roadwork, all the sparring, all the months away from Sandra . . . thinking of the time in camp when I wanted to stay up until eleven-fifteen p.m. to watch a certain movie on The Late Show. But I didn't because I had roadwork the next morning. . . .

"... And I was thinking about how good I'd felt before the fight, as I lay on the table in the dressing room. I remember thinking, 'You're in excellent physical condition, you're in good mental condition—but are you vicious?' But you tell yourself, 'Viciousness is not important now, don't think about it now; a championship fight's at stake, and that's important enough and, who knows? maybe you'll get vicious once the bell rings.'

"... And so you lay there trying to get a little sleep . . . but you're only in a twilight zone, half asleep, and you're interrupted every once in a while by voices out in the hall, some guy's yelling 'Hey, Jack,' or 'Hey, Al,' or 'Hey, get those four-rounders into the ring.' And when you hear that, you think, 'They're not ready for you yet.' So you lay there . . . and wonder, 'Where will I be tomorrow? Where will I be three hours from now?' Oh, you think all kinds of thoughts, some thoughts completely unrelated to the fight . . . you wonder whether you ever paid your mother-in-law back for all those stamps she bought a year ago . . . and you remember that time at two A.M. when Sandra tripped on the steps while bringing a bottle up to the baby . . . and then you get mad and ask: 'What am I thinking about these things for?' . . . and you try to sleep . . . but then the door opens and somebody says to somebody else, 'Hey, is somebody gonna go to Liston's dressing room to watch 'em bandage up?'

"... And so then you know it's about time to get ready . . . . You open your eyes. You get off the table. You glove up, you loosen up. Then Liston's trainer walks in. He looks at you, he smiles. He feels the bandages and later he says, 'Good luck, Floyd,' and you think, 'He didn't have to say that; he must be a nice guy.'

"... And then you go out, and it's the long walk, always a long walk, and you think, 'What am I gonna be when I come back this way?' Then you climb into the ring. You notice Billy Eckstine at ringside leaning over to talk to somebody, and you see the reporters—some you like, some you don't like—and then it's The Star-Spangled Banner, and the cameras are rolling, and the bell rings . . . .

"... How could the same thing happen twice? How? That's all I kept thinking after the knockout. . . . Was I fooling these people all these years? . . . Was I ever the champion? . . . And then they lead you out of the ring . . . and up the aisle you go, past those people, and all you want is to get to your dressing room, fast . . . but the trouble was in Las Vegas they made a wrong turn along the aisle, and when we got to the end there was no dressing room there . . . and we had to walk all the way back down the aisle, past the same people, and they must have been thinking, 'Patterson's not only knocked out, but he can't even find his dressing room. . . .'

"*. . . In the dressing room I had a headache. Liston didn't hurt me physically—a few days later I only felt a twitching nerve in my teeth—it was nothing like some fights I've had: like that Dick Wagner fight in '53 when he beat my body so bad I was urinating blood for days. After the Liston fight, I just went into the bathroom, shut the door behind me, and looked at myself in the mirror. I just looked at myself, and asked, 'What happened?' and then they started pounding on the door, and saying, 'Com'on out, Floyd, com'on out; the press is here, Cus is here, com'on out, Floyd. . . .'*

"*. . . And so I went out, and they asked questions, but what can you say? What you're thinking about is all those months of training, all the conditioning, all the depriving; and you think, 'I didn't have to run that extra mile, didn't have to spar that day, I could have stayed up that night in camp and watched* The Late Show. *. . . I could have fought this fight tonight in no condition. . . .'*"

"Floyd, Floyd," Hanson had said, "let's get back on course. . . ."

Again Patterson would snap out of his reverie, and refocus on the omniscope, and get his flying under control. After landing in New Mexico, and then in Ohio, Floyd Patterson and Ted Hanson brought the little plane into the New York airstrip near the fight camp. The green Cessna that had been flown back by the other pilot was already there, roped to the grass at precisely the same spot it was on this day five months later when Floyd Patterson was planning to fly it toward perhaps another fight—this time a fight with some schoolboys in Scarsdale who had been lifting up his little daughter's dress.

Patterson and Ted Hanson untied the plane, and Patterson got a rag and wiped from the windshield the splotches of insects. Then he walked around behind the plane, inspected the tail, checked under the fuselage, then peered down between the wing and the flaps to make sure all the screws were tight. He seemed suspicious of something. D'Amato would have been pleased.

"If a guy wants to get rid of you," Patterson explained, "all he has to do is remove these little screws here. Then, when you try to come in for a landing, the flaps fall off, and you crash."

Then Patterson got into the cockpit and started the engine. A few moments later, with Hanson beside him, Patterson was racing the little plane over the grassy field, then soaring over the weeds, then flying high above the gentle hills and trees. It was a nice takeoff.

Since it was only a forty-minute flight to the Westchester airport, where Sandra Patterson would be waiting with a car, Floyd Patterson did all the flying. The trip was uneventful until, suddenly behind a cloud, he flew into heavy smoke that hovered above a forest fire. His visibility gone, he was forced to the instruments. And at this precise moment, a fly that had been buzzing in the back of the cockpit flew up front and landed on the instrument panel in front of Patterson. He glared at the fly, watched it crawl slowly up the windshield, then shot a quick smash with his palm against the glass. He missed. The fly buzzed safely past Patterson's ear, bounced off the back of the cockpit, circled around.

"This smoke won't keep up," Hanson assured. "You can level off."

Patterson leveled off.

He flew easily for a few moments. Then the fly buzzed to the front again, zigzagging before Patterson's face, landed on the panel and proceeded to crawl across it. Patterson watched it, squinted. Then he slammed down at it with a quick right hand. Missed.

Ten minutes later, his nerves still on edge, Patterson began the descent. He picked up the radio microphone—"Westchester tower . . . Cessna 2729 uniform . . . three miles northwest . . . land in one-six on final . . ."—and then, after an easy landing, he climbed quickly out of the cockpit and strode toward his wife's station wagon outside the terminal.

But along the way a small man smoking a cigar turned toward Patterson, waved at him, and said, "Say, excuse me, but aren't you . . . aren't you . . . Sonny Liston?"

Patterson stopped. He glared at the man, bewildered. He wasn't sure whether it was a joke or an insult, and he really did not know what to do.

"Aren't you Sonny Liston?" the man repeated, quite serious.

"No," Patterson said, quickly passing by the man, "I'm his brother."

When he reached Mrs. Patterson's car, he asked, "How much time till school lets out?"

"About fifteen minutes," she said. starting up the engine. Then she said, "Oh, Floyd, I just should have told Sister, I shouldn't have. . . ."

"*You* tell Sister; *I'll* tell the boys. . . ."

Mrs. Patterson drove as quickly as she could into Scarsdale, with Patterson shaking his head and telling Ted Hanson in the back, "Really can't understand these school kids. This is a religious school, and they want $20,000 for a glass window—and yet, some of them carry these racial prejudices, and it's mostly the Jews who are shoulder-to-shoulder with us, and. . . ."

"Oh, Floyd," cried his wife, "Floyd, I have to get along here . . . you're not here, you don't live here, I . . . "

She arrived at the school just as the bell began to ring. It was a modern building at the top of a hill, and on the lawn was the statue of a saint, and behind it a large white cross. "There's Jeannie," said Mrs. Patterson.

"Hurry, call her over here," Patterson said.

"Jeannie! Come over here, honey."

The little girl, wearing a blue school uniform and cap, and clasping books in front of her, came running down the path toward the station wagon.

"Jeannie," Floyd Patterson said, rolling down his window, "point out the boys who lifted your dress."

Jeannie turned and watched as several students came down the path; then she pointed to a tall, thin curly-haired boy walking with four other boys, all about twelve to fourteen years of age.

"Hey," Patterson called to him, "can I see you for a minute?"

All five boys came to the side of the car. They looked Patterson directly in the eye. They seemed not at all intimidated by him.

"You the one that's been lifting up my daughter's dress?" Patterson asked the boy who had been singled out.

"Nope," the boy said, casually.

"Nope?" Patterson said, caught off guard by the reply.

"Wasn't him, Mister," said another boy. "Probably was his little brother."

Patterson looked at Jeannie. But she was speechless, uncertain. The five boys remained there, waiting for Patterson to do something.

"Well, er, where's your little brother?" Patterson asked.

"Hey, kid!" one of the boys yelled. "Come over here."

A boy walked toward them. He resembled his older brother; he had freckles on his small, upturned nose, had blue eyes, dark curly hair and, as he approached the station wagon, he seemed equally unintimidated by Patterson.

"You been lifting up my daughter's dress?"

"Nope," the boy said.

"*Nope!*" Patterson repeated, frustrated.

"Nope, I wasn't lifting it. I was just touching it a little. . . ."

The other boys stood around the car looking down at Patterson, and other students crowded behind them, and nearby Patterson saw several white parents standing next to their parked cars; he became self-conscious, began to tap nervously with his fingers against the dashboard. He could not raise his voice without creating an unpleasant scene, yet could not retreat gracefully; so his voice went soft, and he said, finally:

"Look, boy, I want you to stop it. I won't tell your mother—that might get you in trouble—but don't do it again, okay?"

"Okay."

The boys calmly turned and walked, in a group, up the street.

Sandra Patterson said nothing. Jeannie opened the door, sat in the front seat next to her father, and took out a small blue piece of paper that a nun had given her and handed it across to Mrs. Patterson. But Floyd Patterson snatched it. He read it. Then he paused, put the paper down, and quietly announced, dragging out the words, "*She didn't do her religion. . . .*"

Patterson now wanted to get out of Scarsdale. He wanted to return to camp. After stopping at the Patterson home in Scarsdale and picking up Floyd Patterson, Jr., who is three, Mrs. Patterson drove them all back to the airport. Jeannie and Floyd, Jr., were seated in the back of the plane, and then Mrs. Patterson drove the station wagon alone up to camp, planning to return to Scarsdale that evening with the children.

It was four P.M. when Floyd Patterson got back to the camp, and the shadows were falling on the clubhouse, and on the tennis court routed by weeds, and on the big white house in front of which not a single automobile was parked. All was deserted and quiet; it was a loser's camp.

The children ran to play inside the clubhouse; Patterson walked slowly toward his apartment to dress for the workout.

"What could I do with those schoolboys?" he asked. "What can you do to kids of that age?"

It still seemed to bother him—the effrontery of the boys, the realization that he had somehow failed, the probability that, had those same boys heckled someone in Liston's family, the school yard would have been littered with limbs.

While Patterson and Liston both are products of the slum, and while both began as thieves, Patterson had been tamed in a special school with help from a gentle Negro spinster; later he became a Catholic convert, and learned not to hate. Still later he bought a dictionary, adding to his vocabulary such words as "vicissitude" and "enigma." And when he regained his championship from Johansson, he became the Great Black Hope of the Urban League.

He proved that it is not only possible to rise out of a Negro slum and succeed as a sportsman, but also to develop into an intelligent, sensitive, law-abiding citizen. In proving this, however, and in taking pride in it, Patterson seemed to lose part of himself. He lost part of his hunger, his anger—and as he walked up the steps into his apartment, he was saying, "I became the good guy. . . . After Liston won the title, I kept hoping that he would change into a good guy, too. That would have relieved me of the responsibility, and maybe I could have been more of the bad guy. But he didn't. . . . It's okay to be the good guy when you're winning. But when you're losing, it is no good being the good guy."

Patterson took off his shirt and trousers and, moving some books on the bureau to one side, put down his watch, his cuff links and a clip of bills.

"Do you do much reading?" he was asked.

"No," he said. "In fact, you know I've never finished reading a book in my whole life? I don't know why. I just feel that no writer today has anything for me; I mean, none of them has felt any more deeply than I have, and I have nothing to learn from them. Although Baldwin to me seems different from the rest. What's Baldwin doing these days?"

"He's writing a play. Anthony Quinn is supposed to have a part in it."

"Quinn?" Patterson asked.

"Yes."

"Quinn doesn't like me."

"Why?"

"I read or heard it somewhere; Quinn had been quoted as saying that my fight was disgraceful against Liston, and Quinn said something to the effect that he could have done better. People often say that—*they* could have done better! Well I think that if *they* had to fight, *they* couldn't even go through the experience of waiting for the fight to begin. They'd be up the whole night before, and would be drinking, or taking drugs. They'd probably get a heart attack. I'm sure that, if I was in the ring with Anthony Quinn, I could wear him out without even touching him. I would do nothing but pressure him, I'd stalk him, I'd stand close to him. I wouldn't touch him, but I'd wear him out and he'd collapse. But Anthony Quinn's an old man, isn't he?"

"In his forties."

"Well, anyway," Patterson said, "getting back to Baldwin, he seems like a wonderful guy. I've seen him on television and, before the Liston fight in Chicago, he came by my camp. You meet Baldwin on the street and you say, 'Who's this poor slob?'—he seems just like another guy; and this is the same impression *I* give people when they don't know me. But I think Baldwin and me, we have much in common, and someday I'd just like to sit somewhere for a long time and talk to him. . . ."

Patterson, his trunks and sweat pants on, bent over to tie his shoelaces, and then, from a bureau drawer, took out a T-shirt across which was printed *Deauville*. He has several T-shirts bearing the same name. He takes good care of them. They are souvenirs from the high point of his life. They are from the Deauville Hotel in Miami Beach, which is where he trained for the third Ingemar Johansson match in March of 1961.

Never was Floyd Patterson more popular, more admired than during that winter. He had visited President Kennedy; he had been given a $35,000 jeweled crown by his manager; his greatness was conceded by sportswriters—and nobody had any idea that Patterson, secretly, was in possession of a false moustache and dark glasses that he intended to wear out of Miami Beach should he lose the third fight to Johansson.

It was after being knocked out by Johansson in their first fight that Patterson, deep in depression, hiding in humiliation for months in a remote Connecticut lodge, decided he could not face the public again if he lost. So he bought false whiskers and a moustache, and planned to wear them out of his dressing room after a defeat. He had also planned, in leaving his dressing room, to linger momentarily within the crowd and perhaps complain out loud about the fight. Then he would slip undiscovered through the night and into a waiting automobile.

Although there proved to be no need for bringing disguise into the second or third Johansson fights, or into a subsequent bout in Toronto against an obscure heavyweight named Tom McNeeley, Patterson brought it anyway; and, after the first Liston fight, he not only wore it during his thirty-hour automobile ride from Chicago to New York, but he also wore it while in an airliner bound for Spain.

"As I got onto this plane, you'd never have recognized me," he said. "I had on this beard, moustache, glasses and hat—and I also limped, to make myself look older. I was alone. I didn't care what plane I boarded; I just looked up and saw this sign at the terminal reading 'Madrid,' and so I got on that flight after buying a ticket.

"When I got to Madrid I registered at a hotel under the name 'Aaron Watson.' I stayed in Madrid about four or five days. In the daytime I wandered around to the poorer sections of the city, limping, looking at the people, and the people stared back at me and must have thought I was crazy because I was moving so slow and looked the way I did. I ate food in my hotel room. Although once I went to a restaurant and ordered soup. I hate soup. But I thought it was what old people would order. So I ate it. And after a week of this, I began to actually think I was somebody else. I began to believe it. And it is nice, every once in a while, being somebody else."

Patterson would not elaborate on how he managed to register under a name that did not correspond to his passport; he merely explained, "With money, you can do anything."

Now, walking slowly around the room, his black silk robe over his sweat clothes, Patterson said, "You must wonder what makes a man do things like this. Well, I wonder too. And the answer is, I don't know . . . but I think that within me, within every human being, there is a certain weakness. It is a weakness that exposes itself more when you're alone. And I have figured out that part of the reason I do the things I do, and cannot seem to conquer that one word—*myself*—is because . . . is because . . . I am a coward. . . ."

He stopped. He stood very still in the middle of the room, thinking about what he had just said, probably wondering whether he should have said it.

"I am a coward," he then repeated, softly. "My fighting has little to do with that fact, though. I mean you can be a fighter—and a *winning* fighter—and still be a coward. I was probably a coward on the night I won the championship back from Ingemar. And I remember another night, long ago, back when I was in the amateurs, fighting this big, tremendous man named Julius Griffin. I was only a hundred fifty-three pounds. I was petrified. It was all I could do to cross the ring. And then he came at me, and moved close to me . . . and from then on I don't know anything. I have no idea what happened. Only thing I know is, I saw him on the floor. And later somebody said, 'Man, I never saw anything like it. You just jumped up in the air, and threw thirty different punches. . . .'"

"When did you first think you were a coward?" he was asked.

"It was after the first Ingemar fight."

"How does one see this cowardice you speak of?"

"You see it when a fighter loses. Ingemar, for instance, is not a coward. When he lost the third fight in Miami, he was at a party later at the Fountainebleau. Had I lost, I couldn't have gone to that party. And I don't see how he did. . . ."

"Could Liston be a coward?"

"That remains to be seen," Patterson said. "We'll find out what he's like after somebody beats him, how he takes it. It's easy to do anything in victory. It's in defeat that a man reveals himself. In defeat I can't face people. I haven't the strength to say to people, 'I did my best, I'm sorry, and whatnot.'"

"Have you no hate left?"

"I have hated only one fighter," Patterson said. "And that was Ingemar in the second fight. I had been hating him for a whole year before that—not because he beat me in the first fight, but because of what he did after. It was all that boasting in public, and his showing off his right-hand punch on television, his thundering right, his 'toonder and lightening.' And I'd be home watching him on television, and *hating* him. It is a miserable feeling, hate. When a man hates, he can't have any peace of mind. And for one solid year I hated him because, after he took everything away from me, deprived me of everything I was, *he rubbed it in*. On the night of the second fight, in the dressing room, I couldn't wait until I got into the ring. When he was a little late getting into the ring, I thought, 'He's holding me up; he's trying to unsettle me—well, I'll get him!'"

"Why couldn't you hate Liston in the second match?"

Patterson thought for a moment, then said, "Look, if Sonny Liston walked into this room now and slapped me in the face, then you'd see a fight. You'd see the fight of your life because, then, a principle would be involved. I'd forget he was a human being. I'd forget I was a human being. And I'd fight accordingly."

"Could it be, Floyd, that you made a mistake in becoming a prizefighter?"

"What do you mean?"

"Well, you say you're a coward; you say you have little capacity for hate; and you seemed to lose your nerve against those schoolboys in Scarsdale this afternoon. Don't you think you might have been better suited for some other kind of work? Perhaps a social worker, or. . . ."

"Are you asking why I continue to fight?"

"Yes."

"Well," he said, not irritated by the question, "first of all, I love boxing. Boxing has been good to me. And I might just as well ask you the question: 'Why do you write?' Or, 'Do you retire from writing everytime you write a bad story?' And as to whether I should have become a fighter in the first place, well, let's see how I can explain it. . . . Look, let's say you're a man who has been in an empty room for days and days without food . . . and then they take you out of that room and put you into another room where there's food hanging all over the place . . . and the first thing you reach for, you eat. When you're hungry, you're not choosy, and so I chose the thing that was closest to me. That was boxing. One day I just wandered into a gymnasium and boxed a boy. And I beat him. Then I boxed another boy. I beat him, too. Then I kept boxing. And winning. And I said, 'Here, finally, is something I can do!'

"Now I wasn't a sadist," he quickly added. "But I liked beating people because it was the only thing I could do. And whether boxing was a sport or not, I wanted to make it a sport because it was a thing I could succeed at. And what were the requirements? Sacrifice. That's all. To anybody who comes from the Bedford-Stuyvesant section of Brooklyn, sacrifice comes easy. And so I kept fighting, and one day I became heavyweight champion, and I got to know people like you. And you wonder how I can sacrifice, how I can deprive myself so much. You just don't realize where I've come from. You don't understand where I was when it began for me.

"In those days, when I was about eight years old, everything I got—I stole. I stole to survive, and I did survive, but I seemed to hate myself. My mother told me I used to point to a photograph of myself hanging in the bedroom and say, 'I don't like that boy!' One day my mother found three large X's scratched with a nail or something over that photograph of me. I don't remember doing it. But I do remember feeling like a parasite at home. I remember how awful I used to feel at night when my father, a longshoreman, would come home so tired that, as my mother fixed food before him, he would fall asleep at the table because he was that tired. I would always take his shoes off and clean his feet. That was my job. And I felt so bad because here I was, not going to school, doing nothing, just watching my father come home; and on Friday nights it was even worse. He would come home with his pay, and he'd put every nickel of it on the table so my mother could buy food for all the children. I never wanted to be around to see that. I'd run and hide. And then I decided to leave home and start stealing—and I did. And I would never come home unless I brought something that I had stolen. Once I remember I broke into a dress store and stole a whole mound of dresses, at two A.M., and here I was, this little kid, carrying all those dresses over the wall, thinking they were all the same size, my mother's size, and thinking the cops would never notice me walking down the street with all those dresses piled over my head. They did, of course. . . . I went to the Youth House. . . ."

Floyd Patterson's children, who had been playing outside all this time around the country club, now became restless and began to call him, and Jeannie started to pound on his door. So Patterson picked up his leather bag, which contained his gloves, his mouthpiece and adhesive tape, and walked with the children across the path toward the clubhouse.

He flicked on the light switches behind the stage near the piano. Beams of amber streaked through the dimly lit room and flashed onto the ring. Then he walked to one side of the room, outside the ring. He took off his robe, shuffled his feet in the rosin, skipped rope, and then began to shadowbox in front of the spit-stained mirror, throwing out quick combinations of lefts, rights, lefts, rights, each jab followed by a "*hegh-hegh-hegh-hegh*." Then, his gloves on, he moved to the punching bag in the far corner, and soon the room reverberated to his rhythmic beat against the bobbing bag—rat-tat-tat-*tetteta*, rat-tat-tat-*tetteta*, rat-tat-tat-*tetteta*, rat-tat-tat-*tetteta*!

The children, sitting on pink leather chairs moved from the bar to the fringe of the ring, watched him in awe, sometimes flinching at the force of his pounding against the leather bag.

And this is how they would probably remember him years from now: a dark, solitary, glistening figure punching in the corner of a forlorn spot at the bottom of a mountain where people once came to have fun—until the clubhouse became unfashionable, the paint began to peel, and Negroes were allowed in.

As Floyd Patterson continued to bang away with lefts and rights, his gloves a brown blur against the bag, his daughter slipped quietly off her chair and wandered past the ring into the other room. There, on the other side of the bar and beyond a dozen round tables, was the stage. She climbed onto the stage and stood behind a microphone, long dead, and cried out, imitating a ring announcer, "Ladieeees and gentlemen . . . tonight we present. . . ."

She looked around, puzzled. Then, seeing that her little brother had followed her, she waved him up to the stage and began again: Ladiees and gentlemen . . . tonight we present . . . *Floydie Patterson*. . . ."

Suddenly, the pounding against the bag in the other room stopped. There was silence for a moment. Then Jeannie, still behind the microphone and looking down at her brother, said, "Floydie, come up here!"

"*No,*" he said.

"Oh, come up here!"

"*No,*" he cried.

Then Floyd Patterson's voice, from the other room, called: "Cut it out. . . . I'll take you both for a walk in a minute."

He resumed punching—rat-tat-tat-*tetteta*—and they returned to his side. But Jeannie interrupted, asking, "Daddy, how come you sweating?"

"Water fell on me," he said, still pounding.

"Daddy," asked Floyd, Jr., "how come you spit water on the floor before?"

"To get it out of my mouth."

He was about to move over to the heavier punching bag when the sound of Mrs. Patterson's station wagon could be heard moving up the road.

Soon she was in Patterson's apartment cleaning up a bit, patting the pillows, washing the teacups that had been left in the sink. One hour later the family was having dinner together. They were together for two more hours; then, at ten P.M.,

Mrs. Patterson washed and dried all of the dishes, and put the garbage out in the can—where it would remain until the raccoons and skunks got to it.

And then, after helping the children with their coats and walking out to the station wagon and kissing her husband good-bye, Mrs. Patterson began the drive down the dirt road toward the highway. Patterson waved once, and stood for a moment watching the taillights go, and then he turned and walked slowly back toward the house.

SOME DREAMERS OF THE GOLDEN DREAM

J O A N   D I D I O N

Editor's Note—Imagery and Symbolism: The average journalist, historian, or scientist rarely has (or takes) the time to locate imagery or symbolism in a work. The artist of reality does this often, recognizing that, as in fiction, suggestive images bring depth and subtle resonances to a story. In Talese's The Bridge, *the steel structures become ironic images of the ties their builders lack (see pages 63–73). The opening words of Mailer's* The Executioner's Song *offer a subtle evocation of the apple tree and the original fall from grace as our context for meeting Gary Gilmore (see page 102). John Hersey chooses to end his first chapter of* Hiroshima *with the multiply ironic observation that "in the first moment of the atomic age, a human being was crushed by books" (see page 93). Here "books" come to symbolize all of human wisdom.*

Perhaps no artist of reality combs worldly detritus more obsessively, however, than Joan Didion. One of this century's foremost writers of parables, Didion searches for sermons in stones and meaning in the mundane. Didion's 1967 article "Slouching Towards Bethlehem" is often considered the definitive portrait of the "flower children" of the 1960s who flocked to San Francisco in search of peace and love. Her essay "The White Album," written twelve years later, is a quintessential evocation of the entire sixties era. Didion's title, "The White Album," recalls the famous Beatles album of that name, yet it also evokes the image of a blank page (or pages) which the sixties actors sought haplessly and imaginatively to fill. Here again we see the value of images and symbols in the multiple resonances they create in readers' minds.

In her stunning 1983 volume Salvador, *and in many essays since, Didion has shown her gift for exposing the romantic fantasies which often propel both U.S. foreign policy and the lives of individual American citizens. In fact, such "golden" illusions are at the heart of the following 1966 article about a California murder. Through telling imagery and symbolism, Didion enlarges the implications of this murder to regional, even national, importance.*

This is a story about love and death in the golden land, and begins with the country. The San Bernardino Valley lies only an hour east of Los Angeles by the San Bernardino Freeway but is in certain ways an alien place: not the coastal California of the subtropical twilights and the soft westerlies off the Pacific but a harsher California, haunted by the Mojave just beyond the mountains, devastated by the hot dry Santa Ana wind that comes down through the passes at 100 miles an hour and whines through the eucalyptus windbreaks and works on the nerves. October is the bad month for the wind, the month when breathing is difficult and the hills blaze up spontaneously. There has been no rain since April. Every voice seems a scream. It is the season of suicide and divorce and prickly dread, wherever the wind blows.

The Mormons settled this ominous country, and then they abandoned it, but by the time they left the first orange tree had been planted and for the next hundred years the San Bernardino Valley would draw a kind of people who imagined they might live among the talismanic fruit and prosper in the dry air, people who brought with them Midwestern ways of building and cooking and praying and who tried to graft those ways upon the land. The graft took in curious ways. This is the California where it is possible to live and die without ever eating an artichoke, without ever meeting a Catholic or a Jew. This is the California where it is easy to Dial-A-Devotion, but hard to buy a book. This is the country in which a belief in the literal interpretation of Genesis has slipped imperceptibly into a belief in the literal interpretation of *Double Indemnity*, the country of the teased hair and the Capris and the girls for whom all life's promise comes down to a waltz-length white wedding dress and the birth of a Kimberly or a Sherry or a Debbi and a Tijuana divorce and a return to hairdressers' school. "We were just crazy kids," they say without regret, and look to the future. The future always looks good in the golden land, because no one remembers the past. Here is where the hot wind blows and the old ways do not seem relevant, where the divorce rate is double the national average and where one person in every thirty-eight lives in a trailer. Here is the last stop for all those who come from somewhere else, for all those who drifted away from the cold and the past and the old ways. Here is where they are trying to find a new life style, trying to find it in the only places they know to look: the movies and the newspapers. The case of Lucille Marie Maxwell Miller is a tabloid monument to that new life style.

Imagine Banyan Street first, because Banyan is where it happened. The way to Banyan is to drive west from San Bernardino out Foothill Boulevard, Route 66: past the Santa Fe switching yards, the Forty Winks Motel. Past the motel that is nineteen stucco tepees: "SLEEP IN A WIGWAM—GET MORE FOR YOUR WAMPUM." Past Fontana Drag City and the Fontana Church of the Nazarene and the Pit Stop A Go-Go; past Kaiser Steel, through Cucamonga, out to the Kapu Kai Restaurant-Bar and Coffee Shop, at the corner of Route 66 and Carnelian Avenue. Up Carnelian Avenue from the Kapu Kai, which means "Forbidden Seas," the subdivision flags whip in the harsh wind. "HALF-ACRE RANCHES! SNACK BARS! TRAVERTINE ENTRIES! $95 DOWN." It is the trail of an intention gone haywire, the flotsam of the New California. But after a while the signs thin out on Carnelian Avenue, and the houses are no longer the bright pastels of the Springtime Home owners but the faded bungalows of the people who grow a few grapes and keep a few chickens out here, and then the hill gets steeper and the road climbs and even the bungalows are few, and here—desolate, roughly surfaced, lined with eucalyptus and lemon groves—is Banyan Street.

Like so much of this country, Banyan suggests something curious and unnatural. The lemon groves are sunken, down a three- or four-foot retaining wall, so that one looks directly into their dense foliage, too lush, unsettlingly glossy, the greenery of nightmare; the fallen eucalyptus bark is too dusty, a place for snakes to breed. The stones look not like natural stones but like the rubble of some unmentioned upheaval. There are smudge pots, and a closed cistern. To one side of Banyan there is the flat valley, and to the other the San Bernardino Mountains, a dark mass looming too high, too fast, nine, ten, eleven thousand feet, right there above the lemon groves. At midnight on Banyan Street there is no light at all, and no sound except the wind in the eucalyptus and a muffled barking of dogs. There may be a kennel somewhere, or the dogs may be coyotes.

Banyan Street was the route Lucille Miller took home from the twenty-four-hour Mayfair Market on the night of October 7, 1964, a night when the moon was dark and the wind was blowing and she was out of milk, and Banyan Street was where, at about 12:30 A.M., her 1964 Volkswagen came to a sudden stop, caught fire, and began to burn. For an hour and fifteen minutes Lucille Miller ran up and down Banyan calling for help, but no cars passed and no help came. At three o'clock that morning, when the fire had been put out and the California Highway Patrol officers were completing their report, Lucille Miller was still sobbing and incoherent, for her husband had been asleep in the Volkswagen. "What will I tell the children, when there's nothing left, nothing left in the casket," she cried to the friend called to comfort her. "How can I tell them there's nothing left?"

In fact there was something left, and a week later it lay in the Draper Mortuary Chapel in a closed bronze coffin blanketed with pink carnations. Some 200 mourners heard Elder Robert E. Denton of the Seventh-Day Adventist Church of Ontario speak of "the temper of fury that has broken out among us." For Gordon Miller, he said, there would be "no more death, no more heartaches, no more misunderstandings." Elder Ansel Bristol mentioned the "peculiar" grief of the hour. Elder Fred Jensen asked "what shall it profit a man, if he shall gain the whole world, and lose his own soul?" A light rain fell, a blessing in a dry season, and a female vocalist sang "Safe in the Arms of Jesus." A tape recording of the service was made for the widow, who was being held without bail in the San Bernardino County Jail on a charge of first-degree murder.

Of course she came from somewhere else, came off the prairie in search of something she had seen in a movie or heard on the radio, for this is a Southern California story. She was born on January 17, 1930, in Winnipeg, Manitoba, the only child of Gordon and Lily Maxwell, both schoolteachers and both dedicated to the Seventh-Day Adventist Church, whose members observe the Sabbath on Saturday, believe in an apocalyptic Second Coming, have a strong missionary tendency, and, if they are strict, do not smoke, drink, eat meat, use makeup, or wear jewelry, including wedding rings. By the time Lucille Maxwell enrolled at Walla Walla College in College Place, Washington, the Adventist school where her parents then taught, she was an eighteen-year-old possessed of unremarkable good looks and remarkable high spirits. "Lucille wanted to see the world," her father would say in retrospect, "and I guess she found out."

The high spirits did not seem to lend themselves to an extended course of study at Walla Walla College, and in the spring of 1949 Lucille Maxwell met and married Gordon ("Cork") Miller, a twenty-four-old graduate of Walla Walla and of the University of Oregon dental school, then stationed at Fort Lewis as a medical officer. "Maybe you could say it was love at first sight," Mr. Maxwell recalls. "Before they were ever formally introduced, he sent Lucille a dozen and a half roses with a card that said even if she didn't come out on a date with him, he hoped she'd find the roses pretty anyway." The Maxwells remember their daughter as a "radiant" bride.

Unhappy marriages so resemble one another that we do not need to know too much about the course of this one. There may or may not have been trouble on Guam, where Cork and Lucille Miller lived while he finished his Army duty. There may or may not have been problems in the small Oregon town where he first set up private practice. There appears to have been some disappointment about their move to California: Cork Miller had told friends that he wanted to become a doctor, that he was unhappy as a dentist and planned to enter the Seventh-Day Adventist College of Medical Evangelists at Loma Linda, a few miles south of San Bernardino. Instead he bought a dental practice in the west end of San Bernardino County, and the family settled there, in a modest house on the kind of street where there are always tricycles and revolving credit and dreams about bigger houses, better streets. That was 1957. By the summer of 1964 they had achieved the bigger house on the better street and the familiar accouterments of a family on its way up: the $30,000 a year, the three children for the Christmas card, the picture window, the family room, the newspaper photographs that showed "Mrs. Gordon Miller, Ontario Heart Fund Chairman. . . ." They were paying the familiar price for it. And they had reached the familiar season of divorce.

It might have been anyone's bad summer, anyone's siege of heat and nerves and migraine and money worries, but this one began particularly early and particularly badly. On April 24 an old friend, Elaine Hayton, died suddenly; Lucille Miller had seen her only the night before. During the month of May, Cork Miller was hospitalized briefly with a bleeding ulcer, and his usual reserve deepened into depression. He told his accountant that he was "sick of looking at open mouths," and threatened suicide. By July 8, the conventional tensions of love and money had reached the conventional impasse in the new house on the acre lot at 8488 Bella Vista, and Lucille Miller filed for divorce. Within a month, however, the Millers seemed reconciled. They saw a marriage counselor. They talked about a fourth child. It seemed that the marriage had reached the traditional truce, the point at which so many resign themselves to cutting both their losses and their hopes.

But the Millers' season of trouble was not to end that easily. October 7 began as a commonplace enough day, one of those days that sets the teeth on edge with its tedium, its small frustrations. The temperature reached 102° in San Bernardino that afternoon, and the Miller children were home from school because of Teachers' Institute. There was ironing to be dropped off. There was a trip to pick up a prescription for Nembutal, a trip to a self-service dry cleaner. In the early evening, an unpleasant accident with the Volkswagen: Cork Miller hit and killed a German shepherd, and afterward said that his head felt "like it had a Mack truck on it." It was something he often said. As of that evening Cork Miller was $63,479 in debt, including the $29,637 mortgage on the new house, a debt load which seemed oppressive to him. He was a man who wore his responsibilities uneasily, and complained of migraine headaches almost constantly.

He ate alone that night, from a TV tray in the living room. Later the Millers watched John Forsythe and Senta Berger in *See How They Run*, and when the movie ended, about eleven, Cork Miller suggested that they go out for milk. He wanted some hot chocolate. He took a blanket and pillow from the couch and climbed into the passenger seat of the Volkswagen. Lucille Miller remembers reaching over to lock his door as she backed down the driveway. By the time she left the Mayfair Market, and long before they reached Banyan Street, Cork Miller appeared to be asleep.

There is some confusion in Lucille Miller's mind about what happened between 12:30 A.M., when the fire broke out, and 1:50 A.M., when it was reported. She says that she was driving east on Banyan Street at about 35 m.p.h. when she felt the Volkswagen pull sharply to the right. The next thing she knew the car was on the embankment, quite near the edge of the retaining wall, and flames were shooting up behind her. She does not remember jumping out. She does remember prying up a stone with which she broke the window next to her husband, and then scrambling down the retaining wall to try to find a stick. "I don't know how I was going to push him out," she says. "I just thought if I had a stick, I'd push him out." She could not, and after a while she ran to the intersection of Banyan and Carnelian Avenue. There are no houses at that corner, and almost no traffic. After one car had passed without stopping, Lucille Miller ran back down Banyan toward the burning Volkswagen. She did not stop, but she slowed down, and in the flames she could see her husband. He was, she said, "just black."

At the first house up Sapphire Avenue, half a mile from the Volkswagen, Lucille Miller finally found help. There Mrs. Robert Swenson called the sheriff, and then, at Lucille Miller's request, she called Harold Lance, the Miller's lawyer and their close friend. When Harold Lance arrived he took Lucille Miller home to his wife, Joan. Twice Harold Lance and Lucille Miller returned to Banyan Street and talked to the Highway Patrol officers. A third time Harold Lance returned alone, and when he came back he said to Lucille Miller, "O.K. . . . you don't talk any more."

When Lucille Miller was arrested the next afternoon, Sandy Slagle was with her. Sandy Slagle was the intense, relentlessly loyal medical student who used to baby-sit for the Millers, and had been living as a member of the family since she graduated from high school in 1959. The Millers took her away from a difficult home situation, and she thinks of Lucille Miller not only as "more or less a mother or a sister" but as "the most wonderful character" she has ever known. On the night of the accident, Sandy Slagle was in her dormitory at Loma Linda University, but Lucille Miller called her early in the morning and asked her to come home. The doctor was there when Sandy Slagle arrived, giving Lucille Miller an injection of Nembutal. "She was crying as she was going under," Sandy Slagle recalls. "Over and over she'd say, 'Sandy, all the hours I spent trying to save him and now what are they trying to *do* to me?'"

At 1:30 that afternoon, Sergeant William Paterson and Detectives Charles Callahan and Joseph Karr of the Central Homicide Division arrived at 8488 Bella

Vista. "One of them appeared at the bedroom door," Sandy Slagle remembers, "and said to Lucille, 'You've got ten minutes to get dressed or we'll take you as you are.' She was in her nightgown, you know, so I tried to get her dressed."

Sandy Slagle tells the story now as if by rote, and her eyes do not waver. "So I had her panties and bra on her and they opened the door again, so I got some Capris on her, you know, and a scarf." Her voice drops. "And then they just took her."

The arrest took place just twelve hours after the first report that there had been an accident on Banyan Street, a rapidity which would later prompt Lucille Miller's attorney to say that the entire case was an instance of trying to justify a reckless arrest. Actually what first caused the detectives who arrived on Banyan Street toward dawn that morning to give the accident more than routine attention were certain apparent physical inconsistencies. While Lucille Miller had said that she was driving about 35 m.p.h. when the car swerved to a stop, an examination of the cooling Volkswagen showed that it was in low gear, and that the parking rather than the driving lights were on. The front wheels, moreover, did not seem to be in exactly the position that Lucille Miller's description of the accident would suggest, and the right rear wheel was dug in deep, as if it had been spun in place. It seemed curious to the detectives, too, that a sudden stop from 35 m.p.h.—the same jolt which was presumed to have knocked over a gasoline can in the back seat and somehow started the fire—should have left two milk cartons upright on the back floorboard, and the remains of a Polaroid camera box lying apparently undisturbed on the back seat.

No one, however, could be expected to give a precise account of what did and did not happen in a moment of terror, and none of these inconsistencies seemed in themselves incontrovertible evidence of criminal intent. But they did interest the Sheriff's Office, as did Gordon Miller's apparent unconsciousness at the time of the accident, and the length of time it had taken Lucille Miller to get help. Something, moreover, struck the investigators as wrong about Harold Lance's attitude when he came back to Banyan Street the third time and found the investigation by no means over. "The way Lance was acting," the prosecuting attorney said later, "they thought maybe they'd hit a nerve."

And so it was that on the morning of October 8, even before the doctor had come to give Lucille Miller an injection to calm her, the San Bernardino County Sheriff's Office was trying to construct another version of what might have happened between 12:30 and 1:50 A.M. The hypothesis they would eventually present was based on the somewhat tortuous premise that Lucille Miller had undertaken a plan which failed: a plan to stop the car on the lonely road, spread gasoline over her presumably drugged husband, and, with a stick on the accelerator, gently "walk" the Volkswagen over the embankment, where it would tumble four feet down the retaining wall into the lemon grove and almost certainly explode. If this happened, Lucille Miller might then have somehow negotiated the two miles up Carnelian to Bella Vista in time to be home when the accident was discovered. This plan went awry, according to the Sheriff's Office hypothesis, when the car would not go over the rise of the embankment. Lucille Miller might have panicked then—after she had killed the engine the third or fourth time, say, out there on the dark road with the gasoline already spread and the dogs baying and the wind blowing and the unspeakable apprehension that a pair of headlights would suddenly light up Banyan Street and expose her there—and set the fire herself.

Although this version accounted for some of the physical evidence—the car in low because it had been started from a dead stop, the parking lights on because she could not do what needed doing without some light, a rear wheel spun in repeated attempts to get the car over the embankment, the milk cartons upright because there had been no sudden stop—it did not seem on its own any more or less credible than Lucille Miller's own story. Moreover, some of the physical evidence did seem to support her story: a nail in a front tire, a nine-pound rock found in the car, presumably the one with which she had broken the window in an attempt to save her husband. Within a few days an autopsy had established that Gordon Miller was alive when he burned, which did not particularly help the State's case, and that he had enough Nembutal and Sandoptal in his blood to put the average person to sleep, which did: on the other hand Gordon Miller habitually took both Nembutal and Fiorinal (a common headache prescription which contains Sandoptal), and had been ill besides.

It was a spotty case, and to make it work at all the State was going to have to find a motive. There was talk of unhappiness, talk of another man. That kind of motive, during the next few weeks, was what they set out to establish. They set out to find it in accountants' ledgers and double-indemnity clauses and motel registers, set out to determine what might move a woman who believed in all the promises of the middle class—a woman who had been chairman of the Heart Fund and who always knew a reasonable little dressmaker and who had come out of the bleak wild of prairie fundamentalism to find what she imagined to be the good life—what should drive such a woman to sit on a street called Bella Vista and look out her new picture window into the empty California sun and calculate how to burn her husband alive in a Volkswagen. They found the wedge they wanted closer at hand than they might have at first expected, for, as testimony would reveal later at the trial, it seemed that in December of 1963 Lucille Miller had begun an affair with the husband of one of her friends, a man whose daughter called her "Auntie Lucille," a man who might have seemed to have the gift for people and money and the good life that Cork Miller so noticeably lacked. The man was Arthwell Hayton, a well-known San Bernardino attorney and at one time a member of the district attorney's staff.

In some ways it was the conventional clandestine affair in a place like San Bernardino, a place where little is bright or graceful, where it is routine to misplace the future and easy to start looking for it in bed. Over the seven weeks that it would take to try Lucille Miller for murder, Assistant District Attorney Don A. Turner and defense attorney Edward P. Foley would between them unfold a curiously predictable story. There were the falsified motel registrations. There were the lunch dates, the afternoon drives in Arthwell Hayton's red Cadillac convertible. There were the interminable discussions of the wronged partners. There were the confidantes ("I knew everything," Sandy Slagle would insist fiercely later. "I knew every time, places, everything") and there were the words remembered from bad magazine stories ("Don't kiss me, it will trigger things," Lucille Miller remembered telling Arthwell Hayton in the parking lot of Harold's Club in Fontana after lunch one day) and there were the notes, the sweet exchanges: "Hi Sweetie Pie! You are my cup of tea!! Happy Birthday—you don't look a day over 29!! Your baby, Arthwell."

And, toward the end, there was the acrimony. It was April 24, 1964, when Arthwell Hayton's wife, Elaine, died suddenly, and nothing good happened after that. Arthwell Hayton had taken his cruiser, *Captain's Lady*, over to Catalina that weekend; he called home at nine o'clock Friday night, but did not talk to his wife because Lucille Miller answered the telephone and said that Elaine was showering. The next morning the Hayton's daughter found her mother in bed, dead. The newspapers reported the death as accidental, perhaps the result of an allergy to hair spray. When Arthwell Hayton flew home from Catalina that weekend, Lucille Miller met him at the airport, but the finish had already been written.

It was in the breakup that the affair ceased to be in the conventional mode and began to resemble instead the novels of James M. Cain, the movies of the late 1930's, all the dreams in which violence and threats and blackmail are made to seem commonplaces of middle-class life. What was most startling about the case that the State of California was preparing against Lucille Miller was something that had nothing to do with law at all, something that never appeared in the eight-column afternoon headlines but was always there between them: the revelation that the dream was teaching the dreamers how to live. Here is Lucille Miller talking to her lover sometime in the early summer of 1964, after he had indicated that, on the advice of his minister, he did not intend to see her any more: "First, I'm going to go to that dear pastor of yours and tell him a few things. . . . When I do tell him that, you won't be in the Redlands Church any more. . . . Look, Sonny Boy, if you think your reputation is going to be ruined, your life won't be worth two cents." Here is Arthwell Hayton, to Lucille Miller: "I'll go to Sheriff Frank Bland and tell him some things that I know about you until you'll wish you'd never heard of Arthwell Hayton." For an affair between a Seventh-Day Adventist dentist's wife and a Seventh-Day Adventist personal-injury lawyer, it seems a curious kind of dialogue.

"Boy, I could get that little boy coming and going," Lucille Miller later confided to Erwin Sprengle, a Riverside contractor who was a business partner of Arthwell Hayton's and a friend to both the lovers. (Friend or no, on this occasion he happened to have an induction coil attached to his telephone in order to tape Lucille Miller's call.) "And he hasn't got one thing on me that he can prove. I mean, I've got concrete—he has nothing concrete." In the same taped conversation with Erwin Sprengle, Lucille Miller mentioned a tape that she herself had surreptitiously made, months before, in Arthwell Hayton's car.

"I said to him, I said 'Arthwell, I just feel like I'm being used.'. . . He started sucking his thumb and he said 'I love you. . . . This isn't something that happened yesterday. I'd marry you tomorrow if I could. I don't love Elaine.' He'd love to hear that played back, wouldn't he?"

"Yeah," drawled Sprengle's voice on the tape. "That would be just a little incriminating, wouldn't it?"

"Just a *little* incriminating," Lucille Miller agreed. "It really *is*."

Later on the tape, Sprengle asked where Cork Miller was.

"He took the children down to the church."

"You didn't go?"

"No."

"You're naughty."

It was all, moreover, in the name of "love"; everyone involved placed a magical faith in the efficacy of the very word. There was the significance that Lucille Miller saw in Arthwell's saying that he "loved" her, that he did not "love" Elaine. There was Arthwell insisting, later, at the trial, that he had never said it, that he may have "whispered sweet nothings in her ear" (as her defense hinted that he had whispered in many ears), but he did not remember bestowing upon her the special seal, saying the word, declaring "love." There was the summer evening when Lucille Miller and Sandy Slagle followed Arthwell Hayton down to his new boat in its mooring at Newport Beach and untied the lines with Arthwell aboard, Arthwell and a girl with whom he later testified he was drinking hot chocolate and watching television. "I did that on purpose," Lucille Miller told Erwin Sprengle later, "to save myself from letting my heart do something crazy."

January 11, 1965, was a bright warm day in Southern California, the kind of day when Catalina floats on the Pacific horizon and the air smells of orange blossoms and it is a long way from the bleak and difficult East, a long way from the cold, a long way from the past. A woman in Hollywood staged an all-night sit-in on the hood of her car to prevent repossession by a finance company. A seventy-year-old pensioner drove his station wagon at five miles an hour past three Gardena poker parlors and emptied three pistols and a twelve-gauge shotgun through their windows, wounding twenty-nine people. "Many young women become prostitutes just to have enough money to play cards," he explained in a note. Mrs. Nick Adams said that she was "not surprised" to hear her husband announce his divorce plans on the Les Crane Show, and, farther north, a sixteen-year-old jumped off the Golden Gate Bridge and lived.

And, in the San Bernardino County Courthouse, the Miller trial opened. The crowds were so bad that the glass courtroom doors were shattered in the crush, and from then on identification disks were issued to the first forty-three spectators in line. The line began forming at 6 A.M., and college girls camped at the courthouse all night, with stores of graham crackers and No-Cal.

All they were doing was picking a jury, those first few days, but the sensational nature of the case had already suggested itself. Early in December there had been an abortive first trial, a trial at which no evidence was ever presented because on the day the jury was seated the San Bernardino *Sun-Telegram* ran an "inside" story quoting Assistant District Attorney Don Turner, the prosecutor, as saying, "We are looking into the circumstances of Mrs. Hayton's death. In view of the current trial concerning the death of Dr. Miller, I do not feel I should comment on Mrs. Hayton's death." It seemed that there had been barbiturates in Elaine Hayton's blood, and there had seemed some irregularity about the way she was dressed on that morning when she was found under the covers, dead. Any doubts about the death at the time, however, had never gotten as far as the Sheriff's Office. "I guess somebody didn't want to rock the boat," Turner said later. "These were prominent people."

Although all of that had not been in the *Sun-Telegram's* story, an immediate mistrial had been declared. Almost as immediately, there had been another development: Arthwell Hayton had asked newspapermen to an 11 A.M. Sunday morning press conference in his office. There had been television cameras, and flash bulbs popping. "As you gentlemen may know," Hayton had said, striking a note of stiff bonhomie, "there are very often women who become amorous toward their doctor or lawyer. This does not mean on the physician's or lawyer's part that there is any romance toward the patient or client."

"Would you deny that you were having an affair with Mrs. Miller?" a reporter had asked.

"I would deny that there was any romance on my part whatsoever."

It was a distinction he would maintain through all the wearing weeks to come.

So they had come to see Arthwell, these crowds who now milled beneath the dusty palms outside the courthouse, and they had also come to see Lucille, who appeared as a slight, intermittently pretty woman, already pale from lack of sun, a woman who would turn thirty-five before the trial was over and whose tendency toward haggardness was beginning to show, a meticulous woman who insisted, against her lawyer's advice, on coming to court with her hair piled high and lacquered. "I would've been happy if she'd come in with it hanging loose, but Lucille wouldn't do that," her lawyer said. He was Edward P. Foley, a small, emotional Irish Catholic who several times wept in the courtroom. "She has a great honesty, this woman," he added, "but this honesty about her appearance always worked against her."

By the time the trial opened, Lucille Miller's appearance included maternity clothes, for an official examination on December 18 had revealed that she was then three and a half months pregnant, a fact which made picking a jury even more difficult than usual, for Turner was asking the death penalty. "It's unfortunate but there it is," he would say of the pregnancy to each juror in turn, and finally twelve were seated, seven of them women, the youngest forty-one, an assembly of the very peers—housewives, a machinist, a truck driver, a grocery-store manager, a filing clerk—above whom Lucille Miller had wanted so badly to rise.

That was the sin, more than the adultery, which tended to reinforce the one for which she was being tried. It was implicit in both the defense and the prosecution that Lucille Miller was an erring woman, a woman who perhaps wanted too much. But to the prosecution she was not merely a woman who would want a new house and want to go to parties and run up high telephone bills ($1,152 in ten months), but a woman who would go so far as to murder her husband for his $80,000 in insurance, making it appear an accident in order to collect another $40,000 in double indemnity and straight accident policies. To Turner she was a woman who did not want simply her freedom and a reasonable alimony (she could have had that, the defense contended, by going through with her divorce suit), but wanted everything, a woman motivated by "love and greed." She was a "manipulator." She was a "user of people."

To Edward Foley, on the other hand, she was an impulsive woman who "couldn't control her foolish little heart." Where Turner skirted the pregnancy, Foley dwelt upon it, even calling the dead man's mother down from Washington to testify that her son had told her they were going to have another baby because Lucille felt that it would "do much to weld our home again in the pleasant relations that we used to have." Where the prosecution saw a "calculator," the defense saw a "blabbermouth," and in fact Lucille Miller did emerge as an ingenuous conversationalist. Just as, before her husband's death, she had confided in her friends about her love affair, so she chatted about it after his death, with the arresting sergeant. "Of course Cork lived with it for years, you know," her voice was heard to tell Sergeant Paterson on a tape made the morning after her arrest. "After Elaine died, he pushed the panic button one night and just asked me right out, and that, I think, was when he really—the first time he really faced it." When the sergeant asked why she had agreed to talk to him, against the specific instructions of her lawyers, Lucille Miller said airily, "Oh, I've always been basically quite an honest person. . . . I mean I can put a hat in the cupboard and say it cost ten dollars less, but basically I've always kind of just lived my life the way I wanted to, and if you don't like it you can take off."

The prosecution hinted at men other than Arthwell, and even, over Foley's objections, managed to name one. The defense called Miller suicidal. The prosecution produced experts who said that the Volkswagen fire could not have been accidental. Foley produced witnesses who said that it could have been. Lucille's father, now a junior-high-school teacher in Oregon, quoted Isaiah to reporters: *"Every tongue that shall rise against thee in judgment thou shalt condemn."* "Lucille did wrong, her affair," her mother said judiciously. "With her it was love. But with some I guess it's just passion." There was Debbie, the Millers' fourteen-year-old, testifying in a steady voice about how she and her mother had gone to a supermarket to buy the gasoline can the week before the accident. There was Sandy Slagle, in the courtroom every day, declaring that on at least one occasion Lucille Miller had prevented her husband not only from committing suicide but from committing suicide in such a way that it would appear an accident and ensure the double–indemnity payment. There was Wenche Berg, the pretty twenty-seven-year-old Norwegian governess to Arthwell Hayton's children, testifying that Arthwell had instructed her not to allow Lucille Miller to see or talk to the children.

Two months dragged by, and the headlines never stopped. Southern California's crime reporters were headquartered in San Bernardino for the duration: Howard Hertel from the *Times,* Jim Bennett and Eddy Jo Bernal from the *Herald-Examiner*. Two months in which the Miller trial was pushed off the *Examiner's* front page only by the Academy Award nominations and Stan Laurel's death. And finally, on March 2, after Turner had reiterated that it was a case of "love and greed," and Foley had protested that his client was being tried for adultery, the case went to the jury.

They brought in the verdict, guilty of murder in the first degree, at 4:50 P.M. on March 5. "She didn't do it," Debbie Miller cried, jumping up from the spectators' section. "She didn't *do* it." Sandy Slagle collapsed in her seat and began to scream.

"Sandy, for God's sake please *don't*," Lucille Miller said in a voice that carried across the courtroom, and Sandy Slagle was momentarily subdued. But as the jurors left the courtroom she screamed again: "You're murderers. . . . Every last one of you is a *murderer*." Sheriff's deputies moved in then, each wearing a string tie that read "1965 SHERIFF'S RODEO," and Lucille Miller's father, that sad-faced junior-high-school teacher who believed in the word of Christ and the dangers of wanting to see the world, blew her a kiss off his fingertips.

The California Institution for Women at Frontera, where Lucille Miller is now, lies down where Euclid Avenue turns into country road, not too many miles from where she once lived and shopped and organized the Heart Fund Ball. Cattle graze across the road, and Rainbirds sprinkle the alfalfa. Frontera has a softball field and tennis courts, and looks as if it might be a California junior college, except that the trees are not yet high enough to conceal the concertina wire around the top of the Cyclone fence. On visitors' day there are big cars in the parking area, big Buicks and Pontiacs that belong to grandparents and sisters and fathers (not many of them belong to husbands), and some of them have bumper stickers that say "SUPPORT YOUR LOCAL POLICE."

A lot of California murderesses live here, a lot of girls who somehow misunderstood the promise. Don Turner put Sandra Garner here (and her husband in the gas chamber at San Quentin) after the 1959 desert killings known to crime reporters as "the soda-pop murders." Carole Tregoff is here, and has been ever since she was convicted of conspiring to murder Dr. Finch's wife in West Covina, which is not too far from San Bernardino. Carole Tregoff is in fact a nurse's aide in the prison hospital, and might have attended Lucille Miller had her baby been born at Frontera; Lucille Miller chose instead to have it outside, and paid for the guard who stood outside the delivery room in St. Bernadine's Hospital. Debbie Miller came to take the baby home from the hospital, in a white dress with pink ribbons, and Debbie was allowed to choose a name. She named the baby Kimi Kai. The children live with Harold and Joan Lance now, because Lucille Miller will probably spend ten years at Frontera. Don Turner waived his original request for the death penalty (it was generally agreed that he had demanded it only, in Edward Foley's words, "to get anybody with the slightest trace of human kindness in their veins off the jury"), and settled for life imprisonment with the possibility of parole. Lucille Miller does not like it at Frontera, and has had trouble adjusting. "She's going to have to learn humility," Turner says. "She's going to have to use her ability to charm, to manipulate."

The new house is empty now, the house on the street with the sign that says

PRIVATE ROAD
BELLA VISTA
DEAD END

The Millers never did get it landscaped, and weeds grow up around the fieldstone siding. The television aerial has toppled on the roof, and a trash can is stuffed with the debris of family life: a cheap suitcase, a child's game called "Lie Detector." There is a sign on what would have been the lawn, and the sign reads "ESTATE

SALE." Edward Foley is trying to get Lucille Miller's case appealed, but there have been delays. "A trial always comes down to a matter of sympathy," Foley says wearily now. "I couldn't create sympathy for her." Everyone is a little weary now, weary and resigned, everyone except Sandy Slagle, whose bitterness is still raw. She lives in an apartment near the medical school in Loma Linda, and studies reports of the case in *True Police Cases* and *Official Detective Stories*. "I'd much rather we not talk about the Hayton business too much," she tells visitors, and she keeps a tape recorder running. "I'd rather talk about Lucille and what a wonderful person she is and how her rights were violated." Harold Lance does not talk to visitors at all. "We don't want to give away what we can sell," he explains pleasantly; an attempt was made to sell Lucille Miller's personal story to *Life*, but *Life* did not want to buy it. In the district attorney's offices they are prosecuting other murders now, and do not see why the Miller trial attracted so much attention. "It wasn't a very interesting murder as murders go," Don Turner says laconically. Elaine Hayton's death is no longer under investigation. "We know everything we want to know," Turner says.

Arthwell Hayton's office is directly below Edward Foley's. Some people around San Bernardino say that Arthwell Hayton suffered; others say that he did not suffer at all. Perhaps he did not, for time past is not believed to have any bearing upon time present or future, out in the golden land where every day the world is born anew. In any case, on October 17, 1965, Arthwell Hayton married again, married his children's pretty governess, Wenche Berg, at a service in the Chapel of the Roses at a retirement village near Riverside. Later the newlyweds were feted at a reception for seventy-five in the dining room of Rose Garden Village. The bridegroom was in black tie, with a white carnation in his buttonhole. The bride wore a long white *peau de soie* dress and carried a shower bouquet of sweetheart roses with stephanotis streamers. A coronet of seed pearls held her illusion veil.

From **BLOOD AND MONEY**

T H O M A S   T H O M P S O N

*Editor's Note—Enriching the Context through Allusion: Tom Wolfe has
described his first attempt at the Literature of Reality as a "garage sale" piece
containing "vignettes, odds and ends of scholarship, bits of memoir, short bursts
of sociology, apostrophes, epithets, moans, cackles, anything. . . ." Many works
of literary nonfiction are constructed on such collage or garage sale principles.
Narration of the as-it-happened reality is interspersed with newspaper clippings;
psychiatric case studies; poems; songs; quotations from religious, philosophical,
or historical works—anything, in short, which might enrich the context by
providing deeper insight into the subject at hand. In fact, in many of the greatest
works of artful nonfiction, the real event becomes merely a pretense, a
springboard for the author's exploration of more profound truths of the human
spirit, and it is the interjected material which helps shape and sound the way.*

The following excerpts from Thomas Thompson's 1976 best seller Blood and
Money *offer a simple, but vivid illustration of this method of infusing deeper
insights into factual narratives. In 1969, Joan Robinson Hill, a beautiful Houston
horsewoman and the beloved daughter of a Texas millionaire, died under
mysterious circumstances. Her death spurred a series of events which mount, as
Thompson's unfurling Biblical epigraph reveals, into a multiple tragedy of greed,
incestuous obsession, and damnation. Through his repeated allusion to the
biblical book of Revelation, Thompson places his contemporary melodrama in a
broader, richer, and implicitly moral context.*

Book One
Joan
". . . Behold a pale horse. . . "

ONE

During the night an early spring rain washed the city and now, at dawn, the
air was sweet and heavy. Remnants of fog still held to the pavements of
Houston, rolling across the streets like cobweb tumbleweeds, and the
windshields of early commuters were misted and dangerous. The morning seemed
sad, of little promise.

In his bed, the old man sweated and tossed. This night had been worse than most.
He had awakened over and over again, and each time he checked the clock. He was
impatient for the new day to commence so that he could order the flowers. One hundred perfect yellow roses would surely please his daughter. Not until he saw her
laugh again would he sleep well.

Once, during the long darkness, he turned on the light and looked at the photographs which surrounded his bed. Above his head was Joan from a quarter century ago, when she was a child in best white organdy, her knee saucily crossed. To his right, on the wall, was Joan in her late teens, her beauty frozen by soft focus, her features glazed, the classic debutante. And to his left, on the old Grand Rapids dresser, was Joan in recent years, her face ablaze with the triumph of yet another win in the show ring. There were a thousand like these in the big house, filling the walls, pasted into scrapbooks, stuffed into drawers, spilling out of closets. Joan and her horses had become favorite subjects of photographers across the land, and the old man's home was a museum of her image.

But even these familiar suspensions of time could not push away the scene from the night before. Each time he bolted awake, sitting up in bed, throwing a hand across his face to smear the dampness from his eyes, it was still there in all the torment.

"Joan, honey?" He had crept a few steps into the hospital room. It smelled of sterile potions and pain. Two nurses were busy about his daughter with tubes and medical contraptions.

"Pa?" she answered weakly. Normally her voice could boom clear across a cornfield. Her pillow was slightly raised, and on it her hair spilled thin and lifeless, no longer silver white and electric like a noon sun.

"They won't let me stay, honey," he said, fumbling for comfort. "You hurry up and get well, now, and tomorrow morning when you wake up I'm gonna fill your room with yellow roses."

Joan tried to smile. "I'd like that, Pa," she murmured.

"Daddy's gonna do that, Joan," he said. "You know Daddy's gonna do that."

Then one of the nurses pushed expelling hands toward him and he left the room. He stopped for a moment outside and leaned his heavy body against the wall. His heart pumped in alarm. Hadn't the doctors said she would be all right? They had, he reassured himself. He went in search of another one just to hear the words again. . . .

When the door chimes rang just before 6 A.M., the old man heard them. For an instant, in his bed, he opened his eyes and wondered who could be seeking entrance to his home so early, so unexpectedly. But he was weary, not yet ready to wake, and when he heard Ma stirring, he closed his eyes and fell back.

The old woman padded to the front door and opened it with good will. Perhaps, she thought, a neighbor is in distress. But when she saw the people with the gray and tragic faces standing at her threshold, looming out of the mist and fog, her knees buckled. They did not have to speak a word. She knew. She knew exactly what they had come to tell her.

"Oh, my God," the old woman managed as she fell. Pitifully she began to retch, throwing up the whiskey that had helped her find sleep the night before. Her son-in-law, John Hill, watched, but he did not reach down to pick her up. Although a doctor, he lacked the will at this terrible moment. One of the friends who had come with him, another physician, knelt to help Ma. He grasped her gently and lifted her and walked her to the living room. There she fell, breathing hard, onto the sofa. John Hill watched her for a few moments, then he took a tentative step toward the back bedroom where the old man was sleeping. Clearly he dreaded to make this short journey.

It was not Ma's nature to command anyone, for she was a woman who lived an obedient step or two behind her husband and her daughter. Her world was their shadows, and drawn blinds. But now she threw out her hand with an edict.

"Don't wake Pa," she said urgently. "For God's sake, let him sleep. This is the last night he ever will."

And they all sat and waited, fearfully, for Pa to wake and rise and hear the news.

Book Two
John
". . . Behold a pale horse: and his name that
sat on him was Death. . ."

FOURTEEN

Assistant District Attorney I. D. McMaster was a low-key man of great patience, but a fortnight after Joan Robinson Hill was in her grave, he was fed up. "That damned old man," he told a colleague, "is *obsessed*." Several times each day, it seemed, Ash was on the telephone, with some new and damaging tidbit to report. Finally McMaster told the bothersome caller that nothing could be done until Dr. Jachimczyk released the results of his second autopsy. Until then, there was nothing to investigate. A licensed physician—Bertinot—signed the woman's death certificate, and a qualified hospital pathologist—Morse—did an autopsy, even though the conditions were admittedly abnormal.

Ash would not be subdued, no more than a pot of water would cease boiling when flames licked beneath it. His personal loss was enormous, but there was another factor at work: excitement had been injected into an old and eroding life. A mystery to solve! His home became command headquarters to which Ash summoned first his own doctor, a general practitioner named Ed Gouldin, then others who had been friends of John and Joan Hill. The heart surgeon Grady Hallman was one of the first to come, the Mozart-playing Jim Oates was another. They pored over the Sharpstown Hospital case history and discussed the case. The men of medicine agreed that Joan's death was both tragic and unusual but that, until the county coroner made an official ruling, speculating was not only harmful but potentially slanderous.

Very well. In the meantime Ash would not just sit in his easy chair and wait for what surely would be a bolt of lightning from the medical examiner's office. There was no law against assembling material that might be useful someday. He began telephoning people who reportedly had "information" and he scribbled it all down on the pieces of lined notebook paper that were soon spilling from his pockets. His dining-room table became a blizzard of documents, medical charts, textbooks, scraps with cryptic messages that only he could read.

These were some of the stories that Ash pulled out of people while he waited for the coroner:

From a psychiatrist who had lived near the Hills: "When I got over to John's the night of the funeral, he was all alone. Right away he started talking about insurance and business matters. He didn't seem to be grieving much at all. In fact, he was smiling. From his attitude that night, Joan's death seemed to have no more impact on him than the Oilers losing a game—and he was certainly not an Oiler fan. He was much more interested in showing me the music room than in talking about Joan's disease. Mr. Ash, we didn't talk about Joan's disease *at all!* And the reason is clear to me. This was a man who had walked out on his wife when she was in terminal shock—and he knew that I, as a doctor, knew it."

From a nurse who passed along a conversation she overheard in the surgeons' lounge at St. Luke's Hospital: "One doctor says, 'I always suspected old John wanted to get rid of his wife. Wonder what he gave her?' And the other doctor said, 'Maybe an overdose of insulin. It's a natural body substance and impossible to trace.'"

And, from several of the River Oaks women who stood in a black-garbed group after Joan's casket was dropped into the earth: "We were all saying how terrible it was the way John neglected Joan when she got sick. It really was a crime, Pa. Negligence!"

* * *

"Yes . . ." Ann [Kurth] hesitated, then she blurted out a shocker. "He told me how he had killed Joan with a needle, and I knew that he . . ."

As a gasp rushed collectively from the spectators, [the lawyer] Racehorse [Haynes] rocketed out of his chair. He rushed to the bench and asked for a *sotto voce* conference, out of the jury's earshot. This woman's testimony is not worthy of belief, he hissed. What the witness just slipped into the record is prejudicial, inflammatory, and irrevocable, no matter how many times the bench instructs the jury to disregard these statements. With passion to shake a Chatauqua tent, Racehorse demanded a mistrial.

"Overruled," said Judge Hooey quietly, but he announced a luncheon recess. And he left the courtroom looking troubled.

During the break, the prosecutors warned Ann that she must expect exhaustive cross-examination from the defense. Racehorse would try to pulverize her. She smiled demurely, while newspaper photographers' flash bulbs popped around her. "I can handle Mr. Racehorse," she assured them. She always spoke his nickname with a heavy coat of mockery, often telling how disappointed she was at first meeting with the attorney. "I had been hearing about this man called Racehorse," she once remarked, "and I expected to encounter a fantastic stud. Instead, this little squirt walks in to take my deposition. *Quel* disappointment."

Before trial was to resume at 1:30 P.M., Judge Hooey summoned opposing counsel into his chambers. His face was grave. Over the lunch hour he had reviewed the Kurth testimony and Mr. Haynes's motions of opposition to her appearance. "I have decided to grant Mr. Haynes's motion for a mistrial," the judge said.

And suddenly it was over.

Devastated, the district attorney's men urged the judge to change his mind. "We begged, cajoled, pleaded, and cried," McMaster would recall of the moment. "But his honor wouldn't budge." Judge Hooey said he would reset the case for another trial a few months hence. He asked the attorneys to apologize to their other witnesses under subpoena—Racehorse and Don Fullenweider alone had the equivalent of a small hospital staff ready to testify against the state's medical negligence contentions.

When a newspaper reporter asked Ernie Ernst for an explanation of the surprising decision, he said, "It's very simple. The judge just threw our ass out of court." Privately, the two prosecutors came to believe that the judge simply could not accept all of the Kurth testimony. And it had been a mistake for her to quote John Hill as saying he had killed Joan with a needle.

That night the DA's men drank whiskey. They grew rowdy and foolish, Ernst doing a funny imitation of Ann Kurth dodging John Hill's flying hypodermic needles. McMaster laughed, as did everyone else in the room. But in his laughter was the cutting edge of defeat. He knew that the prospects of John Hill being tried again and convicted of murder were lessened now.

* * *

On the flight from Las Vegas to Houston, the plane was filled with members of Houston's plastic surgery community. "If we crash," mused John, "the business is wiped out in Houston." It was a hot Sunday midafternoon when they took off from Vegas. It would be even hotter in Houston, where September is the broiling month. Not far away on the plane sat Nathan Roth, the heavy and moody surgeon who had hired John fresh out of medical training. He had gone before one of the grand juries and given harmful testimony about his onetime protégé's character and professional responsibility. The two men were bitter enemies, but Connie [Hill, John's new wife] every now and then flashed him a mischievous dazzling smile. John knew what she was doing and was amused. Give Connie five minutes with his worst enemy, and she could charm him into a friend. Some of the other surgeons dropped by and chatted with the Hills, grumbling over gambling losses, or speculating on the likelihood of certain Vegas show girls having had breast augmentation.

"Slowly they're forgiving him," thought Connie. "Slowly they're inviting him back into their group. And it's about time!" Before the end of the year, she believed, her husband would be completely accepted by his peers and bear but few scars of his scandal and exile. During the rest of the late afternoon flight John dozed. Now and then Connie nudged him to try out a bit of a speech she was preparing for delivery to a women's group entitled, "Vienna: City of Dreams."

In the taxi home from the Houston airport, Connie snuggled close to John and whispered her thanks for the trip. "Without you, I couldn't have gone to my cousin's wedding, or I couldn't have done San Francisco the way it should be done," she said. Putting her head on John's shoulder, Connie was content. It occurred to her that she and her husband had known each other for almost three years and not one single cross word had been spoken by either. Aside from John's habit of being chronically late, she could find no fault with her quiet husband.

For a few months after the mistrial, she had worried that someone might try to harm him: the hate phone calls kept coming in, and Ash continued his ominous drives past their home. Once, when she went to bed early and fell asleep while waiting for John to return from the hospital, she awoke suddenly at 1 A.M. and found John still absent. Frantically she called the hospital and implored a nurse to search. In the next quarter of an hour Connie paced the great house, imagining that something terrible had happened. Then the phone rang. The nurse had found the plastic surgeon, asleep on a couch in the doctors' lounge. That had been the only disquieting incident in a year and a half. Their lives had settled into a routine. No one save Ash Robinson seemed interested in them any more.

At their pillared mansion, Connie sprang out of the taxi almost before it had parked on the curving driveway. She was eager to see her stepson, Robert, and tell him of the trip. The boy was twelve, sprouting tall, and had somehow managed to survive the tragedy of his mother's death and his father's murder trial with psyche unharmed. He had warmed instantly to Connie, and she knew that he would not settle down for bed until he had visited with his parents. While John paid the cabbie and attended to the luggage, Connie rang the doorbell. Impatiently, she pressed her face to a glass panel beside the door, squashing her features clownishly, hoping to make Robert laugh. But no one came. She rang the bell again, thinking she heard the distant chatter of the television set. Even if Robert was absorbed in some cowboy program, surely John's mother, Myra, who had been "baby sitting," would hurry to the door in greeting.

Then, to her right, through the glass panel, Connie saw a figure approaching, walking through the sunken living room and toward the small step that led to the entrance hall. Connie was not sure, but it seemed that the figure wore a green costume. She prepared to laugh, for Robert was apparently in masquerade. He had concocted a joke for their homecoming. What was he wearing? An odd green something covered his face.

But as the figure drew closer Connie sensed in a fragmented flash that it was not her stepson. Then it must be John's mother. No one else was in the house. But what would Myra Hill be doing with a green hood wrapped around her head? The door opened and Connie laughed, "What's this?" she giggled merrily, going along with the joke. "What now?" Then it registered with her that the figure was too tall for the boy, too short for the erect grandmother. She waited for the figure to cry, "Surprise!" But this was not to be. The person standing before Connie instead reached out with one hand and grabbed a chunk of the cream-colored tailored blouse that she wore inside her suit jacket. Fingers seized a section of the gold chain necklace that was her wedding gift from John. Like a balking horse being led by an angry trainer, she was pulled across the threshold. As she formed a scream, her eyes saw that the figure held a glistening blue-black gun in his right hand and it was rising toward her, like a serpent preparing to strike. The scream died in her throat.

"This is a robbery," the intruder said, and for the first time Connie recognized him to be a man. All of this had passed in the span of five seconds, and she realized that the taxi had sped away and that John Hill was standing behind her. As she by reflex tried to break the man's grasp on her blouse and necklace, John Hill moved in, pushing her away and confronting the robber. "Now wait a minute here . . ." began John as he pushed Connie out of the way, defending her, freeing her to escape. Hysterically she ran sideways, toward a neighbor's house, afraid to run directly for the street and the help of a passing car for fear that she would be in the path of bullets. Just as she reached the white brick walls that borders the property Connie heard the first shot. Then a second. Screaming, falling, she stumbled crazily to a house two down from hers. "My husband's being murdered!" she cried as the neighbor opened the door. Connie was composed enough to telephone the police, then hung up and dialed her lawyer, Don Fullenweider, partner of Racehorse Haynes. He lived just across Kirby Drive and was dozing after a day of fishing. Seconds after he heard Connie's distraught screams on the telephone, he burst out his front door and hurried across the drive to the Hill home. Already sirens were filling the new night. It was just growing dark.

The white colonial house was eerily quiet. The front door was open a crack. Fullenweider pushed it open and gained entrance. The first thing his eyes found was a vase of yellow mums, fallen onto the parquet floor, smashed, blossoms strewn madly about. And then he beheld a sight that he would never be able to shut from his mind. The child, Robert Hill, was standing over the inert form of his father. Hopping up and down because his feet and arms were bound, the little boy was sobbing, a piece of adhesive tape dangling from his lips as if he were a package newly opened.

"They've killed my daddy," he cried. Scooping him up, muttering shushing reassurances, the young lawyer carried Robert outside to the lawn, where neighbors were gathering. An emergency vehicle from the Houston fire department roared up, and an attendant ran into the house. The attorney led him to John Hill. The plastic surgeon lay face down, the lower half of his body on the foyer floor, his head and shoulders sprawled across the step leading down into the sunken living room. Quickly, expertly, the attendant checked for vital signs. He turned over John Hill. Don Fullenweider gasped. The eyes were sealed shut with adhesive tape. So was the mouth and nose. Blood soaked through the tapes and appeared in blobs about the body. The attendant stood up and shook his head. "I'm sorry, mister," he said. "We're too late. . . ."

Fallen between two symbols of his life—one a brooding metallic bust of Beethoven sitting on an end table, the other a framed drawing of horses galloping through a mist—pale, indefinite horses, hurrying toward a gray and distant horizon—John Hill was dead.

Book Three
Pursuit and Trial

". . . Behold a pale horse: and his name that
sat on him was Death,
and Hell followed with him. . . ."
                                    —*Revelation 6:8*

[The judge] read the words once, hurriedly, then shut the paper and leveled his gaze at the old woman standing before him: "We the jury find the defendant [Lilla Paulus] guilty of the offense charged."

She was sentenced to thirty-five years in the state penitentiary [for planning the murder of John Hill] with the anticipation that, given the condition of her health, she would perish there.

Within the hour, Ash Robinson heard the news. He received the verdict in a telephone call from a well-placed source at the courthouse. The old man had cultivated alert ears for more than six years. It was his belief that very little took place in the DA's office that he did not quickly come to know about.

Then the doorbell rang. Ash looked through the peephole. A friend had come to dissect the day's surprising events. The old man was pleased to talk to someone, and he found a half cup of thick coffee left from the dinner pot. The two men settled into chairs and sipped. Clippings were scattered about Ash as if he were a Father Christmas whose stuffing had come out.

"Well," asked Ash, "I wonder what it all means?"

The friend shrugged; he had no answer.

"I suppose that bastard Bennett will keep tryin' to get something on me," Ash went on. His tic jerked his face violently, and he threw his hand to his chest, perhaps to gain reassurance from the beating of his rusted heart. He chuckled ruefully. "You know, it *could* be that Lilla and them made up this story to blackmail me," he suggested. "Man makes a little money in his life, and he's lucky if there's enough left to bury him once the vultures eat their fill."

Oh, he knew Lilla all right. He would own up to it, even if she would not. For a few rambling moments he wandered erratically through their association, and during his journey he became a man who walked to the very brink of confession. But he did not plunge into its purifying waters. "All I ever did—so help me!—was ask Lilla to find things out on John Hill," he wanted his friend to know. At the time, three or four years ago, there had been critical need of malicious information concerning his ex-son-in-law to use as defense against the ingrate's $10-million slander suit. "Lilla told me she could find out everything about John Hill," reminisced the old man. "I offered to pay her all right, but she told me, 'Mr. Robinson, I loved your daughter. Joan was so good to my own child, Mary Jo. Joan put Mary on her first horse. Mr. Robinson, I wouldn't take a nickel off of you. I just want you to get justice.'"

The friend looked at his watch. It was past ten. He knew that the old man traditionally went to bed early. Already Ma was asleep on a couch in the den. The drone of the television was her sedative. But Ash did not want to be left alone with the terrors of this night. He found a sliver of cheesecake and insisted that his friend stay and talk some more. Ash eased his heavy body back down into his chair and put his feet on the throw rug below. On it was woven the faded, almost invisible portrait of a pale horse. Threadbare, soon it would wear away to nothing.

Now the old man tilted his head back and closed his eyes. The friend wondered if he had drifted off to sleep. Perhaps it was best to leave, silently. But Ash jerked back. He had only been peregrinating in his memory. "I went up to the Houston Club this morning," he said. "We have this round table for breakfast. Well, I admit it was kind of macabre, but some of the men there, some of the biggest men in town, mind you, they all gathered around me and they put their arms around my shoulders and they said, 'We don't know what you did or didn't do. But you should have killed the s.o.b. years ago.'"

The friend raised an eyebrow but did not ask the obvious question.

"I know what you're thinking," said Ash, "and the answer is no. *Hell*, no. If they had one iota of evidence against me, they'd of indicted me faster than a Tennessee minute. It's just a bunch of fellas down at the courthouse with political ambitions."

The friend rose. He knew that Ash would, if allowed, continue his meanderings until the sun took away his night fears.

"It's water off a duck's back, anyway," said Ash. He seemed in the courtroom suddenly, defending himself; throwing out his long life for all to see and approve. "I've never had a bill I didn't pay. I don't have to worry about money. Did I tell you about the gas well that came in yesterday?" He searched about his papers for an envelope, found it, opened it, read of tens of thousands of cubic feet of natural gas spewing from the earth and into his pockets. "Ma and me won't be going on the public tit any time soon," he said, as he walked his friend to the door.

In another part of the big house, a telephone was ringing. But the old man did not let it interrupt. He was deep into his own mortality. "They tell me," he finally said, "that at the temple of Abu Simbel, in Egypt, at a certain time in the early morning, for maybe fifteen minutes, the new sun shines through this little hole and it lights up the face of old Radames II. For this little moment of time, there is a golden light. Always has been, always will be. Ain't that a hell of a thing!"

The friend agreed. The image was remarkable, coming as it did on a night when it was time to count bodies and wasted lives and the brutalities of abused power. Ash's money had bought him nothing but tragedy. Even the great horse, Beloved Belinda, had perished in a bizarre accident. After the deaths of Joan and John Hill, the mare broke out of a barn during a thunderstorm, ran into a field, reared up pawing and screaming at the elements, was struck down fatally by a bolt of lightning.

Now, just as the friend took his leave, turning the knob of Ash's front door, grateful to leave as a theatergoer would be to depart the house of Lear, he ventured a rude question. What would Ash have them write on *his* grave?

"Oh, hell, I don't know," said the old man brusquely. "Something like—'Here lies Ash Robinson. He lived and he died and he didn't give a damn what people thought of him.'"

The friend got into his car, but Ash called after him. He had one more thing to say. "You know that son of a bitch John Hill didn't even want to buy my Joan a tombstone! A week before his murder trial, he finally runs out and orders one, just in case it came up in testimony. And have you seen that marker? It's a *crime*."

How Ash Robinson hated the tombstone that memorialized his Joan. In life, she had always been "Joan *Robinson* Hill," and it was thus in all the newspaper accounts, etched on all the silver and gold trophies that were now darkening and unattended on the shelves of his room. They shone no golden light on Ash's face. But in death, the granite slab did not even bear her father's name. She was for the rest of time the chattel of the man Ash hated most—John Hill.

Some night he just might change that. Some night when it was very dark, when men could do their deeds without the glow of stars, the modest monument might topple and split and need to be replaced. That was on the old man's mind. Failing that, it might even be necessary to lift his Joan once more—one last time—raise her from the earth, from the lonely, barren, sunburned grave that her husband had chosen, and carry her to a cool and green place, perhaps under the benevolent shade of a great oak at Chatsworth Farm, just around the bend from Beloved Belinda Walk. In a place like that, Ash could ease his heavy body down beside her. And there, with Joan at last able to sleep at the side of the only man who really loved her—and proved it—only then would their story finally, mercifully, be done.

LAS VEGAS (WHAT?). LAS VEGAS (CAN'T HEAR YOU! TOO NOISY) LAS VEGAS!!!!

TOM WOLFE

Editor's Note—The Pyrotechniques of Print: *In their effort to simulate reality, artists of nonfiction frequently turn to telegraphing typography. In* New York— A Serendipiter's Journey, *Gay Talese describes a telephone operator in this way:*

> *sometimes she wishes she could stop pronouncing numbers*
> *as fo-wer,*
> > *fi-yiv,*
> > > *sev ven,*
> > > > *ni-yen.*
> > > > > *But it is not easy.*

As we have seen in Norman Mailer's The Executioner's Song, *writers even artfully arrange the white space on the page.*

No writer has been more inventive in this regard, however, than Tom Wolfe. Wolfe's style is as flamboyant as his white silk suits, stepped collar vests, collar pins, and spats. "I feel one should suffer for style," says this man who has admitted to owning double-breasted pajamas.

Wolfe earned a doctoral degree in American Studies at Yale University in 1957 and began working as a reporter, first for the Springfield, Massachusetts Union, *and then for the* Washington Post *(1959–1962) and* New York Herald Tribune *(1962–1966). Following the phenomenal success of* The Kandy-Kolored Tangerine-Flake Streamline Baby, *his first collection of articles on the cultural styles of the 1960s, Wolfe brought forth volume after volume of his exuberant self-styled "new journalism." These include* The Pumphouse Gang *(1968),* Radical Chic & Mau-Mauing the Flak Catchers *(1970),* The Painted Word *(1975),* Mauve Gloves & Madmen, Clutter & Vine *(1976),* The Right Stuff *(1979),* In Our Time *(1980), and* From Bauhaus to Our House *(1981).*

Wolfe is at his best when his highly sensory style is matched with a highly sensory subject, like the drug culture he captured in The Electric Kool-Aid Acid Test *(1968), or that most sensory of American cities, Las Vegas. Wolfe has used capital letters at will—for EMphasis. He has extended the exclamation point, parenthesis, ellipsis, and colon :::::::: also for EMphasis. He turns nouns into adjectives and stacks them up like glaring verbal totems of the times. Through these devices Wolfe seeks to reduce the distance between reader and reality by* simulating *reality through the pyrotechniques of print. He wishes us to say (as he repeats so frequently): "But exactly!"*

"**H**ernia, hernia, hernia, hernia, hernia, hernia, hernia, hernia, hernia, hernia, hernia, hernia, hernia, HERNia; hernia, HERNia, hernia, hernia, hernia, hernia, HERNia, HERNia, HERNia; hernia, hernia, hernia, hernia, hernia, hernia, eight is the point, the point is eight; hernia, hernia, HERNia; hernia, hernia, hernia, hernia, all right, hernia, hernia, hernia, hernia, hard eight, hernia, hernia, hernia, HERNia, hernia, hernia, hernia, HERNia, hernia, hernia, hernia, HERNia, hernia, hernia, hernia, hernia. . . ."

"What is all this *hernia hernia* stuff?"

This was Raymond talking to the wavy-haired fellow with the stick, the dealer, at the craps table about 3:45 Sunday morning. The stickman had no idea what this big wiseacre was talking about, but he resented the tone. He gave Raymond that patient arch of the eyebrows known as a Red Hook brush-off, which is supposed to convey some such thought as, I am a very tough but cool guy, as you can tell by the way I carry my eyeballs low in the pouches, and if this wasn't such a high-class joint we would take wiseacres like you out back and beat you into jellied madrilene.

At this point, however, Raymond was immune to subtle looks.

The stickman tried to get the game going again, but every time he would start up his singsong, by easing the words out through the nose, which seems to be the style among craps dealers in Las Vegas—"All right, a new shooter . . . eight is the point, the point is eight" and so on—Raymond would start droning along with him in exactly the same tone of voice, "Hernia, hernia, hernia; hernia, HERNia, HERNia, hernia; hernia, hernia, hernia."

Everybody at the craps table was staring in consternation to think that anybody would try to needle a tough, hip, elite *soldat* like a Las Vegas craps dealer. The gold-lamé odalisques of Los Angeles were staring. The Western sports, fifty-eight-year-old men who wear Texas string ties, were staring. The old babes at the slot machines, holding Dixie Cups full of nickels, were staring at the craps tables, but cranking away the whole time.

Raymond, who is thirty-four years old and works as an engineer in Phoenix, is big but not terrifying. He has the sort of thatchwork hair that grows so low all along the forehead there is no logical place to part it, but he tries anyway. He has a huge, prognathous jaw, but it is as smooth, soft and round as a melon, so that Raymond's total effect is that of an Episcopal divinity student.

The guards were wonderful. They were dressed in cowboy uniforms like Bruce Cabot in *Sundown* and Robert Taylor in many another Western and they wore sheriff's stars.

"Mister, is there something we can do for you?"

"The expression is 'Sir,'" said Raymond. "You said 'Mister.' The expression is 'Sir.' How's your old Cosa Nostra?"

Amazingly, the casino guards were easing Raymond out peaceably, without putting a hand on him. I had never seen the fellow before, but possibly because I had been following his progress for the last five minutes, he turned to me and said, "Hey, do you have a car? This wild stuff is starting again."

The gist of it was that he had left his car somewhere and he wanted to ride up the Strip to the Stardust, one of the big hotel-casinos. I am describing this big goof

Raymond not because he is a typical Las Vegas tourist, although he has some typical symptoms, but because he is a good example of the marvelous impact Las Vegas has on the senses. Raymond's senses were at a high pitch of excitation, the only trouble being that he was going off his nut. He had been up since Thursday afternoon, and it was now about 3:45 a.m. Sunday. He had an envelope full of pep pills—amphetamine—in his left coat pocket and an envelope full of Equanils—meprobamate—in his right pocket, or were the Equanils in the left and the pep pills in the right? He could tell by looking, but he wasn't going to look anymore. He didn't care to see how many were left.

He had been rolling up and down the incredible electric-sign gauntlet of Las Vegas' Strip, U.S. Route 91, where the neon and the par lamps—bubbling, spiraling, rocketing, and exploding in sunbursts ten stories high out in the middle of the desert—celebrate one-story casinos. He had been gambling and drinking and eating now and again at the buffet tables the casinos keep heaped with food day and night, but mostly hopping himself up with good old amphetamine, cooling himself down with meprobamate, then hooking down more alcohol, until now, after sixty hours, he was slipping into the symptoms of toxic schizophrenia.

He was also enjoying what the prophets of hallucinogen call "consciousness expansion." The man was psychedelic. He was beginning to isolate the components of Las Vegas' unique bombardment of the senses. He was quite right about "this *hernia hernia* stuff." Every casino in Las Vegas is, among the other things, a room full of craps tables with dealers who keep up a running singsong that sounds as though they are saying "hernia, hernia, hernia, hernia, hernia" and so on. There they are day and night, easing a running commentary through their nostrils. What they have to say contains next to no useful instruction. Its underlying message is, We are the initiates, riding the crest of chance. That the accumulated sound comes out "hernia" is merely an unfortunate phonetic coincidence. Actually, it is part of something rare and rather grand: a combination of baroque stimuli that brings to mind the bronze gongs, no larger than a blue plate, that Louis XIV, his ruff collars larded with the lint of the foul Old City of Byzantium, personally hunted out in the bazaars of Asia Minor to provide exotic acoustics for his new palace outside Paris.

The sounds of the craps dealer will be in, let's say, the middle register. In the lower register will be the sound of the old babes at the slot machines. Men play the slots too, of course, but one of the indelible images of Las Vegas is that of the old babes at the row upon row of slot machines. There they are at six o'clock Sunday morning no less than at three o'clock Tuesday afternoon. Some of them pack their old hummocky shanks into Capri pants, but many of them just put on the old print dress, the same one day after day, and the old hob-heeled shoes, looking like they might be going out to buy eggs in Tupelo, Mississippi. They have a Dixie Cup full of nickels or dimes in the left hand and an Iron-Boy work glove on the right hand to keep the callouses from getting sore. Every time they pull the handle, the machine makes a sound much like the sound a cash register makes before the bell rings, then the slot pictures start clattering up from left to right, the oranges, lemons, plums, cherries, bells, bars, buckaroos—the figure of a cowboy riding a bucking bronco. The whole sound keeps churning up over and over again in eccentric series all over the place, like one of those random-sound radio symphonies by John Cage. You can hear it at any hour of the day or night all over Las Vegas. You can walk down Fremont Street at dawn and hear it without even walking in a door, that and the spins of the wheels of fortune, a boring and not very popular sort of simplified roulette, as the tabs flap to a stop. As an overtone, or at times simply as a loud sound, comes the babble of the casino crowds, with an occasional shriek from the craps tables, or, anywhere from four P.M. to six A.M., the sound of brass instruments or electrified string instruments from the cocktail-lounge shows.

The crowd and band sounds are not very extraordinary, of course. But Las Vegas' Muzak is. Muzak pervades Las Vegas from the time you walk into the airport upon landing to the last time you leave the casinos. It is piped out to the swimming pool. It is in the drugstores. It is as if there were a communal fear that someone, some-where in Las Vegas, was going to be left with a totally vacant minute on his hands.

Las Vegas has succeeded in wiring an entire city with this electronic stimulation, day and night, out in the middle of the desert. In the automobile I rented, the radio could not be turned off, no matter which dial you went after. I drove for days in a happy burble of Action Checkpoint News, *Monkey No. 9, Donna, Donna, the Prima Donna*, and picking-and-singing jingles for the Frontier Bank and the Fremont Hotel.

One can see the magnitude of the achievement. Las Vegas takes what in other American towns is but a quixotic inflammation of the senses for some poor salary mule in the brief interval between the flagstone rambler and the automatic elevator downtown and magnifies it, foliates it, embellishes it into an institution.

For example, Las Vegas is the only town in the world whose skyline is made up neither of buildings, like New York, nor of trees, like Wilbraham, Massachusetts, but signs. One can look at Las Vegas from a mile away on Route 91 and see no buildings, no trees, only signs. But such signs! They tower. They revolve, they oscillate, they soar in shapes before which the existing vocabulary of art history is helpless. I can only attempt to supply names—Boomerang Modern, Palette Curvilinear, Flash Gordon Ming-Alert Spiral, McDonald's Hamburger Parabola, Mint Casino Elliptical, Miami Beach Kidney. Las Vegas' sign makers work so far out beyond the frontiers of conventional studio art that they have no names them-selves for the forms they create. Vaughan Cannon, one of those tall, blond Westerners, the builders of places like Las Vegas and Los Angeles, whose eyes seem to have been bleached by the sun, is in the back shop of the Young Electric Sign Company out on East Charleston Boulevard with Herman Boernge, one of his designers, looking at the model they have prepared for the Lucky Strike Casino sign, and Cannon points to where the sign's two great curving faces meet to form a narrow vertical face and says:

"Well, here we are again—what do we call that?"

"I don't know," says Boernge. "It's sort of a nose effect. Call it a nose."

Okay, a nose, but it rises sixteen stories high above a two-story building. In Las Vegas no farseeing entrepreneur buys a sign to fit a building he owns. He rebuilds the building to support the biggest sign he can get up the money for and, if neces-sary, changes the name. The Lucky Strike Casino today is the Lucky Casino, which fits better when recorded in sixteen stories of flaming peach and incandescent yellow in the middle of the Mojave Desert. In the Young Electric Sign Co. era signs have become the architecture of Las Vegas, and the most whimsical, Yale-seminar-frenzied devices of the two late geniuses of Baroque Modern, Frank Lloyd Wright and Eero Saarinen, seem rather stuffy business, like a jest at a faculty meeting, compared to it. Men like Boernge, Kermit Wayne, Ben Mitchem and Jack Larsen, formerly an artist for Walt Disney, are the designer-sculptor geniuses of Las Vegas, but their motifs have been carried faithfully throughout the town by lesser men, for gasoline stations, motels, funeral parlors, churches, public buildings, flophouses and sauna baths. A San Francisco artist and jewelry designer, who lived for three years in Plainfield, New Jersey, near unspeakable Route 22, is in Las Vegas for the first time, driving down the Strip. "Wonderful," she says. "New Jersey has spread across the Continental Divide at last."

Then there is a stimulus that is both visual and sexual—the Las Vegas buttocks décolletage. This is a form of sexually provocative dress seen more and more in the United States, but avoided like Broadway message-embroidered ("Kiss Me, I'm Cold") underwear in the fashion pages, so that the euphemisms have not been established and I have no choice but clinical terms. To achieve buttocks décolletage a woman wears bikini-style shorts that cut across the round fatty masses of the buttocks rather than cupping them from below, so that the outer-lower edges of these fatty masses, or "cheeks," are exposed. I am in the cocktail lounge of the Hacienda Hotel, talking to managing director Dick Taylor about the great success his place has had in attracting family and tour groups, and all around me the waitresses are bobbing on their high heels, bare legs and décolletage-bare backsides, set off by pelvis-length lingerie of an uncertain denomination. I stare, but I am new here. At the White Cross Rexall drugstore on the Strip a pregnant brunette walks in off the street wearing black shorts with buttocks décolletage aft and illusion-of-cloth nylon lingerie hanging fore, and not even the old mom's-pie pensioners up near the door are staring. They just crank away at the slot machines. On the streets of Las Vegas, not only the show girls, of which the town has about two hundred fifty, bona fide, in residence, but girls of every sort, including, especially, Las Vegas' little high-school buds, who adorn what locals seeking roots in the sand call "our city of churches and schools," have taken up the chic of wearing buttocks décolletage step-ins under flesh-tight slacks, with the outline of the undergarment showing through fashionably. Others go them one better. They achieve the effect of having been dipped once, briefly, in Helenca stretch nylon. More and more they look like those wonderful old girls out of Flash Gordon who were wrapped just once over in Baghdad pantaloons of clear polyethylene with only Flash Gordon between them and the insane red-eyed assaults of the minions of Ming. It is as if all the hip young suburban gals of America named Lana, Deborah and Sandra, who gather wherever the arc lights shine and the studs steady their coiffures in the plate-glass reflection, have convened in Las Vegas with their bouffant hair above and anatomically stretch-pant-swathed little bottoms below, here on the new American frontier. But exactly!

None of it would have been possible, however, without one of those historic combinations of nature and art that creates an epoch. In this case, the Mojave Desert plus the father of Las Vegas, the late Benjamin "Bugsy" Siegel.

Bugsy was an inspired man. Back in 1944 the city fathers of Las Vegas, their Protestant rectitude alloyed only by the giddy prospect of gambling revenues, were considering the sort of ordinance that would have preserved the town with a kind of Colonial Williamsburg dinkiness in the motif of the Wild West. All new buildings would have to have at least the facade of the sort of place where piano players used to wear garters on their sleeves in Virginia City around 1880. In Las Vegas in 1944, it should be noted, there was nothing more stimulating in the entire town than a Fremont Street bar where the composer of *Deep in the Heart of Texas* held forth and the regulars downed fifteen-cent beer.

Bugsy pulled into Las Vegas in 1945 with several million dollars that, after his assassination, was traced back in the general direction of gangster-financiers. Siegel put up a hotel-casino such as Las Vegas had never seen and called it the Flamingo— all Miami Modern, and the hell with piano players with garters and whatever that was all about. Everybody drove out Route 91 just to gape. Such shapes! Boomerang Modern supports, Palette Curvilinear bars, Hot Shoppe Cantilever roofs and a scalloped swimming pool. Such colors! All the new electrochemical pastels of the Florida littoral: tangerine, broiling magenta, livid pink, incarnadine, fuchsia demure, Congo ruby, methyl green, viridine, aquamarine, phenosafranine, incandescent orange, scarlet-fever purple, cyanic blue, tessellated bronze, hospital-fruit-basket orange. And such signs! Two cylinders rose at either end of the Flamingo—eight stories high and covered from top to bottom with neon rings in the shape of bubbles that fizzed all eight stories up into the desert sky all night long like an illuminated whisky-soda tumbler filled to the brim with pink champagne.

The business history of the Flamingo, on the other hand, was not such a smashing success. For one thing, the gambling operation was losing money at a rate that rather gloriously refuted all the recorded odds of the gaming science. Siegel's backers apparently suspected that he was playing both ends against the middle in collusion with professional gamblers who hung out at the Flamingo as though they had liens on it. What with one thing and another, someone decided by the night of June 20, 1947, that Benny Siegel, lord of the Flamingo, had had it. He was shot to death in Los Angeles.

Yet Siegel's aesthetic, psychological and cultural insights, like Cézanne's, Freud's and Max Weber's, could not die. The Siegel vision and the Siegel aesthetic were already sweeping Las Vegas like gold fever. And there were builders of the West equal to the opportunity. All over Las Vegas the incredible electric pastels were repeated. Overnight the Baroque Modern forms made Las Vegas one of the few architecturally unified cities of the world—the style was Late American Rich— and without the bother and bad humor of a City Council ordinance. No enterprise was too small, too pedestrian or too solemn for The Look. The Supersonic Carwash, the Mercury Jetaway, Gas Vegas Village and Terrible Herbst gasoline stations, the Par-a-Dice Motel, the Palm Mortuary, the Orbit Inn, the Desert Moon, the Blue Onion Drive-In—on it went, like Wildwood, New Jersey, entering Heaven.

The atmosphere of the six-mile-long Strip of hotel-casinos grips even those segments of the population who rarely go near it. Barely twenty-five-hundred feet off the Strip, over by the Convention Center, stands Landmark Towers, a shaft thirty stories high, full of apartments, supporting a huge circular structure shaped like a space observation platform, which was to have contained the restaurant and casino. Somewhere along the way Landmark Towers went bankrupt, probably at that point in the last of the many crises when the construction workers *still* insisted on spending half the day flat on their bellies with their heads, tongues and eyeballs hanging over the edge of the tower, looking down into the swimming pool of the Playboy Apartments below, which has a "nudes only" section for show girls whose work calls for a tan all over.

Elsewhere, Las Vegas' beautiful little high-school buds in their buttocks-décolletage stretch pants are back on the foam-rubber upholstery of luxury broughams peeling off the entire chick ensemble long enough to establish the highest venereal-disease rate among high-school students anywhere north of the yaws-rotting shanty jungles of the Eighth Parallel. The Negroes who have done much of the construction work in Las Vegas' sixteen-year boom are off in their ghetto on the west side of town, and some of them are smoking marijuana, eating peyote buttons and taking horse (heroin), which they get from Tijuana, I mean it's simple, baby, right through the mails, and old Raymond, the Phoenix engineer, does not have the high life to himself.

I am on the third floor of the Clark County Courthouse talking to Sheriff Captain Ray Gubser, another of these strong, pale-eyed Western-builder types, who is obligingly explaining to me law enforcement on the Strip, where the problem is not so much the drunks, crooks or roughhousers, but these nuts on pills who don't want to ever go to bed, and they have hallucinations and try to bring down the casinos like Samson. The county has two padded cells for them. They cool down after three or four days and they turn out to be somebody's earnest breadwinner back in Denver or Minneapolis, loaded with the right credentials and pouring soul and apologiae all over the county cops before finally pulling out of never-never land for good by plane. Captain Gubser is telling me about life and eccentric times in Las Vegas, but I am distracted. The captain's office has windows out on the corridor. Coming down the corridor is a covey of girls, skipping and screaming, giggling along, their heads exploding in platinum-and-neon-yellow bouffants or beehives or raspberry-silk scarves, their eyes appliquéd in black like mail-order decals, their breasts aimed up under their jerseys at the angle of antiaircraft automatic weapons, and, as they swing around the corner toward the elevator, their glutei maximi are bobbing up and down with their pumps in the inevitable buttocks décolletage pressed out against black, beige and incarnadine stretch pants. This is part of the latest shipment of show girls to Las Vegas, seventy in all, for the "Lido de Paris" revue at the Stardust, to be entitled *Bravo!*, replacing the old show, entitled *Voilà*. The girls are in the County Courthouse getting their working papers, and fifteen days from now these little glutei maximi and ack-ack breasts with stars pasted on the tips will be swinging out over the slack jaws and cocked-up noses of patrons sitting at stageside at the Stardust. I am still listening to Gubser, but somehow it is a courthouse where mere words are beaten back like old atonal Arturo Toscanini trying to sing along with the NBC Symphony. There he would be, flapping his little toy arms like Tony Galento shadowboxing with fate, bawling away in the face of union musicians who drowned him without a bubble. I sat in on three trials in the courthouse, and it was wonderful, because the courtrooms are all blond-wood modern and look like sets for TV panel discussions on marriage and the teen-ager. What the judge has to say is no less formal and no more fatuous than what judges say everywhere, but inside of forty seconds it is all meaningless because the atmosphere is precisely like a news broadcast over Las Vegas' finest radio station, KORK. The newscast, as it is called, begins with a series of electronic wheeps out on that far edge of sound where only quadrupeds can hear. A voice then announces that this is Action Checkpoint News. "The news—all the news—flows first through Action Checkpoint!—then reaches You! at the speed of Sound!" More electronic wheeps, beeps and lulus, and then an item: "Cuban Premier Fidel Castro nearly drowned yesterday." Urp! Wheep! Lulu! No news a KORK announcer has ever brought to Las Vegas at the speed of sound, or could possible bring, short of word of the annihilation of Los Angeles, could conceivably compete within the brain with the giddiness of this electronic jollification.

The wheeps, beeps, freeps, electronic lulus, Boomerang Modern and Flash Gordon sunbursts soar on through the night over the billowing hernia—hernia sounds and the old babes at the slots—until it is 7:30 A.M. and I am watching five men at a green-topped card table playing poker. They are sliding their Bee-brand cards into their hands and squinting at the pips with a set to the lips like Conrad Veidt in a tunic collar studying a code message from S.S. headquarters. Big Sid Wyman, the old Big-Time gambler from St. Louis, is there, with his eyes looking like two poached eggs engraved with a road map of West Virginia, after all night at the poker table. Sixty-year-old Chicago Tommy Hargan is there with his topknot of white hair pulled back over his little pink skull and a mountain of chips in front of his old caved-in sternum. Sixty-two-year-old Dallas Maxie Welch is there, fat and phlegmatic as an Indian Ocean potentate. Two Los Angeles biggies are there exhaling smoke from candela-green cigars into the gloom. It looks like the perfect vignette of every Big Time back room, "athletic club," snooker house and floating poker game in the history of the guys-and-dolls lumpen-bourgeoisie. But what is all this? Off to the side, at a rostrum, sits a flawless little creature with bouffant hair and Stridex-pure skin who looks like she is polished each morning with a rotary buffer. Before her on the rostrum is a globe of coffee on a hot coil. Her sole job is to keep the poker players warmed up with coffee. Meantime, numberless uniformed lackeys are cocked and aimed about the edges to bring the five Big Timers whatever else they might desire, cigarettes, drinks, napkins, eyeglass-cleaning tissues, plug-in telephones. All around the poker table, at a respectful distance of ten feet, is a fence with the most delicate golden pickets. Upon it, even at this narcoleptic hour, lean men and women in their best clothes watching the combat of the titans. The scene is the charmed circle of the casino of the Dunes Hotel. As everyone there knows, or believes, these fabulous men are playing for table stakes of fifteen or twenty thousand dollars. One hundred dollars rides on a chip. Mandibles gape at the progress of the battle. And now Sid Wyman, who is also a vice-president of the Dunes, is at a small escritoire just inside the golden fence signing a stack of vouchers for such sums as $4500, all printed in the heavy Mondrianesque digits of a Burroughs business check-making machine. It was as if America's guys-and-dolls gamblers had somehow been tapped upon the shoulders, knighted, initiated into a new aristocracy.

Las Vegas has become, just as Bugsy Siegel dreamed, the American Monte Carlo—without any of the inevitable upper-class baggage of the Riviera casinos. At Monte Carlo there is still the plush mustiness of the nineteenth-century noble lions—of Baron Bleichroden, a big winner at roulette who always said, "My dear friends, it is so easy on Black." Of Lord Jersey, who won seventeen maximum bets in a row—on black, as a matter of fact—nodded to the croupier, and said, "Much obliged old sport, old sport," took his winnings to England, retired to the country and never gambled again in his life. Or of the old Duc de Dinc who said he could win only in the high-toned Club Privé, and who won very heavily one night, saw two Englishmen gaping at his good fortune, threw them every mille note he had in his hands and said, "Here. Englishmen without money are altogether odious." Thousands of Europeans from the lower orders now have the money to go to the Riviera, but they remain under the century-old status pall of the aristocracy. At Monte Carlo there are still Wrong Forks, Deficient Accents, Poor Tailoring, Gauche Displays, Nouveau Richness, Cultural Aridity—concepts unknown in Las Vegas. For the grand debut of Monte Carlo as a resort in 1879 the architect Charles Garnier designed an opera house for the Place du Casino; and Sarah Bernhardt read a symbolic poem. For the debut of Las Vegas as a revue in 1946 Bugsy Siegel hired Abbott and Costello, and there, in a way, you have it all.

I am in the office of Major A. Riddle—Major is his name—the president of the Dunes Hotel. He combs his hair straight back and wears a heavy gold band on his little finger with a diamond sunk into it. As everywhere else in Las Vegas, someone has turned on the air conditioning to the point where it will be remembered, all right, as Las Vegas-style air conditioning. Riddle has an appointment to see a doctor at 4:30 about a crimp in his neck. His secretary, Maude McBride, has her head down and is rubbing the back of her neck. Lee Fisher, the P.R. man, and I are turning ours from time to time to keep the pivots from freezing up. Riddle is telling me about "the French war" and moving his neck gingerly. The Stardust bought and imported a version of the Lido de Paris spectacular, and the sight of all those sequined giblets pooning around on flamingo legs inflamed the tourists. The Tropicana fought back with the Folies Bergère, the New Frontier installed "Paree Ooh La La," the Hacienda reached for the puppets "Les Poupées de Paris," and the Silver Slipper called in Lili St. Cyr, the stripper, which was going French after a fashion. So the Dunes has bought up the third and last of the great Paris girlie shows, the Casino de Paris. Lee Fisher says, "And we're going to do things they *can't* top. In this town you've got to move ahead in quantum jumps."

Quantum? But exactly! The beauty of the Dunes' Casino de Paris show is that it will be beyond art, beyond dance, beyond spectacle, even beyond the titillations of the winking crotch. The Casino de Paris will be a behemoth piece of American calculus, like Project Mercury.

"This show alone will cost us two and a half million a year to operate and one and a half million to produce," Major A. Riddle is saying. "The costumes alone will be fantastic. There'll be more than five hundred costumes and—well, they'll be fantastic.

"And this machine—by the time we get through expanding the stage, this machine will cost us $250,000."

"Machine?"

"Yes. Sean Kenny is doing the staging. The whole set moves electronically right in front of your eyes. He used to work with this fellow Lloyd Wright?"

"Frank Lloyd Wright?"

"Yes. Kenny did the staging for *Blitz*. Did you see it? Fantastic. Well, it's all done electronically. They built this machine for us in Glasgow, Scotland, and it's being shipped here right now. It moves all over the place and creates smoke and special effects. We'll have everything. You can stage a bombardment with it. You'll think the whole theatre is blowing up.

"You'll have to program it. They had to use the same mechanism that's in the Skybolt Missile to build it. It's called a 'Celson' or something like that. That's how complicated this thing is. They have to have the same thing as the Skybolt Missile."

As Riddle speaks, one gets a wonderful picture of sex riding the crest of the future. Whole tableaux of bare-bottomed Cosmonaughties will be hurtling around the Casino de Paris Room of the Dunes Hotel at fantastic speed in elliptical orbits, a flash of the sequined giblets here, a blur of the black-rimmed decal eyes there, a wink of the crotch here and there, until, with one vast Project Climax for our times, Sean Kenny, who used to work with this fellow Frank Lloyd Wright, presses the red button and the whole yahooing harem, shrieking ooh-la-la amid the din, exits in a mushroom cloud.

The allure is most irresistible not to the young but the old. No one in Las Vegas will admit it—it is not the modern, glamorous notion—but Las Vegas is a resort for old people. In those last years, before the tissue deteriorates and the wires of the cerebral cortex hang in the skull like a clump of dried seaweed, they are seeking liberation.

At eight o'clock Sunday morning it is another almost boringly sunny day in the desert, and Clara and Abby, both about sixty, and their husbands, Earl, sixty-three, and Ernest, sixty-four, come squinting out of the Mint Casino onto Fremont Street.

"I don't know what's wrong with me," Abby says. "Those last three drinks, I couldn't even feel them. It was just like drinking fizz. You know what I mean?"

"Hey," says Ernest, "how about that place back 'ere? We ain't been back 'ere. Come on."

The others are standing there on the corner, squinting and looking doubtful. Abby and Clara have both entered old babehood. They have that fleshy, humped-over shape across the back of the shoulders. Their torsos are hunched up into fat little loaves supported by bony, atrophied leg stems sticking up into their hummocky hips. Their hair has been fried and dyed into improbable designs.

"You know what I mean? After a while it just gives me gas," says Abby. "I don't even feel it."

"Did you see me over there?" says Earl. "I was just going along, nice and easy, not too much, just riding along real nice. You know? And then, boy, I don't know what happened to me. First thing I know I'm laying down fifty dollars. . . ."

Abby lets out a great belch. Clara giggles.

"Gives me gas," Abby says mechanically.

"Hey, how about that place back 'ere?" says Ernest.

". . . Just nice and easy as you please. . . ."

". . . get me all fizzed up. . . . "

"Aw, come on. . . ."

And there at eight o'clock Sunday morning stand four old parties from Albuquerque, New Mexico, up all night, squinting at the sun, belching from a surfeit of tall drinks at eight o'clock Sunday morning, and—marvelous!—there is no one around to snigger at what an old babe with decaying haunches looks like in Capri pants with her heels jacked up on decorated wedgies.

"Where do we *come* from?" Clara said to me, speaking for the first time since I approached them on Fremont Street. "He wants to know where we come from. I think it's past your bedtime, sweets."

"Climb the stairs and go to bed," said Abby.

Laughter all around.

"Climb the stairs" was Abby's finest line. At present there are almost no stairs to climb in Las Vegas. Avalon homes are soon to go up, advertising "Two-Story Homes!" as though an incredibly lavish and exotic concept. As I talked to Clara, Abby, Earl and Ernest, it came out that "climb the stairs" was a phrase they brought along to Albuquerque with them from Marshalltown, Iowa, those many years ago, along with a lot of other baggage, such as the entire cupboard of Protestant taboos against drinking, lusting, gambling, staying out late, getting up late, loafing, idling, lollygagging around the streets and wearing Capri pants—all designed to deny a person short-term pleasures so he will center his energies on bigger, long-term goals.

"We was in 'ere"—the Mint—"a couple of hours ago, and that old boy was playing the guitar, you know, 'Walk right in, set right down,' and I kept hearing an old song I haven't heard for twenty years. It has this little boy and his folks keep telling him it's late and he has to go to bed. He keeps saying, 'Don't make me go to bed and I'll be good.' Am I *good*, Earl? Am I *good*?"

The liberated cortex in all its glory is none other than the old babes at the slot machines. Some of them are tourists whose husbands said, *Here is fifty bucks, go play the slot machines*, while they themselves went off to more complex pleasures. But most of these old babes are part of the permanent landscape of Las Vegas. In they go to the Golden Nugget or the Mint, with their Social Security check or their pension check from the Ohio telephone company, cash it at the casino cashier's, pull out the Dixie Cup and the Iron-Boy work glove, disappear down a row of slots and get on with it. I remember particularly talking to another Abby—a widow, sixty-two years old, built short and up from the bottom like a fire hydrant. After living alone for twelve years in Canton, Ohio, she had moved out to Las Vegas to live with her daughter and her husband, who worked for the Army.

"They were wonderful about it," she said. "Perfect hypocrites. She kept saying, you know, 'Mother, we'd be delighted to have you, only we don't think you'll *like* it. It's practically a fron*tier* town,' she says. 'It's so *gar*ish,' she says. So I said, I told her, 'Well, if you'd rather I didn't come. . . .' 'Oh, no!' she says. I wish I could have heard what her husband was saying. He calls me 'Mother.' '*Moth*er,' he says. Well, once I was here, they figured, well, I *might* make a good baby-sitter and dish-washer and duster and mopper. The children are nasty little things. So one day I was in town for something or other and I just played a slot machine. It's fun—I can't describe it to you. I suppose I lose. I lose a little. And *they* have fits about it. 'For God's sake, Grandmother,' and so forth. They always say '*Grand*mother' when I am supposed to 'act my age' or crawl through a crack in the floor. Well, I'll tell you, the slot machines are a *whole lot* better than sitting in that little house all day. They kind of get you; I can't explain it."

The childlike megalomania of gambling is, of course, from the same cloth as the megalomania of the town. And, as the children of the liberated cortex, the old guys and babes are running up and down the Strip around the clock like every-body else. It is not by chance that much of the entertainment in Las Vegas, espe-cially the second-stringers who perform in the cocktail lounges, will recall for an aging man what was glamorous twenty-five years ago when he had neither the money nor the freedom of spirit to indulge himself in it. In the big theatre-dining room at the Desert Inn, The Painted Desert Room, Eddie Fisher's act is on and he is saying cozily to a florid guy at a table right next to the stage, "Manny, you know you shouldn'a sat this close—you know you're in for it now, Manny, baby," while Manny beams with fright. But in the cocktail lounge, where the idea is chiefly just to keep the razzle-dazzle going, there is Hugh Farr, one of the stars of another era in the West, composer of two of the five Western songs the Library of Congress has taped for posterity, *Cool Water* and *Tumbling Tumbleweed*, when he played the violin for the Sons of the Pioneers. And now around the eyes he looks like an aging Chinese savant, but he is wearing a white tuxedo and powder-blue leather boots and playing his sad old Western violin with an electric cord plugged in it for a group called The Country Gentlemen. And there is Ben Blue, looking like a waxwork exhibit of vaudeville, doffing his straw skimmer to reveal the sculptural qualities of his skull. And down at the Flamingo cocktail lounge—Ella Fitzgerald is in the main room—there is Harry James, looking old and pudgy in one of those toy Italian-style show-biz suits. And the Ink Spots are at the New Frontier and Louis Prima is at the Sahara, and the old parties are seeing it all, roaring through the dawn into the next day, until the sun seems like a par lamp fading in and out. The casinos, the bars, the liquor stores are open every minute of every day, like a sempiternal wading pool for the childhood ego. ". . . Don't make me go to bed. . . ."

Finally the casualties start piling up. I am in the manager's office of a hotel on the Strip. A man and his wife, each about sixty, are in there, raging. Someone got into their room and stole seventy dollars from her purse, and they want the hotel to make it up to them. The man pops up and down from a chair and ricochets back and forth across the room, flailing his great pig's-knuckle elbows about.

"What kind of security you call that? Walk right in the god-dern room and just help themselves. And where do you think I found your security man? Back around the corner reading a god-dern detective magazine!"

He had scored a point there, but he was wearing a striped polo shirt with a hip Hollywood solid-color collar, and she had on Capri pants, and hooked across their wrinkly old faces they both had rimless, wraparound French sunglasses of the sort young-punk heroes in *nouvelle vague* movies wear, and it was impossible to give any earnest contemplation to a word they said. They seemed to have the great shiny popeyes of a praying mantis.

"Listen, Mister," she is saying, "I don't care about the seventy bucks. I'd lose seventy bucks at your craps table and I wouldn't think nothing of it. I'd play seventy bucks just like that, and it wouldn't mean nothing. I wouldn't regret it. But when they can just walk in—and you don't give a damn—for Christ's sake!"

They are both zeroing in on the manager with their great insect corneas. The manager is a cool number in a white-on-white shirt and silver tie.

"This happened three days ago. Why didn't you tell us about it then?"

"Well, I was gonna be a nice guy about it. Seventy dollars," he said, as if it would be difficult for the brain to grasp a sum much smaller. "But then I found your man back there reading a god-dern detective magazine. *True Detectives* it was. Had a picture on the front of some floozie with one leg up on a chair and her garter showing. Looked like a god-derned athlete's-foot ad. Boy, I went into a slow burn. But when I am burned up, I am *burned up!* You get me, Mister? There he was, reading the god-derned *True Detectives*."

"Any decent hotel would have insurance," she says.

The manager says, "I don't know a hotel in the world that offers insurance against theft."

"Hold on, Mister," he says, "are you calling my wife a liar? You just get smart, and I'm gonna pop you one! I'll pop you one right now if you call my wife a liar."

At this point the manager lowers his head to one side and looks up at the old guy from under his eyebrows with a version of the Red Hook brush-off, and the old guy begins to cool off.

But others are beyond cooling off. Hornette Reilly, a buttery hipped baggage from New York City, is lying in bed with a bald-headed guy from some place who has skin like oatmeal. He is asleep or passed out or something. Hornette is relating all this to the doctor over the Princess telephone by the bed.

"Look," she says, "I'm breaking up. I can't tell you how much I've drunk. About a bottle of brandy since four o'clock, I'm not kidding. I'm in bed with a guy. Right this minute. I'm talking on the telephone to you and this slob is lying here like an animal. He's all fat and his skin looks like oatmeal—what's happening to me? I'm going to take some more pills. I'm not kidding, I'm breaking up. I'm going to kill myself. You've got to put me in Rose de Lima. I'm breaking up, and I don't even know what's happening to me."

"So naturally you want to go to Rose de Lima."

"Well, yeah."

"You can come by the office, but I'm not sending you to Rose de Lima."

"Doctor, I'm not kidding."

"I don't doubt that you're sick, old girl, but I'm not sending you to Rose de Lima to sober up."

The girls do not want to go to the County Hospital. They want to go to Rose de Lima, where the psychiatric cases receive milieu therapy. The patients dress in street clothes, socialize and play games with the staff, eat well and relax in the sun, all paid for by the State. One of the folk heroines of the Las Vegas floozies, apparently, is the call girl who last year was spending Monday through Friday at Rose de Lima and "turning out," as they call it, Saturdays and Sundays on the Strip, to the tune of $200 to $300 a weekend. She looks upon herself not as a whore, or even a call girl, but as a lady of assignation. When some guy comes to the Strip and unveils the little art-nouveau curves in his psyche and calls for two girls to perform arts upon one another, this one consents to be the passive member of the team only. A Rose de Lima girl, she draws the line.

At the County Hospital the psychiatric ward is latched, bolted, wired up and jammed with patients who are edging along the walls in the inner hall, the only place they have to take a walk other than the courtyard.

A big brunette with the remnants of a beehive hairdo and decal eyes and an obvious pregnancy is the liveliest of the lot. She is making eyes at everyone who walks in. She also nods gaily toward vacant places along the wall.

"Mrs.——— is refusing medication," a nurse tells one of the psychiatrists. "She won't even open her mouth."

Presently the woman, in a white hospital tunic, is led up the hall. She looks about fifty, but she has extraordinary lines on her face.

"Welcome home," says Dr.———.

"This is not my home," she says.

"Well, as I told you before, it has to be for the time being."

"Listen, you didn't analyze me."

"Oh, yes. Two psychiatrists examined you—all over again."

"You mean that time in jail."

"Exactly."

"You can't tell anything from that. I was excited. I had been out on the Strip, and then all that stupid—"

Three-fourths of the 640 patients who clustered into the ward last year were casualties of the Strip or the Strip milieu of Las Vegas, the psychiatrist tells me. He is a bright and energetic man in a shawl-collared black silk suit with brass buttons.

"I'm not even her doctor," he says. "I don't know her case. There's nothing I can do for her."

Here, securely out of sight in this little warren, are all those who have taken the loop-the-loop and could not stand the centripety. Some, like Raymond, who has been rocketing for days on pills and liquor, who has gone without sleep to the point of anoxia, might pull out of the toxic reaction in two or three days, or eight or ten. Others have conflicts to add to the chemical wackiness. A man who has thrown all his cash to the flabby homunculus who sits at every craps table stuffing the take down an almost hidden chute so it won't pile up in front of the customers' eyes; a man who has sold the family car for next to nothing at a car lot advertising "Cash for your car—*right now*" and then thrown that to the homunculus, too, but also still has the family waiting guiltlessly, guilelessly back home; well, he has troubles.

". . . After I came here and began doing personal studies," the doctor is saying, "I recognized extreme aggressiveness continually. It's not merely what Las Vegas can do to a person, it's the type of person it attracts. Gambling is a very aggressive pastime, and Las Vegas attracts aggressive people. They have an amazing capacity to louse up a normal situation."

The girl, probably a looker in more favorable moments, is pressed face into the wall, cutting glances at the doctor. The nurse tells her something and she puts her face in her hands, convulsing but not making a sound. She retreats to her room, and then the sounds come shrieking out. The doctor rushes back.

Other patients are sticking their heads out of their rooms along the hall.

"The young girl?" a quiet guy says to a nurse. "The young girl," he says to somebody in the room.

But the big brunette just keeps rolling her decal eyes.

Out in the courtyard—all bare sand—the light is a kind of light-bulb twilight. An old babe is rocking herself back and forth on a straight chair and putting one hand out in front from time to time and pulling it in toward her bosom.

It seems clear enough to me. "A slot machine?" I say to the nurse, but she says there is no telling.

". . . and yet the same aggressive types are necessary to build a frontier town, and Las Vegas is a frontier town, certainly by any psychological standard," Dr.———— is saying. "They'll undertake anything and they'll accomplish it. The building here has been incredible. They don't seem to care what they're up against, so they do it."

I go out to the parking lot in back of the County Hospital and it doesn't take a second; as soon as I turn on the motor I'm swinging again with Action Checkpoint News, *Monkey No. 9, Donna, Donna, the Prima Donna* and friendly picking and swinging for the Fremont Hotel and Frontier Federal. Me and my big white car are sailing down the Strip and the Boomerang Modern, Palette Curvilinear, Flash Gordon Ming-Alert Spiral, McDonald's Hamburger Parabola, Mint Casino Elliptical and Miami Beach Kidney sunbursts are exploding in the Young Electric Sign Company's Grand Gallery for all the sun kings. At the airport there was that bad interval between the rental-car stall and the terminal entrance, but once through the automatic door the Muzak came bubbling up with *Song of India*. On the upper level around the ramps the slots were cranking away. They are placed like "traps," a word Las Vegas picked up from golf. And an old guy is walking up the ramp, just off the plane from Denver, with a huge plastic bag of clothes slung over the left shoulder and a two-suiter suitcase in his right hand. He has to put the suitcase down on the floor and jostle the plastic bag all up around his neck to keep it from falling, but he manages to dig into his pocket for a couple of coins and get going on the slot machines. All seems right, but walking out to my plane I sense that something is missing. Then I recall sitting in the cocktail lounge of the Dunes at three P.M. with Jack Heskett, district manager of the Federal Sign and Signal Corporation, and Marty Steinman, the sales manager, and Ted Blaney, a designer. They are telling me about the sign they are building for the Dunes to put up at the airport. It will be five thousand square feet of free-standing sign, done in flaming-lake red on burning-desert gold. The d—the D—alone in the word Dunes, written in Cyrillic modern, will be practically two stories high. An inset plexiglas display, the largest revolving, trivision plexiglas sign in the world, will turn and show first the Dunes, with its twenty-two-story addition, then the seahorse swimming pool, then the new golf course. The scimitar curves of the sign will soar to a huge roaring diamond at the very top. "You'll be able to see it from an airplane fifteen miles away," says Jack Heskett. "Fifty miles," says Lee Fisher. And it will be sixty-five feet up in the air—because the thing was, somebody was out at the airport and they noticed there was only one display to be topped. That was that shaft about sixty feet high with the lit-up globe and the beacon lights, which is to say, the control tower. Hell, you can only see that forty miles away. But exactly!

UNIVERSITY DAYS

JAMES THURBER

Editor's Note—Humor: A humorous style is more than simply witty words on paper—although it is that too. It is a special way of perceiving and presenting the world, as the following selections by James Thurber, S. J. Perelman, and John McNulty reveal.

James Thurber described humor as "emotional chaos remembered in tranquility." Thurber was born in Columbus, Ohio, and the chaos he recalls here in "University Days" occurred at The Ohio State University.

Like many artists of nonfiction, Thurber started as a reporter. He wrote for the Columbus Dispatch, *the Paris edition of the* Chicago Tribune, *and the* New York Evening Post *before his friend E. B. White arranged an interview for him with* New Yorker *editor Harold Ross. Thurber was hired to be the magazine's managing editor, but he soon maneuvered his way down the organizational ladder to the more congenial position of staff writer. "I thought you were an editor, goddamn it, but I guess you're a writer, so write. Maybe you have something to say," Harold Ross is said to have told him.*

As it happened, Thurber had much to say—and to draw. His best writing was always from his own experience. He was a New Yorker *writer, but he brought Columbus, Ohio, with him and planted it in New York; it was the secret little garden he kept. The titles of his works—*The Seal in the Bedroom and Other Predicaments, The Middle-Aged Man on the Flying Trapeze, Is Sex Necessary? or, Why You Feel the Way You Do *(written with White), and* Alarms and Diversions—*suggest the apprehensiveness he brought to a world he perceived as full of domestic and foreign terrors.*

Thurber wrote plays and children's books as well as humorous essays. He gave one-man shows of his inimitable drawings, and his book My World and Welcome To It *inspired a 1969 television series. Thurber had a special gift for comic understatement. In "University Days," he writes of the football tackle Bolenciecwcz:* "In order to be eligible to play it was necessary for him to keep up in his studies, a very difficult matter, for while he was not dumber than an ox he was not any smarter." *In those last five words you get it all.*

Thurber also knew how to draw laughs by switching from casual to outrageously formal language. In "University Days," he repeatedly describes the substance he sees in the microscope as "milky white." *Then he beguiles us by referring blithely to* "the familiar lacteal opacity."

Some clever student today should do an update, substituting the computer for the microscope, and a female athlete for Bolenciecwcz.

I passed all the other courses that I took at my University, but I could never pass botany. This was because all botany students had to spend several hours a week in a laboratory looking through a microscope at plant cells, and I could never see through a microscope. I never once saw a cell through a microscope. This used to enrage my instructor. He would wander around the laboratory pleased with the progress all the students were making in drawing the involved and, so I am told, interesting structure of flower cells, until he came to me. I would just be standing there. "I can't see anything," I would say. He would begin patiently enough, explaining how anybody can see through a microscope, but he would always end up in a fury, claiming that I could *too* see through a microscope but just pretended that I couldn't. "It takes away from the beauty of flowers anyway," I used to tell him. "We are not concerned with beauty in this course," he would say. "We are concerned solely with what I may call the *mechanics* of flars." "Well," I'd say, "I can't see anything." "Try it just once again," he'd say, and I would put my eye to the microscope and see nothing at all, except now and again a nebulous milky substance—a phenomenon of maladjustment. You were supposed to see a vivid, restless clockwork of sharply defined plant cells. "I see what looks like a lot of milk," I would tell him. This, he claimed, was the result of my not having adjusted the microscope properly, so he would readjust it for me, or rather, for himself. And I would look again and see milk.

I finally took a deferred pass, as they called it, and waited a year and tried again. (You had to pass one of the biological sciences or you couldn't graduate.) The professor had come back from vacation brown as a berry, bright-eyed, and eager to explain cell-structure again to his classes. "Well," he said to me, cheerily, when we met in the first laboratory hour of the semester, "we're going to see cells this time, aren't we?" "Yes, sir," I said. Students to right of me and to left of me and in front of me were seeing cells; what's more, they were quietly drawing pictures of them in their notebooks. Of course, I didn't see anything.

"We'll try it," the professor said to me, grimly, "with every adjustment of the microscope known to man. As God is my witness, I'll arrange this glass so that you see cells through it or I'll give up teaching. In twenty-two years of botany, I—" He cut off abruptly for he was beginning to quiver all over, like Lionel Barrymore, and he genuinely wished to hold onto his temper; his scenes with me had taken a great deal out of him.

So we tried it with every adjustment of the microscope known to man. With only one of them did I see anything but blackness or the familiar lacteal opacity, and that time I saw, to my pleasure and amazement, a variegated constellation of flecks, specks, and dots. These I hastily drew. The instructor, noting my activity, came back from an adjoining desk, a smile on his lips and his eyebrows high in hope. He looked at my cell drawing. "What's that?" he demanded, with a hint of a squeal in his voice. "That's what I saw," I said. "You didn't, you didn't, you *did*n't!" he screamed, losing control of his temper instantly, and he bent over and squinted into the microscope. His head snapped up. "That's your eye!" he shouted. "You've fixed the lens so that it reflects! You've drawn your eye!"

Another course that I didn't like, but somehow managed to pass, was economics. I went to that class straight from the botany class, which didn't help me any in understanding either subject. I used to get them mixed up. But not as mixed up as another student in my economics class who came there direct from a physics laboratory. He

HE WAS BEGINNING TO QUIVER ALL OVER LIKE LIONEL BARRYMORE

was a tackle on the football team, named Bolenciecwcz. At that time Ohio State University had one of the best football teams in the country, and Bolenciecwcz was one of its outstanding stars. In order to be eligible to play it was necessary for him to keep up in his studies, a very difficult matter, for while he was not dumber than an ox he was not any smarter. Most of his professors were lenient and helped him along. None gave him more hints, in answering questions, or asked him simpler ones than the economics professor, a thin, timid man named Bassum. One day when we were on the subject of transportation and distribution, it came Bolenciecwcz's turn to answer a question. "Name one means of transportation," the professor said to him. No light came into the big tackle's eyes. "Just any means of transportation," said the professor. Bolenciecwcz sat staring at him. "That is," pursued the professor, "any medium, agency, or method of going from one place to another." Bolenciecwcz had the look of a man who is being led into a trap. "You may choose among steam, horse-drawn, or electrically propelled vehicles," said the instructor. "I might suggest the one which we commonly take in making long journeys across land." There was a profound silence in which everybody stirred uneasily, including Bolenciecwcz and Mr. Bassum. Mr. Bassum abruptly broke this silence in an amazing manner. "Choo-choo-choo," he said, in a low voice, and turned instantly scarlet. He glanced appealingly around the room. All of us, of course, shared Mr. Bassum's desire that Bolenciecwcz should stay abreast of the class in economics, for the Illinois game, one of the hardest and most important of the season, was only a week off. "Toot, toot, too-toooooot!" some student with a deep voice moaned, and we all looked encouragingly at Bolenciecwcz. Somebody else gave a fine imitation of a locomotive letting off steam. Mr. Bassum himself rounded off the little show. "Ding, dong, ding, dong," he said, hopefully. Bolenciecwcz was staring at the floor now, trying to think, his great brow furrowed, his huge hands rubbing together, his face red.

"How did you come to college this year, Mr. Bolenciecwcz?" asked the professor. "*Chuf*fa chuffa, *chuf*fa chuffa."

"M'father sent me," said the football player.

"What on?" asked Bassum.

BOLENCIECWCZ WAS TRYING TO THINK

"I git an 'lowance," said the tackle, in a low, husky voice, obviously embarrassed.

"No, no," said Bassum. "Name a means of transportation. What did you *ride* here on?"

"Train," said Bolenciecwcz.

"Quite right," said the professor.

"Now, Mr. Nugent, will you tell us————"

If I went through anguish in botany and economics—for different reasons—gymnasium work was even worse. I don't even like to think about it. They wouldn't let you play games or join in the exercises with your glasses on and I couldn't see with mine off. I bumped into professors, horizontal bars, agricultural students, and swinging iron rings. Not being able to see, I could take it but I couldn't dish it out. Also, in order to pass gymnasium (and you had to pass it to graduate) you had to learn to swim if you didn't know how. I didn't like the swimming pool, I didn't like the swimming, and I didn't like the swimming instructor, and after all these years I still don't. I never swam but I passed my gym work anyway, by having another student give my gymnasium number (978) and swim across the pool in my place. He was a quiet, amiable blond youth, number 473, and he would have seen through a microscope for me if we could have got away with it, but we couldn't get away with it. Another thing I didn't like about gymnasium work was that they made you strip the day you registered. It is impossible for me to be happy when I am stripped and being asked a lot of questions. Still, I did better than a lanky agricultural student who was cross-examined just before I was. They asked each student what college he was in—that is, whether Arts, Engineering, Commerce, or Agriculture. "What college are you in?" the instructor snapped at the youth in front of me. "Ohio State University," he said promptly.

It wasn't that agricultural student but it was another a whole lot like him who decided to take up journalism, possibly on the ground that when farming went to hell he could fall back on newspaper work. He didn't realize, of course, that that would be very much like falling back full-length on a kit of carpenter's tools. Haskins didn't seem cut out for journalism, being too embarrassed to talk to anybody and unable to use a typewriter, but the editor of the college paper assigned him to the cow barns, the sheep house, the horse pavilion, and the animal husbandry department generally. This was a genuinely big "beat," for it took up five times as much ground and got ten times as great a legislative appropriation as the College of Liberal Arts. The agricultural student knew animals, but nevertheless his stories were dull and colorlessly written. He took all afternoon on each of them, on account of having to hunt for each letter on the typewriter. Once in a while he had to ask somebody to help him hunt. "C" and "L," in particular, were hard letters for him to find. His editor finally got pretty much annoyed at the farmer-journalist because his pieces were so uninteresting. "See here, Haskins," he snapped at him one day, "why is it we never have anything hot from you on the horse pavilion? Here we have two hundred head of horses on this campus—more than any other university in the Western Conference except Purdue—and yet you never get any real low down on them. Now shoot over to the horse barns and dig up something lively." Haskins shambled out and came back in about an hour; he said he had something. "Well, start it off snappily," said the editor. "Something people will read." Haskins set to work and in a couple of hours brought a sheet of typewritten paper to the desk; it was a two-hundred word story about some disease that had broken out among the horses. Its opening sentence was simple but arresting. It read: "Who has noticed the sores on the tops of the horses in the animal husbandry building?"

Ohio State was a land grant university and therefore two years of military drill was compulsory. We drilled with old Springfield rifles and studied the tactics of the Civil War even though the World War was going on at the time. At 11 o'clock each morning thousands of freshmen and sophomores used to deploy over the campus, moodily creeping up on the old chemistry building. It was good training for the kind of warfare that was waged at Shiloh but it had no connection with what was going on in Europe. Some people used to think there was German money behind it, but they didn't dare say so or they would have been thrown in jail as German spies. It was a period of muddy thought and marked, I believe, the decline of higher education in the Middle West.

As a soldier I was never any good at all. Most of the cadets were glumly indifferent soldiers, but I was no good at all. Once General Littlefield, who was commandant of the cadet corps, popped up in front of me during regimental drill and snapped, "You are the main trouble with this university!" I think he meant that my type was the main trouble with the university but he may have meant me individually. I was mediocre at drill, certainly—that is, until my senior year. By that time I had drilled longer than anybody else in the Western Conference, having failed at military at the end of each preceding year so that I had to do it all over again. I was the only senior still in uniform. The uniform which, when new, had made me look like an interurban railway conductor, now that it had become faded and too tight made me look like Bert Williams in his bellboy act. This had a definitely bad effect on my morale. Even so, I had become by sheer practice little short of wonderful at squad maneuvers.

One day General Littlefield picked our company out of the whole regiment and tried to get it mixed up by putting it through one movement after another as fast as we could execute them: squads right, squads left, squads on right into line, squads right about, squads left front into line etc. In about three minutes one hundred and nine men were marching in one direction and I was marching away from them at an angle of forty degrees, all alone. "Company, halt!" shouted General Littlefield, "That man is the only man who has it right!" I was made a corporal for my achievement.

The next day General Littlefield summoned me to his office. He was swatting flies when I went in. I was silent and he was silent too, for a long time. I don't think he remembered me or why he had sent for me, but he didn't want to admit it. He swatted some more flies, keeping his eyes on them narrowly before he let go with the swatter. "Button up your coat!" he snapped. Looking back on it now I can see that he meant me although he was looking at a fly, but I just stood there. Another fly came to rest on a paper in front of the general and began rubbing its hind legs together. The General lifted the swatter cautiously. I moved restlessly and the fly flew away. "You startled him!" barked General Littlefield, looking at me severely. I said I was sorry. "That won't help the situation!" snapped the General, with cold military logic. I didn't see what I could do except offer to chase some more flies toward his desk, but I didn't say anything. He stared out the window at the faraway figures of co-eds crossing the campus toward the library. Finally, he told me I could go. So I went. He either didn't know which cadet I was or else he forgot what he wanted to see me about. It may have been that he wished to apologize for having called me the main trouble with the university; or maybe he had decided to compliment me on my brilliant drilling of the day before and then at the last minute decided not to. I don't know. I don't think about it much any more.

NO STARCH IN THE DHOTI, S'IL VOUS PLAÎT

S. J. P E R E L M A N

Editor's Note—Humor: S. J. Perelman displays a style of literary humor quite different from James Thurber's, which is fashioned from personal experiences woefully retold. Perelman, in contrast, required merely a scrap of reality to concoct feasts of verbal delight, as the following ragout "No Starch in the Dhoti, S'il Vous Plaît" reveals. Here a mere aside in a New York Times Magazine *article—that the father of the Indian leader Nehru sent his laundry to Paris—is the yeast from which Perelman brews the most outrageous batch of East/West correspondence never, fortunately, known.*

Perelman was a delicate man, a "sport." He wore tattersall vests and half-glasses down on the bridge of his nose over which he gazed with innocent eyes. He was a small man, and when he drove a car he would peer through the spaces in the steering wheel. This never seemed to faze him. Equally memorable was his passion for the droll retort. Anything could set him off; it was as if he were perpetually transforming the American experience from "Westward Ho" to Westward Ha!

Perelman began as a cartoonist and writer for College Humor *magazine. In the 1930s, however, he found his way to the movies and to the comedian Groucho Marx and his brothers, for whom he wrote the classic films* Monkey Business *and* Horse Feathers. *In 1956, Perelman received an Academy Award for the screenplay of* Around the World in Eighty Days.

Though small in physical stature, Perelman had a massive frame of verbal reference—from several languages. He had a great sense of the particular, for he was not only a reader but a retainer of information. Parodist Peter DeVries summed up Perelman's comic gifts astutely when he noted that Perelman's prose ingeniously blends "high literary allusion, slang, showbiz hype, Yiddishisms, unabashed puns, canyon leaps of the imagination, fantastic coinages of proper names, all compacted into a manner at once densely droll and featherlight."

Throughout his career, Perelman braved the double jeopardy of writing not only nonfiction, but of being a feuilletonist, *a writer of short pieces for magazines. His retort to those perpetually underrating both endeavors is vintage Perelman: "For the past 34 years, I have been approached almost hourly by damp people with foreheads like Rocky Ford melons who urge me to knock off my frivolous career and get started on that novel I'm burning to write. I have no earthly intention of doing any such thing. I don't believe in the importance of scale; to me the muralist is no more valid than the miniature painter. In this very large country, where size is all and where Thomas Wolfe outranks Robert Benchley,* I am content to stitch away at my embroidery hoop."*

---

*Thomas Wolfe—not to be confused with the contemporary cultural critic/satirist Tom Wolfe featured in this volume—wrote massive novels such as *You Can't Go Home Again* and *Look Homeward, Angel.* Robert Benchley, in contrast, was a *New Yorker* humorist—like Perelman. Benchley was a member of the famous Algonquin Hotel Round Table of wits which included Dorothy Parker, George S. Kaufman, Alexander Woollcott, Robert Sherwood, and others. Seriousness was banned at the Round Table.

U p until recently, I had always believed that nobody on earth could deliver a throwaway line with quite the sang-froid of a certain comedian I worked for in Hollywood during the thirties. You probably don't recall the chap, but his hallmark was a big black mustache, a cigar, and a loping gait, and his three brothers, also in the act, impersonated with varying degrees of success a mute, an Italian, and a clean-cut boy. My respect for Julio (to cloak his identity partially) stemmed from a number of pearls that fell from his lips during our association, notably one inspired by an argument over dietary customs. We were having dinner at an off-Broadway hotel, in the noisiest locale imaginable outside the annual fair at Nizhnii Novgorod. There were at least a dozen people in the party—lawyers, producers, agents, brokers, astrologers, tipsters, and various assorted sycophants— for, like all celebrated theatrical personages my man liked to travel with a retinue. The dining room was jammed, some paid-up ghoul from Local 802 was interpreting the "Habanera" on an electric organ over the uproar, and, just to insure dyspepsia, a pair of adagio dancers were flinging themselves with abandon in and out of our food. I was seated next to Julio, who was discoursing learnedly to me on his favorite subject, anatomical deviations among showgirls. Halfway through the meal, we abruptly became aware of a dispute across the table between several of our companions.

"It is *not* just religious!" one was declaring hotly. "They knew a damn sight more about hygiene than you think in those Biblical days!"

"That still don't answer my question!" shouted the man he had addressed. "If they allow veal and mutton and beef, why do they forbid pork?"

"Because it's unclean, you dummy," the other rasped. "I'm trying to tell you— the pig is an unclean animal!"

"What's that?" demanded Julio, his voice slicing through the altercation. "The pig an unclean animal?" He rose from his chair and repeated the charge to be certain everyone within fifty feet was listening. "The pig an unclean animal? Why, the pig is the cleanest animal there is—except my father, of course." And dropped like a falcon back into his chow mein.

As I say, I'd gone along for years considering Julio preeminent in tossing off this kind of grenade, and then one Sunday a few weeks ago, in the *Times* Magazine, I stumbled across an item that leaves no doubt he has been deposed. The new champ is Robert Trumbull, the former Indian correspondent of the paper and a most affable bird with whom I once spent an afternoon crawling around the Qutb Minar, outside New Delhi. In the course of an article called "Portrait of a Symbol Named Nehru," Mr. Trumbull had the following to say: "Nehru is accused of having a congenital distaste for Americans because of their all too frequent habit of bragging and of being patronizing when in unfamiliar surroundings. It is said that in the luxurious and gracious house of his father, the late Pandit Motilal Nehru—who sent his laundry to Paris—the young Jawaharlal's British nurse used to make caustic remarks to the impressionable boy about the table manners of his father's American guests."

It was, of course, the utter nonchalance of the phrase "who sent his laundry to Paris" that knocked me galley-west. Obviously, Trumbull wasn't referring to one isolated occasion; he meant that the Pandit made a practice of consigning his laundry to the post, the way one used to under the academic elms. But this was no callow sophomore shipping his wash home to save money. A man willful and wealthy enough to have it shuttled from one hemisphere to another could hardly have been prompted by considerations of thrift. He must have been a consummate perfectionist, a fussbudget who wanted every last pleat in order, and, remembering my own Homeric wrangles with laundrymen just around the corner, I blenched at the complications his overseas dispatch must have entailed. Conducted long before there was any air service between India and Europe, it would have involved posting the stuff by sea—a minimum of three weeks in each direction, in addition to the time it took for processing. Each trip would have created problems of customs examination, valuation, duty (unless Nehru senior got friends to take it through for him, which was improbable; most people detest transporting laundry across the world, even their own). The old gentleman had evidently had a limitless wardrobe, to be able to dispense with portions of it for three months at a time.

The major headache, as I saw it, though, would have been coping with the *blanchisseur* himself. How did Pandit Motilal get any service or redress out of him at such long range? There were the countless vexations that always arise: the missing sock, the half-pulverized button, the insistence on petrifying everything with starch despite the most detailed instructions.

The more I thought about it, the clearer it became that he must have been enmeshed in an unending correspondence with the laundry owner. I suggest, accordingly, that while the exact nature of his letters can only be guessed at, it might be useful—or, by the same token, useless—to reconstruct a few, together with the replies they evoked. Even if they accomplish nothing else, they should help widen the breach between East and West.

Allahabad,
United Provinces,
June 7, 1903

Pleurniche et Cie.,
124, Avenue de la Grande Armée, Paris.

My Dear M. Pleurniche:

You may be interested to learn—though I doubt that anything would stir you out of your vegetable torpor—that your pompous, florid, and illiterate scrawl of the 27th arrived here with insufficient postage, forcing me to disgorge one rupee three annas to the mailman. How symbolic of your character, how magnificently consistent! Not content with impugning the quality of the cambric in my drawers, you contrive to make me *pay* for the insult. That transcends mere nastiness, you know. If an international award for odium is ever projected, have no fear of the outcome as far as India is concerned. You can rely on my support.

And à propos of symbols, there is something approaching genius in the one that graces your letterhead, the golden fleece. Could any trademark be more apt for a type who charges six francs to wash a cummerbund? I realize that appealing to your sense of logic is like whistling an aria to the deaf, but I paid half that for it originally, and the Muslim who sold it to me was the worst thief in the bazaar. Enlighten me, my dear fellow, since I have never been a tradesman myself—what passes through your head when you mulct a customer in this outrageous fashion? Is it glee? Triumph? Self-approbation at the cunning with which you have swindled your betters? I ask altogether without malice, solely from a desire to fathom the dark intricacies of the human mind.

To revert now to the subject of the drawers. It will do you no good to bombinate endlessly about sleazy material, deterioration from pounding on stones, etc. That they were immersed in an acid bath powerful enough to corrode a zinc plate, that they were wrenched through a mangle with utmost ferocity, that they were deliberately spattered with grease and kicked about the floor of your establishment, and, finally, that a white-hot iron was appliquéd on their seat—the whole sordid tale of maltreatment is writ there for anybody to see. The motive, however, is far less apparent, and I have speculated for hours on why I should be the target of vandalism. Only one explanation fits the facts. Quite clearly, for all your extortionate rates, you underpay your workmen, and one of them, seeking to revenge himself, wreaked his spite on my undergarment. While I sympathize with the poor rascal's plight, I wish it understood that I hold you responsible to the very last sou. I therefore deduct from the enclosed draft nine francs fifty, which will hardly compensate me for the damage to my raiment and my nerves, and remain, with the most transitory assurances of my regard,

Sincerely yours,
Pandit Motilal Nehru

Paris,
July 18, 1903

Pandit Motilal Nehru,
Allahabad, U.P., India.

Dear Pandit Motilal:

I am desolated beyond words at the pique I sense between the lines in your recent letter, and I affirm to you on my wife's honor that in the six generations the family has conducted this business, yours is the first complaint we have ever received. Were I to list the illustrious clients we have satisfied—Robespierre, the Duc d'Enghien, Saint-Saëns, Coquelin, Mérimée Bouguereau, and Dr. Pasteur, to name but a handful—it would read like a roll call of the immortals. Only yesterday, Marcel Proust, an author you will hear more of one of these days, called at our *établissement* (establishment) to felicitate us in person. The work we do for him is peculiarly exacting; due to his penchant for making notes on his cuffs, we must observe the greatest discretion in selecting which to launder. In fine, our function is as much editorial as sanitary, and he stated unreservedly that he holds our literary judgment in the highest esteem. I ask you, could a firm with traditions like these stoop to the pettifoggery you imply?

You can be sure, however, that if our staff has been guilty of any oversight, it will not be repeated. Between ourselves, we have been zealously weeding out a Socialist element among the employees, malcontents who seek to inflame them with vicious nonsense about an eleven-hour day and compulsory ventilation. Our firm refusal to compromise one iota has borne fruit; we now have a hard core of loyal and spiritless drudges, many of them so lackluster that they do not even pause for lunch, which means a substantial time saving and consequently much speedier service for the customer. As you see, my dear Pandit Motilal, efficiency and devotion to our clientele dominate every waking thought at Pleurniche.

As regards your last consignment, all seems to be in order. I ask leave, though, to beg one trifling favor that will help us execute your work more rapidly in future. Would you request whoever mails the laundry to make certain it contains no living organisms? When the current order was unpacked, a small yellow-black serpent, scarcely larger than a pencil but quite dynamic, wriggled out of one of your *dhotis* and spread terror in the workroom. We succeeded in decapitating it after a modicum of trouble and bore it to the Jardin d'Acclimatation, where the curator identified it as a krait, the most lethal of your indigenous snakes. Mind you, I personally thought M. Ratisbon an alarmist—the little émigré impressed me as a rather cunning fellow, vivacious, intelligent, and capable of transformation into a household pet if one had leisure. Unfortunately, we have none, so fervent is our desire to accelerate your shipments, and you will aid us materially by a hint in the right quarter, if you will. Accept, I implore of you, my salutations the most distinguished.

Yours cordially,
Octave-Hippolyte Pleurniche

Allahabad, U.P.,
September 11, 1903

Dear M. Pleurniche:

If I were a hothead, I might be tempted to horsewhip a Yahoo who has the effrontery to set himself up as a patron of letters; if a humanitarian, to garrote him and earn the gratitude of the miserable wretches under his heel. As I am neither, but simply an idealist fatuous enough to believe he is entitled to what he pays for, I have a favor to ask of you, in turn. Spare me, I pray, your turgid rhetoric and bootlicking protestations, and be equally sparing of the bleach you use on my shirts. After a single baptism in your vats, my sky-blue *jibbahs* faded to a ghastly greenish-white and the fabric evaporates under one's touch. Merciful God, whence springs this compulsion to eliminate every trace of color from my dress? Have you now become arbiters of fashion as well as littérateurs?

In your anxiety to ingratiate yourselves, incidentally, you have exposed me to as repugnant an experience as I can remember. Five or six days ago, a verminous individual named Champignon arrived here from Pondichéry, asserting that he was your nephew, delegated by you to expedite my household laundry problems. The blend of unction and cheek he displayed reminiscent of a process server, should have warned me to beware, but, tenderhearted ninny that I am, I obeyed our Brahmin laws of hospitality and permitted him to remain the night. Needless to say, he distinguished himself. After a show of gluttony to dismay Falstaff, he proceeded to regale the dinner table with a disquisition on the art of love, bolstering it with quotations from the Kamasutra so coarse that one of the ladies present fainted dead away. Somewhat later, I surprised him in the kitchen tickling a female servant, and when I demurred, he rudely advised me to stick to my rope trick and stay out of matters that did not concern me. He was gone before daylight, accompanied by a Jaipur enamel necklace of incalculable value and all our spoons. I felt it was a trivial price to be rid of him. Nevertheless, I question your wisdom, from a commercial standpoint, in employing such emissaries. Is it not safer to rob the customer in the old humdrum fashion, a franc here and a franc there, than to stake everything on a youth's judgment and risk possible disaster? I subscribe myself, as always,

> Your well-wisher,
> Pandit Motilal Nehru

> Paris,
> October 25, 1903

Dear Pandit Motilal:

We trust that you have received the bundle shipped five weeks since and that our work continues to gratify. It is also pleasing to learn that our relative M. Champignon called on you and managed to be of assistance. If there is any further way he can serve you, do not hesitate to notify him.

I enclose herewith a cutting which possibly needs a brief explanation. As you see, it is a newspaper advertisement embodying your photograph and a text woven out of laudatory remarks culled from your letters to us. Knowing you would gladly concur, I took the liberty of altering a word or two in places to clarify the meaning and underline the regard you hold us in. This dramatic license, so to speak, in no way vitiates the sense of what you wrote; it is quite usual in theatrical advertising to touch up critical opinion, and to judge from comment I have already heard, you will enjoy publicity throughout the continent of Europe for years to come. Believe us, dear Pandit, your eternal debtor, and allow me to remain

Yours fraternally,
Octave-Hippolyte Pleurniche

Allahabad,
November 14, 1903

Dear M. Pleurniche:

The barristers I retained immediately on perusing your letter—Messrs. Bulstrode & Hawfinch, of Covent Garden, a firm you will hear more of one of these days—have cautioned me not to communicate with you henceforth, but the urge to speak one final word is irresistible. After all, when their suit for a million francs breaks over you like a thunderclap, when the bailiffs seize your business and you are reduced to sleeping along the *quais* and subsisting on the carrot greens you pick up around Les Halles, you may mistakenly attribute your predicament to my malignity, to voodoo, djinns, etc. Nothing of the sort, my dear chap. Using me to publicize your filthy little concern is only a secondary factor in your downfall. What doomed you from the start was the bumbling incompetence, the ingrained slovenliness, that characterizes everyone in your calling. A man too indolent to replace the snaps he tears from a waistcoat or expunge the rust he sprinkles on a brand-new Kashmiri shawl is obviously capable of any infamy, and it ill becomes him to snivel when retribution overtakes him in the end.

Adieu then, *mon brave*, and try to exhibit in the dock at least the dignity you have failed to heretofore. With every good wish and the certainty that nothing I have said has made the slightest possible impression on a brain addled by steam, I am,

Compassionately,
Pandit Motilal Nehru

TWO BUMS HERE WOULD SPEND FREELY EXCEPT FOR POVERTY

J O H N   M C N U L T Y

Editor's Note—Humor: The following article, by John McNulty, is poised at that delicate intersection of humor and heartbreak. McNulty does not offer the dazzling verbal virtuosity of S. J. Perelman. He brings, instead, a humanity to his writing, an intense interest and delight in ordinary people, their lives and their talk.

McNulty was a listener. While others were relaxing in Costello's and other Irish saloons on New York's Third Avenue, McNulty was working. He was listening with keen appreciation. McNulty's ear was legendary. If he could tell a great story, it was because he had heard so many—and he had an infallible instinct for the truths of language. "Girls named Dolores become hairdressers," he insisted. "All ranchers' cats are named Pete." McNulty's favorite book was H. L. Mencken's The American Language, *and, according to James Thurber, he read the* Oxford English Dictionary *"as if it were a novel, filled with wonders and suspense."*

As a boy, McNulty played piano in theatres during the silent movie days.* Afterward, he spent a dozen years in Columbus, Ohio, working on the morning Ohio State Journal *while James Thurber wrote for the afternoon* Dispatch. *McNulty left the Midwest in 1933. He was a fast writer, a newspaper rewriteman supreme, and he found work in New York City at the* New York Mirror, Daily News, *and* Herald Tribune *before joining his friend Thurber at* The New Yorker *in 1937. Brendan Gill has written that as McNulty's pieces began to appear, they took the public by surprise: "They were so offhand, so modest-seeming: paragraphs that gave the impression of having been struck off at random, like tiny sparks of flint."*

Anyone could have witnessed the following scene at Costellos. Only McNulty, however, might have remarked it, and only he could have rendered it in this wondrous way.

Nobody knows how the boss of this saloon on Third Avenue reaches such quick decisions about people who come in, but he does. Like in the case of the two bums who came in Sunday afternoon off the avenue.

It was that time on Sunday afternoon that the inhabitants of this place call the Angelus. That's about four o'clock when late hangovers from Saturday night come in one by one. They stay that way, too, one by one. Each man makes himself into an island, standing in front of the bar, and everyone keeps a space on each side of him the way water is on the sides of islands. These hangovers feel too terrible to talk to each other for a couple of hours yet, anyway. Each of them keeps staring into the

---

*"Come Quick, Indians!" is McNulty's tribute to silent movies, and silent movie piano players. It appears (with "Two Bums") in *The World of John McNulty* (New York: Doubleday, 1957).

mirror in back of the bar and saying to himself, "Look at you, you'll never amount
to anything. You went to school and grew up and everything and now look at you,
you'll never amount to anything." Old veteran Third Avenue bartenders call this
fighting the mirror, and they all think it is very bad for a man. The place is sad and
quiet when a batch of hangovers are doing this and so someone nicknamed this time
of Sunday afternoon the Angelus.

The boss was tending bar himself. He was on the pledge again this Sunday afternoon, so he was standing behind the bar and not saying hardly anything. He is a
sour man when not drinking, because he is a man who doesn't take very well to not
drinking.

The two bums came in walking as if they had the bottoms of rocking chairs for
feet. They had that heel-and-toe walk that punch-drunk fighters have that roll from
heels to toes like a rocking chair rocks from back to front. They were never fighters,
though, these two bums, too frail-built and no cauliflower ears on them.

They were scratch bums. In this neighborhood they call them scratch bums when
they've got as far low as they could get, and don't even try any more to keep themselves without bugs on them. Therefore, scratch bums.

One bum had a version of a straw hat on him he rescued, most likely out of a ash
can in a fashionable neighborhood. It had onetime been one of those peanut straws
they call them that look like a panama that's got sunburned, only cheaper price. The
hat had a hell of a swaggering big brim on it, and looked funny over the scratch
bum's crummy clothes. The other bum carried a closed cigar box under one arm, for
God knows what and nobody ever did find out. The two bums were arm in arm and
they came in without making hardly a sound.

The boss took a drag on his cigarette and laid it down, the way he does when he's
ready to tell bums to turn right around and get out of there, but the bums reached the
bar before he did that. They come rolling up to the bar on the rocking-chair feet and
one bum, the most sad-faced one, dredged up two nickels out of his pocket and
slithered them onto the bar.

"How much is a glass of wine?" the bum asked, and even the hangovers heard
him and looked surprised. Nobody ever asks for a glass of wine hardly in that neighborhood. Except maybe on Christmas Eve some nondrinker might unloosen himself
up that much on account of Christmas. They keep wine only for show-off, so when
the bum asked for wine a couple of the hangovers looked at him and so did the boss.
He didn't seem to believe his ears, but he answered the bum. "Aw, wine is twenty-
five cents," the boss said. He shoved back the puny pair of nickels at the bum.

"Oh!" the bum said. Just plain "Oh." He picked up his two nickels and him and
his pal turned to go out. They took a couple of steps toward the door when all of a
sudden the boss yelled, "Hey, just a minute!" and wiggled a finger on one hand for
them to come back to the bar.

Well, the two bums stood there, wondering what was going to happen. The boss
walked down to the other end of the bar and he reached back and got two of the best
wineglasses and wiped the dust off of them. He walked back with a hell of a flourish
and set the glasses on the bar in front of the two bums. In this place they keep the
imported stuff that's hard to get on account of there's a war in a little locker under

the back end of the bar. The boss stalked back to this locker and out he hauls a bottle of imported Spanish sherry. Not the junk, a bottle of the McCoy, the real stuff, best in the house. He went to the bums and poured out two glasses full. Then he said, "Drink up, fellers, and welcome!"

You'd think the bums might be surprised, but they didn't look it. They seemed to take it in their stride like everything else. They lifted the glasses and drank the wine slow.

"Thank you, sir," the one with the big-brim hat said. "We won't be botherin' you any longer." And the two of them give their mouths a slow swipe with the backs of their hands and swivelled around from the bar and walked out. The bums looked dignified.

"Now, why in the hell did you do that?" one of the hangovers asked the boss.

"Never mind why I done it," the boss said, grumpy. "Those fellers would spend thousands of dollars if it wasn't for they haven't got even a quarter. Only two nick-els. Never mind why I done it."

The boss kept smoking his cigarette a while and paying no attention to the hangover customers. After a couple minutes, damn if he didn't go down again to the far end of the bar and get his hat. He kept trying it on this way and that in front of the mirror.

"I wish to God," he said, "I could get my hat to set on my head the way that hat set on the bum. Now, didn't it have a hell of a jaunty look to it?"

P A R T   III

R E A L I T Y
E N L A R G E D

Parts I and II of this anthology focus on the research and writing of the Literature of Reality. Part III salutes the final product and suggests that the best literary nonfiction not only re-creates reality, but enlarges our understanding of the world as well. Many nonfiction artists reclaim lost stories, enlarging our worlds with the forgotten past. Others bring to our notice facets of everyday life overlooked. Henceforth we view our worlds anew, with heightened appreciation. Other nonfiction writers are confrontational. They seek to challenge traditional or conventional views of "reality" and offer revisionary images of heroes, institutions, and events. Once again our worlds are extended—at times even remade—by these new perspectives.

The desire to enlarge the public's understanding—to bring forward the unnoticed from the shadows of neglect or to offer new views of well-known persons and historical moments—has propelled nonfiction artists throughout history. We believe the persistence of artful nonfiction throughout written record can be explained in part by this endlessly discovering, endlessly revising impulse that we call the enlarging vision.

This final celebratory section begins with Jack Finney's recovery of "The Crime of the [Nineteenth] Century" long lost to most of us today—along with its rich historical context: New York of the 1850s with its "watering places" and dental parlours. It then moves to one of the most literally artful works of nonfiction we know: Art Spiegelman's *Maus II,* the cartoonist's revisionary understanding of his father as a World War II survivor of Hitler's concentration camps. These pieces reveal that illustrations can be yet another tool in the nonfiction artist's repertoire.

St. Clair McKelway's "Some Fun with the F.B.I." provides a humorous, gently chiding, revisionary "take" on that largely unknown institution, while in "Twirling at Ole Miss" and "Praying for Sheetrock," Terry Southern and Melissa Fay Green bring new perspectives to the old story of American racism.

In "Friendly Fire," C. D. B. Bryan brings forth from obscurity the facts surrounding a young soldier's death in Vietnam, both for the boy's grieving parents and for us. Bryan's vision challenged that of the boy's mother, while the Vietnam "Dispatches" of Michael Herr confront the military establishment with glimmering revisionary truths of the Vietnam War. Hunter S. Thompson then re-creates the post-Vietnam world of the 1980s, a world where jogging and marathon races become "the Last Refuge of the Liberal Mind."

We turn, then, from artful re-creation of moments in history to memoirs which, by their very nature, recover the past from the shadows of oblivion. Memoirs place human lives before us—for both instruction and delight. In the excerpt we have chosen from his aptly titled memoir *Stop-Time,* Frank Conroy re-creates a harrowing episode from his prep school days, while Tobias Wolff recalls "borrowing" his stepfather's car in the excerpt we have selected from *This Boy's Life.* Here Wolff's very title suggests a revisionary portrait of American boyhood from that proffered by *Boy's Life,* the popular (but sentimental) magazine of his youth. A final example of artful memoir, the closing chapter of Gay Talese's *Unto the Sons,* brings forth a long hidden story of an immigrant Italian's conflict during World War II— and its impact on his sensitive son.

Science writers, as well as memoirists, can be artists of nonfiction. With Lewis Thomas's "The Lives of the Cell" we demonstrate that the best science writers draw on metaphor, and on even the tiniest organisms, to enlarge our sense of the world.

William Least Heat-Moon takes, not a cell, but one square county in Kansas for his "deep map" of the world. His *PrairyErth* restores to us the historical, geological, cultural, linguistic, and spiritual strata of one grid of land, yet, in the process, Heat-Moon tells much of the story of Kansas and of the Midwest as well. In the closing selection of the volume, Annie Dillard's artful "An Expedition to the Pole," we see one of the greatest nonfiction artists playfully satirizing grade school geography "primers" at the same time she invites us to join her imaginative union of nations, time, space, and spirit. Perhaps it is not too much to say that nonfiction artists not only enlarge our worlds, but, on occasion, show us how unified worlds may be achieved as well.

From THE CRIME OF THE CENTURY

JACK FINNEY

Editor's Note: Jack Finney is best known for his novels and the films that have been made from them, such as Good Neighbor Sam, Assault on a Queen, *and* Invasion of the Body Snatchers (*from* The Body Snatchers). *Finney began in radio, writing singing commercials, and, during the 1940s, 1950s, and 1960s was well known for his short stories which appeared regularly in* Collier's, Good Housekeeping, McCalls, Cosmopolitan, The Saturday Evening Post, *and the* Ladies' Home Journal.

During the late 1960s, Finney began researching the novel Time and Again *in which his central character fulfills a dream long shared by Finney: to travel back in time to the nineteenth century, a century which Finney calls "wonderful" and "varied." Finney's research methods for this volume were exemplary. The process, he confesses, was almost too much fun for the sober label "research":*

> *Day after day I read the* New York Times *[on microfilm], following the excitements of another time. And the* [New York Herald] Tribune. *And* Frank Leslie's Illustrated (weekly) Newspaper, *looking at the pictures. . . .[I] Made notes from the* Times *on what the produce market was selling, so I'd know something of what people were eating. Read the ads to see something of what they were buying and wearing. Stuck pins in a big wall map of an earlier New York to determine for myself where the people in the crime news lived, and where the rich people lived, and had their fun. Read what they were seeing in the theaters, and attended the opening—through a fine lavish description in the* Times *of a glittering new Wallack theater, equipped with a lobby fountain that sprayed perfume. That winter I didn't envy anyone. . . .*

Several years after finishing Time and Again, *Finney found his affection for* Leslie's Illustrated *was still very much alive. Succumbing to his desire, he convinced his state library to send him six bound volumes of* Leslie's *at a time, beginning with the first issue in 1856:*

> *The real thing this time, not microfilm but tall gilt-stamped old books, covers loose, spines sprung. But the pages inside strong and white, the ink as powerfully black, as in the days when* Leslie's *hung from the leaves of vanished New York newsstands. . . .*
>
> *Every page—I turned through them all—of every issue of* Leslie's *right up to nearly the end of that hustling century, when muddy photographs replaced bright woodcuts.*

Leslie's Illustrated *of 1857 presented woodcuts of the principals in the Harvey Burdell murder case. Finney went to the Berkeley campus newspaper room to check the* New York Times *coverage of the murder, and what he found appalled him:*

The Harvey Burdell story turned out to be, not what the few pages of summary in Leslie's *had suggested, but instead what may very well be one of the biggest single stories the* Times *has ever covered. . . . I sat there in Berkeley numbly turning past endless columns of fine newsprint on this story, running day after day after day, and wondering what I was supposed to do now.*

Finney decided to buy the microfilmed Times for 1857 and give one month to reading the mass of material on the Burdell murder and trial. The reading took longer than a month and he emerged with more than one hundred single-spaced pages of typed notes.

It was as though I'd come upon a scattering of small stones, and in trying to dig one out had uncovered a kind of Pompeii. For in the murder of Harvey Burdell I found a forgotten or semiforgotten story of the past so strange and complex, so sensational and endlessly surprising, that it astonishes me yet. It turned out, at least for me, rich in event and character: peopled with as strange a lot, as malevolent, eccentric, and amusing, as any I could ever hope to come across. Reading column after column of directly quoted testimony—hearing, in the old type, these long-ago people speaking, arguing, lying, and shouting in their own words—made them real.

Finney's presentation of "The Crime of the Century" is both as real and as artful as the Leslie's Illustrated woodcuts woven into his text. In the opening paragraphs he takes us on-site to Bond Street in Manhattan and to Saratoga Springs, New York, as well as back in time. He turns himself into our enthusiastic, inquisitive tour guide, raising questions and offering tentative speculations. This casual, conversational narrative style is Finney's counter to the florid journalistic prose of the nineteenth century. It aids the illustrations in creating the piece's "you are there" effect.

In fact, Finney's brilliant weaving of narrative with illustration creates almost a silent movie as he invites us to see, by turns, the fear in Dr. Burdell's eyes and the determination in the eyes of Emma Cunningham. Another artful structuring device is his use of opening and closing windows and doors to direct our gaze into the murder scene. Through it all, Finney strives for objectivity. "I think some understanding is due Mrs. Cunningham," he begins one paragraph, only to follow later with "I think Harvey Burdell deserves some sympathy." Through such rich feeling for the smallest details of nineteenth-century life, Finney enlarges our understanding, not only of that vigorous era, but of human nature as well.

T his is the house I hoped to find still standing at number 31 Bond Street, New York City, when I walked out of the Algonquin Hotel one morning in June a couple of years ago: an unlikely yet not quite impossible hope. I took a bus downtown, camera hung from my neck, a tourist, and found Bond Street where my map said it would be: below Eighth Street between Broadway and the Bowery. From the bus stop I walked back along a fairly busy Broadway, then turned off it, to the right, onto this little two-block-long street: Bond Street today.

Once this was "a fashionable and reputable part of town," said the New York *Tribune* of 1857, although the *Times* thought Bond "simply genteel." But today it looked about as I'd expected; there are a lot of obscure lower Manhattan streets like it. Most of its remaining worn-out old houses have been converted long ago into small-business premises, their upper windows blank and dusty, although people still live in some of them.

Not surprisingly, my number 31 was gone. On its site stood a newer 31; it's there at the right: the one with the fire escape and the arched windows. I didn't go in, though if my 31 had been there still, it would have taken police to have kept me out of it.

Just as unsurprisingly, since lower Manhattan is filled with relics of earlier New Yorks, even though the old 31 was gone there were still a few houses left that, for well over a century, had survived to the present from this moment of a long-ago February day in 1857 when crowds stood along a tree-lined Bond Street staring up at number 31 in awe and excitement at what had just happened inside it.

I think the drawing is accurate. It was made by a *Leslie's Illustrated Newspaper* artist, who then signed it under the tree at lower right; and presently I'll explain why I think it meticulously represents the way Bond Street looked when Copcutt stood with his pad or notebook where I followed with my camera, standing where he stood, a hundred and twenty years later.

You can see from his drawing that several groups of houses on Bond Street then were identical; people called them "pattern" houses. Now look carefully at 31, the house with the crowd on its stoop: notice that like the other beside it, the two dormer windows have angled roofs . . . the lintels over the windows are straight . . . there's an ornamental arch over the doorway . . . a keystone at its top, stone insets along its sides. . . . Now look at the house at left, number 26 Bond Street, still here today. Mentally remove the fire escape and added-on storefront, then compare it

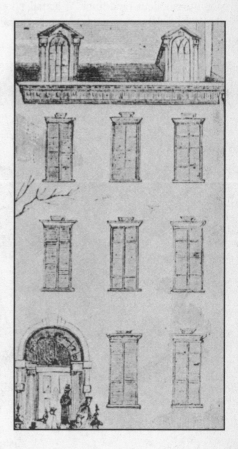

with the drawing I've repeated beside it of the long-vanished 31 for which I came down here looking; and there number 26 Bond Street still stands, as it stood near midnight, Friday, January 30, 1857, when "Murder!" sounded in the darkness and the night air stank of burning wool and leather.

And so I did find something left of the street and the night through which one of its prominent residents once walked for the last time. And as I walked the littered, gritty length of the same street, stopping to stand looking up at these relics (number 50, at left, survives, too), I was almost able to understand that the bloody thing that once happened here, and the astonishing events that followed it . . . really *had* happened; that a living man, fear tight in his stomach, had once walked here, too, under the vanished trees and gaslighting toward 31 Bond Street.

This is the man; it is how he really looked: this and other portraits that follow are precise woodcut renditions of actual photographs from professional studios of the day: Meade, Bacon, Fredrick's, and others.

He is Dr. Harvey Burdell, well-known dentist and physician, of 31 Bond Street—which he owned and in which he conducted a dental practice, becoming rich in consequence, then as now.

On Sunday afternoon, January 25, 1857, he arrived at Bacon studios and spoke to a friend, Mrs. Ann Benjamin, a photographer there. People who knew Harvey Burdell said he talked very rapidly and with a "sort of twang to his voice," said a cousin, "a sort of barking." What he almost surely told Mrs. Benjamin in this odd voice—for by now he was saying it to most everyone—was how frightened he was for his life. And that he wanted his portrait made, right now.

There he sits facing the big wooden camera, Mrs. Benjamin hunched under the black cloth. He is motionless, quite possibly holding his breath, the back of his head held steady by a clamplike device. As he waits for his image to etch the plate for this final portrait of his life he is terrified: this is known. And I think he *looks* frightened, that it shows in his eyes.

If that is so—if that's fear staring out at us across a century—this is the woman who put it there: Emma Augusta Cunningham, thirty-six, widow of a Brooklyn distiller; as formidable in fact as she is in appearance: no fear in those eyes.

They're gray, her hair dark brown, complexion dark, but it isn't easy to see in this portrait—another careful woodcut copy, of an ambrotype—what Harvey Burdell saw in Emma Cunningham when first they met. ". . . we understand she was formerly very prepossessing," a newspaper reporter said, "[but] she is not at the present moment an extra-ordinarily attractive woman." Still: cover her antique dress with one hand, obscure the old hairstyle with the other, then picture her smiling, and possibly you'll see something of the attractiveness Dr. Burdell saw. Or it might have been this: the same reporter said Mrs. Cunningham was "very well preserved, her bust showing considerable fullness," and Burdell liked women, at least in bed: maybe that explains what this portrait doesn't.

But do you agree that a determination can be seen in her eyes, a hardness of purpose? Possibly not, maybe I'm straining, but apparently it could be seen in the living face, because a *Leslie's* reporter wrote: ". . . her lips and mouth generally display remarkable determination." This observation didn't follow after the fact, either: the world didn't yet know the unbelievable—I mean literally unbelievable—extent of this remarkable woman's single-mindedness. One time Harvey Burdell told a cousin, Mary Wilson, as she recalled it, that Emma Cunningham was "'a very dangerous woman. She is always planning, and she told me she had never been thwarted in her life; that whatever plans she attempts she generally carried out.'" This turned out to be true; and Mrs. Cunningham almost literally scared Harvey Burdell to death.

Burdell said they met at "a watering place" in 1854: Saratoga Springs, I expect, because he went there a lot. He thought she was "pleasant, ladylike in her appearance and conduct," he told another of his many cousins, and for a time all was circumspect: he'd stay at Congress Hall, while she went to a boardinghouse—and school—run by Dr. Luther F. Beecher, cousin to Henry Ward Beecher.

There has been some ridiculous fiction written about people traveling back in time to earlier days, but absurd though such books are, I wish they were true. Because my wife and I are mild fanatics about the Saratoga Springs of the last century, and when the Time Machine is invented we're going to nineteenth-century Paris and New York City, including a visit to Bond Street: and to Saratoga Springs, a gorgeous place then. Meanwhile we've made our pilgrimage to today's Saratoga to see what's left. Of course the magnificent old hotels are gone, one of them replaced—a requirement of the twentieth century—by a most ordinary shopping center, with asphalt parking lot, where women once strolled under parasols.

But Congress Hall Park is still marvelously there, many things to be seen in old photos like this, incredibly still there like this.

So again I was able to follow Harvey Burdell's steps, this time as he walked the paths of Congress Hall Park with Emma Cunningham. As they strolled—I picture them arm in arm—I believe she was thinking about marriage, because she would presently show in a variety of startling ways that she did desperately want to marry Harvey Burdell. Out of greed, maybe, for it seemed to be common knowledge that he was rich. Or possibly simply as a haven for her widowed self and five children.

Or even from love or affection, no one can say otherwise, and he seemed to be attractive to women. I wonder also if for his own purposes Harvey Burdell didn't at least hint at marriage as they wandered that park and lovely town.

If he did, it's almost impossible to think he meant it, for some of his acquaintances told a *Tribune* reporter that "he was a confirmed bachelor. He was frequently in the habit of denouncing the sex in the most bitter terms; it was a favorite maxim of his . . . that no man who owned real estate ought to marry." The *Trib* man reported also that Burdell was a "man of large frame, full habit [which I take to mean good physique], very strong, fond of wine and women, and a frequent visitor at houses of pleasure."

So we have a rich, forty-five-year-old, man-of-the-world bachelor who, whatever he did or didn't hint or promise, seems dead set against marriage . . . walking the shady paths of Congress Hall Park with a smiling, attentive woman almost ferociously determined that he will marry her. The stage is set though there is no script; what now began happening to Harvey Burdell was improvised all the way, generally badly. Whoever was first responsible for thoughts of marriage, Dr. Burdell never dreamed where the pleasant paths of Congress Hall Park were leading him.

Back in New York, Mrs. Cunningham pushed the friendship; came to 31 Bond to have the Doctor fix her teeth; brought teenage daughter Augusta to have her teeth fixed. And presently Harvey Burdell was calling regularly at the house Mrs. Cunningham rented on Twenty-fourth Street between Eighth and Ninth. Living with her were two small sons, Willie (or Willy) and George, nine and ten; another teenage daughter, Helen; and two servants. Augusta was away, I don't know why. So Emma Cunningham had six people to feed; wages to pay; a boarding-school bill for Georgiana, her youngest daughter; and possibly she had to send money to Augusta. A man and his wife rented rooms in the house.

All this, incidentally, from the New York *Times* and *Tribune,* but I'll stop naming sources now unless there seems a reason to do it, because nearly everything in this account, and every direct quotation, is from one of those two papers or *Harper's Weekly* and *Leslie's Illustrated Newspaper.* When it isn't, I'll say so.

To me the reported facts of Mrs. Cunningham's life just now suggest that her money could have been running low. She'd received five thousand dollars' insurance at her husband's death, but that was several years ago. Anyway, she gave up the Twenty-fourth Street house, boarded at a Dr. Willington's, then, presently, told Dr. Burdell she had to find other quarters. Meanwhile, she'd need a place to stay temporarily.

That was easy. Burdell leased 31 Bond to a Mrs. Margaret Jones, who ran it as a boarding and lodging house, the Doctor continuing to live and conduct his practice there. Could Mrs. Jones accommodate a friend and her family for a few days? Certainly: Mrs. Jones's livelihood was renting out rooms, and she had several available.

So Emma Cunningham moved into Harvey Burdell's house, taking three attic rooms: for the boys, herself, and Helen. This arrangement of leasing a portion of one's house to a landlady sounds strange now but doesn't seem to have been then. It made sense: Burdell was rich but frugal, even stingy according to his servants, complaining of wasted coal and gas; and the arrangement was convenient and profitable. He collected several hundred dollars' annual rent; retained two large rooms on the second floor, a bedroom and his dental office; had a bathroom, which other rooms did not; and a dental laboratory, the use of which he also rented out: to other dentists of the neighborhood, Bond Street being a street of dentists and doctors. His bed was made daily, linen changed, clothes washed, rooms cleaned. And now, after only a day or so, Mrs. Cunningham said she was so happy here at 31 Bond that she didn't want to leave at all.

This was fine with landlady Jones, and so in addition to all the other benefits, Dr. Burdell had Emma Cunningham living snugly here in his own house. He must have thought he had it made.

I think some understanding is due Mrs. Cunningham. Even today it would be tough for a widow in her mid-thirties with five children on her hands. How was it in 1856? Infinitely tougher, I would suppose, and snaring this well-to-do man she'd met at Saratoga Springs may have seemed her last hope of any bearable future. And he'd promised to marry her, she always said. Installing herself under his roof meanwhile could have seemed the way to make sure he did.

It wasn't. She was under Burdell's roof, but right up under it: in the attic. While among the half-dozen other lodgers and boarders—and living right down on the Doctor's own floor, in the only other bedroom there—was his young cousin, a good-looking twenty-three-year-old separated from her husband and about to be divorced, to resume her name of Demis Hubbard. Mrs. Cunningham came to suspect the nature of the cousins' relationship, and saw Demis as a threat.

So she got herself pregnant, if that's the way to put it. Became pregnant, anyway, I don't know when. There's a lot we won't know of the queer developments of the next few months: it's as though we're seldom allowed inside 31 Bond but must stand waiting outside on the walk. Now and then a window is suddenly raised just long enough to overhear a sentence or two, a few angry words or a fragment of servants' gossip, before it is slammed shut again. Or the front door opens momentarily, and we see a departure or entrance or catch a glimpse of what's happening inside.

These holes and gaps could be filled: with imagined scenes, dialogue invented. But you can do that yourself, so I'll give you fact only and occasionally some surmise. Fact to the extent that I've been able to mine it from what has come down to us; if you read that Mrs. Cunningham's eyes are gray it's because a contemporary said so, and if I say it snowed it's because it did. And the surmise either labeled as such or obviously such. And supported; no idle speculation.

So not until Thanksgiving Day does the white-painted front door of number 31 open for us; and Dr. Burdell walks down the steps, turns east toward the Bowery, and Brooklyn, on an errand of some sort.

Inside the house, we learn from the newly hired cook, Emma Cunningham presently became ill. Helen Cunningham seems to have been out, and if the boys were home they were too young to help. The new cook was Hannah Conlon, described as "a genuine-looking Irish girl, of the most intense kind." Resting in her attic room, she heard Emma Cunningham call out from hers: "'Oh, Doctor [or 'Oh, daughter!'], where are you!'"

The new girl said nothing. Silence for a time. Then it got dark, when things get worse, and Emma Cunningham appeared at Hannah Conlon's door. "'My God, are you going to let me die here!'" she cried out, as Hannah recalled it: her face was smeared with blood, her nose bleeding, Hannah said. She had fallen against the stove, Mrs. Cunningham told her, and cut herself. Hannah got a basin of water, Mrs. Cunningham washed herself, but by now Hannah seems to have understood what was really the matter. "I ran for a doctor," she said.

We're hearing very close to Hannah Conlon's actual words, I think, because both the *Times's* and *Tribune's* accounts jibe about as closely as we could expect of two reporters listening to Hannah Conlon as she described that day, getting her words down as accurately as they could.

But their editors had different notions of what was fit for their readers' eyes. "I ran for a doctor," Hannah tells us in the *Tribune,* "and when I came back, [the chambermaid] and myself perceived that she had miscarried. She said the child belonged to the Doctor." I don't quite believe "perceived that she had miscarried"; and in the *Times* Hannah says, which sounds a little more like it to me, "I ran for a doctor, and when I returned the other girl and myself saw that a fetus was in the chamber. She said that the child belonged to the doctor." Dr. Burdell came home, and—a physician, too—he took over from the doctor Hannah had called in.

So Emma Cunningham had failed, if that pregnancy was planned. But she often failed, usually failed: she simply never gave up. It took a month before she could even come downstairs for meals, Hannah said; but once she was up and around again, she and Harvey Burdell resumed going out together; were seen, for example, at Niblo's Garden, a theater. And since he didn't board with Mrs. Jones, taking his meals at a hotel, Emma Cunningham sometimes invited Dr. Burdell here for dinner. Had him there for dinner that Christmas.

But things weren't really the same, I suspect. I wonder if now, after the miscarriage, Harvey Burdell might have considered himself no longer bound, if he had, in fact, promised marriage. Because—another glimpse inside 31—Mrs. Cunningham now began complaining to landlady Jones that the conversation of some of the Doctor's patients "was not refined and ladylike; she said she thought they came here to laugh and to joke instead of for professional services." Some people said that among his patients Dr. Burdell had more than his share of young prostitutes; maybe Emma Cunningham heard more giggling behind the closed doors of his office than is customary in filling teeth.

But she never quit, and now she said she no longer liked her attic room, and arranged—which must mean she'd made a friend of her—to share Demis Hubbard's room down on the Doctor's floor. Enabling her, of course, to keep an eye on comings and goings there.

People who persevere often get a break. Mrs. Jones now decided not to renew her lease when it expired in the spring, on May 1, so Emma told Harvey she'd like to take over as landlady. That was okay with him, she signed a year's lease, and thus, from temporary resident up in the attic . . . then permanent resident down on the Doctor's own floor . . . Mrs. Cunningham now took over the entire house.

Jones left, and: "The Doctor fixed up the house very nicely, and got new carpets," a friend said. He also took Mrs. Cunningham's note for the annual rental; began taking his meals at the new landlady's table; and they continued going out together, the Broadway Theatre being one at which they were seen.

But Demis was still there. And the Doctor had another female cousin, Lucy Ann Williams; how young or good-looking I don't know, but a widow, and she and Dr. Burdell visited each other often. And then a third threat appeared on the front stoop. The Doctor had just hired the latest of a succession of boys he employed to answer the door for patients, run errands, lay fires, and so on. He was Samuel Ashton, fourteen or fifteen, who had to work, he said, because his father was "out West." The doorbell rang, young Sam answered it, and opened the door on what must have been a startling sight: a handsomely figured woman with a green head—eyes lost behind green-tinted spectacles, features blurred by a green veil. She'd come to see Dr. Burdell, and Sam led the mysterious lady upstairs, where Harvey Burdell took her into his office, and locked the door.

Mrs. Cunningham knew or learned who this visitor was: Sophronia Stevens, wife of Cyrenius Stevens, given names which I think belong in the same league as Demis. And whenever she came to 31 thereafter, which was often, Mrs. Cunningham set Sam to eavesdropping at the closed door of the Doctor's office, and reporting to her. He didn't hear much, but Mrs. Cunningham added Sophronia to the names on her hit list.

And one by one took care of them all. Each in a characteristically nutty way. For along with a determination so unwavering that it would soon astonish the city, the country, and most of Europe, Mrs. Cunningham demonstrated an equally persistent capacity for bungling. She is surely one of the classic screw-ups of all time, and one of the luckiest.

Lucy Ann Williams was first. One day, visiting 31 Bond, she was taken aside by Emma, who told her some disturbing news. They all knew a member of Congress from New Jersey, a Senator Vail; I don't know how. The Senator—actually a representative, says the Biographical Directory of the U.S. Congress, but they seemed to call him "Senator"—had received an anonymous letter, Emma told Lucy Ann, which said Mrs. Williams was not a lady of good character. Naturally Mrs. Williams went home, and wrote the Senator asking about this letter. He replied that it was true he'd received an anonymous letter saying bad things about her, but the odd thing was that he had never shown it to Mrs. Cunningham or told her what it said.

It didn't take Lucy Ann long to puzzle that out, and back she came to 31 Bond to accuse Mrs. Cunningham of writing the letter herself. Who denied it, there was a big blowup, and Burdell calmed things down: said he believed Emma Cunningham because she couldn't have known some of the things mentioned in the letter (which suggests, doesn't it, that they were factual?). He said he suspected one of his relatives had sent it.

Now, this goofy letter could hardly have fooled anyone, assuming, as I certainly do, that Mrs. Cunningham sent it. Yet it worked: Mrs. Williams "dropped Mrs. Cunningham's acquaintance," she said, and kept away from 31 Bond Street.

Demis got it over the Fourth of July. The Fourth came on Friday, Demis went to the country for the long weekend, and when she came back, her former roommate and present landlady simply wouldn't let her into the house. Standing on the stoop arguing, Demis finally had to turn away, walk back down the stairs, and go look for another place to live.

But these awkward victories seem to have come at a price. When eighteen-year-old Augusta, oldest of the three daughters, returned to New York to join her family at 31 Bond, Dr. Burdell and her mother were no longer getting along well; quarreling often, Augusta said. She didn't say what about, but it is a fact that Harvey Burdell said he didn't like the summary ousting of Demis; and it seems impossible that he didn't understand who had written the poison-pen letter about Lucy Ann.

The front door of 31 Bond opens again for us, and Mrs. Cunningham comes down the steps. Women wore hoopskirts then, or puffed out their skirts with layers of starched petticoats, so we can almost see her. Which way she turned I don't know, but quite possibly toward Broadway: lawyers often had offices on this main street of the town. Now—persuasion having failed to make her Mrs. Harvey Burdell—Mrs. Cunningham turned to the law.

In the office of an attorney named B. C. Thayer, who would eventually do far more legal work for this client than either now imagined, she instructed him in what she wanted. He was to prepare the papers for a breach of promise suit, for which she had some spicy material.

Thayer listened, then turned over the actual drawing of the affidavit to another lawyer, Levi Chatfield. This affidavit was later lost, but Chatfield remembered what it said. Emma Cunningham swore that "a contract of marriage," he said, "existed between her and Dr. Burdell sometime in 1855, in the summer or fall, to be performed about the first of June [1856]." What's more, "soon after the contract between them, Dr. Burdell stated to her that he had some property in real estate in New Jersey . . . my recollection is Elizabethtown. . . .That he invited her to go down and see it with him. She went . . . they were engaged in looking at the premises, as I recollect, until after the train left Elizabethtown . . . by design on his part, making it necessary for them to remain overnight . . . . They stopped at the hotel, he came into her room, and . . . after much resistance she finally yielded to his persuasions."

Breach of promise suits were taken seriously, and she had the Thanksgiving Day miscarriage to back up her story, but again she bungled. Someone suggested to her that a complaint of seduction by a thirty-five-year-old woman with nearly grown children might not be impressive. So she brought her affidavit back to Chatfield, "and that part of it was stricken out, so as to leave the matter on the face of the paper as being a forcible thing altogether." She added that Harvey Burdell insisted on examining her as a physician, and that he produced the abortion—not what Hannah Conlon would testify later.

The suit seems to have been an ace in the hole, however, affidavit all signed, a summons on Dr. Burdell, dated September 16, prepared but unserved; she may still have had some lingering hope of marrying Dr. Burdell through persuasion. But now it looks as though possibly he began pressing her for money she couldn't pay. Because only four days later, on September 20, around seven in the evening, the front door of 31 Bond flew open, and Harvey Burdell ran down the steps and over to Broadway—it was this Broadway, the view here photographed in 1859—to call the cops. When he

returned with some cops he'd found there, Dr. Burdell told them that while he'd been napping, Mrs. Cunningham had sneaked in, taken the key to his safe from "his pantaloons pocket," one cop quoted him, unlocked the safe, and stolen back her own note for the annual rent of the house.

In the house, the cop said, Mrs. Cunningham came rushing out of the parlor "in a tremendous rage," telling him not to believe the Doctor, that he had ruined her family and her, and—one of the first threats of violence we know of—that she'd have his "heart's blood, or something to that effect." Another cop arrived, and to him Emma Cunningham said "she was [Burdell's] wife by every tie that could be," and struck Burdell in the chest. "The Doctor replied," said the cop, "that she had been seen with men in a house of assignation, she then stated that he had upstairs instruments for producing abortion, he retorted that if he had them there, she had used them." Then as now in domestic disputes, the cops passed the buck, advising them to settle this between themselves, and got out.

People who knew Harvey Burdell said that while he was quick to excited anger, it seldom lasted long; and he continued taking his meals at Mrs. Cunningham's table. What happened about the note I don't know.

Mrs. Cunningham was tougher. Demis Hubbard showed up again, asking to be allowed back, and Mrs. Cunningham turned her down. As for Sophronia Stevens, one night Emma Cunningham sent a message to Sophronia's husband saying Dr. Burdell wanted to see him right away, right now. Stevens didn't believe it. He knew Burdell well, and there was no conceivable reason for such a message. Besides, he was sixty-seven, and wasn't going anywhere at night; he was afraid of garroters.

These were street robbers who grabbed pedestrians around the neck from behind, holding them half-strangled and helpless—sometimes killing them in the process—while a confederate or confederates robbed them. Our name for them, of course, is muggers; and most people were afraid of them. George Templeton Strong, in his famous diary of his life in New York, says, in 1857: "An epidemic of crime this winter. 'Garroting' stories abound. . . . A man was attacked the other afternoon at his own shop door in the Third Avenue. . . . Most of my friends are investing in revolvers and carry them about at night, and if I expected to have a great deal of late street-walking off Broadway, I think I should make the like provision. . . ."

Stevens did go to number 31 the next morning, was brought into the back parlor, by Tom Callahan, I expect—the Doctor's newest boy-of-all-work—and "I had only just taken my seat," Stevens said, "when a lady came in, took a seat near me, and called me by name. She said she had sent for me, not Dr. Burdell." Emma Cunningham then told Stevens that his wife was carrying on with Dr. Burdell, and also accused Mrs. Stevens of "filching money from me, and making use of Dr. Burdell to deposit it in some bank for her. I told her I would think of the matter, and see her again," but he didn't. "I thought it was all out of whole cloth, and considered she had great nerve. I thought she wanted to make a tool of me by working up my feelings against Dr. Burdell. I thought her motive was to ruin Dr. Burdell's character and get possession of his money."

So he didn't go back, and: "On the Saturday following a gentleman called and wanted to see me. He said his business was from Mrs. Cunningham; he said she had sent him to ask me to come up and see her. He said he was her counsel. He had got her, he said, out of some pretty serious scrapes. I took a chair, and sat down beside him, and asked him if he knew what her business was with me. He said he did not know particularly. I asked him if he knew nothing about it. He represented that she was a wonderful, persevering, smart woman, and always accomplished all she undertook. He said she had money, and plenty of men around her who never failed her." This inexplicable nonsense, just as Stevens recalled it, is typical of the weirdness that so often tinged things Emma Cunningham had a hand in. "He said [his name] was Van Dolan," Stevens continued, "that he was a lawyer, and that his office was at Number 118 Chambers Street." But when he'd left, Stevens couldn't find any "Van Dolan" listed in the city directory as "lawyer," and when he "went down to Chambers Street next day," he "could not find such a name, or any such office; it appeared to be stores."

So Stevens didn't go see Mrs. Cunningham. "I did not know but what some scheme or plot might have been laid for me," he said. "Such curious things take place in this city, that I am a little cautious."

A few days later when he went to Harvey Burdell and told him all this, the Doctor replied that nothing had gone on between him and Sophronia; he had only removed a small tumor or obstruction from her eye. Since Cyrenius knew this was why she'd gone to Dr. Burdell—accounting, I expect, for the tinted glasses and veil—he believed him; believed him anyway, as an old friend. So while Sophronia Stevens, like Demis Hubbard and Lucy Ann Williams, quit coming to 31 Bond, Emma Cunningham had actually messed up once more.

And the Doctor at last quit her table, taking his meals here at the LaFarge House. I can't date this photograph, but I doubt that it's as early as 1856. Still, change in the

last century came more slowly than now, and possibly Harvey Burdell could have recognized this as the tree-lined Broadway and the hotel, in the old New York of low buildings, to which he now walked three times every day for "breakfast, dinner, and supper," the proprietor said. The LaFarge advertised its location as on Broadway "directly opposite Bond Street," so I believe the cross street in the middle distance is Bond, and Burdell's house, therefore, around its corner to the left, a short walk away.

I think Harvey Burdell deserves some sympathy. He was always alone. Never, said the proprietor of the LaFarge, did he see anyone eating with Dr. Burdell. A friend, Alvah Blaisdell, when also asked whether anyone ever ate with the Doctor, said, "I don't think he had anybody . . . he was not the kind of man [to invite a friend to dinner]; he was too close. . . ." So I see Harvey Burdell now, walking out of his house and over to the LaFarge each day to eat his silent meals, as a lonely man, afraid of marriage to Emma Cunningham or anyone else because afraid for his money; and beginning to be afraid of the strange, persistent woman he'd met at Saratoga Springs, who now had a lease on his house.

Afraid with reason: on October 10 Mrs. Cunningham returned to her lawyer, told him to go ahead and serve the Doctor with the already prepared summons charging rape, abortion, and breach of promise; and to draw up another to go along with it, charging slander in having accused her of stealing his note. On the day she so instructed her attorney, Harvey Burdell sat in his rooms and wrote:

"Cousin Demis: I received your letter two days since. You say you are ready to come to New York whenever I say the word. Mrs. Cunningham is about to take some steps to injure me, *I think*. Hold yourself in readiness to come to this city at a moment's warning. Perhaps I may go out after you, but if things go on quietly you had probably better stay where you are.

". . . Mrs. C. has slandered you and Lucy of the worst kind. . . .

"If I do not go to Sackett's Harbor in a few days I will send you some money. I am, in great haste,

"Yours, &c., Harvey Burdell."

A few days later he wrote: "Cousin Demis: . . . The trouble I expected with Mrs. Cunningham may not take place . . ." but he was wrong. On this same day a deputy sheriff, Hugh Crombie, arrived at 31 Bond, served Emma Cunningham's double summons, and arrested the Doctor. "Emma Augusta Cunningham vs. Harvey

Burdell, Action for Breach of Promise, Order of Arrest and $6000 bond," the first was headed, and the second summons, for slander, called for another $6,000 to be posted. When he saw what the papers were, Burdell became "very excited," said Crombie, "and said the suits were to extract money from him. He distinctly repudiated [this is the deputy speaking: everyone seemed more literate then] the idea of making a promise to marry. He said she did steal the note from him. . . ."

He settled the suits, though. And in a strange way. A friend signed a bail bond for him within an hour or so; and a week later Dr. Burdell signed an agreement with Emma Cunningham so peculiar I can't believe a lawyer drew it up. I wonder if they didn't work it out between them, and if he didn't outtalk her, because it read: "In consideration of settling the two suits now pending between Mrs. E. A. Cunningham and myself, I agree as follows:

"First, I agree to extend to Mrs. E. A. Cunningham and family my friendship through life;

"Second, I agree never to do or act in any manner to the disadvantage of Mrs. E. A. Cunningham;

"Third, in case I remain and occupy the house No. 31 Bond Street I now do, I will rent to Mrs. Cunningham the suites of rooms she now occupies 3rd floor, attic and basement at the rate of $800 a year."

Those first two provisions are so curious, and unlawyerlike in language, that I wonder—read them again; see what you think—if they may not be Emma Cunningham's almost pathetic attempt to define and make binding her idea of a husband's obligations, in the absence of marriage itself. And, third, to hang on to the home she had found. To me the document suggests compromise. If Emma Cunningham and her lawyer really did try to get money from him, this tightfisted man simply wouldn't give it; and if she'd hoped the threat of suits might force him to marry her, that didn't work either. But the threat worried him. Crombie said: "He was afraid [the suits] would injure his business reputation if published. The matter seemed to trouble him greatly." For whatever reason, he signed the agreement. Maybe he thought its strange provisions would be unenforceable.

He was furious, though. When he and Emma Cunningham's lawyer, Thayer, showed up at the sheriff's office to notify him that a settlement had been reached and the suits withdrawn: "His tongue was going all the time," Crombie said, "to the effect that they had tried to extort money from him; that he would not marry any woman; and that he had taken her to houses of assignation, and paid her as he had done with other women."

That last sounds doubtful, to say the least. A Bond Street friend of his, Dr. W. R. Roberts, said, "When the Doctor was angry with a person, no matter whether he was relative, friend, or foe, he would say anything to injure them; he would be very friendly afterwards. . . ." And a legal adviser of Burdell's, F. S. Sanxay (F. S. Sanxay: long gone, absolutely forgotten, until you and I momentarily evoke him again) said, "When the Doctor was angry at a person he was the most vituperative man I ever knew, and he did not hesitate to denounce in the most unmeasured terms any person whom he might imagine had injured him. He was quick-tempered and violent. I have known him to speak in terms of praise for an individual, then denounce him, in a few days afterward, most bitterly, and then praise him again. He was very extravagant when praising or denouncing anyone; I never heard such bitter language used by anybody as he used toward his brother William and his near relatives." If this explains what Harvey Burdell said about Emma Cunningham to Deputy Crombie, then I think he comes off as a weak man: blustering, fearful, but with a weak man's stubbornness. Crombie was asked later, "Do you believe he ever thought of marrying her?" and he replied, "Marry her! Why, he'd sooner have committed suicide first."

From MAUS II: A SURVIVOR'S TALE, AND HERE MY TROUBLES BEGAN

ART SPIEGELMAN

Editor's Note: *In December 1991, Art Spiegelman wrote a letter delicately chiding the* New York Times Book Review. *The editors had just selected* Maus II: A Survivor's Tale, And Here My Troubles Began *as one of the ten best books of 1991, but they insisted on placing it on their Best Sellers list for* fiction *instead of* nonfiction.

"If your list was divided into literature and nonliterature, I could gracefully accept the compliment as intended," Spiegelman wrote, "but to the extent that 'fiction' indicates that a work isn't factual, I feel a bit queasy. As an author I believe I might have lopped several years off the 13 I devoted to my two-volume project if I could only have taken a novelist's license while searching for a novelist's structure."

Spiegelman first created "Maus" in 1972 as a three-page story for an underground comic collection titled Funny Animals. *In 1980, installments of this cat and "maus" cartoon became a regular feature of* RAW, *a magazine of avant-garde comics and graphics edited by Spiegelman and his wife, Françoise Mouly. In 1986, the first six chapters of* Maus *were published in book form to great critical and popular success. The book won the Pulitzer Prize, sold 125,000 copies in the United States alone, and was translated into 15 foreign editions.*

That volume, Maus I: A Survivor's Tale, My Father Bleeds History, *presents the early days of Spiegelman's father, Vladek, as a dashing young businessman in 1930s Poland. It chronicles his marriage to an intelligent, rich, sensitive woman named Anja; the birth of their son; Vladek's service in the Polish Army in the early days of World War II; his incarceration as a prisoner of war; and his return to Poland to find his family forced into a ghetto, then into hiding, and finally into Auschwitz (the Nazi death camp) in 1944.* Maus II: A Survivor's Tale, And Here My Troubles Began, *takes up the story in Auschwitz and carries it through to Vladek's death in 1982.*

The "novelist's form" Spiegelman found for his Maus *story is that of* sequential narration *(see Part II, page 94). Like* Maus I, Maus II *alternates Spiegelman's trials in the present with his difficult, miserly father with the story of the father's earlier life in central Europe. As in Truman Capote's* In Cold Blood, *the contrapuntal narratives create suspense, for Spiegelman will halt his account at dramatic moments in his father's concentration camp story to return to his father picking up a piece of string in the present, or to his taking a clever turn in the road. As in* In Cold Blood, *these artful cuttings backward and forward create ironic tensions—and illuminations.* Sequential Narration *also offers Capote and Spiegelman a way of escaping the overwhelming horror of their stories. Spiegelman's segues to the present permit readers to turn away momentarily and reflect upon the atrocities they have been witnessing. This brings relief, and often intensification of understanding as well.*

The following excerpts from the first chapter of Maus II *vividly showcase Spiegelman's narrative technique. To signal his shift from the present to the past, Spiegelman aligns his cartoon panels vertically rather than horizontally, forcing readers literally to alter their perspective (See page 214). Then the Auschwitz story begins in panels brutally larger than any that have gone before. The panels, like the story itself, seem almost overpowering.*

Spiegelman uses mice to represent the Jews, cats for the Nazis, pigs as Poles, and dogs for the Americans. He is not the first to use animal characters to represent people. Spiegelman is working in the tradition of Brer Rabbit and Brer Bear of the Uncle Remus folk tales, as well as following in the path of George Orwell's anti-totalitarian novel Animal Farm *and Franz Kafka's story "Josephine the Singer, or the Mouse Folk" in which Jews are presented as mice. Spiegelman has noted that in* Mein Kampf *Hitler refers to Jews as "vermin," and that one German propaganda film contrasts scenes of Jews in a busy city marketplace with shots of scurrying rats.*

Like Jack Finney's "The Crime of the Century" which begins this section, Maus *shows that visuals can be an integral element of the* Literature of Reality. *According to art critic and historian Adam Gopnik, all forms of cartooning descend from the caricature, which first appeared around 1600 in Italy. Since then, many artists have seen the cartoon as an effective form for political commentary. The eighteenth century Spanish painter Goya believed traditional forms of painting were inadequate for expressing "The Horrors of War," and so signified his outrage in cartoons. In the twentieth century, his countryman Picasso drew on the same tradition in his 1930s political comic strip "The Dream and Lie of Franco."*

According to Gopnik, Spiegelman's Maus *works "not against the grain of the cartoon but within its richest inheritance . . . exploring the deepest possibilities unique to the form." Spiegelman's artfully simple black-and-white drawings capture the look of a 1940s newspaper funnies page. Indeed, Spiegelman says, his "rough, quick drawings make it seem like we found somebody's diary and are publishing facsimiles of it." Although his lines appear bold and broad, a 1992 exhibition of the original panels at the Metropolitan Museum of Modern Art revealed Spiegelman's painstaking craftsmanship: mistakes whited out, and pasted on corrections of both pictures and words.*

Spiegelman constructs his story from hyperrealist detail. We learn how the black market operated within the ghettos, what happened in sequence when the Germans occupied a town, and (in the excerpt below) the countless offhand ways concentration camp prisoners could die. Spiegelman tempers these wrenching particulars by giving his mice essentially the same face. They are both universalized and protected by this "mask." The artist's ear, too, is as good as his eye. Vladek's Yiddish-inflected English is fresh and convincing. It is strangely musical—and all within the tight confines of cartoon balloons.

Spiegelman also refuses to sentimentalize his story. Mouse-Jews betray each other to the cat-Nazis, and Vladek himself is a vexing man. One might argue, in fact, that we tend to believe Vladek's account of Auschwitz precisely because *he wears no halo. Conversely, recovering Vladek's experiences helps both his son and us to understand Vladek's present penurious behaviors.*

Perhaps Maus's *most endearing quality, however, is its disarming manner.*
Spiegelman achieves this quality, not only by modestly beginning the volume with
a sketchbook doodle, but in countless equally artful ways. One clever method of
evoking reality is, paradoxically, to declare your inability to do so. Speaking of the
work he is trying to create, the mouse named Art tells his wife: "I feel so
inadequate. . . . It is so presumptuous of me. . . . Reality is too complex for comic
strips." Here Spiegelman neatly anticipates all the preconceptions readers might
bring to his narrative.

Spiegelman is also disarming in having his mice draw attention to the
artifice of the volume. After a long lament upon the difficulties of telling his
father's story, Mouse-Art says to his mouse wife, "See what I mean . . . in real
life you'd never have let me talk this long without interrupting." Such
comments are not only amusing, but give the cartoon its sophisticated
postmodern "metafunny" charm. Ultimately the style of the entire work
disarms and prepares us to receive a story we are not sure we can bear to hear.
As art historian Gopnik explains:

> *We want an art whose stylizations are as much a declaration of inadequacy*
> *to their subjects as they are a mystical transcendence [of them] . . . . At the*
> *heart of our understanding (or our lack of understanding) of the Holocaust*
> *is our sense that this is both a human and an inhuman experience. . . . This*
> *overlay of the human and the inhuman is exactly what* Maus, *with its odd*
> *form, is extraordinarily able to depict.*

I'VE GOT IT!...PANEL ONE: MY FATHER IS ON HIS EXERCYCLE...

I TELL HIM I JUST MARRIED A FROG...

PANEL TWO: HE FALLS OFF HIS CYCLE IN SHOCK.

SO, YOU AND I GO TO A MOUSE RABBI. HE SAYS A FEW MAGIC WORDS AND **ZAP!**...

BY THE END OF THE PAGE THE FROG HAS TURNED INTO A BEAUTIFUL **MOUSE!**

HMPH

I ONLY CONVERTED TO MAKE VLADEK HAPPY.

YEAH. BUT **NOTHING** CAN MAKE HIM HAPPY.

YOU KNOW, YOU SHOULD HAVE MARRIED WHAT'S-HER-NAME? THE GIRL YOU WERE SEEING WHEN WE FIRST MET?...

SANDRA?

YES. THEN YOU COULD JUST DRAW MICE, NO PROBLEM.

C'MON. I JUST DATED HER TO GET OVER MY PREJUDICE AGAINST MIDDLE-CLASS, NEW YORK, JEWISH WOMEN.

THEY REMIND ME TOO MUCH OF MY **RELATIVES** TO BE EROTIC, SO I JUST—

ART! FRANÇOISE!!

HURRY—YOUR FATHER JUST PHONED US! HE HAD A **HEART ATTACK!**

WHAT?

OH NO!

WHAT A PITY, YOU JUST **GOT** UP HERE...

WE'LL BE BACK.

WE'RE NOT TAKING MUCH LUGGAGE, SO WE HAVE AN EXCUSE NOT TO STAY LONG.

VLADEK SOUNDED HALF-HYSTERICAL ON THE PHONE.

POOR GUY... I FEEL SO SORRY FOR HIM.

YEAH, ME TOO... 'TIL I HAVE TO SPEND ANY TIME WITH HIM— THEN HE DRIVES ME **CRAZY**!

MM.

SIGH.

DEPRESSED AGAIN?

JUST THINKING ABOUT MY BOOK... IT'S SO **PRESUMPTUOUS** OF ME.

I MEAN, I CAN'T EVEN MAKE ANY SENSE OUT OF MY RELATIONSHIP WITH MY FATHER... HOW AM I SUPPOSED TO MAKE ANY SENSE OUT OF AUSCHWITZ?...OF THE HOLOCAUST?...

I KNOW THIS IS INSANE, BUT I SOMEHOW WISH I HAD BEEN IN AUSCHWITZ **WITH** MY PARENTS SO I COULD REALLY KNOW WHAT THEY LIVED THROUGH!

...I GUESS IT'S **SOME** KIND OF GUILT ABOUT HAVING HAD AN EASIER LIFE THAN THEY DID.

And so, the Catskills...

THE SALT HERE, IT'S HALF **FULL**, AND SHE OPENED **ANYWAY** A NEW ONE!

I CAN'T EAT ON MY DIET **ANY** SODIUM. I DON'T NEED EVEN **ONE** CONTAINER SALT, AND HERE IT'S **TWO** OPEN SALTS!

WHERE'S MALA NOW?

TO FLORIDA SHE DROVE. WE'RE BUYING THERE A CONDO. SHE WANTS TO SELL AND TO GRAB OUT THE DEPOSIT MONEY.

BUT THIS SHE **CAN'T** DO. SHE NEEDS MY SIG— **ARTIE! WHAT DO YOU DO?!!**

HUH? I'M JUST LIGHTING MY CIGARETTE...

BETTER YOU **SHOULDN'T** SMOKE: FOR **YOU** IT'S TERRIBLE, AND FOR ME, WITH MY SHORTNESS OF BREATH, IT'S ALSO NO GOOD TO BE **NEAR**...

BUT IF **ANYWAY** YOU'RE SMOKING, PLEASE DON'T USE FROM ME MY **WOODEN** MATCHES. I DON'T HAVE LEFT SO MANY, AND ALREADY TO MAKE **COFFEE** YOU USED ONE.

ONLY TO LIGHT THE **OVEN** I USE THEM. THESE **WOOD** MATCHES I HAVE TO **BUY**! THE PAPER MATCHES I CAN HAVE **FREE** FROM THE LOBBY OF THE PINES HOTEL.

JEEZ! I'LL BUY YOU A WHOLE **BOX** OF WOODEN MATCHES!

IT ISN'T NECESSARY... AT HOME OUR OVEN IS AUTOMATIC, AND HERE I'M STAYING ONLY 15 MORE DAYS.

A few tense hours later...

ACCH, ARTIE, **AGAIN** YOU MADE THE WRONG ADDITION.

BUT LOOK– WE'VE CHECKED IT **TWICE**. IT'S **CORRECT**!

PFAH. IT DOESN'T COME OUT SO AS ON THE STATEMENT. WE'LL HAVE NOW EVERYTHING TO DO AGAIN.

WHA? THAT WOULD TAKE 2 OR 3 HOURS... IT'S OFF BY LESS THAN A **BUCK**. LET'S JUST FORGET IT.

ALWAYS YOU'RE SO **LAZY**! EVERY JOB WE SHOULD MAKE SO AS TO DO IT THE RIGHT WAY.

LAZY?! DAMN IT, YOU'RE DRIVING ME **NUTS**!

WAIT! WHY DON'T YOU TAKE A BREAK? I'LL FIND THE MISTAKE.

YES! WITH FRANÇOISE I CAN DO IT!

UM... I CAN HANDLE IT ALONE. WHY DON'T YOU **BOTH** GO OUT FOR A WALK?

THANKS A LOT.

WELL... DON'T MIX TOGETHER FOR ME ANY OF THE PAPERS. I'LL **REVIEW** WITH YOU WHEN I COME BACK...

...BUT FOR MY LEGS I COULD **USE** NOW THAT WE WALK A LITTLE.

SIGH. OKAY... I'LL GET MY TAPE RECORDER, SO TODAY ISN'T A TOTAL LOSS.

WHAT ARE YOUR PLANS NOW, POP?

WE'LL WALK OVER TO THE PINES HOTEL AND THEN BACK

I MEAN, IN GENERAL, NOW THAT MALA IS GONE.

MAYBE WE'LL TOGETHER STAY TO THE END OF THE SUMMER HERE... IT'S SO BEAUTIFUL...

I TOLD YOU-FRANÇOISE AND I CAN ONLY STAY THROUGH THE WEEKEND.

SO? THEN WHEN YOU GO BACK, I ALSO WILL GO. WHAT HAVE I HERE TO STAY ALL ALONE?

AND THEN?

NU? MAYBE YOU'LL WANT WITH ME IN QUEENS TO STAY?

TO HAVE YOU WITH ME, IT'S ALWAYS A PLEASURE. ...REMEMBER, MY HOUSE IT'S ALSO YOUR HOUSE TOO.

I'M SORRY, POP. I DON'T THINK IT WOULD WORK OUT. I MEAN, WE'VE GOT OUR OWN PLACE TO LIVE, AND—

YES. YOU DON'T HAVE TO ANSWER NOW... ONLY TO THINK OF IT...

UM-CAN I ASK YOU MORE ABOUT YOUR PAST... ABOUT AUSCHWITZ?

OF COURSE, DARLING. TO ME YOU CAN ASK ANYTHING!

WELL...WHAT HAPPENED WHEN YOU AND MOM ARRIVED THERE AND WERE SEPARATED?

WHEN WE CAME, THEY PUSHED IN ONE WAY THE MEN, AND SOMEWHERE ELSE THE WOMEN.

OUT!

I WAVED VERY FAST GOODBYE TO ANJA.

BUT YOU UNDERSTAND, *NEVER* ANJA AND I WERE SEPARATED!

NO??

NO! THE WAR PUT US APART. BUT ALWAYS, BEFORE AND AFTER, WE WERE TOGETHER.

NOT SO LIKE MALA, WHAT GRABS OUT MY MONEY!—

AUSCHWITZ, POP. TELL ME ABOUT AUSCHWITZ.

AUSCHWITZ WAS IN A TOWN CALLED OSWIECIM. BEFORE THE WAR I CAME OFTEN HERE TO SELL MY TEXTILES.

...AND NOW, I CAME AGAIN.

WE CAME TO A BIG HALL AND THEY SHOUTED ON US. GET UNDRESSED! LEAVE YOUR VALUABLES! LINE UP! *SCHNELL!*

I WAS, AT THAT TIME, STILL WITH MY FRIEND MANDELBAUM.

THEY TOOK FROM US OUR PAPERS, OUR CLOTHES AND OUR HAIR—

(PSST- WH-WHAT'S GOING TO HAPPEN TO US?)

(DON'T WORRY..)

WE WERE COLD, AND WE WERE AFRAID.

(IF THEY BROUGHT YOU HERE, THEY'LL PUT YOU TO WORK. THEY'RE NOT READY TO KILL YOU YET.)

(WHAT ABOUT OUR WIVES AND OUR—)

SHUT UP, YIDS! TO THE BATH HOUSE. QUICK!

EVERYWHERE WE HAD TO RUN — SO LIKE *JOGGERS* — AND THEY RAN US TO THE SAUNA...

IN THE SNOW THEY THREW TO US PRISONERS CLOTHINGS.

ONE GUY TRIED TO EXCHANGE.

ALL AROUND WAS A SMELL SO TERRIBLE, I CAN'T EXPLAIN... SWEETISH... SO LIKE RUBBER BURNING. AND FAT.

UNCLE! UNCLE!

WHEN WE CAME INSIDE THE GATES SOMEONE RAN TO US FROM FAR AWAY.

HERE WAS ABRAHAM— MANDELBAUM'S NEPHEW!

SO, UNCLE... YOU'VE ENDED UP HERE TOO.

YOU TOLD US TO COME!

YOU WROTE US ABOUT HOW HAPPY YOU ARE IN HUNGARY—THAT WE SHOULD JOIN YOU RIGHT AWAY! WELL... HERE WE ARE.

HUNGARY. HAH!

THE POLES WHO ARRANGED OUR "ESCAPE" UNDERSTOOD YIDDISH. SO THEY KNEW YOU WERE WAITING TO HEAR IF I WAS SAFE.

IN BIELSKO THE POLES DICTATED THAT LETTER WHILE THE GESTAPO HELD A PISTOL UP TO MY HEAD.

WHAT COULD I DO? THEY'D HAVE SHOT ME THEN AND THERE.

WELL... SO HERE'S OUR HUNGARY...

AND THERE'S ONLY ONE WAY OUT OF HERE FOR ALL OF US ...THROUGH THOSE CHIMNEYS.

ABRAHAM I DIDN'T SEE AGAIN... I THINK HE CAME OUT THE CHIMNEY.

BUT I SAW AGAIN ONCE THE POLES WHO BETRAYED US.

THE GERMANS DIDN'T NEED THEM. SO THEY FINISHED ALSO IN AUSCHWITZ.

WE NEWCOMERS WERE PUT INSIDE A ROOM. OLDTIMERS PASSED AND SAID ALL THE SAME.

YOU SEE THOSE CHIMNEYS?....

OKAY. SO I WAS **MORE** SAD.

I WAS WORN AND SHIVER-ING AND CRYING A LITTLE.

NOBODY EVEN **LOOKER**

BUT FROM ANOTHER ROOM SOMEONE APPROACHED OVER

WHY ARE YOU CRYING, MY SON?

SHOULD I BE HAPPY? AM I AT A CARNIVAL?

LET ME SEE YOUR ARM...

HE WAS A PRIEST...

HMM... YOUR NUMBER STARTS WITH 17. IN HEBREW THAT'S "K'MINYAN TOV." SEVENTEEN IS A VERY GOOD OMEN...

HE WASN'T JEWISH - BUT VERY INTELLIGENT!

IT ENDS WITH 13, THE AGE A JEWISH BOY BECOMES A MAN...

AND **LOOK**! ADDED TOGETHER IT TOTALS 18. THAT'S "CHAI," THE HEBREW NUMBER OF LIFE.

I CAN'T KNOW IF **I'LL** SURVIVE THIS HELL, BUT I'M CERTAIN **YOU'LL** COME THROUGH ALL THIS ALIVE!

I STARTED TO BELIEVE. I TELL YOU, HE PUT ANOTHER LIFE IN ME.

AND WHENEVER IT WAS VERY BAD I LOOKED AND SAID: "YES, THE PRIEST WAS RIGHT! IT TOTALS EIGHTEEN.

WHEW. THAT GUY WAS A **SAINT**!

YES... I NEVER SAW HIM AGAIN.

SOME FUN WITH THE F.B.I.

ST. CLAIR MCKELWAY

Editor's Note: St. Clair McKelway established the division between fact and fiction at The New Yorker. *From 1936 to 1939, the three years he agreed to serve as the magazine's managing editor, McKelway helped create the structure that would insure a staff of writers with the utmost freedom to be themselves. It was McKelway who established the magazine's credo "that no two writers are alike, . . . that every writer's individuality should be nurtured and catered to" and that "writers should be edited with practically reverential concern for their words and for their feelings."*

That McKelway should have originated these policies is not surprising, for he was the most individual of men, a man who shunned formal education and carried a malacca walking stick at the age of nineteen. A handsome man with graceful carriage, he saw journalists as belonging to an aristocracy, a true fourth estate. This, too, was not surprising for he descended from a long line of well-known journalists. His great uncle, also named St. Clair McKelway, was editor of the Brooklyn Eagle *newspaper. His brother became editor of the* Washington Star.

At the age of fourteen, young St. Clair began his career as an office boy for the Washington Times-Herald. *He rose to higher positions at the* Philadelphia Daily News, New York World, New York Herald Tribune, *and* Chicago Tribune *before* The New Yorker *hired him away from the* Bangkok *(Thailand)* Daily Mail.

During his 47 years at The New Yorker, *McKelway wrote articles, humor pieces, and short stories. His profiles of Walter Winchell, dancer Bill "Bojangles" Robinson, and Father Divine (the last with A. J. Liebling) became famous and are models of the profile form. McKelway's reports of unusual criminals and crimes were collected in* True Tales from the Annals of Crime and Rascality. *Among these was his story of a counterfeiter who baffled Treasury agents for years by printing only one dollar bills, as well as the following droll piece, "Some Fun With The F.B.I."*

If there were ever an article that appears to have written itself, this is it. McKelway's style seems artless, yet that is its art. "Some Fun With The F.B.I." is structured in the form of an interview, but in reality it is an extended monologue by Harry Bridges, the F.B.I. suspect. McKelway prepares us to accept this lengthy quotation by writing (in paragraph five) that Bridges "began to talk, slowly and distinctly. . . . I found it unnecessary to ask questions as he went along." We are thus invited to picture McKelway carefully taking down every one of Bridges' "slow," "distinct" words.

In point of fact, however, McKelway is having some fun of his own with journalistic conventions, for it is Bridges, the subject, who politely asks the questions. "Am I taking too much time?" he queries at one point. "Do you want to hear it in this much detail?"

*Our answer, of course, is a breathless "yes," for we, like McKelway, are
enjoying Bridges' good humored send-up of J. Edgar Hoover's formidable
organization.*

Back in 1941, when Harry Bridges was just a militant labor leader and not a
convicted perjurer, I had a talk with him one day at the Hotel Piccadilly. I
had gathered from newspaper stories that from the point of view of the
quarry he was peculiarly familiar with the methods of the F.B.I. For almost a month
that summer, the newspapers said, he had lived at the Hotel Edison, on West Forty-
seventh Street, knowing that his telephone wire was tapped and that two or more
men, whom he identified as F.B.I. agents, were occupying the room next to him. The
newspaper *PM* went so far as to name the agents involved and even produced a
young lady who made an affidavit to the effect that she had been with the agents in
the room next to Bridges for an hour or so, having been invited there by them to listen to the tapped telephone conversation as a sort of lark. Since wire-tapping is a violation of the law, the newspapers were naturally more concerned with what the men
in the next room had done to Bridges than with what Bridges had done to the men in
the next room. Hardly anything was brought out to indicate how Bridges had discovered that he was being shadowed in the first place or how he had treated the men
who were shadowing him and who didn't know he knew they were shadowing him.

"How do you manage to tell when you are being shadowed by the F.B.I.?" I
asked him.

"Well," said Mr. Bridges in a matter-of-fact tone which seems to be characteristic
of him, "there are various ways to determine that. Should I describe the general
ways I use to find out whether they are shadowing me or should I tell you about specific ways I used here in town this summer?"

"Suppose you tell me some of the general ways," I suggested, "and then go into
the specific ways you used at the Edison."

He began to talk, slowly and distinctly, and I found it unnecessary to ask questions as he went along. We sat at a table in a corner of the Piccadilly dining room.
Bridges, whom the government had for some time even then been trying to deport
on the ground that he was a Communist, is an Australian by birth and talked with a
strong Australian accent. He was tall, lean, about thirty-five, and had a candid, vigorous, take-it-or-leave-it manner. I did not ask him about the deportation proceed-
ings, or about his political views, and he did not offer to tell me about them.

"In the first place," he said, "the F.B.I. men like to occupy the room next to yours
in a hotel, if possible. If they can arrange this in advance, as they usually can, you'll
probably be assigned by the management to a room that has a room next to it with a
locked door between it and yours. This locked door almost invariably has a space
under it, sometimes as much as half an inch; I guess in the old days the F.B.I. men in
this other room would look under this door or listen at it, but they've gotten so high-
powered that most of them don't bother nowadays. They consider that kid stuff.
They usually have a man looking into your room with field glasses from a room in

some adjacent building, and usually they have your telephone rigged in such a way that their receiving instruments pick up not only what you say into your telephone but also what you say anywhere in your room. So you look under this connecting door yourself, and you listen. If you see two pairs of men's feet moving around the room and hear no talking except in whispers, you can be fairly certain the room is occupied by F.B.I. men, or at least by men who are not acting like two ordinary men in a hotel room. Of course, you can often see the wire-tapping apparatus—the wires and earphones and so forth—all spread out on the floor of this other room, and then you do not have any further doubts at all.

"Then, too, of course, you get to know how to observe people in the lobby and you look around to see if there are any F.B.I. men there, waiting to follow you around. I usually can spot one or two right away, because I'm suspected, as you know, of being a Communist and I've seen so many F.B.I. men these past years that there are likely to be one or two that I have seen before in the lobby of practically any hotel I am staying at. But if I don't happen to see any F.B.I. men I know, I watch out for men holding newspapers in front of them in a certain peculiar sort of manner. They hold the paper so that it just comes up to the bottom of their eyes, and their eyes are always peering over the top of the paper. They are very easy to pick out because the way their eyes peep over the top of the paper makes them look peculiar. Of course, I don't look at them directly when I am looking for them this way. There are always lots of mirrors in hotel lobbies and I just look in the mirrors and watch them that way—indirectly. Then, if I suddenly start for the door and, just as I'm about to go out, I stop and turn around quickly, one or more of these fellows is likely to have just jumped up to his feet. He will be standing there looking—well, more easygoing like than anybody ever looks who has just gotten up suddenly and stopped in his tracks. If I want to be absolutely sure they are F.B.I. men, of course, I go out and lose anybody that may be following me and then go back and stand in a doorway across the street from the hotel, and when one of the men I've spotted comes out of the hotel, I follow him down to the F.B.I. office when he goes to make his report about what I've been doing. These F.B.I. men are nearly always tall guys, easy to follow in a crowd, and they never seem to suspect that they are being followed.

"Well, those are what you might call the general ways of finding out whether you are being shadowed by the F.B.I. Suppose I tell you now, as you suggested, the story of the events that occurred at the Edison.

"I checked into the Edison first this summer early in July and I was given an ordinary three-fifty room. That was what I had asked for. This room had a small balcony, a sort of narrow terrace, in front of the windows and there was the customary locked door leading into the adjoining room. I was very busy with union business at the time—I am an officer of the C.I.O., you know, as well as president of the International Longshoremen's and Warehousemen's Union—and I just didn't bother right away to find out whether the F.B.I. was on the job or not. But one night I had a half-hour with nothing to do and I climbed out on the balcony and looked into the window of the adjoining room. A man was in there and I looked at him and he looked at me. I don't know whether he was an F.B.I. man or not. I never heard anything about it, in any case. Then I went away—checked out—for the weekend, and when I came back and asked for the same room or some other three-fifty room, I was told that there were none left but that I could have a fine room on another floor at the three-fifty rate. I was shown to a very large room with twin beds and two big windows, and no balcony. It had the locked door leading into the adjoining room, of course. I was still busy and I didn't bother about the F.B.I. I checked out again for a few days and came back on August fourth. This time I was given this very same big room with the twin beds, and when I said I wanted a regular three-fifty room the desk said I could have this big one at the three-fifty rate for as long as I wanted it. I said this certainly was nice of the hotel, and, of course, I began to look around the lobby for the F.B.I. men.

"I was pretty sure I recognized one whom I had known in San Francisco, or in some city out there in the West, in connection with the deportation hearing this spring. Then I went through the business I told you about—watching for guys not reading their newspapers, seeing if they got up when I started out, and so on. I was certain I had three of them spotted before lunchtime that day. Would it interest you to know how I remember the face of an F.B.I. man?"

"Yes, indeed," I said.

"Well," said Bridges, "the way I remember the face of an F.B.I. man is like this: I look at him and get his face clearly in my mind and then I try to think of somebody he reminds me of—like a friend or a movie actor or anybody whose face I know very well. This is better than trying to remember a minute description—better than putting your idea of the F.B.I. man's face into words, if you see what I mean. For instance, one of these three guys I had spotted looked like a longshoreman on the Coast, a very old friend of mine I worked with when I was a longshoreman myself. The second of these three F.B.I. guys reminded me of one of the C.I.O. attorneys on the Coast. The third one had a face very much like the face of Gary Cooper, the movie actor. This way I have of remembering the faces of the F.B.I. men seems to sort of place the face in my mind. Something like those tricks they teach you in memory courses, I guess.

"Well, I thought probably my telephone was tapped, of course, so after I had spotted these three guys and knew I could remember their faces anywhere, I went up to my room and made what I call a test call. I called a friend of mine, one of the officers in the C.I.O. here in town, and I said, 'Look, I've got to see the big shot.' This is the kind of talk that the F.B.I. men are always on the lookout for, you see. They're all sort of like college or high-school boys. My friend at the C.I.O. office, of course, didn't know what I was talking about and said as much, and I said, 'Do I have to tell you who I mean? The big shot! The Number One! Listen,' I said, 'meet me at the drugstore here on the corner in fifteen minutes and I'll explain.'

"So then I went downstairs to a telephone booth and called my friend back and told him what it was all about so he wouldn't bother to meet me at the drugstore. Then I walked around for ten minutes or so and went into the drugstore and, sure enough, one of my three guys came in right after me and sat two seats further down the soda fountain while I drank a milk shake. Another one, the Gary Cooper guy, was standing across the street when I went out. I had pretended to be looking for somebody, expecting somebody to come in, because I didn't want to tip them off that I knew they were shadowing me. I went into a movie-theatre entrance as if I was going to a movie and ducked around and looked out at the street from the other side of the change booth, and I saw the first guy start back for the hotel and the other guy, the Gary Cooper guy, go off in another direction by himself. So I followed him and he got into a taxi. I got into a taxi and followed him down to Foley Square, where he got out and went into the F.B.I. office. Am I taking too much time?"

"Oh, no, not at all," I said.

"Well," said Bridges, "then I went back to the hotel and up to my room. I went in my door very fast and dove over to the connecting door, lay down, and looked under it into the next room. Two pairs of feet went by my eye and I could also see some bunched-up telephone wires on the floor—just dumped there and curled up.

"I wanted to see these guys' faces and find out whether they were the two I had spotted downstairs or whether they were different ones. So I waited in my room for a long time, keeping very quiet and with my door into the corridor open just a little. They must have thought I had left the room, which was what I wanted them to think, because finally I heard their door open and I watched them, through the crack in my door, go down the corridor toward the elevator. I then closed my door softly and opened it again in the usual way and started for the elevator myself. I rode down in it with them. They didn't say a word to each other and one of them kept looking at his fingernails. I got a good look at them, of course. The one looking at his fingernails was the guy that resembles my longshoreman friend and the other one was the guy that resembles the C.I.O. attorney on the Coast.

"After tipping off my friends that I was being tapped, I sort of settled down to have some fun with the F.B.I. I wasn't busy and I had some time on my hands. I knew this hotel we're sitting in now, the Piccadilly, overlooks the Edison, so I went over to Sixth Avenue and rented a pair of field glasses. I put up a deposit on them and agreed to pay fifty cents a day rent, but I eventually bought them because I had so much fun with them. I went back to my room and the two guys were in the next room again. Looking under the door, I could see their feet moving around. I called the hotel operator and told her I was expecting an important long-distance call and to put it right on when she got it, that I'd wait for it. Then I left the room very quietly, ducked out of the hotel, and ducked in and out of a couple of stores just in case any of the lobby guys were following me, and came over to the Piccadilly and went up to the roof garden. I had stayed at the Piccadilly before. I spotted my room at the Edison easily enough with the field glasses because I had left some stuff on the window sill which I could recognize. Then I moved the glasses over to the room next to mine and there were the two guys, stretched out on the twin beds with their earphones on, thinking I was still in the room. It seems that most of the time they listen with the earphones while standing up, but I suppose that this time they must have thought it was going to be a long wait, waiting for the long-distance call, so they had lain down on the beds. It was only about a hundred yards from the roof of the Piccadilly to the room in the Edison, and I could see them quite plainly. I'm afraid I'm taking too long with this. Do you want to hear it in this much detail?"

"I certainly do," I said.

"Well," said Bridges, "I decided to rent a room over here at the Piccadilly so I could watch the F.B.I. men at the Edison more comfortably, and I had the idea, too, of having some of my friends up to watch them while I was in my room at the Edison. I had never had such an easy time with F.B.I. men before, although I have always found it comparatively easy to spot them and so forth. Whenever I left the Edison to come over here to the Piccadilly, I would go around a corner, duck into a store, and watch the Gary Cooper fellow go by looking for me, and then I would come over here. They never had any idea what was going on as far as I can tell. Well, I got the room here and I'd get some of my friends, labor people and so on, to stay in my room at the Piccadilly, and I'd go over to my other room in the Edison, usually taking a friend along with me so I could talk to him and keep the F.B.I. men busy. We'd go into my room at the Edison and my friends at the Piccadilly would see the F.B.I. men get up off their beds and pick up the earphones. Then we'd talk all sorts of silly stuff—about how we were planning, for instance, to take over the Gimbel strike so I could use the pretty Gimbel shopgirls to help me take over the New York longshoremen. Stuff like that. Some of it was a bit complicated, too—figured out sort of carefully to mix them up and confuse their various files on people. Some of it, though, was pretty broad. We couldn't help getting to kidding when we thought of them sitting there listening, but the F.B.I. men apparently took it all in and put it all down. As soon as we'd leave the room, one of them would begin typing very fast on a typewriter at a table in front of the window.

"Then I remembered that one of the things F.B.I. men always do is to get hold of any scraps of paper that are left in the room of a man they are shadowing. They get a key to the room, or they fix up a maid, or something. Well, so we would tear up old letters and things and the next morning leave them in my room at the Edison, and then that afternoon we'd see one of the F.B.I. men sitting at the table at the window in their room pasting little pieces of paper together. A couple of times I tore things up in the shape of six-pointed stars, or five-pointed stars, or in the shape of a row of paper dolls—you know that trick of tearing paper, don't you? I used to do it for my kid. Then we'd see this F.B.I. guy holding up the stars and the rows of dolls next day at the window, studying them.

"We also left some well-used carbon paper in the wastebasket, so they could study that, too. The F.B.I. just loves carbon paper, you know. When they get hold of a piece of carbon paper that has been used for the writing of twenty or thirty letters, they really go to town—chemical processes, magnifying glasses, the whole works—and try to decipher what's been written on the carbon paper. I got a lawyer friend of mine to get me some from his office and another friend of mine got a stenographer he goes around with to bring me some from her office, which is a second-hand-furniture concern. We left them five or six sheets to work on. The guys in the room, of course, wouldn't try to decipher carbon paper themselves; they'd take that kind of thing right down to headquarters.

"Well, that's about all except what's appeared in the newspapers. Since I took the microphone out of my telephone box at the Edison and checked out over there, I haven't seen any F.B.I. men. I still have the microphone, though."

"You found a microphone in your telephone box?" I asked.

"Oh," said Mr. Bridges, "I must have forgot to tell you about that. I'm sorry. Except when the F.B.I. men have lots of time and a completely free hand, you see, they usually just put the microphone in the telephone box. It is a special kind that picks up the two-way conversations on the telephone and also anything that is being said by the people in the room. I looked in the phone box, of course, and saw it there the day I made the test call and they followed me over to the drugstore, but I didn't disturb it until we had finished having our fun with the F.B.I."

TWIRLING AT OLE MISS

TERRY SOUTHERN

Editor's Note: Terry Southern, who wrote the screenplay of Dr. Strangelove, *looked like Bob Dylan with dark glasses during the 1960s when he was working as an editor at* Esquire. *A Texan who ran with George Plimpton's* Paris Review *set, Southern was sent by* Esquire *to Oxford, Mississippi in 1963 to write an article on the Dixie National Baton Twirling Institute. As often happens with the best literary nonfiction, however, Southern found a different story from the one he (and his editors) intended.*

On-site, one might say, Southern enlarged his vision. What Southern saw was a clash between the sheltered romanticism of the Baton Twirling Institute and the reality of racial segregation in the South. Southern underscores this message through the use of sequential narration.* *By cutting back and forth between the sylvan groves of the Institute and the rampant racism everywhere else, he implies that southerners twirl while the South burns.*

Southern's use of "southern" dialect in this article is equally cunning; it does more than merely add charm and local color. His dialect, in actuality, undercuts the various southerners he presents, while his first-person narration and portrayal of himself as a reflective (though hedonistic) outsider, are choices aimed at winning the reader's affection—and allegiance. Southern, for example, will willingly make sport of his own reporter's craft. In so doing, once again he achieves more than merely humor. By undercutting traditional journalistic methods, he implies that the truth of this "story" lies beyond mere journalistic "fact." His "Twirling at Ole Miss" offers an enlarged view of the Dixie Institute— and of much of the nation as well.

I n an age gone stale through the complex of bureaucratic interdependencies, with its tedious labyrinth of technical specialization, each contingent upon the next, and all aimed to converge into a single totality of meaning, it is a refreshing moment indeed when one comes across an area of human endeavor absolutely sufficient unto itself, pure and free, no strings attached—the cherished and almost forgotten *l'art pour l'art.* Such is the work being carried forward now at the Dixie National Baton Twirling Institute, down at the campus of Ole Miss—a visit to which is well worthwhile these days, if one can keep one's wits about.

In my case, it was the first trip South in many years, and I was duly apprehensive. For one thing, the Institute is located just outside Oxford, Mississippi—and, by

---

*For discussion of *sequential narration,* see Truman Capote's "In Cold Blood" in Part II, pages 94–100. For other examples in this section, see Jack Finney's "The Crime of the Century" (pages 182–200), Art Spiegelman's *Maus II* (pages 201–217), Melissa Fay Greene's *Praying for Sheetrock* (pages 234–239), C. D. B. Bryan's *Friendly Fire* (pages 240–255), and Annie Dillard's "An Expedition to the Pole" (pages 312–331).

grotesque coincidence, Faulkner's funeral had been held only the day before my arrival, lending a grimly surreal aura to the nature of my assignment . . . namely, to get the story on the Baton Twirling Institute. Would reverting to the Texas twang and callousness of my youth suffice to see me through?

Arriving in Oxford then, on a hot midday in July, after the three-hour bus ride from Memphis, I stepped off in front of the Old Colonial Hotel and meandered across the sleepy square toward the only sign of life at hand—the proverbial row of shirt-sleeved men sitting on benches in front of the county courthouse, a sort of permanent jury.

"Howdy," I say, striking an easy stance, smiling friendly-like, "Whar the school?"

The nearest regard me in narrow surmise: they are quick to spot the stranger here, but a bit slow to cotton. One turns to another.

"What's that he say, Ed?"

Big Ed shifts his wad, sluices a long spurt of juice into the dust, gazes at it reflectively before fixing me again with gun-blue-cold eyes.

"Reckon you mean, 'Whar the school *at*?', don't you, stranger?"

Next to the benches, and about three feet apart, are two public drinking fountains, and I notice that the one boldly marked "For Colored" is sitting squarely in the shadow cast by the justice symbol on the courthouse facade—to be entered later, of course, in my writer's notebook, under "Imagery, sociochiaroscurian, hack."

After getting directions (rather circuitous, I thought—being farther put off by what I understood, though perhaps in error, as a fleeting reference to "the Till case") I decided to take a cab, having just seen one park on the opposite side of the square.

"Which is nearer," I asked the driver, "Faulkner's house or his grave?"

"Wal," he said without looking around, "now that would take a little studyin', if you were gonna hold a man to it, but offhand I'd say they were pretty damn near the same—about ten minutes from where we're sittin' and fifty cents each. They're in opposite directions."

I sensed the somehow questionable irony of going from either to the Baton Twirling Institute, and so decided to get over to the Institute first and get on with the coverage.

"By the way," I asked after we'd started, "where can a man get a drink of whiskey around here?" It had just occurred to me that Mississippi is a dry state.

"Place over on the county line," said the driver, "about eighteen miles; cost you four dollars for the trip, eight for the bottle."

"I see."

He half turned, giving me a curious look.

"Unless, of course, you'd like to try some 'nigger-pot.'"

"Nigger-pot? Great God yes, man," I said in wild misunderstanding, "let's go!"

It soon developed, of course, that what he was talking about was the unaged and uncolored corn whiskey privately made in the region, and also known as "white lightning." I started to demur, but as we were already in the middle of the colored section, thought best to go through with it. Why not begin the sojourn with a genuine Dixieland experience—the traditional jug of corn?

As it happened the distiller and his wife were in the fields when we reached the house, or hut as it were, where we were tended by a Negro boy of about nine.

"This here's a mighty fine batch," he said, digging around in a box of kindling wood and fetching out unlabeled pints of it.

The taxi driver, who had come inside with me, cocked his head to one side and gave a short laugh, as to show we were not so easily put upon.

"Why, boy," he said, "I wouldn't have thought you was a drinkin' man."

"Nosuh, I ain't no drinkin' man, but I sure know how it suppose to taste—that's 'cause times nobody here I have to *watch* it and I have to *taste* it too, see it workin' right. We liable lose the whole batch I don't know how it suppose to taste. You all taste it," he added, holding out one of the bottles and shaking it in my happy face. "You see if that ain't a fine batch!"

Well, it had a pretty good taste all right—a bit edgy perhaps, but plenty of warmth and body. And I did have to admire the pride the young fellow took in his craft. You don't see much of that these days—especially among nine-year-olds. So I bought a couple of bottles, and the driver bought one, and we were off at last for the Institute.

The Dixie National Baton Twirling Institute holds its classes in a huge, sloping, fairyland grove on the campus of Ole Miss, and it resembles something from another age. The classes had already begun when I stepped out of the cab, and the sylvan scene which stretched before me, of some seven-hundred girls, nymphs and nymphets all, cavorting with their staffs in scanty attire beneath the broadleaf elms, was a sight to spin the senses and quicken the blood. Could I but have donned satyr's garb and rushed savagely among them! But no, there was this job o'work to get on with—dry, factual reportage—mere donkey work, in fact. I decided the correct procedure was to first get some background material, and to this end I sought out Don Sartell, "Mister Baton" himself, Director of the Institute. Mr. Sartell is a handsome and personable young man from north of the Mason-Dixon line, highly intelligent, acutely attuned to the needs of the young, and, needless to say, extremely dexterous *avec les doigts*. (By way of demonstrating the latter he once mastered a year's typing course in a quick six hours—or it may have been six days, though I do recall that it was an impressive and well-documented achievement.)

"Baton twirling," he tells me straight off, "is the second largest girl's youth movement in America—the first, of course, being the Girl Scouts." (Veteran legman. I check this out later. Correct.) "The popularity of baton twirling," he explains, "has a threefold justification: (1) it is a sport which can be practiced alone; (2) it does not, unlike other solo sports (sailing, skiing, shooting, etc.), require expensive equipment; and (3) it does not, again like the aforementioned, require travel, but, on the contrary, may be practiced in one's own living room or backyard."

"Right," I say. "So far, so good, Mister Baton—but what about the intrinsics? I mean, just what is the point of it all?"

"The point, aside from the simple satisfaction of mastering a complex and highly evolved skill, is the development of self-confidence, poise, ambidexterity, disciplined coordination, et cetera."

I asked if he would like a drink of nigger-pot. He declined graciously: he does not drink or smoke. My place, I decided, is in the grove, with the groovy girls—so, limbering up my 600-page, eight-dollar copy of *Who's Who in Baton Twirling*, I take my leave of the excellent fellow and steal toward the sylvan scene below, ready for anything.

The development of American baton twirling closely parallels the history of emancipation of our women. A larger version of this same baton (metal with a knob on the end) was first used, of course, to direct military marching bands, or, prior to that, drum corps—the baton being manipulated in a fairly straight-forward, dum-de-dum, up-and-down manner. The idea of *twirling* it—and finally even *flinging* it—is, obviously, a delightfully girlish notion.

Among those most keenly interested in mastering the skill today are drum majorettes from the high schools and colleges of the South and Midwest, all of which have these big swinging bands and corps of majorettes competing during the half at football games. In the South, on the higher-educational level, almost as much expense and training goes into these groups as into the football team itself, and, to persons of promise and accomplishment in the field, similar scholarships are available. Girls who aspire to become majorettes—and it is generally considered the smartest status a girl can achieve on the Southern campus—come to the Institute for preschool training. Or, if she is already a majorette, she comes to sharpen her technique. Many schools send a girl, or a small contingent of them, to the Institute to pick up the latest routines so that they can come back and teach the rest of the corps what they have learned. Still others are training to be professionals and teachers of baton twirling. Most of these girls come every year—I talked to one from Honey Pass, Arkansas, a real cutie pie, who had been there for eight consecutive years, from the time she was nine. When I asked if she would like a drink of pot, she replied pertly: "*N* . . . *o* . . . spells 'No'!" Such girls are usually championship material, shooting for the Nationals.

Competitions to determine one's degree of excellence are held regularly under the auspices of the National Baton Twirling Association, and are of the following myriad categories: *Advanced Solo; Intermediate Solo; Beginners Solo; Strutting Routine; Beginners Strutting Routine; Military Marching; Flag; Two-Baton; Fire Baton; Duet; Trio; Team; Corps; Boys; Out-of-State*; and others. Each division is further divided into age groups: 0–6, 7–8, 9–10, 11–12, 13–14, 15–16, 17 and over. The winner in each category receives a trophy, and the first five runners-up receive medals. This makes for quite a bit of hardware riding on one session, so that a person in the baton-twirling game does not go too long without at least token recognition—and the general run of *Who's Who* entries ("eight trophies, seventy-three medals") would make someone like Audie Murphy appear rudely neglected.

The rules of competition, however, are fairly exacting. Each contestant appears singly before a Judge and Scorekeeper, and while the Judge observes and relays the grading to the Scorekeeper, the girl goes through her routine for a closely specified time. In Advanced Solo, for example, the routine must have a duration of not less than two minutes and twenty seconds, and not more than two and thirty. She is scored on general qualities relating to her degree of accomplishment—including *showmanship, speed*, and *drops*, the latter, of course, counting against her, though not so much as one might suppose. Entrance fees average about two dollars for each contestant. Some girls use their allowance to pay it.

In the Institute's grove—not unlike the fabled Arcadia—the groups are ranged among the trees in various states of learning. The largest, most central and liveliest of these groups is the one devoted to the mastery of Strutting. Practice and instruction in Strutting are executed to records played over a public-address system at an unusually loud volume—a sort of upbeat rock and roll with boogie-woogie overtones. *Dixie, The Stripper*, and *Potato Peel* were the three records in greatest use for this class—played first at half speed, to learn the motions, then blasted at full tempo. Strutting is, of course, one of the most fantastic body-movement phenomena one is likely to see anywhere. The deliberate narcissistic intensity it requires must exceed even that of the Spanish flamenco dancer. High-style (or "all-out") Strutting is to be seen mainly in the South, and what it resembles more than anything else is a very contemporary burlesque-house number—with the grinds in and the bumps out. It is the sort of dance one associates with jaded and sequin-covered washed-out blondes in their very late thirties—but Ole Miss, as is perhaps well known, is in "the heartland of beautiful girls," having produced two Miss Americas and any number of runners-up, and to watch a hundred of their nymphets practice the Strut, in bathing suits, short shorts, and other such skimp, is a visual treat which cuts anything the Twist may offer the viewer. It is said, incidentally, that the best Strutting is done at the colored schools of the South, and that of these the greatest of all is to be seen at Alabama State Teachers College. That jazz trends have decisively influenced the style of Strutting in recent years is readily acknowledged, and is highly apparent indeed.

At the Institute, the instructor of the Strut stands on a slightly raised platform facing her class, flanked by her two assistants. She wears dark glasses, tight rolled shorts, and looks to be about 34–22–34. She's a swinger from Pensacola, Florida, a former National Senior Champion and Miss Majorette of America, now turned pro. When not at the Dixie Institute at the University of Mississippi, or a similar establishment, she gives private lessons at her own studio, for four to six dollars an hour, and drives a Cadillac convertible.

As for other, more academic, aspects of baton twirling, an exhibition was given the first evening by members of the cadre—all champions, and highly skilled indeed. It is really quite amazing what can be done with a baton, and no one could have been more surprised than your correspondent. The members of the cadre can literally walk those sticks over every inch of the body, almost it seems without touching them. This is especially effective at night when they use a thing called the "fire baton," with a torch flaming at each end.

Instruction in speed and manipulation of this sort is a long and nerve-racking process. There is something almost insane about the amount of sheer effort and perseverance which seems to go into achieving even a nominal degree of real excellence—and practice of four hours a day is not uncommon. And yet the genuine and really impressive skill which is occasionally displayed makes it difficult to consider the art as so totally ridiculous as one would have previously believed—though, of course, another might argue that such achieved excellence only makes it more ridiculous—or perhaps not so much ridiculous as absurd. In fact, in the existentialist sense, it might well be considered as the final epitome of the absurd—I mean, people starving in India and that sort of thing, and then others spending four hours a day skillfully flinging a metal stick about. *Ca alors!* In any case it has evolved now into a highly developed art and a tightly organized movement—though by no means one which has reached full flower. For one thing, a nomenclature—that hallmark of an art's maturity—has not yet been wholly formalized. Theoretically, at least there should be a limit to the number of possible manipulations, each of which could legitimately be held as distinct from all others—that is to say, a repertory which would remain standard and unchanged for a period of time. The art of baton twirling has not yet reached that stage, however, and innovations arise with such frequency that there does not exist at present any single manual, or similarly doctrinaire work, on the subject. Doubtless this is due in large part to the comparative newness of the art, as a large and intensely active pastime—the Dixie National Baton Twirling Institute, for example, having been founded as recently as 1951. The continuing evolution of the art as a whole is reflected in the names of the various manipulations. Alongside the commonplace (or classic) designations, such as *arabesque, tour-jeté, cradles*, etc., are those of more exotic or contemporary flavor: *bat, walk-over, pretzel*, and the like . . . and all, old or new, requiring countless hours of practice.

During the twirling exhibition I fell into conversation with a couple of graduate law students, and afterward went along with them to the campus coffee shop, "Rebel Devil" or whatever it is called—nearly all shops there have the word "Rebel" in them—and we had an interesting talk. Ole Miss prides itself, among other things, on having the only law school in the state which is accredited by the American Bar Association—so that these two graduate law students were not without some claim to representing a certain level of relative advancement in the community of scholars. They were clean-cut young men in their mid-twenties, dressed in summer suits of tasteful cut. In answer to a question of mine, we talked about Constitutional Law for ten minutes before I realized they were talking about *State* Constitutional Law. When it became apparent what I was driving at, however, they were quick to face the issue squarely.

"*We* nevuh had no Negra problem heah," said one of them, shaking his head sadly. He was a serious young man wearing glasses and the mien of a Harvard divinity student. "Theah just *weren't* no problem—wasn't till these *agi-ta-tors* came down heah started all this problem business."

They were particularly disturbed about the possible "trouble, an' I mean *real* trouble" which would be occasioned by the attempted registration of a Negro student [James Meredith] which was threatening to take place quite soon, during that very summer session, in fact. As it happened, the authorities managed to delay it; I did, however, get a preview of things to come.

"Why they'll find *dope* in his room the first night he's heah," the other student said, "dope, a gun, something—*anything*, just plant it in theah an' *find* it! And out he'll go!"

They assured me that they themselves were well above this sort of thing, and were, in fact, speaking as mature and nonviolent persons.

"But now these heah young *unduh* graduates, they're hot-headed. Why, do you know how *they* feel? What *they* say?"

Then to the tune of *John Brown's Body*, the two graduate law students begin to sing, almost simultaneously: *"Oh we'll bury all the niggers in the Mississippi mud . . . "*, singing it rather loudly it seemed to me—I mean if they were just documenting a point in a private conversation—or perhaps they were momentarily carried away, so to speak. In any event, and despite a terrific effort at steely Zen detachment, the incident left me somewhat depressed, so I retired early, to my comfortable room in the Alumni House, where I sipped the white corn and watched television. But I was not destined to escape so easily, for suddenly who should appear on the screen but old Governor Faubus himself—in a gubernatorial campaign rant—with about six cross-purpose facial tics going strong, and in general looking as mad as a hatter. At first I actually mistook it for a rather tasteless and heavy-handed parody of the governor. It could not, I thought, really be Faubus, because why would the network carry an Arkansas primary campaign speech in Mississippi? Surely not just for laughs. Later I learned that while there is such a thing in television as a *nation*wide hookup for covering events of national importance, there is also such a thing as a *South*wide hookup.

The Institute's mimeographed schedule, of which I had received a copy, read for the next day as follows:

7:30	Up and at 'em
8–9	Breakfast—University Cafeteria
9–9:30	Assembly, Limber up, Review—Grove
9:30–10:45	Class No. 4
10:45–11:30	Relax—Make Notes
11:30–12:45	Class No. 5
1–2:30	Lunch—University Cafeteria
2:30–4	Class No. 6
4–5:30	Swim Hour
6:30–7:30	Supper—University Cafeteria
7:30	Dance—Tennis Court
11	Room Check
11:30	Lights Out (NO EXCEPTIONS)

The *"Up and at 'em"* seemed spirited enough, as did the "NO EXCEPTIONS" being in heavy capitals; but the rest somehow offered little promise, so, after a morning cup of coffee, I walked over to the library, just to see if they really had any books there—other than books on Constitutional Law, that is. Indeed they did, and

quite a modern and comfortable structure it was, too, air-conditioned (as was, incidentally, my room at the Alumni House) and well-lighted throughout. After looking
around for a bit, I carefully opened a mint first-edition copy of *Light in August*, and
found "nigger-lover" scrawled across the title page. I decided I must be having a run
of bad luck as, a few minutes later, I suffered still another minor trauma on the steps
of the library. It was one of those incredible bits of irony which sometimes do occur
in life, but are never suitable for fiction—for I had completely put the title-page
incident out of my mind and was sitting on the steps of the library, having a smoke,
when this very amiable gentleman of middle age paused in passing to remark on the
weather (102°) and to inquire in an oblique and courteous way as to the nature of
my visit. An immaculate, pink-faced man, with pince-nez spectacles attached by a
silver loop to his lapel, nails buffed to a gleam, he carried a smart leather briefcase
and a couple of English-literature textbooks which he rested momentarily on the
balustrade as he continued to smile down on me with what seemed to be extraordinary happiness.

"My, but it's a mighty warm day, an' that's no lie," he said, withdrawing a dazzling white-linen handkerchief and touching it carefully to his brow; ". . . an' I
expect you all from up Nawth," he added with a twinkle, "find it especially so!"
Then he quite abruptly began to talk of the "natural tolerance" of the people of
Mississippi, speaking in joyfully objective tones, as though it were, even to him, an
unfailing source of mystery and delight.

"Don't mind nobody's business but yoah own!" he said, beaming and nodding
his head—and it occurred to me this might be some kind of really weirdly obscured
threat, the way he was smiling; but no, evidently he was just remarkably good-
natured. "'Live an' let live!' That's how the people of Mississippi feel—always
have! Why, look at William Faulkner, with all his notions, an' him livin' right ovah
heah in Oxford all the time an' nobody botherin' him—just let him go his own
way—why we even let him teach heah at the University one yeah! That's right! I
know it! Live an' let live—you can't beat it! I'll see you now, you heah?" And his
face still a glittering mask of joviality, he half raised his hand in good-by and hurried on. Who was this strange, happy educator? Was it he who had defaced the title
page? His idea of tolerance and his general hilarity gave one pause. I headed back to
the grove, hoping to recover some equilibrium. There, things seemed to be proceed-
ing pretty much as ever.

"Do you find that your costume is an advantage in your work?" I asked the first
seventeen-year-old Georgia Peach I came across, she wearing something like a
handkerchief-size Confederate flag.

"Yessuh, I *do*," she agreed, with friendly emphasis, tucking her little blouse in a
bit more snugly all around, and continuing to speak in the oddly rising inflection
peculiar to girls of the South, making parts of a reply sound like a question: "Why,
back home near Macon . . . Macon, Georgia? At Robert E. Lee High? . . . we've got
these outfits with *tassels*! And a little red-and-gold skirt? . . . that, you know, sort of
flares out? Well, now they're awful pretty, and of course they're *short* and everything, but I declare those tassels and that little skirt get in my way!"

The rest of the day passed without untoward incident, with my observing the Strut platform for a while, then withdrawing to rest up for the Dance, and perhaps catch the Faub on video again.

The Dance was held on a boarded-over outdoor tennis court, and was a swinging affair. The popular style of dancing in the white South is always in advance of that in the rest of white America; and, at any given moment, it most nearly resembles that which is occurring at the same time in Harlem, which is invariably the forerunner of whatever is to become the national style. I mused on this, standing there near the court foul line, and (in view of the day's events) pursued it to an interesting generalization: perhaps *all* the remaining virtues, or let us say, positive traits, of the white Southerner—folk song, poetic speech, and the occasional warmth and simplicity of human relationships—would seem rather obviously to derive from the colored culture there. Due to my magazine assignment, I could not reveal my findings over the public-address system at the dance—and, in fact, thought best to put them from my mind entirely, and get on with the coverage—and, to that end, had a few dances and further questioned the girls. Their view of the world was quite extraordinary. For most, New York was like another country—queer, remote, and of small import in the scheme of things. Several girls spoke spiritedly of wanting to "get into television," but it always developed that they were talking about programs produced in Memphis. Memphis, in fact, was definitely the mecca, yardstick and *summum bonum*. As the evening wore on I found it increasingly difficult, despite the abundance of cutie pieness at hand, to string along with these values, and so finally decided to wrap it up. It should be noted too, that girls at the Dixie National are under extremely close surveillance both in the grove and out.

The following day I made one last tour, this time noting in particular the instruction methods for advanced twirling techniques: *1-, 2-, 3-finger rolls, wrist rolls, waist roll, neck roll*, etc. A pretty girl of about twelve was tossing a baton sixty feet straight up, a silver whir in the Mississippi sunlight, and she beneath it spinning like an ice skater, and catching it behind her back, not having moved an inch. She said she had practiced it an hour a day for six years. Her hope was to become "the best there is at the high toss and spin"—and she was now up to seven complete turns before making the catch. Was there a limit to the height and number of spins one could attain? No, she guessed not.

After lunch I packed, bid adieu to the Dixie National and boarded the bus for Memphis. As we crossed the Oxford square and passed the courthouse, I saw the fountain was still shaded, although it was now a couple of hours later than the time before. Perhaps it is always shaded—cool and inviting, it could make a person thirsty just to see it.

From PRAYING FOR SHEETROCK

MELISSA   FAY   GREENE

Editor's Note: *In 1975 Melissa Fay Greene graduated from Oberlin College in Ohio and returned to her home state of Georgia with high ideals. As a VISTA (Volunteers in Service to America) worker, she was assigned to the Savannah office of the Georgia Legal Services Program. Into her office came white and black Georgians in need of legal aid, with stories she found unforgettable in their range and nuance.*

"I loved their voices," she confesses. "I gathered material for years with no plot, no book, no story in mind. I just wanted to get their stories before they died. With their deaths would go the last faithful images."

After more than ten years as a dedicated oral historian, Greene recognized she had a story to tell, the story of how the Civil Rights movement came twenty years late to a forgotten county on the Georgia coast. In the salt marshes of McIntosh County (population 7,000), the civil rights revolution of the 1960s seemed "a fabulous tale about distant places," Greene reports. "In every community, there had to be created a local Civil Rights movement, with its own ideology."

Through evocative scenes and sequential narration, *Greene's* Praying for Sheetrock *introduces us to Sheriff Tom Poppell, who ruled McIntosh County as if it were his personal kingdom, and to Thurnell Alston, the black former boilermaker who rose up against him. To add to her stock of stories, Greene interviewed everyone she could find who knew or remembered Sheriff Poppell or Thurnell Alston. These included the dean of the Emory University Law School in Atlanta and lawyers, police officers, restaurant owners, and many others. Greene was seeking "the numberless secret and eccentric tales—unwritten and untold (unless one pries and sits and waits, and comes back another day to sit and wait again for a candle to be carried into a pitch-black, long sealed-up room of the soul)."*

Greene's patience at last brought light. Her deep sense of place, character, and event is evident in the authority of her voice and in her work's profusion of detail. Greene's scenes *awake all the senses. Her arresting opening sentence is followed by passages which make us see the fog, hear the tires squeal, and feel the scrape of metal against metal. Characters come to life through revealing details of dress and manner, and Greene's narrative overflows with voices.*

"At some point it crossed my mind to write [this story] as a novel," Greene acknowledges, "but with material this rich it seems somehow lessened by fiction."

Praying for Sheetrock *was written for those who think all racial problems were corrected in the 1960s. Greene dares to insist that the true civil rights story in America is forged far removed from the glare of cameras, violent confrontations, and charismatic leaders. Where others found only a place to gas up and get back on the road, Greene found the day-to-day meaning of accommodation. In the process she has enlarged our understanding of the civil rights struggle. She asserts, in fact, that the story is still unfolding:*

The life of Thurnell Alston is at this moment being transformed and suffused with meaning, stitched into the quilt of the county's age-old oral history, the stories reaching back to slave times. This quilt is pulled out and shaken and reworked while the black people saw trees, haul in the fish nets, peel the shrimps, sit side by side in the cinder-block juke joints, and circle the smoky grills of backyard barbecue pits, balancing babies and full paper plates.

Prologue

1

June 1971

Two trucks collided on the crisscrossed highways in the small hours of the morning when the mist was thick. The protesting squeal of metal against metal and smashing glass silenced whatever small noises were afoot in the dark county at that hour, the little noises of munching and grunting that arose from the great salt marsh nearby. At seventy miles per hour, the two semitrailers suddenly had found themselves in the coastal lowlands; the blacktops of the rural state routes were slick; and the truck headlights merely illumined the fog from within as if sheets of satin were draped across the road.

The trucks exploded into each other without braking. After that blast of sound and its fallout of hollow chrome pieces dropping onto the road and rolling away, the quietness of the rural county flowed back in, and the muddy sucking and rustling noises arose again from the marsh. The cabs of the big trucks began to burn, pouring their own heavy smoke into the fog.

The McIntosh County Volunteer Fire Department truck arrived first, unfurling a long red scarf of sound on the country roads behind it. It was the night's second accident. The young firemen drenched the burning cabs, while the county ambulance veered into place and departed with the truck drivers. East of Highway 17, the country itself ran out, softening into marsh on its way to the sea.

The county sheriff, awakened by a phone call for the second time that night, stood alone on the highway in the fog and directed cars with a flashlight around the circle of spilled oil and shivered glass. For fifty years before the construction of modern Interstate 95, on the east coast, old U.S. 17 through McIntosh County was the northerners' main route to Florida. Traffic, even in the middle of the night, was fast and constant.

Soon the sun came out of the ocean, the mist dried up, and shrieks of long-necked birds flew back and forth across the breezy morning marshes. The sheriff, a thin, blue-eyed, silver-haired man of fifty, rolled up his sleeves, removed his sunglasses from their case, wiped them with a handkerchief, blotted his face and neck, and prepared for the daylong siege of the white heat of June along Georgia's subtropical coast.

The High Sheriff, Thomas Hardwick Poppell, was five foot nine and 150 pounds, a slender and nattily dressed man in this coastal population of fishermen and lumberjacks. He was a self-made man and was going to die rich. He cursed like a sailor. "He was a little old dried-up fella," said a former state trooper. "He wasn't your typical south Georgia sheriff. He didn't have the pot belly and all that people think of when they think of a south Georgia sheriff. He never dressed the part. He would have on things like white loafers with a pair of bell-bottom slacks during the years when those things were in, a nice-looking pair of bell-bottom slacks. He'd have on an Izod shirt, maybe a white belt. He was a sharp dresser. And of course that hair was just as white as it could be."

"The sheriff could walk in and sit down anywhere in the county," said one local man, "even if it was your own table and it was suppertime."

And others said, "You weren't scared when you saw him coming, but you could feel the power."

Sheriff Tom Poppell, born in McIntosh County in 1921, was in the midst of a thirty-one-year reign. He had inherited the office from his father, old, cranky, tobacco-chewing Sheriff Ad Poppell, who died in 1948. The sheriff's eighty-year-old mother, Janey Poppell, was the county jailer, lived on the top floor of the city jail, and cooked for the prisoners. The sheriff's sister, Maude Poppell Haggard, was the county clerk, and his brother, A. S. "Junior" Poppell, was clerk of superior court. Sheriff Tom Poppell was to be reelected to office every term until his own death, completing the longest-running sheriff's dynasty in the history of Georgia, and after he died the county commission would try to make his *wife* sheriff.

"If he hadn't died, Tom'd *still* be sheriff," many people said in the 1990s. And others remarked, "Yeah, and he died unindicted."

With daylight Sheriff Poppell knew, and the firefighters knew, and the deputies knew, and the people in the cabins in the surrounding woods knew—and if the truck drivers had realized their trucks had crashed in McIntosh County, Georgia (431 miles of swamp, marsh, and forest: population 7,000) *they* would have known—that it was nearing time for a little redistribution of wealth. It was one of the things for which Tom Poppell was famous across the South. It was one of the things that invariably put the sheriff in an excellent mood.

In midmorning the local black population began to gather at the crash site. They parked their cars down the road near the sheriff's jeep and walked north along the highway, shielding their faces against the spray of steam and ash stirred up by the firefighters. The people chatted as they came. Women wore shoulder bags and immense flowered dresses; men in sleeveless undershirts and beaten old fedoras led small children by the hand. The wreck had occurred at the crossroads called Eulonia in the deeply wooded north end of the county. This had been the dark, rich territory of the black people since the end of the Civil War, when William Tecumseh Sherman himself had waved a pistol at the district and given it to the newly freed slaves. Thus, it was a black crowd which assembled that day. Had the crash occurred fifteen miles to the south, closer to the majority-white county seat of Darien, a white crowd would have gathered.

"Good morning, Sheriff!" called the black women in their musical voices, and he, on the road, unsmilingly raised one hand at a slant to return the greeting.

One of the two wrecked trucks had overturned and spilled its cargo onto the highway, and it was around this unidentified heap of goods that the people congregated. The sheriff watched in the distance as a few black men stopped to straighten out and tear open the tumbled-out cartons and learn what he himself had discovered in the dark that morning: the truck had been transporting shoes. The country people sedately divided up the shoe cartons and opened them with a pop-pop-pop of pulled-apart staples, then passed around the fresh shoe boxes. They hummed with pleasure at the beautiful new shoes—red leather, black leather, green leather—lying two-by-two in tissue paper wrappings. The people stacked the purloined shoe boxes in their arms and walked carefully along the highway back to their cars. They drove home to their cabins and house trailers deep in the pine woods, and sat on benches under the trees, calling for the grandchildren to come try some on, and pointing their toes this way and that.

All day long under a sky like white coals the High Sheriff stood spread-legged on the highway, directing traffic; the road crews swept and shoveled; and hundreds of local families quietly harvested shoes. Some called out, "Thank you, sir!" as they left, and others caught the sheriff's eye and nodded or touched a finger to their hats; and Poppell turned his glittering sunglasses and sunburnt face in their direction, his thin lips a straight white line, and as before raised and dropped one hand in response.

"It was the spirit of fleecing the Yankees that was tolerated by even the law-abiding citizens, I suppose," said Woody Hunter, dean of the Emory University Law School and a former resident of McIntosh. "Tom Poppell was Billy the Kid. He was Robin Hood."

"It wasn't like the sheriff encouraged it," said a former volunteer fireman, a white native of McIntosh who had helped to fight the blazing shoe truck twenty years earlier and had watched the people come for their shoes. "We had the postwar South, the poorest-of-the-poor South right here in McIntosh County. It was the dirt-poor type of people swarmed the place like ants, and Tom wasn't about to stop anybody from getting a pair of shoes."

"The sheriff knew people can't walk a damn straight line," said Archie Davis, owner of a restaurant called Archie's, in Darien. "He wasn't a chain-gang recruiter. You're talking about a time when people had no money. Every one of us, if we'd look back, we'd change things—we'd like a clean slate. I don't know how to say it other than he was a regular person. If someone's house burned, he'd be the first one there to help him.

"He had a lot of charisma. He was the kind of guy you might fight him politically, but when it was over and you were in trouble, he was the first one to help you. You build a base with that—I'm talking local people, 95 percent born and bred here. He didn't walk on water, he was just good people. If you weren't careful, he'd be your best friend."

"He would handle everything just as cool and brilliant, just country brilliance is all I know how to describe it," said a Darien lawyer. "Amazing what he could get done with a couple of phone calls. Now the court system is full of all sorts of little junk, but back then the sheriff was judge, jury, and monarch. He'd help a young man out of trouble the first time. But then a lot of people he flat run out of the county because they wouldn't abide by his law. We lived under Poppell's Law, I guess you'd say. He just wrote his own law."

In 1971, Tom Poppell was a dinosaur, the last of his kind. Statewide observers called him "the last of the old-time political bosses in Georgia." Georgia State Troopers, Georgia Bureau of Investigation agents, FBI agents, DEA agents, and U.S. Customs agents up and down the southern coast all agreed with the words of a Brunswick police detective: "The only crime that *existed* in McIntosh County was Tom Poppell's. He was the last of the great old-time High Sheriffs."

2

The shoe truck was not the first wrecked or sabotaged truck on Highway 17 to be looted under the supervision of the McIntosh County Sheriff's Department, nor was it the last truck or even the best, but it was a fine truck and is fondly remembered.

It *was* the first crash site attended by a local black man named Thurnell Alston, who trudged among the others that day and filched a few shoes. He was a boiler-maker living with his wife and children in a narrow cinder-block house ten yards from U.S. 17. He was a tall, thin, chain-smoking black man with bushy, blue-black hair; a long, rather sorrowful face; slate-black skin; and elegant, long hands. He had lived in McIntosh County all his life, and was related by blood or marriage to proba-bly a third of the black community there.

Before the decade was out, Thurnell Alston was advanced by the black commu-nity to challenge the rule of Sheriff Poppell. But on that summer day in 1971, with politics the last thing on his mind, Thurnell idly drifted alongside his neighbors north on U.S. 17 to the overturned truck and rummaged through the boxes. "Sure I got shoes, we all got shoes," he said. "Word just got out there was a truck wrecked in our area. People coming by with shoes. Guys had boxes of shoes all in the woods: 'Come get you a pair of shoes!'

"'Where you get them from?'

"'Man, they got a whole truckload down there!'"

"There was always some truck wrecking down there," he said. "The people around McIntosh get all the benefits from it. All our lives, people always saying, 'Hey, the sheriff give this to me!' These people haven't been nowhere else. The sheriff just really had them hoodwinked. They're just ignorant to what's going on. When there's somebody the sheriff wants elected, you know, you see him and his mother riding around. And these older black people say, 'There go Miss Janey! There go the sheriff! How you doing, Miss Janey? How you doing, Sheriff?' And all this is for votes. The people here were just happy with nothing. It was a plantation mentality. The sheriff was running this county just like an old plantation."

McIntosh County citizens remember fondly not only the shoe truck but trucks full of canned goods, fresh produce and meats, building materials and tools, cookies and cakes, candy and guns, and once, fur stoles and fur coats. All of the cargoes disappeared, and the trucking companies were compelled to report "total loss" to their insurance carriers. "Anything trucks be carrying from Miami to New York, from New York to Miami," said Thurnell Alston, "whatever it was, whatever of value was in those trucks during those times, that's probably in McIntosh County right now today."

Years after the movement for civil equality between the races began to transform the rest of the South, news of it barely had filtered into McIntosh County. In 1971 McIntosh County was a majority-black county with virtually 100 percent black voter registration. Yet the residents had never elected a black person to the mayor's office, the county commission, the city council, or the school board; had never seen a black person appointed to any governing board or selected for grand jury or trial jury service; had not elected a black to state government since the end of Reconstruction; and had not seen any black person hired by any local employer above the level of unskilled laborer, maid, or cook. The black residents saw their children bussed past the white school to an all-black school furnished with used supplies and outdated textbooks.

At the time of the shoe truck in 1971, the black community of McIntosh County was blind and deaf to issues of civil equality, equal employment, and local corruption. On the day of the shoe truck, the people were still years away from balking at Sheriff Poppell's authority. On that day their minds were otherwise occupied. On that day the people had new shoes to try on.

From FRIENDLY FIRE

C . D . B .   B R Y A N

Editor's Note: Courtlandt Dixon Barnes Bryan is the tall, lean stepson of the legendary writer John O'Hara. Bryan graduated from Yale University in 1958 and served in the army in Korea before turning himself to writing fiction and nonfiction in the 1960s.

The most remarkable aspect of Bryan's nonfiction classic Friendly Fire *is not the story itself but the enlarging vision of the author who presents himself as a character in the story. In 1971, Bryan journeyed to the Iowa farm of Peg and Gene Mullen to learn how the loss of a son in the Vietnam War had transformed a "silent majority" family into outspoken war protesters. What begins as a detective story (Bryan's efforts to help the Mullens learn how their son, Michael, died by "friendly" rather than by enemy fire), turns into the story of the effect of this experience upon Peg Mullen, and, by extension, America.*

The excerpts from Friendly Fire *presented here illustrate many of the artful literary techniques Bryan employs to re-create his story. At the height of his sequential narration of events, he will pause to* flash back *to revealing prior moments. Indeed, the volume builds to the final extended flashback to Vietnam and Bryan's careful reconstruction of Michael Mullen's death. At moments, Bryan will also pull back from his compelling story to place the Mullen's quest within the unfolding political context, or to locate himself as the chronicler of the story and reveal his enlarging vision.*

Readers of this progressively horrifying tale repeat the experience of those reading the great tragedies, such as Oedipus Rex *or* King Lear. *Bryan (and then the reader) moves from sympathy for the Mullens to final horror, and to recognition that an act of war has damaged more than its immediate victim. Bryan's vision and revision of the Mullen family story lost him the friendship of Peg Mullen. His self-correcting, enlarging vision proved so haunting that* Friendly Fire *was named the best nonfiction book of 1976 by the* New York Daily News *and was made into a Peabody and Emmy Award-winning docudrama.*

Michael Mullen, like his family, had no reason to believe that the previous President, John Fitzgerald Kennedy, had committed advisers and Special Forces troops to Vietnam for any more sinister reason than that Americans wanted the Vietnamese to have what the Vietnamese were supposed to want for themselves: the freedom to resist Communist aggression, to survive as a nation, to *become like us.* The Mullens believed we were in Vietnam to defend it. They believed Vietnam was a moral war, that if Vietnam fell, all Southeast Asia would fall to Communism with it. They believed it possible to equate our presence in Vietnam with our presence in Korea and our participation in the Second World War. The Mullens believed, in other words, what they were being told.

In February, 1965, President Johnson commenced Operation Rolling Thunder, the sustained air bombardment of North Vietnam. Michael called his mother from Rockhurst, "You remember kidding me about Barry Goldwater?" he asked. "Well, who's 'trigger-happy' now?"

That June U.S. military commanders were authorized to send American troops into combat. One month later President Johnson sanctioned the increase of U.S. forces in Vietnam from 75,000 to 125,000 men. The Mullens were concerned by the growing war and the escalating troop commitment, but they did not protest. They simply hoped the war would end.

La Porte City had by this time grown into a predominantly Protestant, Republican town with a population of a little over 2,000. It had more churches than taverns, and the proud brick fronts of its turn-of-the-century stores had darkened and become grimy with age. The town was clearly losing business to the newer, bigger shopping centers on the road to Waterloo. There was little new construction in La Porte, no more than two or three houses a year. The signboard on the outskirts of town listing the churches and the Rotary and Chamber of Commerce meetings had begun losing its paint. One didn't see many young people lounging about the streets, and La Porte City's only non-Caucasian was an Indian woman on welfare.

The citizens of La Porte thought well of the Mullens, spoke of them as "hard workers." They appreciated how difficult life had been for Peg having to take care of Gene's sick parents and four young kids. They saw, too, that she did not give herself any rest when Gene's parents died in 1960. Instead, to help pay for the hospital and funeral expenses, Peg returned to work. She became an executive secretary for an advertising specialty business in Waterloo. Peg had always been politically active in the local Democratic Party; she attended every state convention and always took time off to meet each candidate who came into town. But she continued active in volunteer work as well and remained teaching catechism classes at the Sacred Heart Catholic Church. By this time Gene had worked his way up to becoming a quality control inspector at John Deere.

The Mullen children, too, were well liked. They stayed out of trouble, got good grades, were popular with their classmates. Peg and Gene Mullen are innately generous, decent people, and they brought up their children to believe in the same basic values with which they themselves had been brought up. When the Mullens spoke of themselves, they described themselves as being "average" or "typical" or "good, solid citizens" in no way different from others in their neighboring communities. They would explain their behavior and responses as that of the "working class," as "farmers," and if they identified themselves as representative of any groups, it was as "Catholics," as "Democrats," "Irish-Americans," or "Iowans" and as being from a background typical of the "Silent Majority."

* * *

That morning the sun had finally broken through the flat pearl-gray overcast that had been brooding over the Mullens' farm. Although the temperature hovered near freezing, the week-long Arctic winds had ceased, and at last it again felt warm enough to be outside.

Gene Mullen walked back from the mailbox to the house. As he climbed the stairs into the kitchen, he called out, "Letter from Mikey." He dropped the bills, the Des Moines *Register* and the second-class mail on the kitchen table and tore open the envelope. Peg wiped her hands on a dish towel and put a kettle of water on to boil.

"What's he say?" she asked. "When did he write it?"

Gene glanced at the top of the letter. "Dated the thirteenth," he said. "Let's see now 'Dear Mom and Dad: Went down off the hill to get a haircut and clean up, but ended up hitching a ride to Chu Lai. Went to the MARS station by chance—they were open and not busy—so got a chance to call. Suppose it was midnight at home and guess you were surprised—'"

"Oh," Peg said, "he must have written this the same day he called." Gene had not been home when Michael had telephoned from Vietnam eight days earlier. Peg had written "Mike called" on an envelope and left it on the kitchen table for Gene to read following the late shift at John Deere. It was twelve thirty by the time Gene returned to the farm, and after reading the note, he woke Peg up. She told him that she had spoken with Michael for only about a minute and a half and that before hanging up, Michael had said, "Good-bye, Mom, it's so bad here. . . ." Peg had been so depressed that she hadn't felt like waiting up to tell Gene when he came home and had simply left him a note. She mixed Gene a mug of instant coffee, brought it to him at the kitchen table and sat down. "What else does he say?"

"He says, '. . . guess you were surprised,' . . . now, here: 'Will be on the bunker line about two more days, then back out into the field.'"

"Ugh!" Peg groaned. "That means more search and destroy."

"No, it doesn't," Gene said. "He's been doing company sweep like he wrote in the other letter."

"Same thing," Peg said.

"No, it isn't," Gene insisted. "A company sweep is—"

Peg waved her hand impatiently. "Go on with the letter."

"All right, all right. He says, 'Glad that all is well—weather here been rather good. Have decided not to take R&R if I can get a drop. So 'til later, hang loose.'" Gene looked at the letter more closely. "Hang loose?"

"Hang loose, you know," Peg said, "take it easy."

Gene shrugged. "'So 'til later, hang loose. Love Michael.'"

"That's it?"

"That's it," Gene said. He passed the letter across the table to his wife.

Peg read through it quickly, "Oh, see," she said, "he's decided for sure to ask for an early drop. You remember the letter before last Michael said he was writing the University of Missouri to get the necessary papers."

Michael hoped to be released early from Vietnam so that he could be readmitted to the Agriculture School. Peg and Gene discussed for a moment what they thought his chances were; Michael himself had written that he felt they were very good. The only part of his letter that bothered them was that he would again be going into the field, that he wouldn't be in the relative safety of the fire base bunker line anymore. Still, in one of his first letters Michael had written that he was in "probably one of the better places over here," a comparatively quiet part of Vietnam.

"So he might be coming home in June," Gene said.

"Looks that way," Peg said, "knock wood."

Gene finished his coffee and stood up "Well, Mother," he said, "I guess I might as well try to fix the television antenna for you."

"What's it like outside?"

"Fine," Gene said. "Cold, but it's fine. The wind's stopped."

He buttoned up his heavy woolen red and black plaid lumber jacket, turned off his hearing aid, put the earplug into his pocket and went outside.

The windblown television antenna was attached to a post near the east side of the farmhouse. Gene was just coming around that east corner, blowing hot breath on his fingertips and trying to remember where he had last put the light wrench he would need when, out of the corner of his eye, he noticed two automobiles turning into his driveway. Without his hearing aid he had not heard them approach and he fumbled beneath his lumber jacket for the earpiece, inserted it and thumbed the volume up.

Gene thought he recognized the first car, believed the parish priest, Father Shimon, had one like it, but that second car. . . . Gene read the black letters painted on the Chevrolet's olive-drab door: U.S. ARMY—FOR OFFICIAL USE ONLY. Gene's chest tightened, and he stood still while the priest and the Army sergeant stepped out of their cars and slammed shut the doors.

Gene watched them walking toward him as if in slow motion, their footsteps thundering across the metallic crust of the drifted snow. He tried to see beyond the country priest's black metal-framed glasses to what might show in his eyes. But Father Shimon's downcast lenses reflected only the snow. Not until the priest forced himself to look up did Gene recognize the fright, the despair, the agony within them, then very quietly Gene asked, "Is my boy dead?"

Father Shimon halted so abruptly that the Army sergeant, who was following, bumped into him from behind. "Gene," the priest said, "this is Sergeant Fitzgerald. He's from Fifth Army Headquarters. He. . . ." Shimon was silent.

Gene looked beyond Father Shimon to the sergeant and asked again, "Is . . . my . . . boy . . . *dead?*"

"Let's go into the house, Gene," Father Shimon said. "I want to talk to you there."

"No!" Gene said, not moving. "I want to *know!* Tell me, *is . . . my . . . boy . . . dead?*"

"I can't tell you here," Father Shimon said, his hand fluttering up toward Gene's shoulder "Come into the house with us . . . please?"

Gene spun away before the priest's pale fingers could touch him.

Peg Mullen heard the back door open, heard Gene rushing up the stairs into the kitchen, heard him shouting, *"It's Mikey! It's Mikey!"* his voice half a sob, half a scream.

She hurried out of the sewing room in time to glimpse the Army uniform entering the kitchen. Peg found Gene standing with his back to the sink, clutching the counter behind him, the Army sergeant halted just to the side of the doorway. Father Shimon, between them, had removed his glasses to wipe away the steam. Peg started to move toward her husband but had to turn away. Never had she seen such terrible devastation in his face, so raw a wound. She looked next at the sergeant, who avoided her eyes by glancing at the priest whose job it was to tell them. But Father Shimon would not stop wiping his glasses, and Peg, feeling herself wanting to scream, to kick over a chair, to thrash about, to do *anything* rather than listen to this awful silence a moment longer, saw her husband's lips move as if to say, "It's Mikey," but no sound would come out.

Peg scowled at the Army sergeant and said, "Michael died on Thursday."

Thursday morning, upon waking up, Peg had burst into tears for no apparent reason. Off and on that entire day she had cried, and so that Gene wouldn't know, she had spent the morning by herself down in the sewing room. She decided to make new curtains for the boys' room, and she sewed and sewed but would have to stop because she would begin crying again and couldn't see the material through her tears. She would wait for the tears to pass, pull herself together and sew some more until finally, a little after two o'clock, when she heard Gene leave for the John Deere plant in Waterloo, she stopped sewing altogether.

The following day, yesterday, Friday, Peg had awakened not sad, just angry. No matter what Gene said to her she snapped back, contradicting him, defying him. And seeing the hurt and confusion in his face, she wanted to apologize but instead became angrier still for feeling that need. At noon Peg felt she simply had to get out of the house. She drove off to spend the day with friends who shared her feelings about the war, with whom she could talk about how worried she was, how frustrated she felt trying to find something meaningful to do.

* * *

Yesterday she had not returned to the farm until dusk and, to keep busy, had begun to clean house. For the next six hours she scrubbed and dusted, waxed and polished, pausing only at ten o'clock for the late evening news on television. There was an account of an accidental shelling at Bien Hoa by South Vietnamese artillery resulting in the deaths of about a dozen American men. The story stuck in Peg's mind when she went back to cleaning, and at midnight she called one of the friends she had seen that afternoon to ask if she had watched the news. They talked about how the accidental shelling seemed to epitomize the stupidity and wastefulness of the Vietnam War. Peg told her friend how busy she had been cleaning, that she had felt this compulsion to polish the house from top to bottom. The friend asked Peg if she were expecting visitors.

"No, none that I know of," Peg had said. "I don't know what's going on with me—I really don't. But whatever it is," she added, "I'm ready."

The Army sergeant did not answer her, so Peg spoke again, "Did Michael die on Thursday?"

"Why do you ask me when he died?" Sergeant Fitzgerald said. "I haven't told you your son is dead."

Peg glared at him with such utter contempt that the sergeant flinched. "You *know* the Army doesn't come to tell parents that their sons are wounded!" Peg said. "You know the Army comes only when they're *dead*!"

The sergeant again turned to the priest, waiting for Father Shimon to break the news, to speak. But the priest was incapable of talking.

Very slowly, deliberately, almost threateningly, Gene Mullen pushed himself away from the sink and moved toward the two men. "Now I want to know the truth!" he told them. "Is . . . my . . . boy . . . dead?"

Sergeant Fitzgerald looked at the priest, then back at Gene and said, "Yes."

And, "Yes-s-s-s," Father Shimon said, too, as if he had been holding his breath all this time. "Yes, Gene, yes, Peg, I'm sorry, yes-s-s-s."

Gene sagged as if hit. He looked at Peg and she at him. Gene stumbled backward until he was again against the sink. He shook his head to and fro like a groggy fighter trying to clear his brain. He began to cry gentle tears that welled up hot in his eyes, overflowed and traced down his cheeks. "Why?" he said to no one in particular. "Why?"

Peg had moved to the kitchen table and stood now gripping the wooden rung of a chairback until she felt herself under enough control to speak. Then she asked the sergeant how Michael had been killed.

Sergeant Fitzgerald sorted through some papers and pulled one out. "I only know the official casualty message given me by Fifth Army Headquarters this morning over the phone."

"Read it," Peg said.

The sergeant lifted the paper to the light. "It states that 'Sergeant (E–5) Michael Eugene Mullen, US 54 93—' so on, 'died while at a night defensive position when artillery fire from friendly forces landed in the area.'" Sergeant Fitzgerald's hand dropped. "I'm sorry . . . I really am very sorry, Mr. and Mrs. Mullen. . . ." He put the paper away and began buttoning up his trench coat as if to leave. "Generally, at this time," he said, "families of casualties prefer to be alone with their priests—"

"Sit down," Peg said quietly.

"Perhaps," Sergeant Fitzgerald was saying, "tomorrow would be a better time to—"

"*Sit down!*" Peg repeated firmly. "We're going to talk about this message, this, this official casualty report."

Gene watched the sergeant leaf back through his papers, start to say, "Mrs. Mullen, I only—"

"Sergeant," Gene ordered, "read that thing again."

Fitzgerald cleared his throat. "'Sergeant (E–5) Michael Eugene Mullen, US 54 93 22 54, died while at a night defensive position when artillery fire from friendly forces landed in the area.'" He looked up from the paper. "That's all it says . . . really."

"Listen," Gene said, "I was a master sergeant in the United States Army, myself, during World War Two, and I . . . and I. . . ." He stopped, no longer certain what the point was that he had wished to make.

"We're going to talk about this message," Peg said. "I want you to explain it to me. This word, what do you mean by 'friendly'?"

"It merely means that it wasn't enemy artillery," the sergeant said. "Your son was killed by friendly fire."

"Friendly fire? *Friendly fire?*" Peg repeated incredulously.

Sergeant Fitzgerald shrugged lamely. "It means any artillery from forces not the enemy."

"*Not* the enemy! *Goddamn you!*" Peg cried, beating the chairback with her fists in frustration. "You couldn't even give him the . . . the decency of being killed by the enemy!" She glared at the sergeant. "These, these 'friendly forces not the enemy,' how come the word 'American' isn't used?"

* * *

Michael's casket was taken inside the Loomis Funeral Home, and Tom Loomis, the director, asked Gene to wait in the vestibule while the casket was opened. Sergeant Fitzgerald followed Loomis, and Gene, Mary and John stayed behind. They sat silently, patiently in the vestibule wondering whether they could be certain it was Michael, worried that his body would have been so shattered by the artillery shell's explosion that they might never be able to know. After about twenty minutes Tom Loomis called down to Gene that he could now view the body. Gene rose and glanced, stricken, at his children.

"We'll be all right, Dad. You go ahead," John said.

Mary gave her father's hand a gentle squeeze. "We'll come up after a while."

Gene Mullen nodded and slowly turned away. He took a few steps and paused at the doorway of the funeral parlor's viewing room. The casket was in a far corner, and he forced himself to raise his eyes to look at it. The casket's lid was up, and Gene noticed Tom Loomis standing somberly to one side. Feeling apprehensive and ill, Gene walked forward until he could see a uniformed body inside. Despairingly, haltingly, he took another step. And another. Then Gene stopped, looked reluctantly at the face and quickly away.

It was Michael, his son. There was no question about it.

Gene Mullen steeled himself, made himself move right next to the coffin, close enough to touch the cold hands so carefully folded across his son's chest. Gene examined the military tunic, the strangeness of its brass buttons, the uniform jacket's lapels with the brass infantry and U.S. insignia, the black Army tie, the starched khaki collar's points, the throat, the lower jaw, the still blue lips, the mustache—the *mustache?* Michael had a mustache! When had he grown a mustache? But it wasn't the mustache that bothered Gene. There was something else. Gene wasn't sure what; he just sensed there was something wrong. Suddenly Gene realized there wasn't a mark on his son.

Gene looked up at the funeral director in bewilderment, then back down. He noticed that Michael's face was a little puffy, his neck seemed swollen, but if it weren't for the uniform, there would be no sign that Michael had been in a war at all. In exasperation and puzzlement, Gene removed his glasses and wiped his hands across his eyes.

"Something wrong, Gene?" the funeral director asked.

"But, Tom, he was supposed to have been killed by *artillery!*"

"When we lifted the body up out of the casket—we had to," Loomis explained; "because it had settled into it a little—I couldn't feel any broken bones or abrasions. . . ."

"Do you think he could have been killed by the concussion?"

"I couldn't say," Loomis said. "I just couldn't tell you that. I don't know." The funeral director leaned forward and traced his finger beneath Michael's khaki shirt collar. "There's some tape along here," he said, "but that's where they embalmed him."

Gene looked again at his son. For some reason Michael's coal black hair (which even when he had left was already thickly flecked with white) had now become a strange and alien brown. He noticed that his son's complexion, which had always been dark, almost mahogany-colored, seemed gray, chalky, a pallor foreign even to death. But Michael's hair and complexion were the only things that seemed wrong, and Gene kept asking himself how could Michael have been killed by an artillery burst, an explosion of burning jagged chunks of shrapnel, and still be perfectly whole? The more Gene tried to understand it, the more agitated and suspicious he became until finally, unable to tolerate it any longer, Gene asked the funeral director where Sergeant Fitzgerald had gone.

"I'm right here, Mr. Mullen," Fitzgerald said. The sergeant had been standing out of the way at the back of the room. He now came forward.

Gene scowled at the sergeant. "Now I want to know *how*-my-son-*died*! I want a death certificate. I want a death certificate stating how my son was killed!"

While Gene waited impatiently, Sergeant Fitzgerald opened an accordion-pleated manila file folder. He fiddled through the papers while Gene grew angrier and angrier, and when the sergeant pulled a sheet of paper from the folder, it was the same paper from which he had read the official casualty message to the Mullens. Fitzgerald simply began to cover it again: ". . . died while at a night defensive position when artillery fire from friendly forces—"

"That's not it! You know that isn't it!" Gene interrupted indignantly. "Look at him! Look at his body! There isn't a mark on him. Now let's get down to the bottom of that stack of papers and find out. I want to know—I want a death certificate. I want this confirmed before I bury that boy, or I'm going to have that body held."

* * *

I didn't know of the Mullens when we lived in Iowa: La Porte City was about seventy-five miles to our north, and we had no reason to travel there. The Mullens' half-page advertisement appeared in the Des Moines *Register* almost a year after we had left. It wasn't until November, 1970, when I stopped off in Iowa for a few days to visit friends, that I heard about the Mullens at all.

Vance Bourjaily, the writer, and his wife, Tina, and I were sitting by the fireplace of their Iowa farmhouse having a drink and watching the late-afternoon sky make up its mind whether to snow or not. We had been talking, naturally, about other writers and their books, but inevitably our conversation drifted to the Vietnam War. Tina asked me if I had heard of Peg Mullen. Vance had met her when they had flown about Iowa in behalf of the 609 amendment. Tina told me how Mrs. Mullen's son had been killed in Vietnam and instead of shutting up about it like a good patriotic Gold Star mother, she had angrily published an antiwar ad. Both Vance and Tina thought Mrs. Mullen might be worth looking into, that it sounded like a good story. "Mom's Apple Pie Gone Sour," I remember, was Tina's phrase. Still, I couldn't help asking myself who was left in America who would be willing to read a story which in any way touched the Vietnam War. I certainly didn't want to write one. Like everybody else, I was sick to death of hearing about Vietnam.

It took me six months to change my mind, six more months of watching the casualty figures on the evening television news before I realized that I was losing my capacity for outrage and shock, that I was simply acquiescing in what this nation's leaders were permitting our country to become.

* * *

The turning point came for me when the President went out to Kansas State and told his audience, "The heart of America is sound. . . . The heart of America is good!" This simply wasn't true.

The heart of America was broken over the deaths of its young in Vietnamese jungles, in bunkers along the Cambodian border, in helicopters over Laos, on campus hilltops in Ohio and in dormitories at Jackson State. If the President thought otherwise, then, it seemed to me, it was a clear case of "The Emperor's Clothes." Could he be so out of touch that he was unaware of the growing hostility and frustration throughout the country? Wherever he went, he was met by protesters and picket signs. It further seemed to me that Mr. Nixon should have come away from his Kansas State experience impressed not, as he had bragged, that it was still possible for him to receive a resounding ovation from college students, but that he should have had to go to a Kansas State to receive one.

* * *

I spent five days with the Mullens that April out on their farm for the most part listening to them talk about their son, Michael, what a fine, hardworking young man he had been, how he had been active in 4-H projects, had worked his way through college and into graduate school, how he would have been the fifth generation of his family to work the same land homesteaded by his great-great-grandfather John Dobshire, 120 years before. What impressed me most was how positive and unshakable they were in their opinions, as though they were responding to issues the morality of which could be clearly and unmistakenly determined—issues which were, therefore, capable of being judged against existing standards of right and wrong.

The intensity of their indignation wasn't all that overwhelmed me. I was astonished, too, by the seemingly inexhaustible volume of sources their outrage fed upon. Local school board elections, telephone company stock manipulations, draft inequities, Nixon's Vietnamization policies, farm subsidy programs, the voting records of incumbent Congressmen and Senators, the machinations of the military-industrial complex, each seemed to contribute to some consummate proof of a conspiracy on the part of the United States government deliberately to deceive and defraud Mr. and Mrs. Oscar Eugene Mullen of La Porte City, Iowa. It became clear, however, that the Mullens' indignation, their sense of betrayal, stemmed from a vision of an America better fitted, perhaps, to an innocent history primer, one capable of expressing a faith in a simpler America—an America which probably never even used to be. One other thing became clear, too, those first five days: the Mullens' surviving son and daughters would never possess so naïve a confidence in this nation's purpose or its leaders. This, in a very real sense, is as great a tragedy as the loss of a son.

* * *

The following week's mail brought letters of consolation from the commanding general of Michael's Americal Division, Lloyd B. Ramsey, and from Stanley R. Resor, the Secretary of the Army. The Mullens read them searching for a sign that their son's sacrifice had had some meaning. "We sincerely hope that your burden may be lightened by the knowledge that Michael was a model soldier," Major General Ramsey wrote, "whose actions and conduct brought credit to himself, the Division and the United States Army. . . . Michael was an exemplary soldier whose ability, spirit and dedication to the service earned for him the respect of his associates and superiors alike. . . . We share your burden and we pray that you will find consolation in the sympathy of your friends, your family and your faith." Peg later sent Major General Ramsey copies of Michael's letters "so that you can see what one of your model, exemplary soldiers thought of you and your war."

Secretary of the Army Resor wrote, "We are proud of his military accomplishments and grateful to him for his contribution to our Nation's strength."

Peg tossed both letters onto the kitchen table pile she reserved for "official mail." The letters landed in such a way that Major General Ramsey's overlapped Lieutenant Colonel Schwarzkopf's just enough to display the date "2 Mar 1970" stamped on both. The rubber stamp infuriated her; it was, to Peg, as if some anonymous Army bureaucrat had simply decided, "Okay, on March 2, send all these letters out." Suddenly she noticed something even more disturbing: the "1970" on the two rubber stamps printed just a hair lower than the "2 Mar" and both "Mar's" seemed to tilt slightly to the left. Of course, Peg realized, the Army purchased rubber date stamps by the thousands, but was it mere coincidence that the battalion's rubber stamp and the division's contained identical flaws? The more likely explanation, she felt, was that the two letters had originated from the same office. The correspondence had been coordinated for but one reason: the Army had something to hide.

Peg had cause to be skeptical. During the week Michael was killed, seven other Iowans died in Vietnam. If Iowa's eight casualties were about average for the losses from the other forty-nine states, it would indicate that at least 400 Americans died that week in Vietnam. Peg already knew that one planeload of bodies had landed in Oakland on Monday and two more landed Tuesday the week Michael's body arrived. The planes carried 75 bodies each. And yet the official casualty figure released for that entire week listed only 88 Americans killed in Vietnam.

When Peg had contacted the parents of that week's seven other Iowa casualties, she discovered the majority of them, too, had been told their sons were "nonbattle" casualties. But not until she learned that the weekly casualty figure reported on the evening television news was for those killed in action only did Peg begin to suspect why the nonbattle casualties were so high. Nonbattle casualties, such as Michael, weren't counted, and she wondered just how many other so-called nonbattle casualties there might have been. (Correspondents covering the Vietnam War in 1970 were already aware that the Army was classifying as nonbattle casualties any soldiers who died in the hospitals as a result of wounds.) Peg was convinced the Army was deliberately disguising the number of casualties suffered to prevent the American people from learning their true losses in the war.

* * *

In early July the Senate rejected (55 to 42) the Hatfield-McGovern 609 amendment calling for the withdrawal of all American troops by the end of the year, and two days later I received a long letter from Peg in response to a large list of questions I had sent. I did not hear again from the Mullens until one afternoon in late July, when Gene telephoned me and excitedly said, "Listen, I've got an ending for your book!"

"Where are you?" I asked.

"We're in Washington again. At the American Friends Office. We're driving up your way tomorrow. May we stop by and see you?"

"Of course," I said, "but what's up?"

"I've gotta run. Peg's got us a cab so I can't say much yet except that I've found him! I've found the man who killed my boy! I located Schwarzkopf," Gene crowed. "We're going to see him this afternoon!"

* * *

But of course, Schwarzkopf *hadn't* killed their son. And I worried about to what awful lengths the Mullens might drive themselves to achieve their next "perfect ending" for me. The Mullens had already demonstrated a surprisingly sophisticated awareness of the impact media exposure might have. The enormous attention they had received as a result of their first antiwar advertisement could not help having seemed heady stuff indeed. National prominence once achieved—no matter how momentary and elusive—creates a craving for ever more attention. Inevitably the different media, television especially, not only report news but inspire, influence, feed upon and demand ever more news. The temptation to create "perfect endings" was the corruption I wanted the Mullens spared. The only way I could achieve this was by finding out for them exactly what had happened to their son. I believed I already knew. I believed, also, that they knew, too. Colonel Valentin Kuprin, the artillery battalion commander, had told them. It had not, however, been what they had wanted to hear.

* * *

By twilight Charlie Company's defensive perimeter was set. The men's foxholes and sleeping positions had been dug, the machine-gun emplacements finished. The men were able to relax, eat their C rations, talk and move quietly around. Over on the north side of the hill in the 3rd Platoon's area, Culpepper had waited for the light to fade, then strung his hammock five inches above the ground. He could not sleep where the leeches could reach him. He would rather take his chances on waking up if trouble arose and having time to get into his foxhole. He stood now looking from his machine-gun pit out over the cliff. Abe Aikins wandered over and, looking down, said, "Jesus, Pep, you'd better not do any walking in the middle of the night. That must be a hundred feet straight down!"

"Straight up, too." Culpepper smiled. "Nobody's climbing that. Tonight I'm gonna get me some sleep!"

Willard Polk was sitting with Michael Mullen on the lip of the foxhole they had dug. Michael had finished the fruit in his C ration can of peaches and, with great pleasure, was drinking the syrup. Polk liked Michael, called him Mulligan. Mullen never hassled him. He was like a chaplain in some ways, Polk felt, because he was always so concerned with other people's problems. Polk had been telling Michael about the trouble he had been in in Detroit. "I'd been locked up for misdemeanors, trespassing on Ford property, simple larceny, things like that. I was with some dudes who knocked out a store window and got busted for carrying a concealed weapon, assault on a police officer. . . ."

Michael looked at him with surprise.

"I was drunk at the time," Polk explained. "And besides, he was hassling me. I got drafted just after I got out of jail. I'd been in for sixty days on account of violation of parole, you know. And the only reason why my mother paid to get me out was because I had this draft notice waiting, see. She knew they'd put me in the Army—she didn't know they'd send me here, though. But I'll tell you, Mulligan, I'm gonna get me outta here. One way or another I'll get out." Polk slapped at some mosquitoes. "Hey, you got a cigarette?"

"Don't smoke," Michael said.

Polk shrugged and took a pack of Salems from his fatigue shirt pocket and lit one. "What're you gonna do when you get out?"

"I'll have to see. There's a girl I like. I've been thinking I'd like to get me something like a VW bus and drive around the country, see all the different states. Just take it easy for a while."

"You're getting 'short,' aren't you?"

"If I get my early drop, it'll be about a hundred days."

Polk picked up his can of bug spray and sprayed his fatigue pants. "Fuckin' mosquitoes, fuckin' leeches, there ain't *nothing* good about this place."

"Sergeant Mullen?"

Polk and Michael looked up. It was their platoon leader, Second Lieutenant Joslin. Michael rose to his feet. "Sir?"

"Tell your squad to put on their steel pots and to get in their foxholes. The artillery is going to fire the DTs."

"All right, sir." Michael went to the members of his squad but could not find the Prince. He knew Samuels shared a foxhole with Leroy Hamilton, so Michael asked Hamilton if he'd seen the Prince.

"He was talking to the chaplain," Hamilton said.

"Where's he?"

"By the CP, I think," Hamilton said.

Michael met the Prince walking back to his foxhole. "They're going to fire the DTs," Michael warned him.

"I heard," Samuels said. "You know what the chaplain's name is? It's Do-Good, can you believe it? It's spelled D-U-I-good."

"What's he doing here?" Michael asked.

The Prince shrugged. "Don't know. He just said he thought he ought to be here." He slipped into the foxhole and squatted down. Mullen's foxhole was just to the right.

Over in the 3rd Platoon area, Sergeant Webb was telling Martin Culpepper and Russell Schumacher to put their helmets on.

"What good do they do?" Schumacher asked.

"Won't stop nothing," Culpepper grumbled.

"Put 'em on," Webb said wearily. "Lieutenant Rocamora said they were going to fire the DTs now."

It was eight thirty and almost dark. The men sat in their foxholes, talking quietly. They were all tired after having had to chop their way up the hill, dig their foxholes and carry the extra heavy load the five-day operation required. After an hour had passed and the DTs had still not been fired, some of the men left their foxholes, stretched out in their sleeping positions and dozed off.

* * *

The artillery radio crackled, and the reconnaissance sergeant leaned closer to it. Aikins, in the nearby foxhole, could barely hear what was said. The recon sergeant woke Lieutenant Rocamora. "Sir? They're going to fire our DTs now. Do you want me to wake the men?"

Rocamora looked at the luminous dial of his watch. It was a quarter to three. There had already been one false alarm. The DTs were being fired 400 meters out, more than 1,300 feet from the closest man. "Let them sleep," Rocamora told his sergeant. "You'd better inform the captain, though."

"I'll do it," Aikins said.

Captain Cameron, asleep in his flak jacket, wearing both his helmet and glasses, awoke quickly. Aikins explained that the DTs were to be fired. Cameron waved his hand to show he had heard and lay back, still half asleep. "Roger. W.P. Airburst. Fifty meters," the recon sergeant was saying.

Moments later Cameron heard the white phosphorous marking round chuff overhead. There was a loud, hollow, *Whaing*! and the shell exploded 400 meters southwest of their position 50 feet in the air. The recon sergeant looked over at Rocamora. Rocamora nodded back. The round had exploded exactly where they wanted it. No corrections were needed.

The next round would automatically be the high explosive, the HE.

Lying there in the dark, Cameron heard the HE round coming and for some reason he just *knew*. He could tell. His brain clicked, *That sonuvabitch isn't going to make it!*

The pitch was different. It was a strange, flat rumbling noise, the sound of a shell pushing the air in front of it rather than away and over his head. Cameron heard the shell coming, there was an instantaneous awareness. He didn't have time to speak, to shout any warning, to take any evasive action. There was nothing Cameron could do but listen to that terrible, low, flat, terrifying rumbling coming closer and closer and closer until it hit.

There was a sudden blinding light, the bright incandescence of thousands of flashbulbs popping all about, then a sharp, immediate, echoless, explosive CRACK! followed by a hurricane of shrapnel, dirt, stones, tree limbs, loose equipment. Small limbs hit Cameron's head and shoulders, the explosion pushed him into the ground, and he couldn't see. His first thought was, *God, stop them before they fire again!* He knew it had been one of their own rounds. There was no question in his mind whatsoever. "CEASE FIRE!" he shouted to the radio operators. "CEASE FIRE!"

Cameron could hear Rocamora shouting over the artillery radio, and he yelled at Rocamora, "TELL THEM NOT TO FIRE AGAIN!"

Cameron heard people running, could smell the cordite in the air. His eyes began to clear, and he was able to see wisps of smoke in the trees and dust drifting down to the ground.

Aikins heard Cameron and Rocamora shouting and then silence. He didn't feel any pain, but he was dazed and unsure of what had happened. Instinctively he put his hands up to his face and brought them back down to look for blood. His head hurt, but he could not see any blood. He shook his head to clear it.

Samuels, too, had been dazed by the explosion. He felt it had happened directly overhead. Specialist Fourth Class Rodriguez ran by shouting, "Prince! Grab your rifle! We're being overrun!" Samuels sat up, reached for his rifle and instantly knew something was wrong. His hand, brushing his leg to grasp his rifle had come up wet, covered with blood. There was blood all over his fatigue pants, but he couldn't feel any pain. He couldn't feel a thing! Cautiously, Samuels looked down and saw that his left leg was flipped crazily to one side midway down from the knee. There was no way his leg could be lying like that and still be . . . and still be attached! Rodriguez, too, had stopped suddenly, turned back in midstride to stare in horror at the Prince's leg. And Samuels, seeing confirmed in Rodriguez' expression what he himself had dared not believe, let out a high, keening, animal cry of terrible bewilderment and pain.

"Get the medic over here!" Rodriguez shouted. "Get a medic to the Prince!"

Someone else was yelling, "A light! I need a light! Get me a light!"

The Prince was screaming, "Doc! DOC! Oh, God, help me, DOC!" Aikins, who had had to run back to the sleeping area for his medical kit, was hurrying back. Cameron's senior radio operator was calling Schwarzkopf, "Black Smoke One, Black Smoke One? This is Black Smoke Six. Do you read me?"

"This is Black Smoke One," Schwarzkopf answered.

"This is Black Smoke Six. We need an immediate dust-off. An urgent dust-off."

Schwarzkopf had monitored Charlie Company's call for a cease-fire, but he had no means of knowing how bad things were. "Are you sure you need a dust-off? Let me talk to your company commander." It was pitch-black. Foggy. Schwarzkopf knew how difficult it would be for the med-evac helicopter to find them.

Cameron took the hand mike from the radio operator, "Black Smoke One? This is Black Smoke Six. We took a short round. We need an immediate dust-off. We may even need a jungle penetrator. I don't know yet."

The jungle penetrator is a basket device lowered by winch from a helicopter hovering overhead. The helicopter must hold its position and guide the basket through the openings in the jungle canopy. The procedure is dangerous and difficult and utilized only when absolutely necessary. Cameron had mentioned the jungle penetrator because he could not yet determine whether or not he would be able to get a landing zone with enough clearance for the medical evacuation helicopter to put down.

When the shell hit, Culpepper found himself lying on the ground clutching his rifle. He did not even remember how he got there. "Jesus, Schumacher! What was that?"

"An arty round!"

"*What?*"

"Those stupid sons of bitches!" Schumacher yelled. "They're supposed to be shooting out there, but they're shooting at us! If we'd given ourselves as a target, they couldn't have done any better."

* * *

Polk didn't know what had happened either. He had heard and felt the shell explode, awoke to find Cactus screaming to his left, the scream a thin, metallic ringing in Polk's ears. He saw blood on Cactus' face, felt the terror hot, like fire, surge from his stomach to his chest. Polk sat up, patted his body searching for blood, then rolled toward Michael Mullen, asking "Mulligan? Mulligan, you all right?"

Michael didn't move. Polk heard only the hiss of escaping air.

"MULLIGAN!" Polk wailed, the panic rising heavier, hotter, higher through him. He saw the blood, heard the screaming and jerked himself like a puppet to his feet. Polk, babbling in terror, ran past the new 1st Platoon sergeant, Wetsel, and saw that he, too, was wounded. Polk didn't stop. He ran over the lip of his foxhole, fell to his knees and vomited over and over and over again.

* * *

Samuels, Polk, Culpepper, Aikins, Cameron. Each separately confirmed the details of the incident which had brought about Michael's death. Each of them had been on that hill that night; each of them furthered my conviction that Schwarzkopf had told the Mullens the truth.

I felt, therefore, that I had come to the end of the story. Inasmuch as any man can know another's death, I now knew Michael's. That is why, as I approached the last gentle, rolling hill on Route 218 south of the Mullens' hometown, I felt a sense of relief. It was a relief born out of the naïve anticipation that at last I could offer the Mullens some comfort. I could relieve their anguish, bestow on them a kind of peace. I still believed that the truth, inevitably, would set them free.

I never wanted to be in this book. I had intended only to be a journalist: unbiased, dispassionate, receptive to all sides. I knew my only chance for articulating the tragedy of this war, the only way I could explain, as I had set out to do, the people's estrangement from their government, their increasing paranoia and distrust, lay in limiting my focus.

By concentrating on one specific incident, the death of Michael Mullen, but restricting myself to this one isolated Iowa farm family's story, I had hoped somehow to encompass the whole. This technique, I later came to recognize, was not a journalist's but a novelist's; and it led inevitably not only to my own participation and inclusion in the Mullens' story but also to that awful sadness and disappointment I now felt. I knew because I thought them wrong about Schwarzkopf, they believed I had passed judgment against everything they had done. I knew they were wondering whether they could trust me, or had I, too, become a part of the conspiracy to hide the truth? Vietnam did that to us. It dragged us all in, made us choose sides. Had not Peg herself said, "There's only one side when you lose your son"?

That I disagreed with them about Schwarzkopf was beside the point. I did agree with them on principle: Michael's death was an unforgivable tragedy—as Schwarzkopf, too, would have been and was among the first to agree. The colonel further recognized, however, that their opinion of him was a symptom and consequence of the injuries they had received. He was the one who said, "But it's an even more terrible thing that has happened to the Mullens themselves." They, like their son, like the nation itself, had become casualties of the war. And my sadness lay in knowing nothing I could say or write could change that, just as nothing they could say or do could bring back their son.

From DISPATCHES

MICHAEL HERR

Editor's Note: Michael Herr's Dispatches *became an international best seller when it was published in 1978. C. D. B. Bryan and Tobias Wolff called it "the best book to have been written about the Vietnam War." John le Carré described it as "the best book I have ever read on men and war in our time."*

Herr began sending his "Dispatches" from Vietnam in 1968. Published originally in Esquire *and then in book form, they offer an unsettling reappraisal of American actions in that conflict. Through his staccato, Morse Code, "SOS" vignettes, Herr criticizes military and political leaders for hiding the reality of the war from the American public; he reproaches fellow journalists for ignoring the human stories all around them.*

Herr's dispatches capture the soldiers' voices and pass along their tales. He deliberately uses the "grunts'" language and provides the reader no helpful decoding of acronyms such as VC, DMZ, AFVN, and NVA. These choices permit him both to create authentic scenes and to give those of us at home a sense of how very far away we are from the war's reality.

Herr was an oddity in Vietnam, for he was one of the few there by choice. "I went to cover the war and the war covered me," he admitted. In the end, Dispatches *suggests how difficult it is to know and to face the truth about Vietnam. Herr's stories pile up—like the Vietnam body counts—until they become unbearable. It is not surprising, then, that Francis Ford Coppola would turn to Herr for the narration of his film* Apocalypse Now, *or that Stanley Kubrick would tap him to coauthor* Heavy Metal Jacket.

What they say is totally true, it's funny the things you remember. Like a black paratrooper with the 101st who glided by and said, "I been *scaled* man, I'm *smooth* now," and went on, into my past and I hope his future, leaving me to wonder not what he meant (that was easy), but where he'd been to get his language. On a cold wet day in Hue our jeep turned into the soccer stadium where hundreds of North Vietnamese bodies had been collected, I saw them, but they don't have the force in my memory that a dog and a duck have who died together in a small terrorist explosion in Saigon. Once I ran into a soldier standing by himself in the middle of a small jungle clearing where I'd wandered off to take a leak. We said hello, but he seemed very uptight about my being there. He told me that the guys were all sick of sitting around waiting and that he'd come out to see if he could draw a little fire. What a look we gave each other. I backed out of there fast, I didn't want to bother him while he was working.

This is already a long time ago, I can remember the feelings but I can't still have them. A common prayer for the overattached: You'll let it go sooner or later, why not do it now? Memory print, voices and faces, stories like filament through a piece of time, so attached to the experience that nothing moved and nothing went away.

"First letter I got from my old man was all about how proud he was that I'm here and how we have this *duty* to, you know, *I* don't fucking know, whatever . . . and it really made me feel great. Shit, my father hardly said good morning to me before. Well, I been here eight months now, and when I get home I'm gonna have all I can do to keep from killing that cocksucker. . . ."

Everywhere you went people said, "Well, I hope you get a story," and everywhere you went you did.

"Oh, it ain't so bad. My last tour was better though, not so much mickeymouse, Command gettin' in your way so you can't even do your job. Shit, last three patrols I was on we had fucking *orders* not to return fire going through the villages, that's what a fucked-up war it's gettin' to be anymore. My *last* tour we'd go through and that was it, we'd rip out the hedges and burn the hootches and blow all the wells and kill every chicken, pig and cow in the whole fucking ville. I mean, if we can't shoot these people, what the fuck are we doing here?"

Some journalists talked about no-story operations, but I never went on one. Even when an operation never got off the ground, there was always the strip. Those were the same journalists who would ask us what the fuck we ever found to talk to grunts about, who said they never heard a grunt talk about anything except cars, football and chone. But they all had a story, and in the war they were driven to tell it.

"We was getting killed and the Dinks was panicking, and when the choppers come in to get us out, there wasn't enough room for everybody. The Dinks was screaming and carrying on, grabbing hold of the treads and grabbing hold of our legs till we couldn't get the choppers up. So we just said smack it, let these people get their own fucking choppers, and we started shooting them. And even then they kept on coming, oh man it was wild. I mean they could sure as shit believe that Charlie was shooting them, but they couldn't believe that we was doing it too. . . ."

That was a story from the A Shau Valley years before my time there, an old story with the hair still growing on it. Sometimes the stories were so fresh that the teller was in shock, sometimes they were long and complex, sometimes the whole thing was contained in a few words on a helmet or a wall, and sometimes they were hardly stories at all but sounds and gestures packed with so much urgency that they became more dramatic than a novel, men talking in short violent bursts as though they were afraid they might not get to finish, or saying it almost out of a dream, innocent, offhand and mighty direct, "Oh you know, it was just a firefight, we killed some of them and they killed some of us." A lot of what you heard, you heard all the time, men on tape, deceitful and counterarticulate, and some of it was low enough, guys whose range seemed to stop at "Git some, git some, harharhar!" But once in a while you'd hear something fresh, and a couple of times you'd even hear something high, like the corpsman at Khe Sanh who said, "If it ain't the fucking incoming it's the fucking outgoing. Only difference is who gets the fucking grease, and that ain't no fucking difference at all."

The mix was so amazing; incipient saints and realized homicidals, unconscious lyric poets and mean dumb mother-fuckers with their brains all down in their necks; and even though by the time I left I knew where all the stories came from and where they were going, I was never bored, never even unsurprised. Obviously, what they really wanted to tell you was how tired they were and how sick of it, how moved they'd been and how afraid. But maybe that was me, by then my posture was shot: "reporter." ("Must be pretty hard to stay detached," a man on the plane to San Francisco said, and I said, "Impossible.") After a year I felt so plugged in to all the stories and the images and the fear that even the dead started telling me stories, you'd hear them out of a remote but accessible space where there were no ideas, no emotions, no facts, no proper language, only clean information. However many times it happened, whether I'd known them or not, no matter what I'd felt about them or the way they'd died, their story was always there and it was always the same: it went, "Put yourself in my place."

* * *

In the first week of December 1967 I turned on the radio and heard this over AFVN: "The Pentagon announced today that, compared to Korea, the Vietnam War will be an economy war, provided that it does not exceed the Korean War in length, which means that it will have to end *sometime* in 1968."

By the time that Westmoreland came home that fall to cheerlead and request-beg another quarter of a million men, with his light-at-the-end-of-the-tunnel collateral, there were people leaning so far out to hear good news that a lot of them slipped over the edge and said that they could see it too. (Outside of Tay Ninh City a man whose work kept him "up to fucking here" in tunnels, lobbing grenades into them, shooting his gun into them, popping CS smoke into them, crawling down into them himself to bring the bad guys out dead or alive, he almost smiled when he heard that one and said, "What does that asshole know about tunnels?")

A few months earlier there had been an attempt Higher to crank up the Home For Christmas rumor, but it wouldn't take, the troop consensus was too strong, it went, "Never happen." If a commander told you he thought he had it pretty well under control it was like talking to a pessimist. Most would say that they either had it wrapped up or wound down; "He's all pissed out, Charlie's all pissed out, booger's shot his whole wad," one of them promised me, while in Saigon it would be restructured for briefings, "He no longer maintains in our view capability to mount, execute or sustain a serious offensive action," and a reporter behind me, from *The New York Times* no less, laughed and said, "Mount this, Colonel." But in the boonies, where they were deprived of all information except what they'd gathered for themselves on either side of the treeline, they'd look around like someone was watching and say, "I dunno, Charlie's up to something. Slick, slick, that fucker's *so* slick. Watch!"

The summer before, thousands of Marines had gone humping across northern I Corps in multi-division sweeps, "Taking the D out of DMZ," but the North never really broke out into the open for it, hard to believe that anyone ever thought that they would. Mostly it was an invasion of a thousand operation-miles of high summer dry season stroke weather, six-canteen patrols that came back either contactless or chewed over by ambushes and quick, deft mortar-rocket attacks, some from other Marine outfits. By September they were "containing" at Con Thien, sitting there while the NVA killed them with artillery. In II Corps a month of random contact near the Laotian border had sharpened into the big war around Dak To. III Corps, outside of Saigon, was most confusing of all, the VC were running what was described in a month-end, sit/rep handout as "a series of half-hearted, unambitious ground attacks" from Tay Ninh through Loc Ninh to Bu Dop, border skirmishes that some reporters saw as purposely limited rather than half-hearted, patterned and extremely well coordinated, like someone was making practice runs for a major offensive. IV Corps was what it had always been, obscure isolated Delta war, authentic guerrilla action where betrayal was as much an increment as bullets. People close to Special Forces had heard upsetting stories about the A Camps down there, falling apart from inside, mercenary mutinies and triple cross, until only a few were still effective.

That fall, all that the Mission talked about was control: arms control, information control, resources control, psycho-political control, population control, control of the almost supernatural inflation, control of terrain through the Strategy of the Periphery. But when the talk had passed, the only thing left standing up that looked true was your sense of how out of control things really were. Year after year, season after season, wet and dry, using up options faster than rounds on a machine-gun belt, we called it right and righteous, viable and even almost won, and it still only went on the way it went on. When all the projections of intent and strategy twist and turn back on you, tracking team blood, "sorry" just won't cover it. There's nothing so embarrassing as when things go wrong in a war.

From THE CURSE OF LONO

HUNTER S. THOMPSON

Editor's Note: Hunter S. Thompson is one of the few writers who can claim to have ridden with both the Hell's Angels and Richard Nixon. Few authors, too, have run for political office (Sheriff of Aspen, Colorado), or inspired a Doonesbury cartoon character: the profligate "Uncle Duke."

During the 1960s, Thompson gradually evolved from a reporter with ties to such establishment newspapers as the National Observer *and the* New York Herald Tribune *into one of the most idiosyncratic and successful freelance writers in America. Like Norman Mailer, Thompson has been ready to confront every aspect of American experience, from politics to the Super Bowl, and to create an outrageous narrative persona in the process.*

Thompson's early works include Hell's Angels: The Strange and Terrible Saga of the Outlaw Motorcycle Gangs, Fear and Loathing in Las Vegas: A Savage Journey to the Heart of the American Dream, *and* Fear and Loathing on the Campaign Trail '72. *Since then, his articles have been collected in* The Great Shark Hunt: Strange Tales from a Strange Time, Generation of Swine: Tales of Shame and Degradation in the '80s, Songs of the Doomed: More Notes on the Death of the American Dream, *and* Better Than Sex: Confessions of a Political Junkie Trapped Like a Rat in Mr. Bill's Neighborhood.

Thompson has described his writing as "Gonzo" journalism, a term meaning "crazy" or "off-the-wall," which he borrowed from Boston Globe Sunday Magazine *editor Bill Cardozo during the 1968 New Hampshire primary. In point of fact, Thompson's Gonzo mix of paranoia, nightmare, and black humor has revealed more truth about American politics, sports, and entertainment than has the reporting of much of the "establishment" media.*

In 1967, Thompson enlarged our sense of an American pageant staged annually in his hometown of Louisville, Kentucky. In "The Kentucky Derby is Decadent and Depraved," Thompson and his British illustrator and alter ego, Ralph Steadman, met the enemy and found, as Pogo said, that it is "us." The following excerpt from Thompson's 1983 volume The Curse of Lono *records another Thompson adventure with Ralph Steadman, this time in Hawaii. Marathon running might have seemed like the healthiest of pastimes. At least it did until Thompson unleashed this scathing reappraisal.*

May 23, 1980

Hunter S. Thompson
c/o General Delivery
Woody Creek, CO

Dear Hunter:
   To keep a potential screed down to a few lines, we would like you to
cover the Honolulu Marathon. We will pay all expenses and an excellent
fee. Please contact us.

   Think about it. This is a good chance for a vacation.

Sincerely,

Paul Perry
Executive Editor,
Running Magazine

October 25, 1980
Owl Farm

Dear Ralph,

   I think we have a live one this time, old sport. Some dingbat named
Perry up in Oregon wants to give us a month in Hawaii for Christmas and
all we have to do is cover the Honolulu Marathon for his magazine, a thing
called Running. . . .
   Yeah, I know what you're thinking, Ralph. You're pacing around over
there in the war room at the Old Loose Court and thinking, "Why me? And
why now? Just when I'm getting respectable?"
   Well . . . let's face it, Ralph; anybody can be respectable, especially in
England. But not everybody can get paid to run like a bastard for 26 miles
in some maniac hype race called the Honolulu Marathon.
   We are both entered in this event, Ralph, and I feel pretty confident about
winning. We will need a bit of training, but not much.

The main thing will be to run as an entry and set a killer pace for the first three miles. These body-nazis have been training all year for the supreme effort in this Super Bowl of marathons. The promoters expect 10,000 entrants, and the course is 26 miles; which means they will all start slow . . . because 26 miles is a hell of a long way to run, for any reason at all, and all the pros in this field will start slow and pace themselves very carefully for the first 20 miles.

But not us, Ralph. We will come out of the blocks like human torpedoes and alter the whole nature of the race by sprinting the first three miles shoulder-to-shoulder in under 10 minutes.

A pace like that will crack their nuts, Ralph. These people are into running, not racing—so our strategy will be to race like whorehounds for the first three miles. I figure we can crank ourselves up to a level of frenzy that will clock about 9:55 at the three-mile checkpoint . . . which will put us so far ahead of the field that they won't even be able to see us. We will be over the hill and all alone when we hit the stretch along Ala Moana Boulevard still running shoulder-to-shoulder at a pace so fast and crazy that not even the judges will feel sane about it . . . and the rest of the field will be left so far behind that many will be overcome with blind rage and confusion.

I've also entered you in the Pipeline Masters, a world class surfing contest on the north shore of Oahu on Dec. 26.

You will need some work on your high-speed balance for this one, Ralph. You'll be shot through the curl at speeds up to 50 or even 75 miles an hour, and you won't want to fall.

I won't be with you in the Pipeline gig, due to serious objections raised by my attorney with regard to the urine test and other legal ramifications.

But I will enter the infamous Liston Memorial Rooster Fight, at $1,000 per unit on the universal scale—e.g., one minute in the cage with one rooster wins $1,000 . . . or five minutes with one rooster is worth $5,000 . . . and two minutes with five roosters is $10,000 . . . etc.

This is serious business, Ralph. These Hawaiian slashing roosters can tear a man to shreds in a matter of seconds. I am training here at home with the peacocks—six 40-pound birds in a 6' × 6' cage, and I think I'm getting the hang of it.

The time has come to kick ass, Ralph, even if it means coming briefly out of retirement and dealing, once again, with the public. I am also in need of a rest—for legal reasons—so I want this gig to be easy, and I know in my heart that it will be.

Don't worry, Ralph. We will bend a few brains with this one. I have already secured the Compound: two homes with a 50-meter pool on the edge of the sea on Alii Drive in Kona, where the sun always shines.

OK
HST

* * *

We were in downtown Honolulu now, cruising along the waterfront. The streets were full of joggers fine-tuning their strides for the big race. They ignored passing traffic, which made Skinner nervous.

"This running thing is out of control," he said. "Every rich liberal in the Western world is into it. They run ten miles a day. It's a goddamn religion."

"Do *you* run?" I asked.

He laughed. "Hell yes, I run. But never with empty hands. We're *criminals*, Doc. We're not *like* these people and I think we're too old to learn."

"But we *are* professionals," I said. "And we're here to cover the race."

"Fuck the race," he said. "We'll cover it from Wilbur's front yard—get drunk and gamble heavily on the football games."

John Wilbur, a pulling guard on the Washington Redskins team that went to the Super Bowl in 1973, was another old friend from the white-knuckle days of yesteryear, who had finally settled down enough to pass for a respectable businessman in Honolulu. His house on Kahala Drive in the high-rent section was situated right on the course for this race, about two miles from the finish line. . . . It would be a perfect headquarters for our coverage, Skinner explained. We would catch the start downtown, then rush out to Wilbur's to watch the games and abuse the runners as they came by the house, then rush back downtown in time to cover the finish.

"Good planning," I said. "This looks like my kind of story."

"Not really," he said. "You've never seen anything as dull as one of these silly marathons . . . but it's a good excuse to get crazy."

"That's what I mean," I said. "I'm *entered* in this goddamn race." He shook his head. "Forget it," he said. "Wilbur tried to pull a Rosie Ruiz a few years ago, when he was still in top shape—he jumped into the race about a half mile ahead of everybody at the twenty-four-mile mark, and took off like a bastard for the finish line, running at what he figured was his normal 880 speed. . . ." He laughed. "It was horrible," he continued. "Nineteen people passed him in two miles. He went blind from vomiting and had to crawl the last hundred yards." He laughed again. "These people are *fast*, man. They ran right over him."

"Well," I said, "so much for that. I didn't want to enter this goddamn thing anyway. It was Wilbur's idea."

"That figures," he said. "You want to be careful out here. Even your best friends will lie to you. They can't help themselves."

* * *

We spent the next few days in deep research. Neither one of us had the vaguest idea what went on at a marathon, or why people ran in them, and I felt we should ask a few questions and perhaps mingle a bit with the runners.

This worked well enough, once Ralph understood that we were not going to Guam and that *Running* was not a political magazine. . . . By the end of the week we were hopelessly bogged down in a maze of gibberish about "carbo-loading," "hitting the wall," "the running divorce," "heel-toe theories," along with so many pounds of baffling propaganda about the Running Business that I had to buy a new Pierre Cardin seabag to carry it all.

We hit all the prerace events, but our presence seemed to make people nervous and we ended up doing most of our research in the Ho Ho Lounge at the Hilton. We spent so many hours talking to runners that I finally lost track of what it all meant and began setting people on fire.

It rained every day, but we learned to live with it . . . and by midnight on the eve of the race, we felt ready.

The Doomed Generation

We arrived at ground zero sometime around four in the morning—two hours before starting time, but the place was already a madhouse. Half the runners had apparently been up all night, unable to sleep and too cranked to talk. The air was foul with a stench of human feces and Vaseline. By five o'clock huge lines had formed in front of the bank of chemical privies set up by Doc Scaff and his people. Prerace diarrhea is a standard nightmare at all marathons, and Honolulu was no different. There are a lot of good reasons for dropping out of a race, but bad bowels is not one of them. The idea is to come off the line with a belly full of beer and other cheap fuel that will burn itself off very quickly. . . .

Carbo-power. No meat. Protein burns too slow for these people. They want the starch. Their stomachs are churning like rat-bombs and their brains are full of fear.

Will they finish? That is the question. They want that "Finishers" T-shirt. Winning is out of the question for all but a quiet handful: Frank Shorter, Dean Matthews, Duncan MacDonald, Jon Sinclair. . . . These were the ones with the low numbers on their shirts: 4, 11, 16, and they would be the first off the line.

The others, the *Runners*—people wearing four-digit numbers—were lined up in ranks behind the Racers, and it would take them a while to get started. Carl Hatfield was halfway to Diamond Head before the big number people even tossed their Vaseline bottles and started moving, and they knew, even then, that not one of them would catch a glimpse of the winner until long after the race was over. Maybe get his autograph at the banquet. . . .

We are talking about two very distinct groups here, two entirely different marathons. The Racers would all be finished and half drunk by 9:30 in the morning, or just about the time the Runners would be humping and staggering past Wilbur's house at the foot of "Heartbreak Hill."

At 5:55 we jumped on the tailgate of Don Kardong's KKUA radio press van, the best seats in the house, and moved out in front of the pack at exactly 11.5 miles per hour, or somewhere around the middle of second gear. The plan was to drop us off at Wilbur's house and then pick us up again on the way back.

Some freak with four numbers on his chest came off the line like a hyena on speed and almost caught up with our van and the two dozen motorcycle cops assigned to run interference . . . but he faded quickly.

We jumped off the radio van at Wilbur's and immediately set up a full wet-bar and Command Center next to the curb and for the next few minutes we just stood there in the rain and heaped every conceivable kind of verbal abuse on the Runners coming up.

"You're doomed, man, you'll never make it."

"Hey, fat boy, how about a beer?"

"*Run*, you silly bastard."

"Lift those legs."

"Eat shit and die," was Skinner's favorite.

One burly runner in the front ranks snarled back at him, "I'll see you on the way back."

"No, you won't. You'll never make it back. You won't even finish! You'll collapse."

It was a rare kind of freedom to belch any kind of cruel and brutal insult that came to mind because the idea of anybody stopping to argue was out of the question. Here was this gang of degenerates hunkered down by the side of the racecourse with TV sets, beach umbrellas, cases of beer and whiskey, loud music and wild women, smoking cigarettes.

It was raining—a light warm rain, but steady enough to keep the streets wet, so we could stand on the curb and hear every footfall on the pavement as the runners came by.

The front-runners were about thirty seconds behind us when we jumped off the still-moving radio van, and the sound of their shoes on the wet asphalt was not much louder than the rain. There was no sound of hard rubber soles pounding and slapping on the street. That noise came later, when the Racers had passed and the first wave of Runners appeared.

The Racers run smoothly, with a fine-tuned stride like a Wankel rotary engine. No wasted energy, no fighting the street or bouncing along like a jogger. These people *flow*, and they flow very fast.

The Runners are different. Very few of them flow, and not many run fast. And the slower they are, the more noise they make. By the time the four-digit numbers came by, the sound of the race was disturbingly loud and disorganized. The smooth rolling *hiss* of the Racers had degenerated into a hell broth of slapping and pounding feet.

We followed the race by radio for the next hour or so. It was raining too hard to stand out by the curb, so we settled down in the living room to watch football on TV and eat the big breakfast that Carol Wilbur had fixed "for the drunkards" before leaving at four in the morning to run in the Marathon. (She finished impressively, around 3:50.) It was just before eight when we got a call from Kardong in the radio van to be out on the curb for a rolling pickup on the way to the finish line.

Duncan MacDonald, a local boy and previous two-time winner, had taken command of the race somewhere around the 15-mile mark and was so far ahead that the only way he could lose this race would be by falling down—which was not likely, despite his maverick reputation and good-natured disdain for traditional training habits. Even drunk, he was a world-class racer, and a hard man for anybody to catch once he got out in front.

There was nobody near him when he passed the 24-mile mark in front of Wilbur's house, and we rode the final two miles to the finish line on the tailgate of the radio van, about 10 yards ahead of him . . . and when he came down the long hill from Diamond Head, surrounded by motorcycle cops and moving like Secretariat in the stretch at Churchill Downs, he looked about 10 feet tall.

"Jesus Christ," Skinner muttered. "Look at that bastard run."

Even Ralph was impressed. "This is beautiful," he said quietly, "this man is an *athlete*."

Which was true. It was like watching Magic Johnson run the fast break or Walter Payton turning the corner. A Racer in full stride is an elegant thing to see. And for the first time all week, the Running Business made sense to me. It was hard to imagine *anything* catching Duncan MacDonald at that point, and he was not even breathing hard.

We hung around the finish line for a while to watch the Racers coming in, then we went back to Wilbur's to have a look at the Runners. They straggled by, more dead than alive, for the rest of the morning and into the afternoon. The last of the finishers came in a few minutes after six, just in time to catch the sunset and a round of applause from the few rickshaw drivers still loitering in the park by the finish line.

Marathon running, like golf, is a game for *players*, not winners. That is why Wilson sells golf clubs, and Nike sells running shoes. The Eighties will not be a healthy decade for games designed only for winners—except at the very pinnacle of professional sport; like the Super Bowl, or the Heavyweight Championship of the World. The rest of us will have to adjust to this notion, or go mad from losing. Some people will argue, but not many. The concept of victory through defeat has already taken root, and a lot of people say it makes sense. The Honolulu Marathon was a showcase example of the New Ethic. The main prize in this race was a gray T-shirt for every one of the four thousand "Finishers." That was the test, and the only ones who failed were those who dropped out.

There was no special shirt for the winner, who finished so far ahead of the others that only a handful of them ever saw him until the race was long over . . . and not

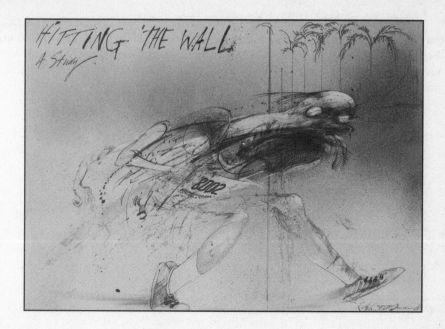

one of them was close enough to MacDonald, in those last two miles before the finish, to see how a real winner runs.

The other five or six or even seven or eight thousand entrants were running for their own reasons . . . and *this* is the angle we need; the *raison d'être* as it were. . . . Why do those buggers run? Why do they punish themselves so brutally, for no prize at all? What kind of sick instinct would cause eight thousand supposedly smart people to get up at four in the morning and stagger at high speed through the streets of Waikiki for 26 ball-busting miles in a race that less than a dozen of them have the slightest chance of winning?

These are the kind of questions that can make life interesting for an all-expense-paid weekend at the best hotel in Honolulu. But that weekend is over now, and we have moved our base to Kona, 150 miles downwind—the "gold coast" of Hawaii, where anybody even half hooked in the local real estate market will tell you that life is better and bigger and lazier and . . . yes . . . even *richer* in every way than on any one of the other islands in this harsh little maze of volcanic zits out here in the middle of the Pacific Ocean, 5,000 miles from anywhere at all.

There's no sane reason at all for these runners. Only a fool would try to explain why four thousand Japanese ran at top speed past the USS *Arizona*, sunken memorial in the middle of Pearl Harbor, along with another four or five thousand certified American *liberals* cranked up on beer and spaghetti and all taking the whole thing so seriously that only one in two thousand could even smile at the idea of a 26-mile race featuring four thousand Japanese that begins and ends within a stone's throw of Pearl Harbor on the morning of December 7, 1980. . . .

Thirty-nine years later. What are these people celebrating? And why on this bloodstained anniversary?

It was a weird gig in Honolulu, and it is even weirder now. We are talking, here, about a thing with more weight than we know. What looked like a paid vacation in Hawaii has turned into a nightmare—and at least one person has suggested that we may be looking at the Last Refuge of the Liberal Mind, or at least the Last Thing that *Works*.

From STOP-TIME

FRANK CONROY

Editor's Note: Since The Confessions of Saint Augustine *in the fourth century A.D., autobiographies and memoirs have captivated readers, particularly when they are artful, like Frank Conroy's 1967* Stop-Time. *We read memoirs just as we read fiction, to enter imaginatively into other people's lives and, in so doing, to explore the world and ourselves. In truth, we may invest even more of ourselves in memoirs than in fiction, for we believe them to be the certifiable Literature of Reality.*

Frank Conroy published Stop-Time *at the age of thirty-one. The volume presents events from his earliest memories to his first day at Haverford College at age eighteen. Conroy draws his title* Stop-Time *from a moment at the age of eleven when he woke from a serious illness. At that second he remembers thinking, "I don't know who I am, but it doesn't bother me. The white walls, the sunlight, the voices all exist in absolute purity." They are sufficient, and Conroy constructs his memoir from just such purely recollected stopped moments in time.*

In the opening five paragraphs Conroy creates an unforgettable portrait of his father by alternating facts about his father's life and disabling nervous condition, with acutely recalled moments of their interaction. Paragraph two, for example, offers five revealing incidents, one after another, without any transition between. This approach imitates the free association of the mind, and together these five images capture the reckless gallantry of Conroy's sire.

With paragraph six Conroy begins the first of four separate scenes *from his life in a progressive boarding school in Pennsylvania where he lived year-round from age nine to eleven. As with his re-creation of his father, Conroy gains depth in his characterizations of his boarding school headmaster and schoolmates through the cool intensity of his interest in them.*

"A child has no choice but to accept the immediate experiences of his life at face value," Conroy explains. "He isn't moving on; he simply is." Conroy's complete acceptance of his life is what makes his memoir compelling. He does not feel sorry for himself and is neither self-justifying nor self-reproaching. Rather, his observations of himself and his fellows are often startling, as when he notes that "Children are swept away by morality" and that "brutality happens easily."

And he delivers it all in lean but colorful prose, using ordinary language with such precision that not only events, but the feelings and undertones of events, are revealed.

1

SAVAGES

My father stopped living with us when I was three or four. Most of his adult life was spent as a patient in various expensive rest homes for dipsomaniacs and victims of nervous collapse. He was neither, although he drank too much, but rather the kind of neurotic who finds it difficult to live for any length of time in the outside world. The brain tumor discovered and removed toward the end of his life could have caused his illness, but I suspect this easy out. To most people he seemed normal, especially when he was inside.

I try to think of him as sane, yet it must be admitted he did some odd things. Forced to attend a rest-home dance for its therapeutic value, he combed his hair with urine and otherwise played it out like the Southern gentleman he was. He had a tendency to take off his trousers and throw them out the window. (I harbor some secret admiration for this.) At a moment's notice he could blow a thousand dollars at Abercrombie and Fitch and disappear into the Northwest to become an outdoorsman. He spent an anxious few weeks convinced that I was fated to become a homosexual. I was six months old. And I remember visiting him at one of the rest homes when I was eight. We walked across a sloping lawn and he told me a story, which even then I recognized as a lie, about a man who sat down on the open blade of a penknife embedded in a park bench. (Why, for God's sake would he tell a story like that to his eight-year-old son?)

At one point in his life he was analyzed or took therapy with A. A. Brill, the famous disciple of Freud, with no apparent effect. For ten or fifteen years he worked as a magazine editor, and built up a good business as a literary agent. He died of cancer in his forties.

I visited him near the end. Half his face was paralyzed from the brain-tumor operation and jaundice had stained him a deep yellow. We were alone, as usual, in the hospital room. The bed was high to my child's eye. With great effort he asked me if I believed in universal military training. Too young even to know what it was, I took a gamble and said yes. He seemed satisfied. (Even now I have no idea if that was the answer he wanted. I think of it as some kind of test. Did I pass?) He showed me some books he had gotten to teach himself to draw. A few weeks later he died. He was six feet tall and at the end he weighed eighty-five pounds.

Against the advice of his psychiatrists my mother divorced him, a long, tedious process culminating a year before his death. One can hardly blame her. At his worst he had taken her on a Caribbean cruise and amused himself by humiliating her at the captain's table. Danish, middle-class, and not nearly as bright, she was unable to defend herself. Late one night, on deck, his fun and games went too far. My mother thought he was trying to push her over the rail and screamed. (This might be the time to mention her trained mezzo-soprano voice and lifelong interest in opera.) My father was taken off the ship in a strait jacket, to yet another (Spanish-speaking) branch of the ubiquitous rest home he was never to escape.

I was twelve when my father died. From the ages of nine to eleven I was sent to an experimental boarding school in Pennsylvania called Freemont. I wasn't home more than a few days during these years. In the summer Freemont became a camp and I stayed through.

The headmaster was a big, florid man named Teddy who drank too much. It was no secret, and even the youngest of us were expected to sympathize with his illness and like him for it—an extension of the attitude that forbade the use of last names to make everyone more human. All of us knew, in the mysterious way children pick things up, that Teddy had almost no control over the institution he'd created, and that when decisions were unavoidable his wife took over. This weakness at the top might have been the key to the wildness of the place.

Life at Freemont was a perpetual semihysterical holiday. We knew there were almost no limits in any direction. A situation of endless, dreamlike fun, but one that imposed a certain strain on us all. Classes were a farce, you didn't have to go if you didn't want to, and there were no tests. Freedom was the key word. The atmosphere was heavy with the perfume of the nineteen-thirties—spurious agrarianism, group singing of proletarian chants from all countries, sexual freedom (I was necking at the age of nine), sentimentalism, naïveté. But above all, filtering down through the whole school, the excitement of the *new thing*, of the experiment—that peculiar floating sensation of not knowing what's going to happen next.

One warm spring night we staged a revolution. All the Junior boys, thirty or forty of us, spontaneously decided not to go to bed. We ran loose on the grounds most of the night, stalked by the entire faculty. Even old Ted was out, stumbling and crashing through the woods, warding off the nuts thrown from the trees. A few legitimate captures were made by the younger men on the staff, but there was no doubt most of us could have held out indefinitely. I, for one, was confident to the point of bravado, coming out in the open three or four times just for the fun of being chased. Can there be anything as sweet for a child as victory over authority? On that warm night I touched heights I will never reach again—baiting a thirty-year-old man, getting him to chase me over my own ground in the darkness, hearing his hard breath behind me (ah, the *wordlessness* of the chase, no words, just action), and finally leaping clean, leaping effortlessly over the brook at exactly the right place, knowing he was too heavy, too stupid as an animal, too old, and too tired to do what I had done. Oh God, my heart burst with joy when I heard him fall, flat out, in the water. Lights flashed in my brain. The chase was over and I had won. I was untouchable. I raced across the meadow, too happy to stop running.

Hours later, hidden in a bower, I heard the beginning of the end. A capture was made right below me. Every captured boy was to join forces with the staff and hunt the boys still out. My reaction was outrage. Dirty pool! But outrage dulled by recognition—"Of course. What else did you expect? They're clever and devious. Old people, with cold, ignorant hearts." The staff's technique didn't actually work as planned, but it spread confusion and broke the lovely symmetry of us against them. The revolution was no longer simple and ran out of gas. To this day I'm proud that I was the last boy in, hours after the others. (I paid a price though—some inexplicable loss to my soul as I crept around all that time in the dark, looking for another holdout.)

We went through a fire period for a couple of weeks one winter. At two or three in the morning we'd congregate in the huge windowless coat-room and set up hundreds of birthday candles on the floor. They gave a marvelous eerie light as we sat around telling horror stories. Fire-writing became the rage—paint your initials on the wall in airplane glue and touch a flame to it. At our most dramatic we staged elaborate take-offs on religious services, complete with capes and pseudo-Latin. We were eventually discovered by our bug-eyed counselor—a homosexual, I recognize in retrospect, who had enough problems caring for thirty-five boys at the brink of puberty. As far as I know he never touched anyone.

Teddy announced a punishment that made the hair rise on the backs of our necks. After pointing out the inadequacies of the fire-escape system he decreed that each of us would be forced to immerse his left hand in a pot of boiling water for ten seconds, the sentence to be carried out two days hence. Frightened, morbidly excited, we thought about nothing else, inevitably drawn to the image of the boiling water with unhealthy fascination. We discussed the announcement almost lovingly till all hours of the night, recognizing a certain beauty in the phrasing, the formal specification of the "left hand," the precision of "immersed for ten seconds"—it had a medieval flavor that thrilled us.

But Teddy, or his wife (it was done in her kitchen), lost his nerve after the screams and tears of the first few boys. The flame was turned off under the pot and by the time my turn came it didn't hurt at all.

The only successful bit of discipline I remember was their system to get us to stop smoking. We smoked corn silk as well as cigarettes. (The preparation of corn silk was an important ritual. Hand-gathered in the field from only the best ears, it was dried in the sun, rubbed, aged, and rolled into pipe-sized pellets. We decimated Freemont's corn crop, ineptly tended in the first place, by leaving ten stripped ears rotting on the ground for every one eventually harvested. No one seemed to mind. Harvest day, in which we all participated, was a fraudulent pastoral dance of symbolic rather than economic significance.) With rare decisiveness Teddy got organized about the smoking. The parents of the only non-scholarship student in the school, a neat, well-to-do Chinese couple, removed him without warning after a visit. The faculty believed it was the sight of students lounging around the public rooms with cigarettes hanging expertly from their rosy lips, while we maintained it was the toilet-paper war. The parents had walked through the front door when things were reaching a crescendo—endless white rolls streaming down the immense curved stairway, cylindrical bombs hurtling down the stairwell from the third-floor balcony to run out anticlimactically a few feet from the floor, dangling like exhausted white tongues. The withdrawal of the only paying student was a catastrophe, and the smoking would have to stop.

Like a witch doctor, some suburban equivalent of the rainmaker, Mr. Kleinberg arrived in his mysterious black panel truck. Members of the staff were Teddy,

George, or Harry, but this outsider remained Mister Kleinberg, a form of respect to which it turned out he was entitled. We greeted him with bland amusement, secure in the knowledge that no one could do anything with us. A cheerful realist with a big smile and a pat on the shoulder for every boy in reach, he was to surprise us all.

The procedure was simple. He packed us into a small, unventilated garage, unloaded more cigarettes than the average man will see in a lifetime, passed out boxes of kitchen matches, and announced that any of us still smoking after ten packs and five cigars was excluded from the new, heavily enforced ban on smoking. None of us could resist the challenge.

He sat behind his vast mound with a clipboard, checking off names as we took our first, fresh packs. Adjusting his glasses eagerly and beaming with friendliness, he distributed his fantastic treasure. The neat white cartons were ripped open, every brand was ours for the asking—Old Gold, Pall Mall (my brand), Chesterfields, Wings, Camels, Spud, Caporals, Lucky Strike (*Loose Sweaters Mean Floppy Tits*), Kools, Benson & Hedges. He urged us to try them all. "Feel free to experiment, boys, it may be your last chance," he said, exploding with benevolent laughter.

I remember sitting on the floor with my back against the wall. Bruce, my best friend, was next to me.

"We're supposed to get sick," he said.

"I know."

We lighted up a pair of fat cigars and surveyed the scene. Forty boys puffed away in every corner of the room, some of them lined up for supplies, keeping Mr. Kleinberg busy with his paperwork. The noise was deafening. Gales of nervous laughter as someone did an imitation of John Garfield, public speeches as so-and-so declared his intention to pass out rather than admit defeat, or his neighbor yelled that he'd finished his fourth pack and was still by God going strong. One had to scream through the smoke to be heard. It wasn't long before the first boys stumbled out, sick and shamefaced, to retch on the grass. There was no way to leave quietly. Every opening of the door sent great shafts of sunlight across the smoky room, the signal for a derisive roar—boos, hoots, whistles, razzberries—from those sticking it out. I felt satisfaction as an enemy of mine left early, when the crowd was at its ugliest.

The rest of us followed eventually, of course, some taking longer than others, but all poisoned. Mr. Kleinberg won and smoking ended at Freemont. With dazed admiration we watched him drive away the next day in his black truck, smiling and waving, a panetela clamped between his teeth.

A rainy day. All of us together in the big dorm except a fat boy named Ligget. I can't remember how it started, or if any one person started it. A lot of talk against Ligget, building quickly to the point where talk was not enough. When someone claimed to have heard him use the expression "nigger-lipping" (wetting the end of a cigarette), we decided to act. Ligget was intolerable. A boy was sent to find him.

I didn't know Ligget. He had no friends even though he'd been at school longer than the rest of us. There was some vagueness about his origins, probably his parents were dead and relatives cared for him. We knew he was in the habit of running away. I remember waking up one night to see three men, including a policeman, carrying him back to his bed. He fought with hysterical strength, although silently, as if he were afraid to wake the rest of us. All three had to hold him down for the hypodermic.

On this rainy day he didn't fight. He must have known what was up the moment he walked through the door, but he didn't try to run. The two boys assigned to hold his arms were unnecessary. Throughout the entire trial he stood quite still, only his eyes, deep in the pudgy face, swiveling from side to side as he followed the speakers. He didn't say anything.

The prosecutor announced that first of all the trial must be fair. He asked for a volunteer to conduct Ligget's defense. When it became clear no one wanted the job a boy named Herbie was elected by acclamation. It seemed the perfect choice: Herbie was colorless and dim, steady if not inspired.

"I call Sammy as a witness," said the prosecutor. There was a murmur of approval. Sammy was something of a hero to us, as much for his experiences in reform school as for his fabulous condition. (An undescended testicle, which we knew nothing about. To us he had only one ball.) "The prisoner is charged with saying 'nigger-lip.' Did you hear him say it?"

"Yes. He said it a couple of days ago. We were standing over there in front of the window." Sammy pointed to the end of the room. "He said it about Mark Schofield." (Schofield was a popular athletic star, a Senior, and therefore not in the room.)

"You heard him?"

"Yes. I got mad and told him not to talk like that. I walked away. I didn't want to hear him."

"Okay. Now it's your turn, Herbie."

Herbie asked only one question. "Are you sure he said it? Maybe he said something else and you didn't hear him right."

"He said it, all right." Sammy looked over at Ligget. "He said it."

"Okay," said the prosecutor, "I call Earl." Our only Negro stepped forward, a slim, good-looking youth, already vain. (A sin so precocious we couldn't even recognize it.) He enjoyed the limelight, having grown used to it in the large, nervous, and visit-prone family that had spoiled him so terribly. He got a package every week, and owned a bicycle with gears, unheard of before his arrival.

"What do you know about this?" asked the prosecutor.

"What do you mean?"

"Did you ever hear him say what he said?"

"If he ever said that around me I'd kill him."

"Have you noticed anything else?"

"What?"

"I mean, well, does he avoid you or anything?"

Herbie suddenly yelled, "But he avoids everybody!" This was more than we had expected from old Herbie. He was shouted down immediately.

"I don't pay him no mind," said Earl, lapsing uncharacteristically into the idiom of his people.

The trial must have lasted two hours. Witness after witness came forward to take a stand against race prejudice. There was an interruption when one of the youngest boys, having watched silently, suddenly burst into tears.

"Look, Peabody's crying."

"What's wrong, Peabody?" someone asked gently.

Confused, overwhelmed by his emotions, Peabody could only stammer, "I'm sorry, I'm sorry, I don't know what's the matter. . . . It's so horrible, how could he . . . "

"What's horrible?"

"Him saying that. How could he say that? I don't understand," the boy said, tears falling from his eyes.

"It's all right, Peabody, don't worry."

"I'm sorry, I'm sorry."

Most of the testimony was on a high moral plane. Children are swept away by morality. Only rarely did it sink to the level of life. From the boy who slept next to Ligget: "He smells."

We didn't laugh. We weren't stupid boys, nor insensitive, and we recognized the seriousness of such a statement.

"His bed smells, and his clothes, and everything he has. He's a smelly, fat slob and I won't sleep next to him. I'm going to move my bed."

Sensing impatience in the room, the prosecutor called the prisoner himself. "Do you have anything to say?"

Ligget stood stock still, his hidden eyes gleaming. He was pale.

"This is your last chance, you better take it. We'll all listen, we'll listen to your side of it." The crowd voiced its agreement, moved by an instant of homage to fair play, and false sympathy. "Okay then, don't say you didn't have a chance."

"Wait a second," said Herbie. "I want to ask him something. Did you say 'nigger-lip' to Sammy?"

It appeared for a moment that Ligget was about to speak, but he gave up the effort. Shaking his head slowly, he denied the charge.

The prosecutor stepped forward. "All those who find him guilty say aye." A roar from forty boys. "All those who find him innocent say nay." Silence. (In a certain sense the trial was a parody of Freemont's "town meetings" in which rather important questions of curriculum and school policy were debated before the students and put to a vote.)

The punishment seemed to suggest itself. We lined up for one punch apiece.

Although Ligget's beating is part of my life (past, present, and future coexist in the unconscious, says Freud), and although I've worried about it off and on for years, all I can say about it is that brutality happens easily. I learned almost nothing from beating up Ligget.

There was a tremendous, heart-swelling excitement as I waited. The line moved slowly, people were taking their time. You got only one punch and you didn't want to waste it. A ritual of getting set, measuring the distance, perhaps adjusting the angle of his jaw with an index finger—all this had to be done before you let go. A few boys had fluffed already, only grazing him. If you missed completely you got another chance.

It wasn't hurting Ligget that was important, but rather the unbelievable opportunity to throw a clean, powerful punch completely unhindered, and with none of the sloppiness of an actual fight. Ligget was simply a punching bag, albeit the best possible kind of punching bag, one in human form, with sensory equipment to measure the strength of your blows.

It was my turn. Ligget looked at me blankly. I picked a spot on his chin, drew back my arm, and threw as hard a punch as I could muster. Instant disappointment. I hadn't missed, there was a kind of snapping sound as my fist landed, and his head jerked back, but the whole complex of movements was too fast, somehow missing the exaggerated movie-punch finality I had anticipated. Ligget looked at the boy behind me and I stepped away. I think someone clapped me on the back.

"Good shot."

Little Peabody, tear-stained but sober, swung an awkward blow that almost missed, grazing Ligget's mouth and bringing a little blood. He moved away and the last few boys took their turns.

Ligget was still on his feet. His face was swollen and his small eyes were glazed, but he stood unaided. He had kept his hands deep in his pockets to prevent the reflex of defense. He drew them out and for a moment there was silence, as if everyone expected him to speak.

Perhaps it was because we felt cheated. Each boy's dreams-of-glory punch had been a shade off center, or not quite hard enough, or thrown at the wrong angle, missing perfection by a maddeningly narrow margin. The urge to try again was strong. Unconsciously we knew we'd never have another chance. This wild freedom was ours once only. And perhaps among the older boys there were some who harbored the dream of throwing one final, superman punch, the knock-out blow to end all knock-out blows. Spontaneously, the line formed again.

After three or four blows Ligget collapsed. He sank to the floor, his eyes open and a dark stain spreading in his crotch. Someone told him to get up but it became clear he couldn't understand. Eventually a boy was sent to get the nurse. He was taken to the hospital in an ambulance.

X rays revealed that Ligget's jaw was broken in four places. We learned this the day after the beating, all of us repentant, sincerely unable to understand how it had happened. When he was well enough we went to visit him in the hospital. He was friendly, and accepted our apologies. One could tell he was trying, but his voice was thin and stiff, without a person behind it, like a bad actor reading lines. He wouldn't see us alone, there had to be an adult sitting by him.

No disciplinary action was taken against us. There was talk for a while that Sammy was going to be expelled, but it came to nothing. Ligget never returned.

From THIS BOY'S LIFE

T O B I A S   W O L F F

Editor's Note: "I started out jotting things down about my childhood, because I felt them slipping away, and I wanted to have some sort of record," explains Tobias Wolff about the origin of his moving 1989 memoir This Boy's Life. *As Wolff wrote, he saw patterns emerging. Then he began to hear a voice, telling the story.*

"I recognized that my childhood made a good story," he acknowledges. "For years I had seen people perk up when I told them some of the things that happened when I was a kid."

This Boy's Life *is our century's* Adventures of Huckleberry Finn, *only in artful* nonfiction *rather than fiction. Adolescent Toby Wolff, like Huck, has "lit out for the Territory,"· the Northwest Territory to be exact, and we watch him literally forging a new identity through acts of rebellion and imagination. The memoir opens on the continental divide in the 1950s, with ten-year-old Toby heading west with his mother "to get away from a man my mother was afraid of and to get rich on uranium." The two end up in Chinook, Washington, a camp town owned by Seattle City Light, and in the excerpt reprinted here Toby, now fourteen, is under the thumb of Dwight, his mother's abusive second husband.*

Wolff published two collections of short stories and the award-winning novella Barracks Thief *before turning to nonfiction. Perhaps for this reason, each chapter of* This Boy's Life *reads like a highly concentrated short story. Careful study of this excerpt will reveal how Wolff achieves this effect. Though appearing almost seamless in its chronological flow, the excerpt is actually crafted from nine separate* scenes—*the longest 27 paragraphs, the shortest, two. In fact, five of the nine scenes consist of just two or three vivid paragraphs.*

In his two longest scenes, Wolff shows himself a master of terse, pointed dialogue. "I have a good memory, and I was lucky—most of the people I lived with repeated themselves a lot," Wolff explains. He insists, in fact, that memory is the story: "Our memories are what make us."

Wolff says he was also fortunate in having an almost Dickensian villain in his stepfather, Dwight, who was chillingly re-created by Robert DeNiro in the 1993 film of Wolff's memoir. "I had this complete creep around me all the time who had no virtues and all the faults," he says. "I was going to push against whatever man was around anyway, but what a wonderful thing that the man I had to push against was Dwight."

Clearly that is the view of the adult writer rather than of the beleaguered boy whose blunt, taut language carries the burden of the narration. Wolff says he was drawn to writers like Frank Conroy, "people willing to confront their past and the truth of their past and the truth of what it's like to grow up in this country, wanting a piece of the action, and what it costs you."

He also was influenced by the late "minimalist" short story writer Raymond Carver, whom he met when both taught at Stanford University in the 1970s: "I

was already pretty much writing the way I write. But reading Ray's work gave me
a sense of confirmation about what I was doing. I felt an immediate affinity for his
standards of honesty and exactness, his refusal to do anything cheap in a story, to
destroy his characters with irony that proved his own virtue."

Wolff says he deliberately kept his own adult perspective from intruding much
in his memoir:

> *I think that would have compromised the integrity of [the boy's] experience,*
> *to come in with a comforting adult voice all the time. I don't like that tone in*
> *childhood memoirs, generally, letting the kid off the hook with this very*
> *adult ironical humor, when things really are quite serious. One of the things*
> *I took to heart when I was preparing myself to write the book was Graham*
> *Greene's* A Sort of Life, *in which he says that memoirs frequently go bad*
> *because writers fail to give due gravity to the things that were grave and*
> *serious matters when they were young. . . .*
>
> *Was it being coy to withhold [the later perspective]? I would rather run*
> *the risk of being coy than of crowding the kid out. You have to make those*
> *decisions when you write anything, and you always risk one thing to get*
> *another. You have to decide what you want most. I most wanted the reader*
> *to have a sense of this kid very much on his own, which he was. My mother*
> *was certainly a loving person and would give whatever support she could,*
> *but she couldn't always give substantial support because her circumstances*
> *didn't allow it.*

Circumstances did offer a dog as an unwanted intruder into young Toby Wolff's
homelife. It is the adult writer, Tobias Wolff, who turns this battered, cowering
weimaraner into a subtle symbol *of himself and his potential fate.*

Likewise his memoir's title, This Boy's Life, *is an ironic allusion to the cheery*
boy's magazine Boy's Life, *reminding readers of the discrepancy between the*
ideal boyhood portrayed in that magazine and the reality of Wolff's, and many
others', lives.

However, hope as well as hardship march side by side through Wolff's memoir.
The hard-edged humor mother and son cultivate becomes a survival mechanism.
This humor offers the reader both comic relief from the cruelty of their condition
and comic intensification of it. It adds to the rich mix of violence, love,
deprivation, compassion, and raw optimism which makes This Boy's Life *such a*
powerfully realistic American narrative.

The boy Toby Wolff did survive into manhood. He joined the army in 1964,
trained as a member of the Special Forces, and departed from the army in 1968
after serving in Vietnam. Wolff then found his way to Oxford University where he
earned bachelor's and master's degrees. He also holds a master's degree from
Stanford University where he won a Wallace Stegner Fellowship in creative
writing. A hint of this future is suggested in the following excerpt, for, in an
emblematic moment, young Toby finds his voice on the open road, and learns
lessons never intended by the narrow Dwight.

When I got home from Concrete one night there was a big dog sleeping on the floor of the utility room. It was an ugly dog. Its short yellow coat was bare in patches, and one ear hung in pennant-like shreds. It had a pink, almost hairless tail. As I began to walk past, the dog came awake. Its eyes were yellow. At first it just looked at me, but when I moved again it gave a low growl. I yelled for someone to come.

Dwight stuck his head throught the doorway and the dog got up and started licking his hands. Dwight asked what the problem was and I told him the dog had growled at me.

Dwight said, "Good, he's supposed to. He doesn't know you yet. Champion," he said, "this is Jack. Let him smell your hands," he told me. "Go on, he won't bite."

I held my hand out and Champion sniffed it. "*Jack*," Dwight said to him. "*Jack*."

I asked Dwight whose dog it was. He told me it was mine.

"Mine?"

"You said you wanted a dog."

"Not this one."

"Well, he's yours. You paid for him," he added.

I asked what he meant, I paid for him, but Dwight wouldn't tell me. I found out a few minutes later. Something was wrong in my room. Then I saw that my Winchester was gone. I stared at the pine rack I had made for it in shop. I stared at the rack as if I'd overlooked the rifle the first time, and only needed to look more carefully to see it. I sat on my bed for a while, then I stood up and walked out to the living room, where Dwight was watching television.

I said, "My Winchester is gone."

"That dog is purebred weimaraner," Dwight said, keeping his eyes on the TV.

"I don't want it. I want my Winchester."

"Then you're shit out of luck, because your Winchester is on its way to Seattle."

"But that was *my* rifle!"

"And Champ's your dog! Jesus! I trade some old piece of crap for a valuable hunting dog and what do you do? Piss and moan, piss and moan."

"I'm not pissing and moaning."

"The hell you aren't. You can just make your own deals from now on."

My mother was at a political conference. She had done some local organizing for the Democratic party in the last state election, and now they were trying to get her to work for Adlai Stevenson. When she got home the next day I met her outside and told her about the rifle.

She nodded as if she'd already heard the story. "I knew he'd do something," she said.

They had it out after I went to bed. Dwight made some noise but she backed him down. The rifle belonged to me, she said. He could yell all he wanted but on that point there was nothing to discuss. She made Dwight agree that when Champion's owner sent up the AKC papers he'd promised to send, papers that would prove the dog's illustrious line of descent, Dwight would call him and arrange to drive Champion down to Seattle and get my rifle back. He couldn't do that now because he didn't know the man's last name or address.

In this way the affair was settled to my satisfaction, except that the man some-how forgot to send the papers.

We took Champion hunting for the first time at a gravel quarry where mergansers liked to congregate. These ducks were considered bad eating, so most people didn't shoot them. But Dwight would shoot at anything. He was a poor hunter, restless and unobservant and loud, and he never got the animals he went after. This made him furious; on the way back to the car he would kill anything he saw. He killed chip-munks, squirrels, blue jays and robins. He killed a great snowy owl with a 12-gauge from ten feet away and took potshots at bald eagles as they skimmed the river. I never saw him get a deer, a grouse, a quail, a pheasant, an edible duck, or even a large fish.

He thought his equipment was to blame. To his collection of target rifles he added two hunting rifles, a Marlin 30/30 and a Garand M–1 with a telescopic sight. He had a double-barreled 12-gauge shotgun for waterfowl and a semiautomatic 16-gauge that he called his "bush gun." To spot the game he never got close to he car-ried a pair of high-powered Zeiss binoculars. To dress the game he never killed he carried a Puma hunting knife.

For all the talk of Champion being my dog, I understood that he was supposed to be part of Dwight's total hunting system.

When we reached the quarry, Dwight threw a stick into the water to stimulate Champion's retrieving instincts and to demonstrate the softness of his mouth. He said weimaraners were famous for their mouths. "You won't see one tooth mark on that stick," he told me. Champion ran up to the water, then stopped. He looked back at us and whimpered. He was quaking like a chihuahua. "Go on, boy," Dwight said. Champion whimpered again. He bent one paw, stuck it in the water, pulled it out and started barking at the stick.

"Smart dog," Dwight said. "Knows it's not a bird."

The mergansers came in at dusk. They must have seen us, but as if they knew what they tasted like they showed no fear. They flew in low and close together. Dwight fired both barrels at them. One duck dropped like a stone and the rest rushed up again, quacking loudly. They circled the quarry long enough for Dwight to reload and fire. This time he didn't hit anything, and the mergansers flew away.

The bird he'd brought down was floating in the water about twenty feet from shore. Its bill was under the surface, its wings outstretched. It wasn't moving. Dwight broke the shotgun and pulled out the shells. "Get 'er, Champ," he said. But Champion did not get the duck. He wasn't even on the shore now, or anywhere else in sight. Dwight called to him in tones of friendliness, command, and threat, but he did not return. I offered to bring the duck in by throwing rocks behind it. Dwight said not to bother, it was just a garbage bird.

We found Champion under the car. Dwight had to sweet-talk him for several minutes before he bellied out, yelping softly and cowering. "He's a little gun-shy is all," Dwight said. "We can fix that."

Dwight decided to fix that by taking Champion goose hunting in eastern Washington. He talked my mother into going along. They were supposed to be away for about a week, but came back on unfriendly terms after three days. My mother told me that Champion had run off across the fields after the first shot, and that it took Dwight most of the afternoon to find him. They kept him in the car the next day but he pissed and crapped all over the seats. That was when they decided to come home.

"He cleaned it up," she added, "Every bit of it. I wouldn't go near it."

I hadn't asked. I guess she just thought I'd like to know.

Champion didn't always growl when I came in. Usually he ignored me, and in time I would let down my guard, and then he would do it again and scare the hell out of me. One night he gave me such a fright that I grabbed a sponge mop and hit him over the head. Champion snarled and I hit him again and kept hitting him, screaming myself hysterical while he tried to get away, his paws scrabbling on the wooden floor. Finally he stuck his head behind the water heater and kept it there as I worked the rest of him over. At some point I got tired, and saw what I was doing, and stopped.

I was alone in the house. I tried to pace off the jangling I felt, and the guilt. I could forgive myself for most things, but not cruelty.

I went back to the utility room. Champion was lying on his blanket again. I prodded his bones and examined him for cuts. He seemed okay. The sponge had taken the force of the blows. While I checked him over, Champion whined and licked my hands. I spoke gently to him. This was a mistake. It gave him the idea that I liked him, that we were pals. From that night on he wanted to be with me all the time. Whenever I passed through the utility room he groveled and abased himself, hoping to keep me there, then barked and hurled himself against the door as I went outside.

This caused me some trouble. For almost a year now, ever since I started high school, I'd been sneaking out of the house after midnight to take the car for joy rides. Dwight wouldn't teach me to drive—he claimed to believe that I would kill us both— so I had taken the teaching function upon myself. After Champion attached himself to me, I had to bring him along or he would raise the household with his cries.

With Champion beside me on the front seat, gazing out the window like a real passenger or snapping his chops at the wind, I cruised the empty streets of the camp. When I got bored I took the car to a stretch of road halfway to Marblemount where I could get it up to a hundred miles an hour without having to make any turns. As Champion placidly watched the white line shivering between the headlights I chattered like a gibbon and wept tears of pure terror. Then I stopped the car in the middle of the road, turned it around, and did the same thing headed the other way. I drove a little farther each time. Someday, I thought, I would just keep going.

One morning I backed the car into a ditch while turning it around for my run home. I spun the wheels for a while, then got out and looked things over. I spun the wheels some more, until I was dug in good and deep. Then I gave up and started the trek back to camp. It was nearly three o'clock, and the walk home would take at least four hours. They would find me missing before I got there. The car too. I let off a string of swear words, but they seemed to be coming at me, not from me, and I soon stopped.

Champion ran ahead through the forest that crowded the road on both sides. The mountains were black all around, the stars brilliant in the inky sky. My footsteps were loud on the roadway. I heard them as if they came from somebody else. The movement of my legs began to feel foreign to me, and then the rest of my body, foreign and unconvincing, as if I were only pretending to be someone. I watched this body clomp along. I was outside it, watching it without belief. Its imitation of purpose seemed absurd and frightening. I did not know what it was, or what was watching it so anxiously, from so far away.

And then a voice bawled, "Oh Maybelline!" I knew that voice. It was mine, and it was loud, and I got behind it. I sang "Maybelline" and another song, and another. I kept singing at the top of my voice. A couple of times I broke off to try to think up an excuse for my situation—Look, I know you won't believe this, but I just kind of woke up and there I was, *driving the car*!—but all of these ideas led me to despair, and I went back to singing songs. I sang every song I knew, and it began to amaze me how many of them there were. And I became aware that I didn't sound that bad out here where I could really cut loose—that I sounded pretty good. I took different parts. I did talking songs, like "Deck of Cards" and "Three Stars." I sang falsetto. I began to enjoy myself.

I was halfway to Chinook when I heard an engine behind me. I faced the lights and flagged the driver down. He stopped his truck in the road, engine running, a man I didn't know. "That your car back there?" he asked.

I said it was.

"How'd you do that, anyway?"

"It's hard to explain," I said.

He told me to get in. I started yelling for Champion. "Wait a minute," he said. "Who's this Champ? You didn't say anything about any Champ."

"My dog."

The man peered into the darkness while I tried to call Champion in. He was afraid of what was out there and afraid of me, and his fear made me feel dangerous. Finally he said, "I'm going," but just then Champion bounded out of the trees. The man looked at him. "God almighty," he said, but he opened the door for us and drove us back to the car. He was silent during the drive and silent while he winched the car up onto the road. When I thanked him, he just nodded slightly and drove away.

I made it into bed not long before my mother came to wake me. "I don't feel so good," I told her.

She put her hand on my forehead, and at that gesture I wanted to tell her everything, the whole scrape, not by way of confession but in my exhilaration at having gotten out of it. She liked hearing stories about close calls; they confirmed her faith in luck. But I knew that I couldn't tell her without at least promising never to take the car again, which I had every intention of doing, or at worst forcing her to betray me to Dwight.

She looked down at me in the gray light of dawn. "You don't have a fever," she said. "But I have to admit, you look awful." She told me I could stay home from school that day if I promised not to watch TV.

I slept until lunchtime. I was sitting up in bed, eating a sandwich, when Dwight came to my room. He leaned in the doorway with his hands in his pockets like a mime acting out Relaxation. It made me wary.

"Feeling better?" he asked.

I said I was.

"Wouldn't want you to come down with anything serious," he said. "Get some sleep, did you?"

"Yes sir."

"You must've needed it."

I waited.

"Oh, by the way, you didn't happen to hear a funny little pinging noise in the engine, did you?"

"What engine?"

He smiled.

Then he said he'd been at the commissary a few minutes ago with Champion, and that he'd met a man there who recognized the dog and told a pretty interesting story of how they happened to cross paths earlier that morning. What did I think about that?

I said I didn't know what he was talking about.

Then he was on me. He caught me with one hand under the covers and the other holding the sandwich, and at first, instead of protecting myself, I jerked the sandwich away as if that was what he wanted. His open hands lashed back and forth across my face. I dropped the sandwich and covered my face with my forearm, but I couldn't keep his hands away. He was kneeling on the bed, his legs on either side of me, locking me in with the blankets. I shouted his name, but he kept hitting me in a fast convulsive rhythm and I knew he was beyond all hearing. Somehow, with no conscious intention, I pulled my other arm free and hit him in the throat. He reared back, gasping. I pushed him off the bed and kicked the covers away, but before I could get up he grabbed my hair and forced my face down hard against the mattress. Then he hit me in the back of the neck. I went rigid with the shock. He tightened his grip on my hair. I waited for him to hit me again. I could hear him panting. We stayed like that for a while. Then he pushed me away and got up. He stood over me, breathing hoarsely. "Clean up this mess," he said. He turned at the door and said, "I hope you learned your lesson."

I learned a couple of lessons. I learned that a punch in the throat does not always stop the other fellow. And I learned that it's a bad idea to curse when you're in trouble, but a good idea to sing, if you can.

Champion had seen his last merganser. He turned out to be a cat killer. Three times he brought dead cats back to the house between those famously soft jaws of his. Dwight dropped them in the river and yelled at Pearl and me for letting him out. But Champ was under suspicion, and one day he got into someone's back yard and tore a Persian kitten to pieces under the eyes of the little girl who owned it. The camp director knocked on the door that evening and told Dwight that Champion had to go, now. Dwight said he'd need a few days to find him another home, but the camp director said that what he meant by now was *now*, as soon as he left.

Dwight stayed in the utility room for some time. After a spell of silence I heard him rummaging around. Then he said, "Come on, Champ." My mother and I were reading in the living room. We looked at each other. I went to the window and watched Dwight walking into the dusk, Champion sniffing the ground ahead of him. Dwight was carrying the 30/30. He let Champion into the car and drove away, upriver.

Dwight was only gone for a little while. I knew he hadn't buried Champion, because he came back so soon and because we didn't own a shovel.

My mother and I liked to watch *The Untouchables*. On one episode Al Capone confronted a man who had disappointed him. He listened to the man's tortured explanation with a look of sympathy and understanding. Then he said, softly, "Why don't you take a little ride with Frank?" The man's eyes bulged. He looked at Frank Nitti, then turned back to Al Capone and cried, "No, Mr. Capone, wait, I'll make it up to you . . ." But Mr. Capone was reading some papers on his desk. The next shot showed a long black car parked on a country road.

After Champion, whenever I did something wrong my mother would say to me, "Why don't you take a little ride with Dwight?"

From UNTO THE SONS

GAY TALESE

Editor's Note: In 1982, having written about the New York Times *in* The Kingdom and the Power, *the Mafia in* Honor Thy Father, *and sex and censorship in America in* Thy Neighbor's Wife, *Gay Talese decided it was time to turn from spectator to subject. "For 37 years I had been a sympathetic observer of other people's challenges and conflicts," he notes. "Now I would turn the spotlight on my family and myself in order to tell the story of Italian immigration to America."*

Unto the Sons, *the resulting volume published in 1992, represents Talese's most ambitious research and writing to date. "The intoxication of research is that you never know where it will take you," he acknowledges. From 1982 to 1987 Talese made three extended visits to a remote mountain village in southern Italy. There, in Maida, his ancestors had settled, and there many Taleses remain to this day. Talese traced his family name back to the fourteenth century and the village itself back to the ancient Greeks.*

"I hired an Italian interpreter, and during the days I would interview my relatives (through the interpreter) about our family history," he recalls. "At night I would read histories of Italy and Europe to absorb a sense of the larger events, the historical stage on which my ancestors were merely players—minor players but worthy of notice nevertheless."

Following the trail of his father's immigration to America in 1922, Talese stopped in Paris and then spent eight months in Ambler, Pennsylvania, a small suburb north of Philadelphia where many southern Italian stonecutters, like his grandfather and namesake Gaetano Talese, found work. From Ambler he journeyed southeast by train to Ocean City, New Jersey, a resort island south of Atlantic City where Joseph, his father, would make his home, establishing a tailor shop at exactly the latitude of his home village in Italy.

The final chapter of Unto the Sons, *reprinted here, takes place in Ocean City during World War II. It enlarges our sense of that "good war," by presenting a side rarely noted by historians or novelists. Proud to be a new American citizen, Joseph Talese is yet torn by conflict as he watches his adopted country at war with his native Italy. That the casualties of war included more than the soldiers at the front is the unspoken message of Talese's story. Indeed the war would reach out to strike twelve-year-old Gay himself.*

The climactic scene of this chapter was engraved indelibly in Talese's mind— and body. Nevertheless, he conducted 60 formal interviews with his father and mother in order to be able to re-create accurately their actions and emotions. He realized that his family's store also offered an advantage for any information gatherer: "My parent's store was like a town center. People talked about their own lives, and about each other." Ocean City's first war victim, Edgar Ferguson, had been a customer in the store. However, Talese verified his death and gathered other historic and scenic details for this chapter by paging through the Ocean City Sentinel Ledger *from 1920 to 1945. That newspaper and dozens of books on*

fascism in America prepared Talese to report the local mood toward the Italian
dictator Benito Mussolini.

The result is a lost story regained, and our enlarged vision of both the
immigrant experience and the conflicts of war. "I recognize now that I have been
trying to write this story—of my father, of myself, and of other Italo-Americans—
for the past 40 years," Talese confesses. "I believe the most average life is
extraordinary, if you can just get to the truth of it. Artists of nonfiction can bring to
people an enlarged clarification of their lives."

Throughout the winter of 1944, Joseph prayed several times each day in the living room of his home, kneeling on the red velvet of the prie-dieu under the portrait of the saint, ignoring the store bell below and leaving the operation of his business largely to his wife. He did this at Catherine's suggestion, for he had been hospitalized after the Christmas holidays with appendicitis, and after returning to work he had become so uncharacteristically curt with the customers that he realized the business would be better served by his absence. A high percentage of the clientele now were American servicemen on shore leave, young men demanding quick service, often insisting that their uniforms be pressed or their newly earned chevrons be sewn on while they waited; and among such customers, many of whom had returned from triumphant tours in Sicily and Italy, Joseph could not always conceal the humiliation and divided loyalty he felt as an emotional double agent.

He had dutifully attended the memorial service for the town's first war victim— Lieutenant Edgar Ferguson, a customer's son who had died in Italy (Joseph had hesitated only briefly before approaching the victim's family to express his condolences)—and Joseph had punctually participated in his daily shore patrol assignments along the boardwalk, on the lookout for German submarines with his fellow Rotarians, until his hospitalization had interfered; but since his release from the hospital in early February 1944, he had tried to isolate himself from his friends and business associates on this island that had become increasingly jingoistic as the war's end seemed to be nearing and victory for the Allies seemed inevitable. He had stopped having lunch as usual at the corner restaurant near his shop because he was weary of the war talk at the counter, and tired of hearing such tunes on the jukebox as "Praise the Lord and Pass the Ammunition." He ceased attending the ten-fifteen Mass on Sunday mornings and went instead to an earlier one, at seven, which was less crowded and fifteen minutes shorter; it came without the sermon, which tended to be patriotic, and without the priest's public prayers that singled out for blessing only the servicemen of the Allies.

Joseph continued to keep up with the war news in the daily press, but now he bought the papers at a newsstand beyond the business district, a six-block trip instead of the short walk to the corner cigar store, because he wanted to avoid the neighborhood merchants and his other acquaintances who lingered there and might try to draw him into their discussions about the war in Italy. The last time he had gone there, during the summer before his illness, Mussolini had dominated the headlines (he had just been imprisoned by the Italian king) and as Joseph left with his papers underarm, he heard a familiar voice calling out from the rear of the store: "Hey, Joe, what's gonna happen to your friend now?"

Joseph glared at the men gathered around the soft-drink stand, and spotted his questioner—a thin, elderly man named Pat Malloy, who wore a white shirt and black bow tie and had worked for years behind the counter of the corner restaurant.

"He's no friend of mine!" Joseph shouted, feeling his anger rise as he stepped down to the sidewalk and went quickly up the avenue with his papers folded inward so that the headlines and the photographs of the jowly-faced interned dictator were covered. Joseph did not make eye contact with the soldiers and sailors he saw among the strollers, although he could hardly avoid the American flags that flapped across the sidewalk in front of every shop on Asbury Avenue, including his own; and it was never possible at night to forget the ongoing war: the town was completely blacked out—all the streetlamps were painted black; lowered shades and drawn curtains hid the lighted rooms within houses; and few people drove their automobiles after dark, not only because there was a gas shortage but also because the required black paint on their headlights induced automobile accidents and collisions with pedestrians and wandering dogs.

Although there had been no new German submarine attacks in the area since an American tanker had been torpedoed ten miles south of Ocean City a year before, the island's continuing blackout had introduced new problems: gangs of hoodlums from the mainland regularly ransacked vacant summer homes during the winter months; they also operated a flourishing trade in pilfered cars, having an abundance of parked vehicles to choose from during the nocturnal hours, when it was more difficult to drive cars than to steal them.

Joseph secured his dry-cleaning trucks each night in a garage, and he chained the bumper of his 1941 Buick to a stone wall in the lot behind his shop. Before driving it he often had to hammer the ice off the lock, but he accepted such delays as by-products of the war and the blackout—a blackout which, in his case, extended well beyond the boundaries of his island. He had been cut off from communication with his family in Italy, and his cousin in Paris, for many months. Antonio's last letter, received in the spring of 1943, before the Allies had attacked Sicily, described the Maida relatives as sustaining themselves but expecting the worst, and added that the POW husband of Joseph's sister (captured by the British in North Africa) might have been shot while trying to escape; in any case, no official word of his whereabouts had been received. Whether Joseph's brother Domenico was dead or alive was also questionable; he had not been heard from in more than a year. Antonio had passed on the report that Domenico was possibly with a German-led Italian infantry division near the Russian front—Antonio had received this information from a contact in the Italian Foreign Ministry—but he had emphasized to Joseph that the report was unsubstantiated. Since the arrival of Antonio's last letter, the Allied invasion of southern Italy had begun; Mussolini had been rescued from prison by Germans to serve as Hitler's puppet; and Joseph was now trying to recuperate on this island where he had lived compatibly for almost twenty-two years but on which he currently felt estranged as never before.

While his withdrawal was voluntary, having not been prompted by flagrant personal slights or expressions of ostracism toward his business, Joseph felt powerless to free himself from his remoteness and the hostile emotion that too often erupted within him after such remarks as Pat Malloy's. It was possible that Malloy's referring to Mussolini as Joseph's "friend" was a casual remark, made without ill intent. Joseph was, after all, the town's most prominent Italian-born resident, one who had delivered lectures on Italian history and politics to community groups on the island and the mainland; and there had also been no derisive tone in Pat Malloy's voice, to say nothing of the cordial informality he had always shown toward Joseph in the restaurant. Furthermore, to be linked with Mussolini in Ocean City was not necessarily insulting, for the anti-union, Communist-baiting policies of the Duce had long been popular among the staunch Republicans who governed the island; and even in recent years, as the Fascist and Nazi regimes had closed ranks, Mussolini gained from whatever *was* to be gained in the United States by being identified as less odious and murderous than Hitler.

Still, during this winter, Joseph dwelled in a state of exile, adrift between the currents of two warring countries; he would read the newspapers at the breakfast table until nearly ten A.M., his children having already left for school and his wife gone down into the shop, and would then exit down the side stairwell of the building and out the back door, wearing his overcoat and homburg and with a heavy woolen scarf wrapped around his neck, and proceed across the lot to the railroad tracks, and then onward through the black ghetto toward the bay—in the opposite direction from the ocean and his binoculared submarine-searching friends and acquaintances who were lined up with their feet on the lower railings of the boardwalk and their eyes squinting toward the sea. The bayfront district was the most desolate section of town during the winter months; a few black men and women ambled through the bungalow- and shack-lined streets and the weedy fields cluttered with rusting car parts and other rubble, but there was no other sign of human life back here, save for the motorists driving along Bay Avenue, and the white workmen who sometimes scraped the bottoms of overturned dinghies and sloops in the boatyards, and repaired the docks in front of the vacated yacht club. There were hardly any sea gulls around the bay, where the scavenging possibilities could not compare with those offered by the ocean; and never during Joseph's excursions did he meet pedestrians whom he knew well enough to feel obliged to pause and converse with, and explain why he was off by himself traipsing about on the broken concrete sidewalks and frosty fields of this black, backwater part of town. His doctor had not suggested that daily walks would be beneficial to the restoration of his health, although Joseph had said so in explaining to his employees his comings and goings from the store; and it also became the excuse his wife gave to those regular customers who inquired, as some did, why he was constantly out of the shop and spotted frequently by them as they motored along Bay Avenue. Joseph had full confidence in Catherine's ability to make whatever he did seem plausible and proper, and meanwhile to carry on the business without him. She was assisted of course by her saleswomen, and by the old retired tailor from Philadelphia, who now worked a six-day week on the island; and she was supported as well by the reliable Mister Bossum, the black deacon and bootlegger who supervised the dry-cleaning plant and had taken over the responsibilities for the punctuality of the irresponsible pressers, especially the one presser everybody called Jet, the flat-footed, carbuncled ex-jazz musician who even on snowy days arrived for work wearing sandals and short-sleeved silk Hawaiian shirts.

Joseph passed close to Jet's boardinghouse each morning en route to the bayfront, and he was sometimes tempted to stop in and see if Jet had left for work yet; but Joseph resisted, having more urgent concerns. His mother was rarely out of his thoughts during his walks, although he found himself chiding her as much as praying for her. If only she had followed his father to America, Joseph told himself again and again, all the family would now be better off. They would be living with Joseph, or near him, somewhere in America, sparing him his present anxieties about their welfare, and his nagging suspicion that he had somehow abandoned them. If only he had some confirmation that his mother and the rest of his family were alive, that the Allied troops had skirted Maida and left the village undestroyed, he believed, he would no longer be the reclusive and petulant man he had become.

But the war news from southern Italy was scant and inconclusive as far as Maida was concerned. From the Philadelphia and Atlantic City papers he purchased each morning, and from the *New York Times* he received each afternoon in the mail, sometimes two days late, he knew only that the Allies were pushing back the Germans from several locations in the general vicinity of Naples. But Maida was too small, or too insignificant militarily, to warrant mention in the reports; and whatever damage had occurred there, or was occurring now, was left to Joseph's ever-darkening imagination.

When he returned from his walk, by noon if not sooner, he would unlock the rear door on the north side of the building and ascend to the apartment by the walled-in staircase without being seen by anyone in the shop. He would then press once on the wall buzzer near the living room door, signaling to his wife at her desk downstairs that he was home; and usually within seconds she would acknowledge his message with a return signal, and would press twice if she wanted him to pick up the phone extension to discuss something she thought he should know before she closed the shop at five-thirty and came up for the evening. Only on rare occasions did Catherine press twice, however, for there was hardly anything about the business that she could not handle at least as well as he could—a fact that they were both aware of, but that neither discussed. Catherine felt herself sensitive to his every mood and vulnerability, particularly at this point in the war, and in the aftermath of his illness. Having lived under the same roof with him virtually every hour of their almost fifteen years of marriage, except for the recent fortnight of his hospitalization, she thought she knew his strengths, his weaknesses, and his daily routine perhaps better than she knew her own. She knew that when he returned from the bayfront walk, he would first hang up his coat and hat in their bedroom closet in the rear of the apartment, then walk through the corridor back into the living room to kneel briefly at the prie-dieu. A quick lunch would follow in the kitchen, invariably consisting of a plain omelet with crisp unbuttered toast, and a cup of reheated coffee left over from breakfast. He ate little during the day and preferred eating alone. He washed and dried his dishes, but never put them away, leaving this chore for his daughter, Marian, when she came home from school.

Catherine did not leave the shop at lunchtime; instead she had the saleswomen who had their lunches at the nearby five-and-ten soda fountain bring back a milk shake for her. If it was relatively quiet in the shop at midday, as it nearly always was in wintertime, Catherine could hear her husband walking through the corridor after lunch to the mahogany Stromberg-Carlson console in the far corner of the living room, near his record collection. By this time she had already turned off the two particular neon lights in the front of the shop that caused most of the static upstairs on the radio; and if she did not hear him pacing the floor as he listened to the war news, she assumed Joseph was seated in the faded velvet armchair next to the set, leaning forward while twirling his steel-rimmed glasses. He would usually switch stations every three or four minutes, turning the console's large brown asbestos knob slowly and cautiously, as if fearing what the next broadcast might bring. At night she had often observed the intensity with which he listened to the news, await-ing each battlefront bulletin with his face so close to the set that his soulful expres-sion varied in color as the console's green "eye" fluttered in and out of frequency. The children were asleep at this time, these nightly reports often being broadcast well beyond midnight; Catherine herself usually retired shortly after closing the children's bedroom doors, having earlier helped them with their homework. But for hours afterward she lay awake restlessly, not because of the softly tuned radio that continued to absorb her husband's attentions in the living room, nor because of the pink light from the corridor torchère that was reflected forty feet away on the ceiling above the L-shaped ten-foot-high mirror-faced divider that masked the marital bed-room. She was disturbed instead by her husband's pacing back and forth in the liv-ing room *after* he had turned off the set, pacing that continued sometimes until dawn, to end only when he had fallen asleep on the sofa, fully clothed. In the morn-ing, hoping not to wake him, Catherine would whisper as she alerted the children for school; but he was always up before they had finished breakfast, and before shaving he would come into the kitchen in his rumpled suit to greet the children for-mally and then address his wife more gently, usually speaking to her in Italian so the children would not understand.

Except when disciplining them, Joseph paid a minimum of attention to the chil-dren during this troublesome winter. Each had been assigned daily chores, both in the apartment and in the store. Even when the chores were performed punctually and competently, Joseph regularly found things to criticize. His complaints were expressed as assertively to eight-year-old Marian as to twelve-year-old Gay. Of the two, only Marian was bold enough to defend herself against his accusations; she alone had the nerve to defy him. While she agreeably carried her mother's shopping list to the neighborhood grocery store, where the family had a charge account—it was actually a barter arrangement dating back to the Depression, when her father and the grocer began exchanging goods and services, making up the difference with gifts at Christmastime after the annual rallying—Marian was far less cooperative in her parents' store. She dusted the glass cases carelessly, swept the floors of the fit-ting rooms grudgingly when she did so at all, and reacted to her father's reprimands sometimes by dropping the broom or dustpan and stomping out of the shop, ignor-ing her father's promises of punishment.

"You're more stubborn than my mother," he once shouted at Marian, whom he had named in honor of his mother, although physically she clearly favored his wife's side of the family. Marian had her mother's fair complexion and the red hair of her mother's father, Rosso. She did not appear to be the sibling of her olive-skinned, dark-haired brother, who, while more tractable and less defiant than she, was also more capable of remaining out of their father's sight. Only during his father's illness and self-imposed exile from the shop did Gay enter it without feeling tense and apprehensive—and return to it after school without fear of being late, for his mother was not a clock-watcher; and thus in the winter of 1944 he began taking a more leisurely route home each afternoon, stopping first at the Russell Bakery Shop on Asbury Avenue, where a friend, the baker's grandson, could be counted on to bring a few éclairs out to the alley for a delicious, hastily consumed treat, and then play catch for a few minutes with the rubber ball that Gay always carried in his schoolbag.

Later, in the pressing room, after delivering to Jet and the other presser, Al, enough hangers-with-guards to fulfill their needs for at least a half-hour, Gay had the option of exiting through the back door via the steam screen provided by the pressers, and practicing his pitching form in the lot behind the shop—hurling the rubber ball against the brick wall of the neighboring hardware store's annex, and at times letting it carom off the roof of his father's chained Buick before catching it. He was secure in the knowledge that his father spent the afternoons up in the apartment on his knees, or sitting in the living room listening to operas or news broadcasts, and so he was stunned one afternoon to hear the thumping sounds of his ball punctuated by the urgent rapping of his father's knuckles against the rear window that overlooked the lot.

Gay ran back into the safety of the pressers' steam and quickly resumed the task of affixing guards to hangers, and also sandpapering and unbending those rusty and crooked hangers that customers had provided in response to the store's advertised appeal, and its promise to pay half a penny for each wire hanger, because of the wartime metal shortage. As he worked, he feared the appearance of his father and some form of retribution that might well be overdue. In recent weeks, he had received a failing report card after the midterm examinations; and he had been warned repeatedly by his father to discontinue making his prized model airplanes, for the glue used in sealing their parts cast a hypnotic and possibly toxic odor throughout the apartment. His father had furthermore charged that the glue was most likely the cause of his son's daydreaming and general dimwittedness in school, the lack of scholarship that had been noted, in kinder terms, by the Mother Superior on the bottom of the recently received report card.

Gay anxiously worked at the hangers, still awaiting his father's arrival in the workroom, knowing that he could expect no protection from Mister Bossum, or Jet, or Al, or the old tailor. But as the minutes continued to register on the misty-faced clock that hung on the workroom wall, and he sandpapered one hanger after another without interruption, he lost track of the time until he saw in front of him his mother's high-heeled shoes and heard her consoling voice suggesting that he was working too hard. It was also closing time, she said, as she extended a hand to help him up from his crouched position.

He was surprised to see that the tailor and the pressers had already left; now only slight sizzling sounds rose from the valves of the machines. Marian also stood waiting, holding a light bundle of groceries in the cloth sack their mother had made because of the paper scarcity. Gay walked up the interior staircase behind his mother and sister, then entered the living room and saw his father seated near the console with his back turned, leaning forward with his head in his hands. The radio was off. He could hear his father softly crying.

His sister, who seemed unaware of it, headed toward the kitchen with the groceries. Gay followed her. Catherine hastened toward her husband and placed a hand on his shoulder. For several minutes they could be heard speaking quietly in Italian. Then she left him and went into the kitchen to prepare the children's dinner; she explained to them that their father was feeling worse than usual, and added that after they had finished dinner they were to go to their rooms and close their doors, and, as long as they kept down the volume, they could listen to their radios. There was no homework to worry about. It was Friday night. Tomorrow a more leisurely day was in the offing, the always welcomed Saturday that brought no school bus or any chores in the shop until after ten A.M.

Joseph spent Friday night on the sofa, having hardly touched the dinner on the tray Catherine had placed on the coffee table in front of him. She had remained in the living room with him until midnight, continuing to speak in Italian. English was heard only when Catherine went to warn Marian that her radio was too loud, and to remind her that she should soon turn off the bed lamp because the following morning she would be picked up by the parents of one of her classmates, with whom she would be attending a birthday party on the mainland.

On Saturday morning after nine, when Gay got up, he saw that his sister had already left. Her door was open, her bed unmade. His parents' bedroom door was shut, as usual, but he knew his mother was downstairs, opening the store for the busy Saturday trade. He could hear the bell downstairs as customers opened and closed the shop's main door on Asbury Avenue. It was a sound he associated with Saturdays, and he always found the tones reassuring, signals of his family's financial stability. In the kitchen, as he poured himself some orange juice, he noticed that there were newspapers on the table that had not been there the night before. Returning to the front of the apartment, he saw no sign of his father. He found it odd to be in the apartment by himself and uniquely exhilarating to be able to walk around freely and privately, answerable to no one. As he approached the console, he noticed that its usual gleaming mahogany exterior was now smudgy with fingerprints. He then saw his father's bathrobe lying on the floor behind the sofa, and the ashtray filled with cigarette butts, and sections of newspapers that had been crumpled up and hurled in the other corner, and had come to rest near the piano. Since his father had always been the family's enforcer of tidiness and order, Gay could not even venture a guess as to the cause of this laxity.

Back in the kitchen, sitting in front of a bowl of dry cereal that his mother had left for him, he looked at the headlines and photographs on the front pages of the newspapers. One was an Italian-language paper that he of course could not read; another was the *New York Times*, which he refused to read because it did not have comics. But on this day he was drawn to the front pages of these and other papers because most of them displayed pictures of the devastation left after recent air raids—smoke was rising out of a large hilltop building that American bombers had attacked in Italy, and had completely destroyed. The headlines identified the ruins as the Abbey of Monte Cassino, located in southern Italy, northwest of Naples. The articles described the abbey as very old, dating back to the sixth century. They called it a cradle of learning throughout the Dark Ages, a scholarly center for Benedictine monks, who had occupied it for fourteen centuries; it was built on a hill that Nazi soldiers had taken over during the winter of 1943–1944. The raid on February 15, 1944, had involved more than a hundred forty of America's heaviest bombers, the B–17 Flying Fortresses; these, together with the medium-sized bombers that followed, released nearly six hundred tons of bombs on the abbey and its grounds. It was the first time the Allies had deliberately made a target of a religious building.

After breakfast, while brushing his teeth in the bathroom, dressed and ready to go down to the store, Gay heard strange noises in the apartment, a pounding on the walls and the cursing of an angry male voice. When he opened the door, he saw his father, in overcoat and hat, swatting down the model airplanes suspended from Gay's bedroom ceiling by almost invisible threads.

"*Stop it, they're mine!*" Gay screamed, horrified at the sight of his carefully crafted American bombers and fighter planes, framed with balsa wood and covered with crisp paper, being smashed into smithereens by his father. "*Stop, stop, stop— they're mine, get out of my room, get out!*" Joseph did not seem to hear, but kept swinging wildly with both hands until he had knocked out of the air and crushed with his feet every single plane that his son had for more than a year taken countless evening hours to make. They were two dozen in number—exact replicas of the United States' most famous fighter planes and bombers—the B–17 Flying Fortress, the B–26 Marauder, the B–25 Mitchell, the Bell P–39 Airacobra fighter plane, the P–38 Lockheed Lightning, the P–40 Kittyhawk; Britain's renowned Spitfire, Hurricane Lancaster; and other Allied models that until this moment had been the proudest achievement of Gay's boyhood.

"I hate you, I hate you," he cried at his father before running out of the apartment, and then down the side staircase to the first landing, where he grabbed his roller skates. "I hate you!" he yelled again, looking up toward the living room door, but seeing no sign of his father. Crying, he continued to the bottom of the staircase and out onto the avenue, then thrust his skates around his shoe tops without bothering to tighten them; and as quickly as he could, he headed up Asbury Avenue, thrashing his arms through the cold wind and sobbing as he sped between several bewildered people who suddenly stepped aside. As he passed the Russell Bakery Shop, he lost his balance and swerved toward the plate-glass window. People were lined up in front of the pastry counter, and two women screamed as they saw the boy, his hands outstretched, crash into the window and then fall bleeding with glass cascading down on his head.

Unconscious until the ambulance arrived, and then embarrassed by the crowds staring silently behind the ropes that the police held in front of the bakery's broken window, he turned toward his father, who was embracing him in bloody towels, crying and saying something in Italian that the boy did not understand.

"*Non ti spagnare*," Joseph said, over and over—don't be afraid—using the old dialect of southern Italians who had lived in fear of the Spanish monarchy. "*Non ti spagnare*," Joseph went on, cradling his son's head with his bloody hands, and closing his eyes as he heard his son repeating, tearfully, "I hate you."

Joseph then became silent, watching the ambulance crew arrive with a stretcher as the police ordered the people in the crowd to keep their distance. When Joseph next spoke, he did so in English, although his son found him no less bewildering than before, even as Joseph repeated: "Those who love you, make you cry. . . ."

THE LIVES OF A CELL

LEWIS THOMAS

Editor's Note: In the spring of 1975, an unusual complication arose within the National Book Award nominating committee. A single volume, Dr. Lewis Thomas's The Lives of a Cell: Notes of a Biology Watcher, *was nominated by both the Science and the Arts-and-Letters panels. A friendly tug-of-war ensued between the two panels and, in the end, the 1974 National Book Award was conferred on* The Lives of a Cell, *not as the best book of the year in science, but in arts and letters. This outcome came as a pleasant surprise to Dr. Thomas, who, although an admirer of such earlier physician writers as Oliver Wendell Holmes and a nearly lifelong poet himself, nevertheless had devoted his professional career to science, specifically immunology and experimental pathology. At his retirement, Thomas served as Chancellor of the Memorial Sloan-Kettering Cancer Center in New York City.*

Now six books later, it is possible to suggest that posterity may regard Thomas's greater contribution to be to literature rather than to science. Simply put, he is one of the best writers of short essays in the English language. Thomas's great gift has been to construct a genial literary persona whose optimistic spirit unifies his entire body of artful science writing. Thomas turns himself into our good doctor evincing surprise and delight at the world's interconnections.

Thomas never talks down to his readers. He calls a mitochondria a mitochondria, and centrioles, centrioles. However, by combining these terms with swift comparisons to the reader's own familiar experiences, he makes such technical subject matter understandable.

In the following title essay from The Lives of a Cell, *Thomas uses himself to illustrate his message: that we are all interconnected, and that unity is greater than differentiation. Joyce Carol Oates, who has used Thomas's volumes to teach students how to structure essays, has stated: "One might as well rise to the higher speculation that [Thomas's work] anticipates, the kind of writing that will appear more and more frequently, as scientists take on the language of poetry in order to communicate human truths too mysterious for old-fashioned common sense."*

W e are told that the trouble with Modern Man is that he has been trying to detach himself from nature. He sits in the topmost tiers of polymer, glass, and steel, dangling his pulsing legs, surveying at a distance the writhing life of the planet. In this scenario, Man comes on as a stupendous lethal force, and the earth is pictured as something delicate, like rising bubbles at the surface of a country pond, or flights of fragile birds.

But it is illusion to think that there is anything fragile about the life of the earth; surely this is the toughest membrane imaginable in the universe, opaque to probability, impermeable to death. We are the delicate part, transient and vulnerable as cilia. Nor is it a new thing for man to invent an existence that he imagines to be above the rest of life; this has been his most consistent intellectual exertion down the millennia. As illusion, it has never worked out to his satisfaction in the past, any more than it does today. Man is embedded in nature.

The biologic science of recent years has been making this a more urgent fact of life. The new, hard problem will be to cope with the dawning, intensifying realization of just how interlocked we are. The old, clung-to notions most of us have held about our special lordship are being deeply undermined.

Item. A good case can be made for our nonexistence as entities. We are not made up, as we had always supposed, of successively enriched packets of our own parts. We are shared, rented, occupied. At the interior of our cells, driving them, providing the oxidative energy that sends us out for the improvement of each shining day, are the mitochondria, and in a strict sense they are not ours. They turn out to be little separate creatures, the colonial posterity of migrant prokaryocytes, probably primitive bacteria that swam into ancestral precursors of our eukaryotic cells and stayed there. Ever since, they have maintained themselves and their ways, replicating in their own fashion, privately, with their own DNA and RNA quite different from ours. They are as much symbionts as the rhizobial bacteria in the roots of beans. Without them, we would not move a muscle, drum a finger, think a thought.

Mitochondria are stable and responsible lodgers, and I choose to trust them. But what of the other little animals, similarly established in my cells, sorting and balancing me, clustering me together? My centrioles, basal bodies, and probably a good many other more obscure tiny beings at work inside my cells, each with its own special genome, are as foreign, and as essential, as aphids in anthills. My cells are no longer the pure line entities I was raised with; they are ecosystems more complex than Jamaica Bay.

I like to think that they work in my interest, that each breath they draw for me, but perhaps it is they who walk through the local park in the early morning, sensing my senses, listening to my music, thinking my thoughts.

I am consoled, somewhat, by the thought that the green plants are in the same fix. They could not be plants, or green, without their chloroplasts, which run the photosynthetic enterprise and generate oxygen for the rest of us. As it turns out, chloroplasts are also separate creatures with their own genomes, speaking their own language.

We carry stores of DNA in our nuclei that may have come in, at one time or another, from the fusion of ancestral cells and the linking of ancestral organisms in symbiosis. Our genomes are catalogues of instructions from all kinds of sources in nature, filed for all kinds of contingencies. As for me, I am grateful for differentiation and speciation, but I cannot feel as separate an entity as I did a few years ago, before I was told these things, nor, I should think, can anyone else.

Item. The uniformity of the earth's life, more astonishing than its diversity, is accountable by the high probability that we derived, originally, from some single cell, fertilized in a bolt of lightning as the earth cooled. It is from the progeny of this parent cell that we take our looks; we still share genes around, and the resemblance of the enzymes of grasses to those of whales is a family resemblance.

The viruses, instead of being single-minded agents of disease and death, now begin to look more like mobile genes. Evolution is still an infinitely long and tedious biologic game, with only the winners staying at the table, but the rules are beginning to look more flexible. We live in a dancing matrix of viruses; they dart, rather like bees, from organism to organism, from plant to insect to mammal to me and back again, and into the sea, tugging along pieces of this genome, strings of genes from that, transplanting grafts of DNA, passing around heredity as though at a great party. They may be a mechanism for keeping new, mutant kinds of DNA in the widest circulation among us. If this is true, the odd virus disease, on which we must focus so much of our attention in medicine, may be looked on as an accident, something dropped.

Item. I have been trying to think of the earth as a kind of organism, but it is no go. I cannot think of it this way. It is too big, too complex, with too many working parts lacking visible connections. The other night, driving through a hilly, wooded part of southern New England, I wondered about this. If not like an organism, what is it like, what is it *most* like? Then, satisfactorily for that moment, it came to me: it is *most* like a single cell.

From PRAIRYERTH

WILLIAM LEAST HEAT-MOON

Editor's Note: William Trogdon derived his pen name, William Least Heat-Moon, from his Osage Indian heritage. When Trogdon's father, a Kansas City lawyer, became a Boy Scoutmaster, he took the name "Heat Moon" to honor an Osage kinsman who may have been born in July, the hottest month of the year. When Trogdon's older brother became a Scout, he became "Little Heat Moon," leaving younger brother Bill resigned to be "Least Heat Moon."

Young Bill grew up to be a scholar of the Renaissance with four college degrees when, in the late 1970s, he embarked on a 13,000 mile odyssey through the back roads of America which he chronicled in the 1983 volume Blue Highways. *The book's title derives from the color mapmakers used to trace the winding side roads off the beaten interstates. "I'm a map freak," confesses Heat-Moon, who always carries a well-worn atlas upon which he has marked—with a yellow pencil—every road he has ever driven.*

Blue Highways *became a bestseller in 1983 and has sold more than a million copies. In 1984 Heat-Moon turned his attention from the long highway to one small county in the center of America: Chase County, Kansas, population 3,013. For the next four years, he wandered the 744 truly square miles of Chase County, from its Flint Hills in the east to the nation's last remaining tallgrass prairie in the west. Dividing the square county into its 12 equally square geographical survey sections, Heat-Moon walked and talked, but mostly listened and observed.*

PrairyErth, *the resulting volume published in 1991, takes its name from an old geological term for prairie soil. Heat-Moon's multilayered book is subtitled "A Deep Map," for the book is a foray (simultaneously) through space, time, mind, and emotion.*

"PrairyErth is about the connection of land and memory," Heat-Moon explains, and he has structured his palimpsest in twelve sections, one for each section of the county. Each section begins with a map, followed by pages of quotations from Heat-Moon's "Commonplace Book," his collection of memorable passages from his reading. Then follow stories of and ruminations on the terrain, including excerpts from pioneer diaries; reflections upon fence posts, arrowheads, and the nesting habits of pack rats; and a re-creation of the 1931 Chase County airplane crash which killed Notre Dame football hero Knute Rockne.

Heat-Moon superbly captures the Kansas idiom, introducing us to coyote hunters and conservationists, feminist ranchers and cafe owners, and other feisty Kansans of all kinds. He pays loving tribute to the 140 ways to spell Kansas, including Kaw, the name of the Native American tribe at home on the prairie before white settlers uprooted them. Heat-Moon has confessed to hearing the voices of his Indian ancestors as he has written his artful nonfiction. Parts of PrairyErth, *he confirms, "do not seem as though they are my voice."*

Many mornings as he sat down to work on PrairyErth, *Heat-Moon would pick up and rub one of the ancient rocks he keeps on his desk. Sometimes he would hold the rock high, his arms reaching toward the sky in a stance many Native Americans use in prayer. "If I didn't do that," he says, "I didn't write as well."*

PrairyErth offers tales of tornadoes, fires, and floods, such as the scene excerpted below. Heat-Moon gives us survivors, and the forces still threatening survival. His PrairyErth enlarges our sense of place. As John Skow has noted: "'Emptiness' turned out to be only apparent, and 'near nothing' jostling and crowded."

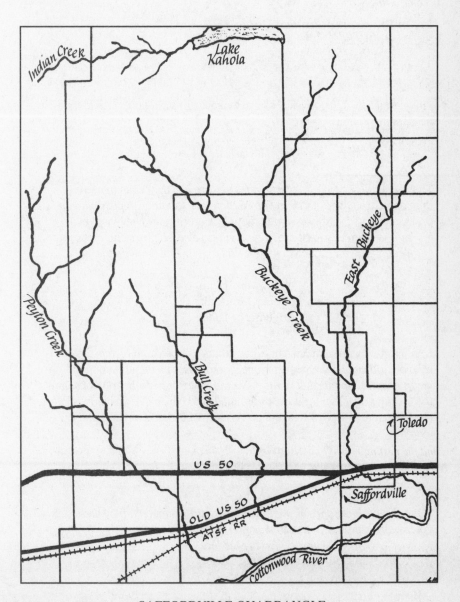

SAFFORDVILLE QUADRANGLE

From the Commonplace Book:
Saffordville

I must describe it. Its physical characteristics are somehow close to the heart of the matter.
                         -Mark Helprin,
                           "Mar Nueva" (1988)

There is no describing [the prairies]. They are like the ocean in more than one particular but in none more than this: the utter impossibility of producing any just impression of them by description. They inspire feelings so unique, so distinct from anything else, so powerful, yet vague and indefinite, as to defy description, while they invite the attempt.
                         -John C. Van Tramp,
                      Prairie and Rocky Mountain
                           Adventures *(1860)*

Creeds and carrots, catechisms and cabbages, tenets and turnips, religion and rutabagas, governments and grasses all depend upon the dewpoint and the thermal range. Give the philosopher a handful of soil, the mean annual temperature and rainfall, and his analysis would enable him to predict with absolute certainty the characteristics of the nation.
                         -John James Ingalls,
                      "In Praise of Blue Grass" (1875)

                              * * *

"Things have a life of their own," the gypsy proclaimed with a harsh accent. "It's simply a matter of waking up their souls."
                         -Gabriel García Márquez,
                    One Hundred Years of Solitude *(1967)*

Each hamlet or village or town should be a **place***, its* **own** *place. This is not a matter of fake historicism or artsy-craftsy architecture. It is a*

*matter of respect for things existing, subtle patterns of place woven
from vistas and street widths and the siting and color and scale of
stores, houses, and trees. . . . If the countryside is to prosper, it must be
different from city or suburb. . . . That difference is in part the simple
business of containing our towns and giving them boundaries.*
-Robert B. Riley,
"New Mexico Villages in a Future
Landscape" (1969)

*Gain! Gain! Gain! Gain! Gain! is the beginning, the middle and the end,
the alpha and omega of the founders of American towns.*
-Morris Birkbeck,
Notes on a Journey in America *(1818)*

*We always need theres, spots which happily aren't like ours, to validate
heres. Mostly theres are inert supports, silent witnesses to the quality of
here.*
-Robert B. Heilman,
"We're Here" (1987)

*Chase County has 2,839 people. There is one blind person, one insane
person, and 745 voters.*
-News item,
Chase County News *(1873)*

*Maybe you never heard of Cottonwood Falls, but the philosopher who
said that the whole universe was reflected in a drop of dew may have
had that particular town in mind.*
-King Features news item,
"Here's America's Progress at
a Glance" (1936)

In the Quadrangle:
Saffordville

I n 1952, when I first crossed Chase County, I was twelve years old and riding in
the front seat as navigator while my father drove our Pontiac Chieftain with its
splendid hood ornament, an Indian's head whose chromium nose we followed

for half a decade over much of America. In the last weeks, I've probed my memory to find even one detail of that initial passage into the western prairies. What did I see, feel? Nothing now except our route returns. My guess is that I found the grasslands little more than miles to be got over—after all, that's the way Americans crossed Kansas. Still do.

In 1965, when I came out of the navy, I drove across the prairie again on a visit to California, and the grasslands looked different to me, so alive and varied, and now I believe that two years of watching the Atlantic Ocean changed the way I viewed landscape, especially levelish, rolling things. I also began to see the prairies as native ground, the land my hometown sat just out of sight of, and I began to like them not because they demand your attention like mountains and coasts but because they almost defy absorbed attention. At first, to be *here*, to be here *now*, was hard for me to do on the prairie. I liked the clarity of line in a place that seemed to require me to bring something to it and to open to it actively: see far, see little. I learned a prairie secret: take the numbing distance in small doses and gorge on the little details that beckon. Like its moisture, the prairie doesn't give up anything easily, unless it's horizon and sky. Search out its variation, its colors, its subtleties. It's not that I had to learn to think flat—the prairies rarely are—but I had to begin thinking open and lean, seeing without set points of obvious focus, noticing first the horizon and then drawing my vision back toward middle distance where so little appears to exist. I came to understand that the prairies are nothing but grass as the sea is nothing but water, that most prairie life is *within* the place: under the stems, below the turf, beneath the stones. The prairie is not a topography that shows its all but rather a vastly exposed place of concealment, like the geodes so abundant in the county, where the splendid lies within the plain cover. At last I realized I was not a man of the sea or coasts or mountains but a fellow of the grasslands. Once I understood that, I began to find all sorts of reasons why, and here comes one:

I am driving west of Emporia, Kansas, on highway 50 where it takes up the course of the two-mile-wide and shallow valley of the east-running Cottonwood River, and I've just entered the prairie hills through a trough of a wooded bottom on this route that runs some way into the uplands before it rises out of the floodplain to reveal the open spread of grasses. The change is sudden, stark, surprising. If I kept heading west, I would ride among the grasses—tall, middle, short—until I crossed the prairie and the plains (the words are not synonyms) and climbed into the foothills of the Rockies. By following route 50 into Chase County, up out of the shadowed woodlands, out of the soybean and sorghum bottoms and into the miles of something too big, too wild to be called a meadow, I am recapitulating human history, retracing in an hour the sixty-five-million-year course of our evolution from some small, bottom-dwelling mammal that began to crawl trees and evolve and then climb down and move into the East African savannahs. It was tall grass that made man stand up: to be on all fours, to crouch in a six-foot-high world of thick cellulose, is to be blind and vulnerable. People may prefer the obvious beauty of mountains and seacoasts, but we are bipedal because of savannah; we are human because of tallgrass. When I walk the prairie, I like to take along the notion that, while something primal in me may long for the haven of the forest, its apprenticeship in the trees, it also recognizes this grand openness as the kind of place where it became itself.

Now: I am in the grasses, my arms upraised: spine and legs straight, everything upright like the bluestem, and I can walk a thousand miles over this prairie, but I can't climb a tree worth a damn.

On highway 50, two miles west of the eastern Chase County line exactly (man-made things are often exact distances here because they grow up along section-line junctures), a gravel road crosses the highway; I am walking it southward, toward where it passes over old route 50 and then over the old Santa Fe tracks, then over the new tracks, and then drops steeply down the high grade to the oldest route 50 and runs a mile to the Cottonwood River. Between tracks and river stand four houses, a brick school, and, off in a grove, a wooden depot used as a storage shed, and the sign still says, although fading, SAFFORDVILLE.

Saffordville: population five, the youngest fifty-five, the oldest eighty-two. The village, briefly called Kenyon (I haven't discovered why), takes its name from a Kansas judge who advocated passage of the Homestead Act of 1862. I am in the grass and scrub where the town once was, and I climb concrete steps leading to nothing, shuffle down native-stone sidewalk slabs going nowhere, and ahead is the concrete cooler of a grocery and, behind it, the block shell of an auto garage. In 1940, two hundred people lived here. No town in the county has increased its popu-lation since World War II, and what I am about to say is true of other villages nearby, the twin towns of Cottonwood and Strong excepted; as a form of shorthand, let me call this dying the Saffordville Syndrome: in the thirties, the town had a doc-tor, three stores, two schools, one hotel, a blacksmith shop, lumberyard, grain eleva-tor, implement dealer, creamery, café, barber and butcher shops, bank, garage, a church, and five "lodges" (Masons, Woodmen, Eastern Star, Royal Neighbors, Ladies' Aid). These happened: farmers needed fewer hands to get a good crop from the rich bottoms, and bigger implements required more land to make them pay; automobiles and paved roads opened the commerce of Emporia (so properly named); county schools consolidated.

That much is general American history. Saffordville added a detail that, in one Kansan's words, *capped the climax*. Town speculators trying to make a killing by inventing towns and then selling lots laid out Saffordville not just between Buckeye and Bull creeks, but also on the first terrace of the Cottonwood River so that heavy rains rush the village from three sides, and, on the south, a bluff forces the Cottonwood in flood northward toward Saffordville where the railroad grade dams it. The effect is something like building a town at the bottom of a funnel; even after the citizens cut away a loop in the river, it didn't drain fast enough during flood. In the 1940s, an old raconteur wrote:

> The Indians used to warn settlers who settled near the river. They said they
> had seen the water from bluff to bluff. The settlers did not pay any attention
> to the Indian warnings, and in 1904, there came a flood and the Cottonwood
> River overflowed its banks and flooded Everything. Two weeks later it

> *overflowed again, which was the last flood for nineteen years. Again in*
> *1923, there came another flood. It was the last one until 1926. In 1929 there*
> *were two floods—one in June and the other in November. From 1923 to*
> *1929, the river overflowed eight times.*

And then, as if to prove these were not mere and rare chances of nature, in 1951 the Cottonwood flooded four times, the last the worst in white man's memory. Less than a hundred feet wide here, this river, which had caught fire from an oil well spill a generation earlier and two generations before that had gone dry (countians tell of walking the twelve miles to Emporia on the river bed and of helplessly standing by their empty wells and watching their houses burn to the ground that summer), this same river gathered the waters of its tributaries running full of July rains, and went overnight from five feet deep to thirty feet, and took off once again across the valley, just as it was to do in 1965, 1973, 1985. Had there been an economic reason for Saffordville to continue, these repetitions of muddy water would have been serious drawbacks, but, without reasons beyond the inertia of initial settlement, the Cottonwood, like a wronged red man, finally drove out the town. A fellow told me, *That river ate our dinner once too often.* The residents packed up possessions, picked up their houses and church and even some of the stone-slab sidewalks, and moved a mile north to the higher ground of faceless Toledo, a mere cluster of buildings that happen to stand in some proximity. Since the big flood of 1951, only two families have stayed on in Saffordville, and, a couple of decades ago, another moved in. To my knowledge, no one around here thinks them crazy.

Upon the First Terrace

1

Now this is Tom Bridge: *Most of the dust storms in southeastern Colorado blew in from the north. I was a boy—seven, eight, nine—in the early thirties, Dust Bowl days. For a long distance we could see them coming, the dusters. We looked north and there was a curtain of brown dust, sometimes black. The storm came on like a cliff. The sun shone right into the irregularities in that wall, and it was like looking into a canyon. There was a period of quiet: the air got still as the dust came on. It was hundreds of feet high. And then the high-velocity winds that were riding over the top of the storm roared in. It turned so dark I could hardly see the end of my arm. We watched from the house, and we felt the grit between our teeth, and pressure changes pulled dust into the house and into everything—linens, trunks, hatboxes. Lids weren't any use, so my mother hung wet towels over the windows, and when we went out, she had us wrap wet cloths over our mouths and noses. The dust was silt—fine quartz sand pulled up off the alluvial fan east of the Rockies.*

I am at the dinner table in the Bridges' house, a solid, one-and-a-half-story, red-brick, red-tile-roofed place built in 1921 in Saffordville. Although it's not a big home, even today it stands out in the county. For twenty-two years, Tom Bridge, tall and angular, has taught geology at Emporia State University, but he grew up on the Colorado grasslands at the foot of the Front Range.

After a duster, we'd go out and hunt arrowheads: the wind had carried off the lighter topsoil and the flint points lay shining on the hardpan. I had cigar boxes of them "dug up" by the wind. We lived near a leg of the Santa Fe Trail, where the ruts were compacted so hard that the wind would blow away the soil around them, and following a storm we'd find ruts raised like railroad tracks. We never had to open a gate after a duster: the fences would catch the tumbleweed and make a windbreak, and the drifts covered the barbed wire. We rode our horses right over the fences.

In 1966, he got lost and drove into Saffordville and asked the old banker's son for directions to a piece of land Tom was considering buying. The son said he might sell him his house, and later he did, and all along Bridge knew that the house sat in the floodplain of the Cottonwood River. Anybody who grows up inhaling dry bits of the Rocky Mountains might do the same. He moved in with his wife, Syble, and their four children, and it's quite possible that they will be the last citizens in Saffordville. From 1966 to 1973 they averaged a flood a year, but the water never got higher than the basement. Tom didn't complain about the flooding but he did about Syble's overstocking canned goods because they seemed a needless burden. In 1985 the river began to swell, and the Bridges began raising furniture, but they were soon out of bricks and concrete blocks, and they started setting cans of corn, tomato soup, and V-8 juice under the furniture legs. Of the three inhabited houses remaining in Saffordville, the Bridges' is the farthest from the river but on the lowest ground, and it isn't feasible to raise the brick house as their neighbors the Staedtlers did their big, two-story frame place. So, while the radio crackled out flood updates, the Bridges put down cans of chili, and pork and beans, their sole defense against the river and not much more effective than wet towels against dusters.

As goes the Cottonwood River, so goes Chase County: through the quarter-billion-year-old limestone hills, the typically slow waters have cut a sixty-mile dogleg trough, northeast, east. Before the recent building of several impoundments, all the storm runoff in the county, but for two small portions in the south, as well as much of the drainage of Marion County, rolled past Saffordville. While nearly every village in Chase sits in the valley of the Cottonwood or one of its tributaries, only Saffordville on the east, sooner or later, gets the runoff from seventeen hundred square miles, an immense drainage for such a small channel.

Without the Cottonwood watershed there would never have been much settlement in Chase or agriculture other than upland grazing, and the railroad and highway 50 would not likely have passed this way, since transport crosses the hills through the gaps cut by the Cottonwood and South Fork. The valleys hold the towns and the cultivation, but only fourteen percent of the county is bottomland, and it is the rain that falls on the other eighty-six percent, the uplands, that creates floods. Like Kane, the ancient Hawaiian shark-god, the Cottonwood gives life and destruction with equal nonchalance.

Now the river is rising:

the uplands in saturation, they can no longer hold the rain, and they slough it down the slopes to the creeks, where a few days earlier quiet waters flowed blue-gray, the color of moonstone, but now they climb banks and rip off ledges with mad turnings of earthen roil, and where they join larger streams they meet walls of water and back up until the whole county, its veinings of waterways become a massive thrombus, starts to overflow, and the word goes out by radio, by neighbors in pickups: *River's on the rise!* And all the time it's raining, raining so long that the *Emporia Gazette* has time to print front-page jokes about it. *If you've been saving for a rainy day, brother, this is it.* Raining, and the Cottonwood, now thirty feet deep, tops out and starts across the bottoms and begins losing its hundred serpentines as it straightens itself to fit the more linear contours of the valley, and the word goes out, *Take high ground!* and people wonder, *Am I high enough?* and now only parallel lines of cottonwoods and sycamores and willows mark the usual river course, and a man stands on a bridge and remembers how last week his rowboat hardly moved in the slow river when he fished east of the old milldam, and now the silent river has voice, loud, and one fellow says to his son, *It's that sound I don't like,* and farmers start their combines and tractors (and one machine won't fire up) and move them to higher ground: *How high is high enough?* and, *Is there time to get the cattle out?* and everywhere along the South Fork and the Cottonwood the usual argument: *I'm not leaving. This is where I live. This is mine.* And the old, benign river turns malevolent, and a farmer shouts at his wife, *It's sweeping us away!* and she won't listen because women here are always the last to leave, and out back the corn and milo are slipping under, green to brown, and she shouts, *I'm going upstairs!* and he shouts too, *No you're not!* And she: *It's not taking my house while I stand up on the bluff, not this river!* And he: *It ain't no river now!* It's a thing moving as if it knows what made this valley and knows its million-year right of tenancy, and it's going to tear out the fences and flush the squatters and their privies away and scrub the valley of the septic intrusion and let them go down with their hogs and stories of Noah:

the river has risen.

This is Syble Bridge, small and trim. She says to me: *The problem isn't the water really: it's the mud that stays behind. The water drains out but the mud settles.* And Tom says, and he is thinking of Dust Bowl days too: *We get that same layer, that same type of dust or mud precipitated out of water.* I'm laughing and I say, all your life you keep getting soil in your house from one agency or another. You're an earth scientist and earth keeps coming in to live with you. It must make you glad you're not an entomologist. Or a mortician.

I ask, where did you see the water first, and she says: *In '85 I opened the basement door, and it was coming up the stairs at me. It was rising faster than we'd seen it do before. I'd already gotten my home-canned goods from down below, and then they went under up here: sweet pickles and dills. Afterward, we were afraid to eat them, but we ate the stuff in tin cans. Two dozen jars of pickles, still pretty and green, went to the dump along with some furniture and mattresses and rugs: three flatbed truckloads. You understand, in '85 we never left the house. That's the way it is for us here—our neighbors don't leave either. We have one room upstairs, and Tom and I go up to it, but we come down in our rubber boots and sit in the water to eat at the table. The man who built this house, Bill ImMasche, the banker, did the same thing: went upstairs and waited it out. During a flood, Stanley North would come up to the back of the house in a rowboat to bring Bill his paper and mail and milk every day. In '51 they took the screen off the upstairs window to pass things in. Before he pulled away, Stanley said, "You want this screen back on?" "No," says Bill. "Leave it off. I'll swat flies. It'll give me something to do." The floods never bothered him, but people say that his wife's severe heart trouble came from worrying over this house flooding. He watched his pennies, but she shook him loose to build this place.*

The Bridges have lived here twenty-two years, and I ask why they don't at least build a levee around the house, a four-foot berm should do it, and Tom says, *When we get time.* I ask whether living here makes them watch the sky, and he says, *We've had floods when we've had no rain on our place. We have to listen to the radio, go down to the bridge to check on the river, especially at night when we can't see it coming over the fields.*

Syble says, *When the forecast is for flood, Tom starts moving vehicles to higher ground, and I mow the lawn so the grass clippings will wash away. If the forecast was for flooding tomorrow, I'd head right now for the canned goods, especially juice cans, the forty-six-ounce size. Two years ago it was ten inches in this room, but in '51 it was five feet, and that's what damaged the house. When we bought it, we had to put everything inside back together. We decorated with the idea that things would probably get wet.* Now Syble is setting the table to serve a roast and mashed potatoes and broccoli, and she says, *In high water it gets quiet. About all we hear is the water slopping outside.*

Tom: *This house is a riverboat that won't float. I'll look out a window and see carp jumping on the lawn. Frogs in the basement. Cordwood floating off the porch.*

And Syble: *I looked out the window in '85 and saw the workbench float out the garage. An eddy carried it away. It wasn't a regular workbench: it was an old grand piano that had been gutted, but it had fancy carved legs. We kept tools and nails sitting on. We watched it float out, go past the house, moving right along. It stopped over east in Edith's field, tools still on top of it.*

Tom: *I had three Honda motorcycles in the garage. They went beneath. There isn't time to get everything, so we go for the books first, then things in the basement. I turn off the electricity if water's coming upstairs. Syble got shocked the last time. You'll feel the electric current in the water, a kind of vibrating: it can kill you. We take oil lamps to the second floor. The toilet stops working, the bathtub backs up with foul stuff. There's no question a flood's inconvenient.*

Syble: *You don't live in a floodplain and get excited about water. Now, a tornado gets us excited. Tom calls us collectors who need a flood every so often to clear things out anyway. When the water drops, we get the brooms and hose and squirt it and keep the water riled up, make it take the mud back out. If you let the mud dry, it's like concrete. We pump out the basement.*

The Bridges have no flood insurance, and Tom tells me he sold their canoe, and Syble says, *I wouldn't want out in a flood in a canoe or anything else.* They don't have a CB to make up for losing the telephone when the buried lines short out. I ask Tom if he will see water in this house again, and he says, *That's a real possibility, but I don't worry about it. Our lives aren't threatened. Our possessions, yes.*

The meal is over, and we are talking about geology, and someone has said that the Kansas pioneers' great fear was drought. I say, since erosion is the primary geologic force in Kansas, isn't it appropriate for a geologist to live amidst the cycle of flood, erosion, and deposition, and Tom says, *Twenty-two years here now and I really understand sedimentary layering, what made these hills.*

II

Edith McGregor lives across the road—that's all it can be called now, although it once was Hunt Street—from the Bridges, and she also knows that sedimentary layering is the real enemy. Her home is a large, two-story frame house, immaculately white, the kind you find along old, tree-lined, front-porch streets in America, and she isn't much slowed by her eighty-two years, she of the young hands. Her husband died a few years ago, yet she's a jolly woman, a former schoolteacher as are all five people who live in Saffordville, and, like the others, she owns no boat and would have to be unconscious before she would take to the flood in anything other than the second floor of her house. She has a master's degree in psychology. I am seated at her kitchen table in front of the window where, six months ago, she watched the tornado come down on Toledo, a mile north, and she says, *I didn't go to the basement. I wasn't turning my back on that thing,* and she sets down thick slices of her wheat bread and pushes the butter toward me; she has already explained how she gets fresh Chase County wheat from the small grain elevator by the Santa Fe tracks and how she grinds it to add to her store flour. It's ten in the morning, and she's wiping off a jar of home-canned pears.

Dean and I came here in 1947, and we saw floods about every year, but the water never got out of the yard until '51. It came up early on Wednesday morning, and it rolled across those west bean fields like a wall, it seems. We didn't have much time before it started up the porch steps and under the front door and then through the windows. They're low like old windows are. This is the highest house here: built in 1913 for seven thousand dollars and paid for with one crop of alfalfa seed. My husband was head wire-chief in Emporia, in telegraph communications for the Santa Fe, and whenever it looked like high water, he'd take out for town so he wouldn't get cut off. That Wednesday he got the horse to higher ground and went on to work. I was here with my daughter and son, both still in school. First we crated up the chickens and took them up to the sun porch on the second floor, and that was our mistake: it took too much time to run down three dozen fryers. We got the dining table up on boxes and the piano up on something—got it up a foot or so—we thought that was enough, and she smiles at her naïveté and says, *They tell that the Indians believed a big flood would come every hundred years, but our people who build on high ground have their wells go dry in the summer: we located down in here to have water. My well's been polluted by floods, but it's never gone dry.*

There's a story of the woman who in the drought of 1929 prayed hard for rain, even asking that the river overflow and water their dying corn, and it began raining, and the Cottonwood rose and washed out their whole crop, and I ask, did you pray? and she says, *I suppose we did. My son got scared when the water started rising in the house, but he got over it. The first floor is four feet above the yard: I measured the water in this kitchen, and it came to the top of the table, thirty-three inches. We took canned goods upstairs: I remember a lot of hominy and mackerel. Haven't eaten hominy since.*

Edith sets preserves and a glass of cold water on the table, and she says, *When the river's coming on, I always fill the bathtub so we can wash up and flush the toilet. Somebody will bring us drinking water. In '51, a boat was at the house by noon to pick us up, but when the water's six feet deep with a current like we get here, I don't go outside.* She says that as if speaking of spring showers. *That boat wasn't big enough. I can't swim. Besides, I had no reason to get out. I like to stay and take care of things. I guess I'm an old river rat.*

She slows as she recalls the details, and she says, *We stayed and watched the river rise: the chicken coop washed away, and that was it for us raising chickens. The soybean crop went, but the wheat we'd already harvested. Then, the second day my son got restless, and he went up on the roof with the dog and his twenty-two and shot at trash floating by. An airplane flew over and saw him and passed word that the McGregors were signaling for help. I wasn't scared, really wasn't. My husband couldn't get away from all the stopped trains in Emporia: every stranded passenger wanted to send a message. He didn't come home until Monday. But every night he drove up to the south bluff to see if the oil lamp was burning in the window—that was our signal that we were all right. On Friday I started stirring the water with a broom so the mud would go out with it. I went round and round the rooms, and finally, when the water was out of the house, I went to the porch time and again and brought in buckets of water to throw on the floors. You don't wait until you need a shovel. These pine floors held up, but all the veneer furniture and the doors and the piano just fell apart.*

She's watching to see whether I find all this eccentric, and she says, *I walked out of the house Sunday, but my son put a bundle of clean clothes over his head and waded out Saturday evening—went to town for a good meal. When I came out, first thing I did was get a drink of cold water and a big slice of fruit pie someone brought—peach it was. Then strangers started coming out to stare and pick through our fields and houses. They carried off more than the river did.* For the first time she shows irritation.

She says, *I remember that before the water started rising, animals did strange things. Groundhogs, skunks, snakes all moving: they weren't waiting for the water. A mother skunk got trapped in the barn with her two little ones, and my son lifted the babies up on a feed box, and then the mother climbed up but never raised her tail. She seemed to understand. A neighbor, the French war bride, stopped her pickup on the highway and opened the door to see if a big old hog was all right. He climbed up in the seat and sat down beside her, she said, "just like he knowed me."*

Now Edith is looking out the window where she could once count eight houses along Hunt Street. She says this seriously: *If people don't know any better than to live down here, they'll have to suffer the consequences, but I never knew anyone to die in our floods.*

III

In the early summer of 1951, Frances Staedtler's husband's parents jacked up their big house, added three feet to the foundation, and set the house back down on it. Six days later the Cottonwood was at the door, and then in the kitchen, the living room, and the family went upstairs. Frances spoke to me for a while about the floods, her story paralleling the others', and, when she began talking about her mother-in-law taking the ironing board to the second floor in case she needed a raft, Frances had to stop, and she struggled to say, *I'm afraid I can't go on. It's too much remembering how we all were in those days, when we were strong enough to fight it. We were together.*

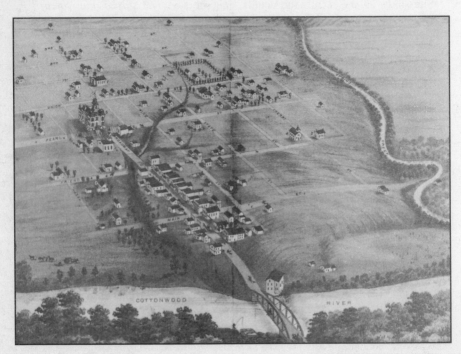

Cottonwood Falls, Kansas   Drawn by D. D. Morse, 1878

These people of Saffordville, the whole population, all five of them, as they talk their way back into the big floods, grow animated, and sorrows and smiles come and go so quickly about their faces that I almost don't see them, and their eyes are widened and keen. They are not boastful, but they relish, not having beaten the river, but having held their own with it and not yielding to it other than by climbing a flight of stairs, and the whole time they realize the battle is a little foolish—just the way they want it. They recognize but do not say how the river whets a fine edge on their lives, and I never heard any of them speak love for the river, or hate. These are not people locked in the floodplain by poverty; they are held here by recollections of what the river has given them: hours of a family bound tightly like shocks of wheat, of moments when all their senses were almost one with the land, of times when they earned the right to be tenants on the first terrace of the Cottonwood River. One afternoon, Edith McGregor said to me: *Not everybody gets the chance to live like this.*

AN EXPEDITION TO THE POLE

A N N I E   D I L L A R D

Editor's Note: Annie Dillard describes writers as those daring to float free—in midair:

> *Every morning you climb several flights of stairs, enter your study, open the French doors, and slide your desk and chair out into the middle of the air. The desk and chair float thirty feet from the ground, between the crowns of maple trees. The furniture is in place; you go back for your thermos of coffee. Then, wincing, you step out again through the French doors and sit down on the chair and look over the desktop. . . . Get to work. Your work is to keep cranking the flywheel that turns the gears that spin that belt in the engine of belief that keeps you and your desk in midair.*

Dillard's "An Expedition to the Pole" is an illustration of an engine of belief in grand prix form. An astonishing blend of research, experience, deep reflection, vast imagination, and humor, "An Expedition to the Pole" both pleases and instructs.

The form of the essay is itself original. In titling individual sections "The Land," "The People," and "The Technology," Dillard offers a gentle parody of grade school geography primers. As her narrative quickly discloses, however, these facets of the human landscape are inextricably intertwined.

Dillard's three roman numeraled sections mark the unfolding of time. Part I presents the fundamental human condition: we, like the polar explorers, are bumbling our way toward the ultimate. We are seeking "working compromises between the sublimity of our ideas and the absurdity of the fact of us." Part II signals the passing of time: "Months have passed; years have passed. Whatever ground gained has slipped away. New obstacles arise, and faintness of heart, and dread." Still we strive, and in the final section Dillard abandons both solitude and dignity to offer a sublime vision of the community of faith.

Annie Dillard did not set out to be an artist of nonfiction. She wanted to write short stories for women's magazines. When editors rejected her fiction, she gave up smoking and, needing something to do with her hands, she began copying passages from books on nature and religion into a spiral notebook. She soon switched to 4" x 6" index cards, eventually amassing 1,100. These became the foundation of Pilgrim at Tinker Creek, *a work which, like Thoreau's* Walden, *represents a rare mixture of nature writing, mysticism, and art. It won the Pulitzer Prize for 1974.*

Since then Dillard has written eight books: poetry (Tickets for a Prayer Wheel), *essays* (Teaching a Stone to Talk), *a record of her* Encounters with Chinese Writers, *an extended meditation on human suffering* (Holy the Firm), *a memoir* (An American Childhood), *two books on writing* (Living by Fiction *and* The Writing Life), *and, most recently, a novel* (The Living). *"I don't think I've written a personal book yet," she states. "The world is the great subject."*

Dillard's statement is true. Even her childhood memoir takes the child's consciousness as its subject. Her own youth is merely an example. Now a writer in residence at Middlebury College in Connecticut, Dillard writes all morning seven days a week. Her favorite writers are theologians, naturalists, and poets. "I like the big guys who really go after the big game," she states.

Dillard admits to having, in some respects, a nineteenth-century sensibility. However, she believes the possibilities for prose writing are more interesting in this century than last. She has, for example, more irony in her writing than Melville, Emerson, and Thoreau.

Dillard encourages young writers to avoid attractive workplaces. "One wants a room with no view," she insists, "so imagination can meet memory in the dark." She also urges apprentice writers to be profligate with their literary intuitions:

> *spend it all, shoot it, play it, lose it, all, right away, every time. Do not hoard what seems good for a later place in the book, or for another book; give it, give it all, give it now. . . . something more will arise for later, something better. These things fill from behind, from beneath, like well water. Similarly, the impulse to keep to yourself what you have learned is not only shameful, it is destructive. Anything you do not give freely and abundantly becomes lost to you. You open your safe and find ashes.*

Dillard believes that the more literary a piece of writing is—"the more purely verbal, crafted sentence by sentence, the more imaginative, reasoned, and deep"—the greater chance that people will read it and that it will endure:

> *The line of words is heading out past Jupiter this morning. Traveling 150 kilometers a second, it makes no sound. . . . The line of words speeds past Jupiter and its cumbrous, dizzying orbit; it looks neither to the right nor to the left. It will be leaving the solar system soon, single-minded, rapt, rushing heaven like a soul.*

I

There is a singing group in this Catholic church today, a singing group which calls itself "Wildflowers." The lead is a tall, square-jawed teen-aged boy, buoyant and glad to be here. He carries a guitar; he plucks out a little bluesy riff and hits some chords. With him are the rest of the Wildflowers. There is an old woman, wonderfully determined; she has long orange hair and is dressed country-and-western style. A long embroidered strap around her neck slings a big western guitar low over her pelvis. Beside her stands a frail, withdrawn fourteen-year-old boy, and a large Chinese man in his twenties who seems to want to enjoy himself but is not quite sure how to. He looks around wildly as he sings, and shuffles his feet. There is also a very tall teen-aged girl, presumably the lead singer's girl friend; she is delicate of feature, half serene and half petrified, a wispy soprano. They straggle out in front of the altar and teach us a brand-new hymn.

It all seems a pity at first, for I have overcome a fiercely anti-Catholic upbringing in order to attend Mass simply and solely to escape Protestant guitars. Why am I here? Who gave these nice Catholics guitars? Why are they not mumbling in Latin and performing superstitious rituals? What is the Pope thinking of?

But nobody said things were going to be easy. A taste for the sublime is a greed like any other, after all; why begrudge the churches their secularism now, when from the general table is rising a general song? Besides, in a way I do not pretend to understand, these people—all the people in all the ludicrous churches—have access to the land.

THE LAND

The Pole of Relative Inaccessibility is "that imaginary point on the Arctic Ocean farthest from land in any direction." It is a navigator's paper point contrived to console Arctic explorers who, after Peary and Henson reached the North Pole in 1909, had nowhere special to go. There is a Pole of Relative Inaccessibility on the Antarctic continent, also; it is that point of land farthest from salt water in any direction.

The Absolute is the Pole of Relative Inaccessibility located in metaphysics. After all, one of the few things we know about the Absolute is that it is relatively inaccessible. It is that point of spirit farthest from every accessible point of spirit in all directions. Like the others, it is a Pole of the Most Trouble. It is also—I take this as given—the pole of great price.

THE PEOPLE

It is the second Sunday in Advent. For a year I have been attending Mass at this Catholic church. Every Sunday for a year I have run away from home and joined the circus as a dancing bear. We dancing bears have dressed ourselves in buttoned clothes; we mince around the rings on two feet. Today we were restless; we kept dropping onto our forepaws.

No one, least of all the organist, could find the opening hymn. Then no one knew it. Then no one could sing anyway.

There was no sermon, only announcements.

The priest proudly introduced the rascally acolyte who was going to light the two Advent candles. As we all could plainly see, the rascally acolyte had already lighted them.

During the long intercessory prayer, the priest always reads "intentions" from the parishioners. These are slips of paper, dropped into a box before the service begins, on which people have written their private concerns, requesting our public prayers. The priest reads them, one by one, and we respond on cue. "For a baby safely delivered on November twentieth," the priest intoned, "we pray to the Lord." We all responded, "Lord, hear our prayer." Suddenly the priest broke in and confided to our bowed heads, "That's the baby we've been praying for the past two months! The woman just kept getting more and more pregnant!" How often, how shockingly often, have I exhausted myself in church from the effort to keep from laughing out loud? I often laugh all the way home. Then the priest read the next intention: "For my son, that he may forgive his father. We pray to the Lord." "Lord, hear our prayer," we responded, chastened.

A high school stage play is more polished than this service we have been rehearsing since the year one. In two thousand years, we have not worked out the kinks. We positively glorify them. Week after week we witness the same miracle: that God is so mighty he can stifle his own laughter. Week after week, we witness the same miracle: that God, for reasons unfathomable, refrains from blowing our dancing bear act to smithereens. Week after week Christ washes the disciples' dirty feet, handles their very toes, and repeats, It is all right—believe it or not—to be people.

Who can believe it?

During communion, the priest handed me a wafer which proved to be stuck to five other wafers. I waited while he tore the clump into rags of wafer, resisting the impulse to help. Directly to my left, and all through communion, a woman was banging out the theme from *The Sound of Music* on a piano.

THE LAND

Nineteenth-century explorers set the pattern for polar expeditions. Elaborately provisioned ships set out for high latitudes. Soon they encounter the pack ice and equinoctial storms. Ice coats the deck, spars, and rigging; the masts and hull shudder; the sea freezes around the rudder, and then fastens on the ship. Early sailors try ramming, sawing, or blasting the ice ahead of the ship before they give up and settle in for the winter. In the nineteenth century, this being "beset" in the pack often killed polar crews; later explorers expected it and learned, finally, to put it to use. Sometimes officers and men move directly onto the pack ice for safety; they drive tent stakes into the ice and pile wooden boxes about for tables and chairs.

Sooner or later, the survivors of that winter or the next, or a select polar party, sets off over the pack ice on foot. Depending on circumstances, they are looking either for a Pole or, more likely, for help. They carry supplies, including boats, on sledges which they "manhaul" on ropes fastened to shoulder harnesses. South Polar expeditions usually begin from a base camp established on shore. In either case, the terrain is so rough, and the men so weakened by scurvy, that the group makes only a few miles a day. Sometimes they find an island on which to live or starve the next winter; sometimes they turn back to safety, stumble onto some outpost of civilization, or are rescued by another expedition; very often, when warm weather comes and the pack ice splits into floes, they drift and tent on a floe, or hop from floe to floe, until the final floe lands, splits, or melts.

In 1847, according to Arctic historian L. P. Kirwan, the American ship *Polaris* "was struck by an enormous floe. And just as stores, records, clothing, equipment, were being flung from the reeling ship, she was swept away through the Arctic twilight, with most, but not all, of her crew on board. Those left behind drifted for thirteen hundred miles on an ice-floe until they were rescued, starving and dazed, off the coast of Labrador."

Polar explorers were chosen, as astronauts are today, from the clamoring, competitive ranks of the sturdy, skilled, and sane. Many of the British leaders, in particular, were men of astonishing personal dignity. Reading their accounts of life *in extremis*, one is struck by their unending formality toward each other. When Scott's Captain Oates sacrificed himself on the Antarctic peninsula because his ruined feet were slowing the march, he stepped outside the tent one night to freeze himself in a blizzard, saying to the others, "I am just going outside and may be some time."

Even in the privacy of their journals and diaries, polar explorers maintain a fine reserve. In his journal, Ernest Shackleton described his feelings upon seeing, for the first time in human history, the Antarctic continent beyond the mountains ringing the Ross Ice Shelf: "We watched the new mountains rise from the great unknown that lay ahead of us," he wrote, "with feelings of keen curiosity, not unmingled with awe." One wonders, after reading a great many such firsthand accounts, if polar explorers were not somehow chosen for the empty and solemn splendor of their prose styles—or even if some eminent Victorians, examining their own prose styles, realized, perhaps dismayed, that from the look of it, they would have to go in for polar exploration. Salomon Andrée, the doomed Swedish balloonist, was dying of starvation on an Arctic island when he confided in his diary, with almost his dying breath, "Our provisions must soon and richly be supplemented, if we are to have any prospect of being able to hold out for a time."

THE PEOPLE

The new Episcopalian and Catholic liturgies include a segment called "passing the peace." Many things can go wrong here. I know of one congregation in New York which fired its priest because he insisted on their passing the peace—which involves nothing more than shaking hands with your neighbors in the pew. The men and women of this small congregation had limits to their endurance; passing the peace was beyond their limits. They could not endure shaking hands with people to whom they bore lifelong grudges. They fired the priest and found a new one sympathetic to their needs.

The rubric for passing the peace requires that one shake hands with whoever is handy and say, "Peace be with you." The other responds, "Peace be with *you*." Every rare once in a while, someone responds simply "Peace." Today I was sitting beside two teen-aged lugs with small mustaches. When it came time to pass the peace I shook hands with one of the lugs and said, "Peace be with you," and he said, *"Yeah."*

THE TECHNOLOGY: THE FRANKLIN EXPEDITION

The Franklin expedition was the turning point in Arctic exploration. The expedition itself accomplished nothing, and all its members died. But the expedition's failure to return, and the mystery of its whereabouts, attracted so much publicity in Europe and the United States that thirty ships set out looking for traces of the ships and men; these search parties explored and mapped the Arctic for the first time, found the northwest passage which Franklin had sought, and developed a technology adapted to Arctic conditions, a technology capable of bringing explorers back alive. The technology of the Franklin expedition, by contrast, was adapted only to conditions in the Royal Navy officers' clubs in England. The Franklin expedition stood on its dignity.

In 1845, Sir John Franklin and 138 officers and men embarked from England to find the northwest passage across the high Canadian Arctic to the Pacific Ocean. They sailed in two three-masted barques. Each sailing vessel carried an auxiliary steam engine and a twelve-day supply of coal for the entire projected two or three years' voyage. Instead of additional coal, according to L. P. Kirwan, each ship made room for a 1,200-volume library, "a hand-organ, playing fifty tunes," china place settings for officers and men, cut-glass wine goblets, and sterling silver flatware. The officers' sterling silver knives, forks, and spoons were particularly interesting. The silver was of ornate Victorian design, very heavy at the handles and richly patterned. Engraved on the handles were the individual officers' initials and family crests. The expedition carried no special clothing for the Arctic, only the uniforms of Her Majesty's Navy.

The ships set out in high dudgeon, amid enormous glory and fanfare. Franklin uttered his utterance: "The highest object of my desire is faithfully to perform my duty." Two months later a British whaling captain met the two barques in Lancaster Sound; he reported back to England on the high spirits of officers and men. He was the last European to see any of them alive.

Years later, civilization learned that many groups of Inuit—Eskimos—had hazarded across tableaux involving various still-living or dead members of the Franklin expedition. Some had glimpsed, for instance, men pushing and pulling a wooden boat across the ice. Some had found, at a place called Starvation Cove, this boat, or a similar one, and the remains of the thirty-five men who had been dragging it. At Terror Bay the Inuit found a tent on the ice, and in it, thirty bodies. At Simpson Strait some Inuit had seen a very odd sight: the pack ice pierced by the three protruding wooden masts of a barque.

For twenty years, search parties recovered skeletons from all over the frozen sea. Franklin himself—it was learned after twelve years—had died aboard ship. Franklin dead, the ships frozen into the pack winter after winter, their supplies exhausted, the remaining officers and men had decided to walk to help. They outfitted themselves from ships' stores for the journey; their bodies were found with those supplies they had chosen to carry. Accompanying one clump of frozen bodies, for instance, which incidentally showed evidence of cannibalism, were place settings of sterling silver flatware engraved with officers' initials and family crests. A search party found, on the ice far from the ships, a letter clip, and a piece of that very backgammon board which Lady Jane Franklin had given her husband as a parting gift.

Another search party found two skeletons in a boat on a sledge. They had hauled the boat sixty-five miles. With the two skeletons were some chocolate, some guns, some tea, and a great deal of table silver. Many miles south of these two was another skeleton, alone. This was a frozen officer. In his pocket he had, according to Kirwan, "a parody of a sea-shanty." The skeleton was in uniform: trousers and jacket "of fine blue cloth . . . edged with silk braid, with sleeves slashed and bearing five covered buttons each. Over this uniform the dead man had worn a blue greatcoat, with a black silk neckerchief." That was the Franklin expedition.

Sir Robert Falcon Scott, who died on the Antarctic peninsula, was never able to bring himself to use dogs, let alone feed them to each other or eat them. Instead he struggled with English ponies, for whom he carried hay. Scott felt that eating dogs was inhumane; he also felt, as he himself wrote, that when men reach a Pole unaided, their journey has "a fine conception" and "the conquest is more nobly and splendidly won." It is this loftiness of sentiment, this purity, this dignity and self-control, which makes Scott's farewell letters—found under his body—such moving documents.

Less moving are documents from successful polar expeditions. Their leaders relied on native technology, which, as every book ever written about the Inuit puts it, was "adapted to harsh conditions."

Roald Amundsen, who returned in triumph from the South Pole, traveled Inuit style; he made good speed using sleds and feeding dogs to dogs on a schedule. Robert E. Peary and Matthew Henson reached the North Pole in the company of four Inuit. Throughout the Peary expedition, the Inuit drove the dog teams, built igloos, and supplied seal and walrus clothing.

There is no such thing as a solitary polar explorer, fine as the conception is.

THE PEOPLE

I have been attending Catholic Mass for only a year. Before that, the handiest church was Congregational. Week after week I climbed the long steps to that little church, entered, and took a seat with some few of my neighbors. Week after week I was moved by the pitiableness of the bare linoleum-floored sacristy which no flowers could cheer or soften, by the terrible singing I so loved, by the fatigued Bible readings, the lagging emptiness and dilution of the liturgy, the horrifying vacuity of the sermon, and by the fog of dreary senselessness pervading the whole, which existed alongside, and probably caused, the wonder of the fact that we came; we returned; we showed up; week after week, we went through with it.

Once while we were reciting the Gloria, a farmer's wife—whom I knew slightly—and I exchanged a sudden, triumphant glance.

Recently I returned to that Congregational church for an ecumenical service. A Catholic priest and the minister served grape juice communion.

Both the priest and the minister were professionals, were old hands. They bungled with dignity and aplomb. Both were at ease and awed; both were half confident and controlled and half bewildered and whispering. I could hear them: "Where is it?" "Haven't you got it?" "I thought *you* had it!"

The priest, new to me, was in his sixties. He was tall; he wore his weariness loosely, standing upright and controlling his breath. When he knelt at the altar, and when he rose from kneeling, his knees cracked. It was a fine church music, this sound of his cracking knees.

THE LAND

Polar explorers—one gathers from their accounts—sought at the Poles something of the sublime. Simplicity and purity attracted them; they set out to perform clear tasks in uncontaminated lands. The land's austerity held them. They praised the land's spare beauty as if it were a moral or a spiritual quality: "icy halls of cold sublimity," "lofty peaks perfectly covered with eternal snow." Fridtjof Nansen referred to "the great adventure of the ice, deep and pure as infinity . . . the eternal round of the universe and its eternal death." Everywhere polar prose evokes these absolutes, these ideas of "eternity" and "perfection," as if they were some perfectly visible part of the landscape.

They went, I say, partly in search of the sublime, and they found it the only way it can be found, here or there—around the edges, tucked into the corners of the days. For they were people—all of them, even the British—and despite the purity of their conceptions, they man-hauled their humanity to the Poles.

They man-hauled their frail flesh to the Poles, and encountered conditions so difficult that, for instance, it commonly took members of Scott's South Polar party several hours each morning to put on their boots. Day and night they did miserable, niggling, and often fatal battle with frostbitten toes, diarrhea, bleeding gums, hunger, weakness, mental confusion, and despair.

They man-hauled their sweet human absurdity to the Poles. When Robert E. Peary and Matthew Henson reached the North Pole in 1909, Peary planted there in the frozen ocean, according to L. P. Kirwan, the flag of the Dekes: "the colours of the Delta Kappa Epsilon Fraternity at Bowdoin College, of which Peary was an alumnus."

Polar explorers must adapt to conditions. They must adapt, on the one hand, to severe physical limitations; they must adapt, on the other hand—like the rest of us—to ordinary emotional limitations. The hard part is in finding a workable compromise. If you are Peary and have planned your every move down to the last jot and tittle, you can perhaps get away with carrying a Deke flag to the North Pole, if it will make you feel good. After eighteen years' preparation, why not feel a little good? If you are an officer with the Franklin expedition and do not know what you are doing or where you are, but think you cannot eat food except from sterling silver tableware, you cannot get away with it. Wherever we go, there seems to be only one business at hand—that of finding workable compromises between the sublimity of our ideas and the absurdity of the fact of us.

They made allowances for their emotional needs. Over-wintering expedition ships commonly carried, in *addition* to sufficient fuel, equipment for the publication of weekly newspapers. The brave polar men sat cooling their heels *in medias* nowhere, reading in cold type their own and their bunkmates' gossip, in such weeklies as Parry's *Winter Chronicle and North Georgia Gazette*, Nansen's *Framsjaa*, or Scott's *South Polar Times* and *The Blizzard*. Polar explorers also amused themselves with theatrical productions. If one had been frozen into the pack ice off Ross Island near Antarctica, aboard Scott's ship *Discovery*, one midwinter night in 1902, one could have seen the only performance of *Ticket of Leave, a screaming comedy in one act*. Similarly, if, in the dead of winter, 1819, one had been a member of young Edward Parry's expedition frozen into the pack ice in the high Arctic, one could have caught the first of a series of fortnightly plays, an uproarious success called *Miss in her Teens*. According to Kirwan, "'This,' Parry dryly remarked, 'afforded to the men such a fund of amusement as fully to justify the expectations we had formed of the utility of theatrical entertainments.'" And you yourself, Royal Navy Commander Edward Parry, were you not yourself the least bit amused? Or at twenty-nine years old did you still try to stand on your dignity?

THE LAND

God does not demand that we give up our personal dignity, that we throw in our lot with random people, that we lose ourselves and turn from all that is not him. God needs nothing, asks nothing, and demands nothing, like the stars. It is a life with God which demands these things.

Experience has taught the race that if knowledge of God is the end, then these habits of life are not the means but the condition in which the means operates. You do not have to do these things; not at all. God does not, I regret to report, give a hoot. You do not have to do these things—unless you want to know God. They work on you, not on him.

You do not have to sit outside in the dark. If, however, you want to look at the stars, you will find that darkness is necessary. But the stars neither require nor demand it.

THE TECHNOLOGY

It is a matter for computation: how far can one walk carrying how much silver? The computer balks at the problem; there are too many unknowns. The computer puts its own questions: Who is this "one"? What degree of stamina may we calculate for? Under what conditions does this one propose to walk, at what latitudes? With how many companions, how much aid?

THE PEOPLE

The Mass has been building to this point, to the solemn saying of those few hushed phrases known as the Sanctus. We have confessed, in a low, distinct murmur, our sins; we have become the people broken, and then the people made whole by our reluctant assent to the priest's proclamation of God's mercy. Now, as usual, we will, in the stillest voice, stunned, repeat the Sanctus, repeat why it is that we have come:

> Holy, holy, holy Lord,
> God of power and might,
> heaven and earth are full of your glory . . .

It is here, if ever, that one loses oneself at sea. Here, one's eyes roll up, and the sun rolls overhead, and the floe rolls underfoot, and the scene of unrelieved ice and sea rolls over the planet's pole and over the world's rim wide and unseen.

Now, just as we are dissolved in our privacy and about to utter the words of the Sanctus, the lead singer of Wildflowers bursts onstage from the wings. I raise my head. He is taking enormous, enthusiastic strides and pumping his guitar's neck up and down. Drooping after him come the orange-haired country-and-western-style woman; the soprano, who, to shorten herself, carries her neck forward like a horse; the withdrawn boy; and the Chinese man, who is holding a tambourine as if it had stuck by some defect to his fingers and he has resolved to forget about it. These array themselves in a clump downstage right. The priest is nowhere in sight.

Alas, alack, oh brother, we are going to have to *sing* the Sanctus. There is, of course, nothing new about singing the Sanctus. The lead singer smiles disarmingly. There is a new arrangement. He hits a chord with the flat of his hand. The Chinese man with sudden vigor bangs the tambourine and looks at his hands, startled. They run us through the Sanctus three or four times. The words are altered a bit to fit the strong upbeat rhythm:

> Heaven and earth
> (Heaven and earth earth earth earth earth)
> Are full (full full full)
> Of your glory . . .

Must I join this song? May I keep only my silver? My backgammon board, I agree, is a frivolity. I relinquish it. I will leave it right here on the ice. But my silver? My family crest? One knife, one fork, one spoon, to carry beneath the glance of heaven and back? I have lugged it around for years; I am, I say, superlatively strong. Don't laugh. I am superlatively strong! Don't laugh; you'll make *me* laugh. The answer is no. We are singing the Sanctus, it seems, and they are passing the plate. I would rather, I think, undergo the famous dark night of the soul than encounter in church the dread hootenanny—but these purely personal preferences are of no account, and maladaptive to boot. They are passing the plate and I toss in my schooling; I toss in my rank in the Royal Navy, my erroneous and incomplete charts, my pious refusal to eat sled dogs, my watch, my keys, and my shoes. I was looking for bigger game, not little moral lessons; but who can argue with conditions?

"Heaven and earth earth earth earth earth," we sing. The withdrawn boy turns his head toward a man in front of me, who must be his father. Unaccountably, the enormous teen-aged soprano catches my eye, exultant. A low shudder or shock crosses our floe. We have split from the pack; we have crossed the Arctic Circle, and the current has us.

THE LAND

We are clumped on an ice floe drifting over the black polar sea. Heaven and earth are full of our terrible singing. Overhead we see a blurred, colorless brightness; at our feet we see the dulled, swift ice and recrystallized snow. The sea is black and green; a hundred thousand floes and bergs float in the water and spin and scatter in the current around us everywhere as far as we can see. The wind is cool, moist, and scented with salt.

I am wearing, I discover, the uniform of a Keystone Kop. I examine my hat: a black cardboard constable's hat with a white felt star stapled to the band above the brim. My dark Keystone Kop jacket is nicely belted, and there is a tin badge on my chest. A holster around my hips carries a popgun with a cork on a string, and a red roll of caps. My feet are bare, but I feel no cold. I am skating around on the ice, and singing, and bumping into people who, because the ice is slippery, bump into other people. "Excuse me!" I keep saying, "I beg your pardon woops there!"

When a crack develops in our floe and opens at my feet, I jump across it—skillfully, I think—but my jump pushes my side of the floe away, and I wind up leaping full tilt into the water. The Chinese man extends a hand to pull me out, but alas, he slips and I drag him in. The Chinese man and I are treading water, singing, and collecting a bit of a crowd. It takes a troupe of circus clowns to get us both out. I check my uniform at once and learn that my rather flattering hat is intact, my trousers virtually unwrinkled, but my roll of caps is wet. The Chinese man is fine; we thank the clowns.

This troupe of circus clowns, I hear, is poorly paid. They are invested in bright, loose garments; they are a bunch of spontaneous, unskilled, oversized children; they joke and bump into people. At one end of the floe, ten of them—red, yellow, and blue—are trying to climb up on each other to make a human pyramid. It is a wonderfully funny sight, because they have put the four smallest clowns on the bottom, and the biggest, fattest clown is trying to climb to the top. The rest of the clowns are doing gymnastics; they tumble on the ice and flip cheerfully in midair. Their crucifixes fly from their ruffled necks as they flip, and hit them on their bald heads as they land. Our floe is smaller now, and we seem to have drifted into a faster bit of current. Repeatedly we ram little icebergs, which rock as we hit them. Some of them tilt clear over like punching bags; they bounce back with great splashes, and water streams down their blue sides as they rise. The country-and-western-style woman is fending off some of the larger bergs with a broom. The lugs with the mustaches have found, or brought, a Frisbee, and a game is developing down the middle of our floe. Near the Frisbee game, a bunch of people including myself and some clowns are running. We fling ourselves down on the ice, shoulders first, and skid long distances like pucks.

Now the music ceases and we take our seats in the pews. A baby is going to be baptized. Overhead the sky is brightening; I do not know if this means we have drifted farther north, or all night.

THE PEOPLE

The baby's name is Oswaldo; he is a very thin baby who looks to be about one. He never utters a peep; he looks grim, and stiff as a planked shad. His parents—his father carrying him—and his godparents, the priest, and two acolytes, are standing on the ice between the first row of pews and the linoleum-floored sacristy. I am resting my bare feet on the velvet prie-dieu—to keep those feet from playing on the ice during the ceremony.

Oswaldo is half Filipino. His mother is Filipino. She has a wide mouth with much lipstick, and wide eyes; she wears a tight black skirt and stiletto heels. The father looks like Ozzie Nelson. He has marcelled yellow hair, a bland, meek face, and a big, meek nose. He is wearing a brown leather flight jacket. The godparents are both Filipinos, one of whom, in a pastel denim jump suit, keeps mugging for the Instamatic camera which another family member is shooting from the aisle.

The baby has a little red scar below one eye. He is wearing a long white lace baptismal gown, blue tennis shoes with white rubber toes, and red socks.

The priest anoints the baby's head with oil. He addresses to the parents several articles of faith: "Do you believe in God, the Father Almighty, creator of Heaven and earth?" "Yes, we believe."

The priest repeats a gesture he says was Christ's, explaining that it symbolically opens the infant's five senses to the knowledge of God. Uttering a formal prayer, he lays his hand loosely over Oswaldo's face and touches in rapid succession his eyes, ears, nose, and mouth. The baby blinks. The priest, whose voice is sometimes lost in the ruff at his neck, or blown away by the wind, is formal and gentle in his bearing; he knows the kid is cute, but he is not going to sentimentalize the sacrament.

Since our floe spins, we in the pews see the broken floes and tilting bergs, the clogged, calm polar sea, and the variously lighted sky and water's rim, shift and revolve enormously behind the group standing around the baby. Once I think I see a yellowish polar bear spurting out of the water as smoothly as if climbing were falling. I see the bear splash and flow onto a distant floeberg which tilts out of sight.

Now the acolytes bring a pitcher, a basin, and a linen towel. The father tilts the rigid baby over the basin; the priest pours water from the pitcher over the baby's scalp; the mother sops the baby with the linen towel and wraps it over his head, so that he looks, proudly, as though he has just been made a swami.

To conclude, the priest brings out a candle, for the purpose, I think, of pledging everybody to Christian fellowship with Oswaldo. Actually, I do not know what it is for; I am not listening. I am watching the hands at the candlestick. Each of the principals wraps a hand around the brass candlestick: the two acolytes with their small, pale hands at its base, the two families—Oswaldo's and his godparents'—with their varicolored hands in a row, and the priest at the top, as though he has just won the bat toss at baseball. The baby rides high in his father's arms, pointing his heels in his tennis shoes, silent, wanting down. His father holds him firmly with one hand and holds the candlestick beside his wife's hand with the other. The priest and the seated members of Wildflowers start clapping then—a round of applause for everybody here on the ice!—so we clap.

II

Months have passed; years have passed. Whatever ground gained has slipped away. New obstacles arise, and faintness of heart, and dread.

THE LAND

Polar explorers commonly die of hypothermia, starvation, scurvy, or dysentery; less commonly they contract typhoid fever (as Stefansson did), vitamin A poisoning from polar bear liver, or carbon monoxide poisoning from incomplete combustion inside tents sealed by snow. Very commonly, as a prelude to these deaths, polar explorers lose the use of their feet; their frozen toes detach when they remove their socks.

Particularly vivid was the death of a certain Mr. Joseph Green, the astronomer on Sir James Cook's first voyage to high latitudes. He took sick aboard ship. One night "in a fit of the phrensy," as a contemporary newspaper reported, he rose from his bunk and "put his legs out of the portholes, which was the occasion of his death."

Vitus Bering, shipwrecked in 1740 on Bering Island, was found years later preserved in snow. An autopsy showed he had had many lice, he had scurvy, and had died of a "rectal fistula which forced gas gangrene into his tissues."

The bodies of various members of the Sir John Franklin expedition of 1845 were found over the course of twenty years, by thirty search expeditions, in assorted bizarre postures scattered over the ice of Victoria Strait, Beechey Island, and King William Island.

Sir Robert Falcon Scott reached the South Pole on January 17, 1912, only to discover a flag that Roald Amundsen had planted there a month earlier. Scott's body, and the bodies of two of his companions, turned up on the Ross Ice Shelf eleven miles south of one of their own supply depots. The bodies were in sleeping bags. His journals and farewell letters, found under his body, indicated that the other two had died first. Scott's torso was well out of his sleeping bag, and he had opened wide the collar of his parka, exposing his skin.

Never found were the bodies of Henry Hudson, his young son, and four men, whom mutineers in 1610 had lowered from their ship in a dinghy, in Hudson's Bay, without food or equipment. Never found were the bodies of Sir John Franklin himself, or of Amundsen and seventeen other men who set out for the Arctic in search of a disastrous Italian expedition, or the bodies of Scott's men Evans and Oates. Never found were most of the drowned crew of the United States ship *Polaris* or the body of her commander, who died sledging on the ice.

Of the United States Greely expedition to the North Pole, all men died but six. Greely himself, one of the six survivors, was found "on his hands and knees with long hair in pigtails." Of the United States De Long expedition to the North Pole in the *Jeannette*, all men died but two. Of the *Jeannette* herself and her equipment, nothing was found until three years after she sank, when, on a beach on the other side of the polar basin, a Greenlander discovered a pair of yellow oilskin breeches stamped *Jeannette*.

THE PEOPLE

Why do we people in churches seem like cheerful, brainless tourists on a packaged tour of the Absolute?

The tourists are having coffee and doughnuts on Deck C. Presumably someone is minding the ship, correcting the course, avoiding icebergs and shoals, fueling the engines, watching the radar screen, noting weather reports radioed in from shore. No one would dream of asking the tourists to do these things. Alas, among the tourists on Deck C, drinking coffee and eating doughnuts, we find the captain, and all the ship's officers, and all the ship's crew. The officers chat; they swear; they wink a bit at slightly raw jokes, just like regular people. The crew members have funny accents. The wind seems to be picking up.

On the whole, I do not find Christians, outside of the catacombs, sufficiently sensible of conditions. Does anyone have the foggiest idea what sort of power we so blithely invoke? Or, as I suspect, does no one believe a word of it? The churches are children playing on the floor with their chemistry sets, mixing up a batch of TNT to kill a Sunday morning. It is madness to wear ladies' straw hats and velvet hats to church; we should all be wearing crash helmets. Ushers should issue life preservers and signal flares; they should lash us to our pews. For the sleeping god may wake someday and take offense, or the waking god may draw us out to where we can never return.

The eighteenth-century Hasidic Jews had more sense, and more belief. One Hasidic slaughterer, whose work required invoking the Lord, bade a tearful farewell to his wife and children every morning before he set out for the slaughterhouse. He felt, every morning, that he would never see any of them again. For every day, as he himself stood with his knife in his hand, the words of his prayer carried him into danger. After he called on God, God might notice and destroy him before he had time to utter the rest, "Have mercy."

Another Hasid, a rabbi, refused to promise a friend to visit him the next day: "How can you ask me to make such a promise? This evening I must pray and recite 'Hear, O Israel.' When I say these words, my soul goes out to the utmost rim of life. . . . Perhaps I shall not die this time either, but how can I now promise to do something at a time after the prayer?"

ASSORTED WILDLIFE

Insects

I like insects for their stupidity. A paper wasp—*Polistes*—is fumbling at the stained-glass window on my right. I saw the same sight in the same spot last Sunday: Pssst! Idiot! Sweetheart! Go around by the door! I hope we seem as endearingly stupid to God—bumbling down into lamps, running half-wit across the floor, banging for days at the hinge of an opened door. I hope so. It does not seem likely.

Penguins

According to visitors, Antarctic penguins are . . . adorable. They are tame! They are funny!

Tourists in Antarctica are mostly women of a certain age. They step from the cruise ship's rubber Zodiacs wearing bright ship's-issue parkas; they stalk around on the gravel and squint into the ice glare; they exclaim over the penguins, whom they find tame, funny, and adorable; they take snapshots of each other with the penguins, and look around cheerfully for something else to look around at.

The penguins are adorable, and the wasp at the stained-glass window is adorable, because in each case their impersonations of human dignity so evidently fail. What are the chances that God finds our failed impersonation of human dignity adorable? Or is he fooled? What odds do you give me?

III

THE LAND

Several years ago I visited the high Arctic and saw it: the Arctic Ocean, the Beaufort Sea. The place was Barter Island, inside the Arctic Circle, in the Alaskan Arctic north of the North Slope. I stood on the island's ocean shore and saw what there was to see: a pile of colorless stripes. Through binoculars I could see a bigger pile of colorless stripes.

It seemed reasonable to call the colorless stripe overhead "sky," and reasonable to call the colorless stripe at my feet "ice," for I could see where it began. I could distinguish, that is, my shoes, and the black gravel shore, and the nearby frozen ice the wind had smashed ashore. It was this mess of ice—ice breccia, pressure ridges, and standing floes, ice sheets upright, tilted, frozen together and jammed—which extended out to the horizon. No matter how hard I blinked, I could not put a name to any of the other stripes. Which was the horizon? Was I seeing land, or water, or their reflections in low clouds? Was I seeing the famous "water sky," the "frost smoke," or the "ice blink"?

In his old age, James McNeill Whistler used to walk down to the Atlantic shore carrying a few thin planks and his paints. On the planks he painted, day after day, in broad, blurred washes representing sky, water, and shore, three blurry light-filled stripes. These are late Whistlers; I like them very much. In the high Arctic I thought of them, for I seemed to be standing in one of them. If I loosed my eyes from my shoes, the gravel at my feet, or the chaos of ice at the shore, I saw what newborn babies must see: nothing but senseless variations of light on the retinas. The world was a color-field painting wrapped round me at an unknown distance; I hesitated to take a step.

There was, in short, no recognizable three-dimensional space in the Arctic. There was also no time. The sun never set, but neither did it appear. The dim round-the-clock light changed haphazardly when the lid of cloud thickened or thinned. Circumstances made the eating of meals random or impossible. I slept when I was tired. When I woke I walked out into the colorless stripes and the revolving winds, where atmosphere mingled with distance, and where land, ice, and light blurred into a dreamy, freezing vapor which, lacking anything else to do with the stuff, I breathed. Now and then a white bird materialized out of the vapor and screamed. It was, in short, what one might, searching for words, call a beautiful land; it was more beautiful still when the sky cleared and the ice shone in the dark water.

THE TECHNOLOGY

It is for the Pole of Relative Inaccessibility I am searching, and have been searching, in the mountains and along the seacoasts for years. The aim of this expedition is, as Pope Gregory put it in his time, "To attain to somewhat of the unencompassed light, by stealth, and scantily." How often have I mounted this same expedition, has my absurd barque set out half-caulked for the Pole?

THE LAND

"These incidents are *true*," I read in an 1880 British history of Arctic exploration. "These incidents are *true*,—the storm, the drifting ice-raft, the falling berg, the sinking ship, the breaking up of the great frozen floe: these scenes are *real*,—the vast plains of ice, the ridged hummocks, the bird-thronged cliff, the far-stretching glacier."

Polar exploration is no longer the fashion it was during the time of the Franklin expedition, when beachgoers at Brighton thronged to panoramas of Arctic wastes painted in shopwindows, and when many thousands of Londoners jammed the Vauxhall pleasure gardens to see a diorama of polar seas. Our attention is elsewhere now, but the light-soaked land still exists; I have seen it.

THE TECHNOLOGY

In the nineteenth century, a man deduced Antarctica.

During that time, no one on earth knew for certain whether there was any austral land mass at all, although the American Charles Wilkes claimed to have seen it. Some geographers and explorers speculated that there was no land, only a frozen Antarctic Ocean; others posited two large islands in the vicinity of the Pole. That there is one continent was not in fact settled until 1935.

In 1893, one John Murray presented to the Royal Geographic Society a deduction of the Antarctic continent. His expedition's ship, the *Challenger*, had never come within sight of any such continent. His deduction proceeded entirely from dredgings and soundings. In his presentation he posited a large, single continent, a speculative map of which he furnished. He described accurately the unknown continent's topology: its central plateau with its permanent high-pressure system, its enormous glacier facing the Southern Ocean, its volcanic ranges at one coast, and at another coast, its lowland ranges and hills. He was correct.

Deduction, then, is possible—though no longer fashionable. There are many possible techniques for the exploration of high latitudes. There is, for example, such a thing as a drift expedition.

When that pair of yellow oilskin breeches belonging to the lost crew of the *Jeannette* turned up after three years in Greenland, having been lost north of central Russia, Norwegian explorer Fridtjof Nansen was interested. On the basis of these breeches' travels he plotted the probable direction of the current in the polar basin. Then he mounted a drift expedition: in 1893 he drove his ship, the *Fram*, deliberately into the pack ice and settled in to wait while the current moved north and, he hoped, across the Pole. For almost two years, he and a crew of twelve lived aboard ship as the frozen ocean carried them. Nansen wrote in his diary, "I long to return to life . . . the years are passing here . . . Oh! at times this inactivity crushes one's very soul; one's life seems as dark as the winter night outside; there is sunlight upon no other part of it except the past and the far, far distant future. I feel as if I *must* break through this deadness."

The current did not carry them over the Pole, so Nansen and one companion set out one spring with dog sledges and kayaks to reach the Pole on foot. Conditions were too rough on the ice, however, so after reaching a record northern latitude, the two turned south toward land, wintering together finally in a stone hut on Franz Josef Land and living on polar bear meat. The following spring they returned, after almost three years, to civilization.

Nansen's was the first of several drift expeditions. During World War I, members of a Canadian Arctic expedition camped on an ice floe seven miles by fifteen miles; they drifted for six months over four hundred miles in the Beaufort Sea. In 1937, an airplane deposited a Soviet drift expedition on an ice floe near the North Pole. These four Soviet scientists drifted for nine months while their floe, colliding with grounded ice, repeatedly split into ever-smaller pieces.

THE LAND

I have, I say, set out again.

The days tumble with meanings. The corners heap up with poetry; whole unfilled systems litter the ice.

THE TECHNOLOGY

A certain Lieutenant Maxwell, a member of Vitus Bering's second polar expedition, wrote, "You never feel safe when you have to navigate in waters which are completely blank."

Cartographers call blank spaces on a map "sleeping beauties."

On our charts I see the symbol for shoals and beside it the letters "P.D." My neighbor in the pew, a lug with a mustache who has experience of navigational charts and who knows how to take a celestial fix, tells me that the initials stand for "Position Doubtful."

THE LAND

To learn the precise location of a Pole, choose a clear, dark night to begin. Locate by ordinary navigation the Pole's position within an area of several square yards. Then arrange on the ice in that area a series of loaded cameras. Aim the cameras at the sky's zenith; leave their shutters open. Develop the film. The film from that camera located precisely at the Pole will show the night's revolving stars as perfectly circular concentric rings.

THE TECHNOLOGY

I have a taste for solitude, and silence, and for what Plotinus called "the flight of the alone to the Alone." I have a taste for solitude. Sir John Franklin had, apparently, a taste for backgammon. Is either of these appropriate to conditions?

You quit your house and country, quit your ship, and quit your companions in the tent, saying, "I am just going outside and may be some time." The light on the far side of the blizzard lures you. You walk, and one day you enter the spread heart of silence, where lands dissolve and seas become vapor and ices sublime under unknown stars. This is the end of the Via Negativa, the lightless edge where the slopes of knowledge dwindle, and love for its own sake, lacking an object, begins.

THE LAND

I have put on silence and waiting. I have quit my ship and set out on foot over the polar ice. I carry chronometer and sextant, tent, stove and fuel, meat and fat. For water I melt the pack ice in hatchet-hacked chips; frozen salt water is fresh. I sleep when I can walk no longer. I walk on a compass bearing toward geographical north.

I walk in emptiness; I hear my breath. I see my hand and compass, see the ice so wide it arcs, see the planet's peak curving and its low atmosphere held fast on the dive. The years are passing here. I am walking, light as any handful of aurora; I am light as sails, a pile of colorless stripes; I cry "heaven and earth indistinguishable!" and the current underfoot carries me and I walk.

The blizzard is like a curtain; I enter it. The blown snow heaps in my eyes. There is nothing to see or to know. I wait in the tent, myself adrift and emptied, for weeks while the storm unwinds. One day it is over, and I pick up my tent and walk. The storm has scoured the air; the clouds have lifted; the sun rolls round the sky like a fish in a round bowl, like a pebble rolled in a tub, like a swimmer, or a melody flung and repeating, repeating enormously overhead on all sides.

My name is Silence. Silence is my bivouac, and my supper sipped from bowls. I robe myself mornings in loose strings of stones. My eyes are stones; a chip from the pack ice fills my mouth. My skull is a polar basin; my brain pan grows glaciers, and icebergs, and grease ice, and floes. The years are passing here.

Far ahead is open water. I do not know what season it is, know how long I have walked into the silence like a tunnel widening before me, into the horizon's spread arms which widen like water. I walk to the pack ice edge, to the rim which calves its floes into the black and green water; I stand at the edge and look ahead. A scurf of candle ice on the water's skin as far as I can see scratches the sea and crumbles whenever a lump of ice or snow bobs or floats through it. The floes are thick in the water, some of them large as lands. By my side is passing a flat pan of floe from which someone extends an oar. I hold the oar's blade and jump. I land on the long floe.

No one speaks. Here, at the bow of the floe, the bright clowns have staked themselves to the ice. With tent stakes and ropes they have lashed their wrists and ankles to the floe on which they lie stretched and silent, face up. Among the clowns, and similarly staked, are many boys and girls, some women, and a few men from various countries. One of the men is Nansen, the Norwegian explorer who drifted. One of the women repeatedly opens and closes her fists. One of the clowns has opened his neck ruffle, exposing his skin. For many hours I pass among these staked people, intending to return later and take my place.

Farther along I see that the tall priest is here, the priest who served grape juice communion at an ecumenical service many years ago, in another country. He is very old. Alone on a wind-streaked patch of snow he kneels, stands, and kneels, and stands, and kneels. Not far from him, at the floe's side, sitting on a packing crate, is the deducer John Murray. He lowers a plumb bob overboard and pays out the line. He is wearing the antique fur hat of a Doctor of Reason, such as Erasmus wears in his portrait; it is understood that were he ever to return and present his findings, he would be ridiculed, for his hat. Scott's Captain Oates is here; he has no feet. It is he who stepped outside his tent, to save his friends. Now on his dignity he stands and mans the sheet of a square linen sail; he has stepped the wooden mast on a hillock amidships.

From the floe's stern I think I hear music; I set out, but it takes me several sleeps to get there. I am no longer using the tent. Each time I wake, I study the floe and the ocean horizon for signs—signs of the pack ice which we left behind, or of open water, or land, or any weather. Nothing changes; there is only the green sea and the floating ice, and the black sea in the distance speckled by bergs, and a steady wind astern which smells of unknown mineral salts, some ocean floor.

At last I reach the floe's broad stern, its enormous trailing coast, its throngs, its many cooking fires. There are children carrying babies, and men and women painting their skins and trying to catch their reflections in the water to leeward. Near the water's edge there is a wooden upright piano, and a bench with a telephone book on it. A woman is sitting on the telephone book and banging out the Sanctus on the keys. The wind is picking up. I am singing at the top of my lungs, for a lark.

Many clowns are here; one of them is passing out Girl Scout cookies, all of which are stuck together. Recently, I learn, Sir John Franklin and crew have boarded this floe, and so have the crews of the lost *Polaris* and the *Jeannette*. The men, whose antique uniforms are causing envious glances, are hungry. Some of them start rough-housing with the rascally acolyte. One crewman carries the boy on his back along the edge to the piano, where he abandons him for a clump of cookies and a seat on the bench beside the short pianist, whose bare feet, perhaps on account of the telephone book, cannot reach the pedals. She starts playing "The Sound of Music." "You know any Bach?" I say to the lady at the piano, whose legs seem to be highly involved with those of the hungry crewman; "You know any Mozart? Or maybe 'How Great Thou Art'?" A skeletal officer wearing a black silk neckerchief has located Admiral Peary, recognizable from afar by the curious flag he holds. Peary and the officer together are planning a talent show and skits. When they approach me, I volunteer to sing "Antonio Spangonio, That Bum Toreador" and/or to read a piece of short fiction; they say they will let me know later.

Christ, under the illusion that we are all penguins, is crouched down posing for snapshots. He crouches, in his robe, between the lead singer of Wildflowers, who is joyfully trying to determine the best angle at which to hold his guitar for the camera, and the farmer's wife, who keeps her eyes on her painted toenails until the Filipino godfather with the camera says "Cheese." The country-and-western woman, singing, succeeds in pressing a cookie upon the baby Oswaldo. The baby Oswaldo is standing in his lace gown and blue tennis shoes in the center of a circle of explorers, confounding them.

In my hand I discover a tambourine. Ahead as far as the brittle horizon, I see icebergs among the floes. I see tabular bergs and floebergs and dark cracks in the water between them. Low overhead on the underside of the thickening cloud cover are dark colorless stripes reflecting pools of open water in the distance. I am banging on the tambourine, and singing whatever the piano player plays; now it is "On Top of Old Smoky." I am banging the tambourine and belting the song so loudly that people are edging away. But how can any of us tone it down? For we are nearing the Pole.

CREDITS

C. D. B. BRYAN, excerpts from *Friendly Fire* by C. D. B. Bryan. Copyright ©1976 by Courtlandt Dixon Barnes Bryan. Reprinted by permission of The Putnam Publishing Group.

TRUMAN CAPOTE, excerpts from *In Cold Blood* by Truman Capote. Copyright ©1965 by Truman Capote and renewed in 1993 by Alan U. Schwartz. Reprinted by permission of Random House, Inc.

FRANK CONROY, excerpt from *Stop-Time* by Frank Conroy. Copyright ©1965, 1966, 1967 by Frank Conroy. Used by permission of Viking Penguin, a division of Penguin Books USA, Inc.

JOAN DIDION, "Some Dreamers of the Golden Dream" from *Slouching Towards Bethlehem* by Joan Didion. Copyright ©1966, 1968 by Joan Didion. Reprinted by permission of Farrar, Straus & Giroux, Inc.

ANNIE DILLARD, "An Expedition to the Pole" (pp. 17–52) from *Teaching a Stone to Talk* by Annie Dillard. Copyright ©1982 by Annie Dillard. Reprinted by permission of HarperCollins Publishers, Inc.

JACK FINNEY, excerpts from *Forgotten News: The Crime of the Century and Other Lost Stories*. Copyright ©1983 by Jack Finney. Reprinted by permission of Don Congdon Associates, Inc.

MELISSA FAY GREENE, excerpt from *Praying for Sheetrock* (pp. 1–8). Copyright ©1991 by Melissa Fay Greene. Reprinted by permission of Addison-Wesley Publishing Company, Inc.

WILLIAM LEAST HEAT-MOON, excerpts from *PrairyErth: A Deep Map*. Copyright ©1991 by William Least Heat-Moon. Reprinted by permission of Houghton Mifflin Co. All rights reserved.

MICHAEL HERR, excerpts from *Dispatches* by Michael Herr. Copyright ©1977 by Michael Herr. Reprinted by permission of Alfred A. Knopf, Inc.

JOHN HERSEY, "A Noiseless Flash" from *Hiroshima* by John Hersey. Copyright ©1946, 1973 by John Hersey. Reprinted by permission of Alfred A. Knopf, Inc.

INDEX